THE

# BEGINNER'S LATIN BOOK.

BY

WILLIAM C. COLLAR, A.M.,
HEAD-MASTER ROXBURY LATIN SCHOOL,

AND

M. GRANT DANIELL, A.M.,
PRINCIPAL CHAUNCY-HALL SCHOOL, BOSTON.

*Longum iter est per praecepta, breve et efficax per exempla.*
SENECA.

BOSTON:
GINN & COMPANY.
1887.

J. S. Cushing & Co., Printers, Boston.

# PREFACE.

THE aim of this book is to serve as a preparation for reading, writing, and, to a less degree, for speaking Latin. It is designed primarily for boys and girls who are to begin the study of Latin at an early age; but as all who would get from Latin the best mental discipline, or lay a broad and firm foundation for Latin scholarship, must traverse pretty much the same road, and as Latin is begun in this country by most learners before any other foreign language is studied, a beginner's Latin book for those who take up the study at the age of ten or twelve need not be essentially different from one designed for learners of fourteen or fifteen. The most important difference would lie in the knowledge of the terminology and principles of English grammar that might be deemed an indispensable prerequisite. As a matter of fact, children come to the study of Latin with all degrees of ignorance of English grammar, and the minimum of necessary knowledge for the beginner is unquestionably very small. What minimum is considered essential for those who use this book, is indicated on page 6. It is hoped, therefore, that the contents of the book will justify its title; that it does not assume too much, and is not too difficult for the least mature who are likely to use it, and that it will not be found too much simplified,—too juvenile, for those who begin Latin in high schools and academies. Simplicity, clearness, and directness have been studied throughout. The system of inflected forms, which is seldom mastered, but the mastery of which is an indispensable condition of further pleasant, successful, and profitable study, is slowly but very fully developed, with the addition of abundant and varied exercises. For convenience, as well as on educational grounds, the paradigm of the verb is given in one block, instead of in fragments detached and dispersed, and everywhere the active and passive forms are placed side by side, to be compared, and learned as they are treated, simultaneously.

The idea underlying and controlling the plan is the maximum of practice with the minimum of theory, on the principle that the thorough acquisition of the elements of Latin must be more of art than science, — more the work of observation, comparison, and imitation, than the mechanical following of rules, or the exercise of analysis and conscious inductive reasoning.

The book contains: —

1. A brief introduction explaining the Roman and English methods of pronunciation, the necessary paradigms, an outline of the most important principles of syntax, and a large number of exercises for translation into English and into Latin, accompanied by short explanatory notes.

2. About twenty-five simple Latin dialogues, added to as many chapters. Some of these are on subjects of the lessons, and include a good many grammatical terms; some are on various topics of school and holiday life; and others on subjects historical and mythological.

3. Easy selections for translation, consisting besides a number of fables, of extracts from Viri Romae, Nepos, Ovid, Catullus, Cæsar, and Cicero, some interspersed with the lessons, others added at the end of the book.

Those who seek in a first Latin book a complete presentation of the facts and principles of the Latin language, will not be satisfied with this volume. But, in the opinion of the authors, there is no error in elementary instruction in Latin more common and more deplorable than that of failing to discriminate between the relatively important and unimportant; between what is suited to the beginning and what to the more advanced stages of the study. It is not too much to say that a very great part of the barrenness and futility of the teaching and study of Latin in schools is due to this lack of discrimination, and to a false conception of thoroughness. It is not intended to imply that a hard and fast line can be drawn, still less is this book offered as a realization in this respect of the ideal. The ideal is never realized. But it has been the constant aim to make just this distinction: to determine everywhere, in the light of much observation and reflection and of long experience, what should be made the subject of immediate study, and what should be postponed; what is entitled to prominence, and what ought to be subordinated. Some excellent teachers think that the subjunctive mood should have no place in a preparatory Latin book; and undoubtedly the syntax of the subjunctive does involve too many and too great difficulties for such a work, if anything more than an outline of some commoner uses is attempted. On the other hand, the learner can hardly read any Latin without encountering forms of the subjunctive. The best way then seems to be to construct a large number of very short sentences for practice on the forms, which shall exhibit, in the briefest compass, some important and most frequently recurring uses of the mood, more especially because the ways of translating the subjunctive cannot be illustrated from the isolated forms in the paradigms, as in the other moods. This idea has been worked out in part in Chapter LIV., the forms having been previously left untranslated.

The *colloquia* have been added, not as an integral and necessary part of the lessons, but to serve as an incentive to the moderate use of Latin orally in recitation, and to afford convenient exercises for training the ear and for enlarging the vocabulary of the learner. The grammatical terms have been drawn chiefly from the *Institutiones* of Rudimann. The *colloquium* on page 5 has been borrowed from Dr. H. Meurer's *Lateinisches Lesebuch*, and suggestions and parts of the materials for a very few others have been derived from the same source ; also two or three of the passages for translation, and here and there some sentences in the exercises. Whoever examines these *colloquia* with a critical eye, will find some words which are confined to the vocabularies of grammarians and commentators, and a very few others employed in senses for which it would be embarrassing to be required to cite classical authority. For example, the word *pensum* is used often in the sense of *a schoolboy's task, something to be done or learned, a lesson.* This word doubtless meant strictly *a spinner's task.* But in classical Latin it had already approached the meaning *task* in general, and it is but a very slight extension of its application to employ it as it is in the *colloquia.* Such a moderate decanting of new wine into old bottles, it is hoped may be excused. Still if any teacher thinks that the Latinity of his pupils will be injured by the use of the *colloquia*, it is optional with him to omit them altogether, without losing the continuity of the lessons.

The complaint is very common, and its justice must be acknowledged, that first Latin books are often excessively and needlessly arid and wooden. Accordingly an effort has been made, while following a rigorously scientific method in the development of the successive subjects, to impart something of attractiveness, interest, freshness, and variety to the study of the elements of Latin by means of the *colloquia*, the choice of extracts for translation (introduced as early as possible), and the mode of treatment in every part, extending even to the choice of Latin words, and to the construction of many of the exercises.

Usage is not fixed in respect to the so-called principal parts of verbs, a few of the later school manuals giving the nominative masculine of the perfect participle, instead of the supine, except in the case of neuter or intransitive verbs. It has been thought better in this book to follow the prevailing practice, only to treat the form that has been called the supine in this connection, not as the supine,—which in most cases it is not and cannot be, since, as is well known, only about 230 verbs can be proved to have a supine,—but as the neuter of the perfect participle.[1] Thus the learner is guarded against errors and is spared the perplexity of having to memorize now one, now another form.

It is hoped that this book can be finished and reviewed by the average learner in a year, and that the transition then to Viri Romae, Nepos, or Cæsar will not prove too difficult. More than two-thirds of the words used belong to the vocabulary of Cæsar, and only a trifle less than two-thirds to that of Nepos. In the case of young pupils it may be advisable to omit the translation of the English exercises into Latin, beginning with Chapter LV., till after the selections for translation at the end of the book have been read.

It remains to acknowledge the generous assistance of several scholars. Professor George M. Lane, of Harvard University, Professor George L. Kittredge, of Exeter Academy, N.H., George F. Forbes, A.M., and D. O. S. Lowell, A.M., both of the Roxbury Latin School, and Marshall W. Davis, A.B., of Thayer Academy, Braintree, read and criticised the work in manuscript. Mr. Forbes and Mr. Lowell also read the proof-sheets and made important suggestions and corrections. The authors feel especially indebted to John Tetlow, A.M., Head-Master of the Boston Girls' High and Latin Schools, and author of *Inductive Lessons in Latin*, for critically reading the proof-sheets, and for materially contributing to the improvement of the book by

[1] This plan has been followed by Dr. R. F. Leighton in his *First Steps in Latin.*

the correction of errors, and by the suggestions of his conscientious and exact scholarship.

Thanks are due to Mr. J. S. Cushing, under whose personal direction the book has been printed, for the patience, care, and skill which he has constantly exercised to make the work typographically as faultless as possible.

WM. C. COLLAR.
M. GRANT DANIELL.

BOSTON, Sept. 1, 1886.

# CONTENTS.

# BEGINNER'S LATIN BOOK.

## CHAPTER I.

### INTRODUCTORY.

**It is suggested to teachers who are not experienced in teaching Latin that this chapter may, perhaps, be most profitably used for reference. Pupils will catch pronunciation quickly from the lips of the teacher; and as they make mistakes, they will be interested in being referred to the rules of pronunciation. It is therefore advised that the teacher begin with the *Colloquium*, page 5, pronouncing slowly each sentence, the pupils following successively, and then together. In the same way the teacher might then construe literally.**

**1.** ALPHABET. — The Latin alphabet has no *w*. Otherwise it is the same as the English.

**2.** VOWELS.—Vowels may be long (marked thus ¯), short (marked thus ˘), or common[1] (marked thus ˘̄). The long vowel occupies double the time of the short in pronouncing.

**3.** CONSONANTS. — Of the consonants

| | | |
|---|---|---|
| The mutes are: | P-mutes . . . | **p, b, f** |
| | T-mutes . . . | **t, d** |
| | K-mutes . . . | **k, c, g, q (u)** |
| The liquids are | . . . . . . . . | **l, m, n, r** |
| The sibilant is | . . . . . . . . | **s** |
| The double consonants are | . . . | **x = cs,**[2] **z = ds.** |

---

[1] That is, sometimes long and sometimes short.

[2] Also represents the combinations **hs, qus, gs, vs.**

## 4. Sounds of the Letters, Roman Method.

### *Vowels.*

| | | | |
|---|---|---|---|
| ā | is sounded | like | the last *a* in *papä'*. |
| ă | " | " | the first *a* in *papä'*. |
| ē | " | " | *e* in *they*. |
| ĕ | " | " | *e* in *met*. |
| ī | " | " | *i* in *machine*. |
| ĭ | " | " | *i* in *pin*. |
| ō | " | " | *o* in *holy*. |
| ŏ | " | " | *o* in *wholly*.[1] |
| ū[2] | " | " | *oo* in *boot*. |
| ŭ | " | " | *oo* in *foot*. |

### *Diphthongs.*

| | | | |
|---|---|---|---|
| ae | is sounded | like | *ai* in *aisle*. |
| au | " | " | *ou* in *our*. |
| ei | " | " | *ei* in *eight*. |
| oe | " | " | *oi* in *boil*. |
| eu | " | " | *eu* in *feud*. |
| ui | " | " | *we*. |

### *Consonants.*

Consonants generally have the same sounds as in English. But observe the following: —

| | | | |
|---|---|---|---|
| c | is sounded | like | *c* in *come*. |
| g | " | " | *g* in *get*. |
| j | " | " | *y* in *yes*. |
| s | " | " | *s* in *sun*.[3] |
| t | " | " | *t* in *time*.[4] |
| v | " | " | *w* in *wine*. |
| ch | " | " | *k* in *kite*. |

[1] That is, as the word is commonly pronounced; the sound heard in *holy*, shortened.

[2] In *qu*, and also commonly in *gu* and *su* before a vowel, *u* is a semi-vowel or consonant, and is pronounced like *w*.

[3] Never like *z*. [4] Never like *sh*.

**5.** Syllables.

1. A syllable consists of a vowel or diphthong with or without one or more consonants. Hence a word has as many syllables as it has vowels and diphthongs: **ae-gri-tū′-dō,** *sickness.*

2. When a word is divided into syllables, a single consonant is joined with the vowel following: **a-mā′-bi-lis,** *amiable.*

3. If there are two or more consonants between two vowels, as many are joined with the following vowel as can be pronounced at the beginning of a word or syllable: **im′-pro-bus,** *bad;* **ho-spes,** *guest.*

4. But in compound words the division must show the component parts: **ab′-est (ab,** *away;* **est,** *he is*), *he is away.*

5. The last syllable of a word is called the *ultima;* the one next to the last, the *penult;* the one before the penult, the *antepenult.*

**6.** Quantity.

1. A vowel is short before a vowel (with few exceptions) or *h*, also probably before *nt* and *nd*: **pŏ-ē′-ma,** *poem;* **grā′-tĭ-ae,** *thanks;* **nĭ′-hil,** *nothing;* **a′-mănt,** *they love;* **mo-nĕn′-dus,** *to be advised.*

2. Diphthongs, vowels representing diphthongs, vowels resulting from contraction, and vowels followed by *nf*, *ns*, *j*, and commonly *gn*, are long: **in-ī′-quus (inaequus),** *unequal;* **cō′-gō (cŏăgō),** *collect;* **cōn′-fe-rō,** *bring together;* **mēn′-sa,** *table;* **hū′-jus,** *of him;* **mā′-gnus,** *great.* In this book only long vowels are marked, unless for some special reason.

3. A syllable is long when it contains a long vowel or a diphthong: **vō′-cēs,** *voices;* **ae′-dēs,** *temple.*

4. A syllable is long if it has a short vowel followed by two or more consonants (except a mute followed by *l* or *r*), or by *x* or *z*; but the short vowel is still pronounced short: **sunt,**[1] *they are;* **tem′-plum,** *temple;* **dux,**[1] *leader.*

5. A syllable is common if it has a short vowel followed by a mute with *l* or *r*: **te′-ne͝-brae,** *darkness.* The vowel is pronounced short.

The above statements are useful in determining the place of the accent.

**7.** Accent.

1. Words of two syllables have the accent on the first: **tu′-ba,** *trumpet.*

2. Words of more than two syllables have the accent on the penult when the penult is long, otherwise on the antepenult: **prae-dī′-cō,** *foretell;* **prae′-di-cō,** *declare;* **ille′-ce͝-brae,** *snares;* **pa-ter′-nus,**[2] *paternal.*

(1) Several words, called enclitics, of which the commonest are **ne,** the sign of a question, and **que,** *and,* are appended to other words, and such words are then accented on the syllable preceding the **ne** or **que**: **amat′-ne,** *does he love?* **dōna′-que,** *and gifts.*

**8.** English Method of Pronunciation.—By this method the above rules relating to syllables (**5**) and accent (**7**) are observed, and words are pronounced substantially as in English; but final *es* is sounded as in English *ease,* and final *ōs* (acc. plur.) as in *dose.*

[1] **u** pronounced like *oo* in *foot.*

[2] Here, though the *vowel* of the penult is short, the *syllable* is long by **6. 4.**

The following *colloquium* may be used, if the teacher wishes, for practice, and to illustrate the foregoing statements. See introductory note, page 1.

## 9. COLLOQUIUM.

| | |
|---|---|
| *Augustus.* Quid tibi vīs? | *What do you wish (for yourself)?* |
| *Iūlus.* Tēcum ambulāre velim. | *I should like to take a walk with you.* |
| *A.* Ego nōlō; domī manēre mālō. | *I don't want to; I prefer to stay at home.* |
| *I.* Cūr māvīs? | *Why do you prefer (that)?* |
| *A.* Ego et frāter vesperī cum patre ambulāre mālumus. | *My brother and I had rather take a walk at evening with our father.* |
| *I.* Cūr mēcum per silvās vagārī nōn vultis? | *Why don't you want to roam with me through the woods?* |
| *A.* Quod vesperī amoenitāte fruī mālumus quam sōlis ardōre. | *Because we had rather enjoy the pleasantness of evening than the heat of the sun.* |
| *I.* At jam saepe mēcum ambulāre nōluistī. | *But often before now you have not wanted to walk with me.* |
| *A.* Nōn rēctē dīcis; nōn est causa cūr tēcum ambulāre nōlim; at cum hortus avī satis amplus sit et lacum silvamque contineat, ibi mālumus lūdere. Sī vīs, nōbīscum venī. | *What you say is not true; there is no reason why I should not want to walk with you; but since grandfather's garden is quite large, and has a pond and a grove, we had rather play there. If you like, come with us.* |

**10. Cases.**

1. The names of the cases in Latin are: *nominative, vocative, genitive, dative, accusative, ablative.*

2. The vocative is the case of address, but it does not differ in form from the nominative, except in the singular of nouns and adjectives in *us* of the second declension, and hence is not elsewhere given separately in the paradigms.

3. Another case, the *locative*, which denotes the place of an action, is mostly confined to proper names, and has the form of the ablative (sometimes dative) singular or plural, or of the genitive singular.

**11.** GENDER.—The gender of Latin nouns is determined partly, as in English, by the meaning, but much oftener by the termination.

1. Nouns denoting males are *masculine:* **agricola,** *farmer;* **Cicerō,** *Cicero.*

2. Nouns denoting females are *feminine:* **rēgīna,** *queen;* **Tullia,** *Tullia.*

3. Names of rivers, winds, and months are *masculine:* **Padus,** *Po;* **aquilō,** *north wind;* **Jānuārius,** *January.*

4. Names of countries, towns, islands, and trees, are *feminine:* **Āfrica,** *Africa;* **Rōma,** *Rome;* **Sicilia,** *Sicily;* **pirus,** *pear-tree.*

5. Indeclinable nouns are neuter: **fās,** *right.*

Other rules of gender will be given under the several declensions.

---

It is assumed that the learner knows the names and functions of the parts of speech in English, and the meanings of the common grammatical terms, such as *subject and predicate, case, mood, tense, voice, declension, conjugation,* etc. So much knowledge is absolutely essential for entering upon the study of the following lessons.

# CHAPTER II. 1.

## FIRST DECLENSION.

**12.** The stem[1] ends in *a*.

**13.** GENDER.—The gender is feminine; but see general rules, **11.**

**14.** PARADIGM.

| SINGULAR. | | PLURAL. | |
|---|---|---|---|
| N.V. | tub**a**, *a trumpet.* | N.V. | tub**ae**, *trumpets.* |
| G. | tub**ae**, *of a trumpet.* | G. | tub**ārum**, *of trumpets.* |
| D. | tub**ae**, *to* or *for a trumpet.* | D. | tub**īs**, *to* or *for trumpets.* |
| Ac. | tub**am**, *a trumpet.* | Ac. | tub**ās**, *trumpets.* |
| Ab. | tub**ā**,[2] *with a trumpet.* | Ab. | tub**īs**, *with trumpets.* |

1. For the reason why the vocative case is not given separately in the paradigm see **10.** 2.

2. Examples of the locative case (**10.** 3) in this declension are: **Rōmae**, *at Rome;* **Athēnīs**, *at Athens.*

**15.** TERMINATIONS.—These consist of case-endings, joined with the final letter of the stem. But sometimes the final letter of the stem is lost, and sometimes the case-ending.

| | SINGULAR. | PLURAL. |
|---|---|---|
| N.V. | **a** | **ae** |
| G. | **ae** | **ārum** |
| D. | **ae** | **īs** |
| Ac. | **am** | **ās** |
| Ab. | **ā** | **īs** |

[1] The stem is the common base to which certain letters are added to express the relation of the word to other words.

[2] The ablative is variously rendered, according to its connection. It is therefore recommended that, in declining words, no translation of the ablative be given till its use has been illustrated. See p. 20, n. 1.

**16.** Observe that the genitive and dative singular and nominative plural are alike; also the dative and ablative plural.

**17.** In Latin there is no article: **tuba** may be translated *a trumpet*, *the trumpet*, or *trumpet*.

**18.** The pupil should commit to memory the table of terminations.

## 2.

**19.** VOCABULARY.

| NOUNS. | ADJECTIVES.[3] |
|---|---|
| **aquila**, F., *eagle*. | **alba**, *white*. |
| **cauda**, F., *tail*. | **bona**, *good*. |
| **columba**, F., *dove*. | **dūra**, *hard*. |
| **fīlia**,[1] F., *daughter*. | **lāta**, *wide, broad*. |
| **puella**, F., *girl*. | **longa**, *long*. |
| **rēgīna**, F., *queen*. | **māgna**, *large*. |
| **rosa**,[2] F., *rose*. | **mala**, *bad*. |
| **via**, F., *road, street, way*. | **parva**, *small, little*. |

VERBS.

| | |
|---|---|
| **est**, (*he, she, it*) *is*. | **habet**, (*he, she, it*) *has*. |
| **sunt**, (*they*) *are*. | **habent**, (*they*) *have*. |

**20.** Observe that in the above verb-forms the singular ends in *t*, and the plural in *nt*.

### NOMINATIVE AND ACCUSATIVE.

**21.** EXERCISES.

I.[4] 1. Viae lātae. 2. Via lāta. 3. Viās lātās. 4. Viam lātam. 5. Cauda longa. 6. Caudās longās. 7. Caudam longam. 8. Caudae longae. 9. Columbās parvās. 10. Co-

[1] **Fīlia** and **dea**, *goddess*, have a dative and ablative plural in *-ābus*, but this is mostly confined to legal and religious language.

[2] CAUTION: Do not pronounce *s* like *z*, if you use the Roman method. See page 2, note 3.

[3] The masculine and neuter of adjectives will be taken up in connection with nouns of the second declension.

[4] Observe that the adjective takes the case and number of the noun to which it belongs.

lumbae parvae. 11. Columba parva. 12. Columbam parvam. 13. Rosam albam. 14. Rosae albae. 15. Rosa alba. 16. Rosās albās. 17. Rēgīna mala. 18. Rēgīnās malās.

II. In like manner give the nominative and accusative in both numbers of the words meaning *little girl*, *great eagle*, *good queen*, *wide street*. Decline together **rosa alba, via longa, bona puella**.

## 3.

**22.** EXERCISES.

I. 1. Via est longa. 2. Dūra est via. 3. Puellae rosās habent. 4. Rēgīna columbam habet. 5. Rosae sunt albae. 6. Cauda est alba. 7. Caudae sunt longae. 8. Aquila caudam habet. 9. Puellae tubās habent. 10. Aquilae sunt māgnae.

II. 1. Via dūra est longa. 2. Puella bona rosam habet. 3. Columba caudam parvam habet. 4. Rēgīnae albās rosās habent. 5. Rosa parva est alba. 6. Aquila māgna est alba. 7. Tubae māgnae sunt longae. 8. Puella tubam longam habet. 9. Fīliae bonae columbās habent. 10. Aquila māgna lātam caudam habet.

**23.** Notice the order of the words in the above sentences, and see wherein it differs from the order in English. You will find that —

1. The adjective is commonly placed after its noun. When placed before the noun it is for emphasis.

2. The verb commonly comes at the end of the sentence, but **est** and **sunt** are less frequently so placed.

3. The object commonly comes before the verb.

**24.** Observe that the subject is in the nominative case, and that the verb agrees with it in number, as in English.

**25.** Observe that the verb **habet** (**habent**) is transitive, and has its object in the accusative.

**26.** Rule of Syntax. — **The direct object of a transitive verb is in the accusative case.**

## 4.

**27.** EXERCISES.

I. 1. The roads are broad. 2. The streets are long. 3. Queens have doves. 4. The girl has a rose. 5. Eagles have tails. 6. The dove is white. 7. The girl has a trumpet. 8. The eagle is large. 9. The rose is white. 10. The girls are small.

II. 1. The long way is hard. 2. Good girls have roses. 3. Doves have small tails. 4. Great eagles have broad tails. 5. The good queen has a dove. 6. The little girls have large trumpets. 7. The little dove is white. 8. The queen is good. 9. The good queen has a little daughter. 10. A little girl has a white rose.

**28.** *Answer the following in Latin:*[1]—

1. Estne[2] via lāta? 2. Habetne puella rosam? 3. Habentne aquilae caudās longās? 4. Quid (*what*) habet rēgīna bona? 5. Quid habent puellae bonae? 6. Habentne columbae caudās?

## 5.

**29.** VOCABULARY.

NOUNS.

**āla**, F., *wing*.
**Britannia**, F., *Britain*.
**Cornēlia**, F., *Cornelia*.
**Galba**, M., *Galba*.
**hōra**, F., *hour*.
**lūna**, F., *moon*.

ADJECTIVES.

**multa**, *much* (pl. *many*).
**plēna**, *full*.
**prīma**, *first*.
**secunda**, *second*.

VERBS.

**amat**, (*he, she, it*) *loves*.
**amant**, (*they*) *love*.
**dat**, (*he, she, it*) *gives*.
**dant**, (*they*) *give*.

CONJUNCTION.

**et**, *and*.

ADVERB.

**nōn**, *not*.

---

[1] Every answer should form a complete sentence. To the question **est-ne via longa**? the answer should be **via est longa.**

[2] The particle **ne** is appended to some word in a sentence, often the verb, as a sign of a question, and is not to be translated by any separate word.

## Genitive and Dative.

**30.** EXERCISES.

I. 1. Lūnae plēnae. 2. Lūnārum plēnārum. 3. Lūnīs plēnīs. 4. Hōrārum prīmārum. 5. Hōrīs prīmīs. 6. Fīlia Galbae.[1] 7. Fīliīs Cornēliae. 8. Rosīs albīs. 9. Columbae parvae. 10. Aquilārum ālārum.

II. 1. The queen's daughter. 2. The queens' daughters. 3. For the girl's rose. 4. Of the wings of the dove. 5. For Cornelia's daughter. 6. Of Britain. 7. For eagles. 8. Of the long streets. 9. For the little girls. 10. To the small trumpet.

## 6.

**31.** EXERCISES.

I. 1. Puellae (*dative*) est rosa. 2. Puella rosam habet. 3. Rēgīnīs sunt columbae. 4. Rēgīnae columbās habent. 5. Rosa puellae est alba. 6. Rosae puellārum sunt albae. 7. Galba fīliae[2] columbam dat. 8. Cornēlia puellīs rosās dat. 9. Galba Cornēliae aquilam dat. 10. Galba et Cornēlia fīliās habent.

II. 1. Fīliae Cornēliae rosās albās habent. 2. Cornēlia puellae parvae rosam māgnam dat. 3. Est[3] hōra prīma lūnae plēnae. 4. Hōra est[3] secunda et lūna est plēna. 5. Māgna est rosa puellae parvae. 6. Galba puellae tubam parvam dat. 7. Columbae albae fīliae bonae sunt. 8. Multae et longae sunt Britanniae viae. 9. Britannia rēgīnam bonam habet. 10. Galba fīliīs bonae rēgīnae rosās multās dat.

**32.** The first sentence in I. is literally translated *to the girl is a rose*. Evidently the meaning is *the girl has a rose*, the same as that of the second. The dative thus used with **est** or **sunt** is called the **Dative of the Possessor**, or the **Possessive Dative**.

[1] *Galba's daughter.* The genitive is often to be translated by the English possessive.

[2] Translate, *his daughter.*

[3] *It is.*

**33.** Examine the seventh sentence in I. The transitive verb **dat** has a direct object, **columbam**; but it also has a dative limiting it, **fīliae**. This dative is called an **Indirect Object**. Find other illustrations of the following:

**34.** Rule of Syntax.—**The indirect object is put in the dative.**

## 7.

**35.** EXERCISES.

1. Before turning the following sentences into Latin, translate mentally 2, 6, and 10, in **31**. II., taking the words as they stand. Observe that the indirect object precedes the direct.

2. In the following exercises try to cast each sentence into the Latin form before thinking of the Latin words. Thus, the sixth sentence will take the form, *the girl to the queen a rose gives;* and the eighth, *to a girl little is a rose little*, or *a girl little a rose little has.*

I. 1. It[1] is the first hour. 2. There[2] is a full moon. 3. The moon is full. 4. The dove is small. 5. The tail of the eagle is broad. 6. The girl gives the queen[3] a rose. 7. The queen's roses are white. 8.[4] A little girl has a little rose. 9. The first hour is a long one.[2] 10. Galba gives the girls some[2] roses.

II. 1. The queen's daughter has a white rose. 2. The queen of Britain gives the girl a great rose. 3. It is the second hour of the full moon. 4. The daughters of Cornelia are small girls.[5] 5. The daughters of Cornelia are good little[6] girls.[5] 6. The little dove's tail is a long one. 7. The wings of eagles are long and broad. 8. Eagles have long, broad[7] wings. 9. The little dove has a white tail. 10.[4] Many doves have white tails.

---

[1] Omit. Compare **31**. II. 3 and 4.

[2] Omit.

[3] That is, *to the queen*. Compare **31**. I. 7, 8, and 9; and **31**. II. 2, 6, and 10.

[4] Translate in two ways, like **31**. I., 1 and 2, 3 and 4.

[5] Nominative.

[6] In Latin, *good and little.*

[7] *Long and broad.*

# CHAPTER III. 1.

## SECOND DECLENSION.

**36.** The stem ends in *o*.

**37.** Gender. — Nouns ending in *um* are neuter; most others are masculine; but see general rules for gender, **11.** 4.

**38.** PARADIGMS.[1]

| **Hortus**, *garden*. | | | **Bellum**, *war*. | | |
|---|---|---|---|---|---|
| | SINGULAR. | PLURAL. | | SINGULAR. | PLURAL. |
| N.V. | hort**us**, **ĕ** | hort**ī** | N.V. | bell**um** | bell**a** |
| G. | hort**ī** | hort**ōrum** | G. | bell**ī** | bell**ōrum** |
| D. | hort**ō** | hort**īs** | D. | bell**ō** | bell**īs** |
| Ac. | hort**um** | hort**ōs** | Ac. | bell**um** | bell**a** |
| Ab. | hort**ō** | hort**īs** | Ab. | bell**ō** | bell**īs** |

**39.** The vocative singular of nouns in *us* of this declension ends in *ĕ*.

1. As these are the only Latin nouns having a form for the vocative different from the nominative, this peculiarity is best regarded and treated as an exception.

**40.** Examples of the locative case (**10.** 3) in this declension are: **Corinthī**, *at Corinth*; **Thūriīs**, *at Thurii*.

**41.** TERMINATIONS.

| | SINGULAR. | | PLURAL. | |
|---|---|---|---|---|
| | *Masc.* | *Neut.* | *Masc.* | *Neut.* |
| N.V. | **us, ĕ** | **um** | **ī** | **a** |
| G. | **ī** | **ī** | **ōrum** | **ōrum** |
| D. | **ō** | **ō** | **īs** | **īs** |
| Ac. | **um** | **um** | **ōs** | **a** |
| Ab. | **ō** | **ō** | **īs** | **īs** |

**42.** Although the stem ends in *o*, the *o* does not appear except in the dat. and abl. singular and in the gen. and acc. plural.

---

[1] For peculiarities of nouns in *ius* and *ium* see **79**.

## 2.

**43.** VOCABULARY.

NOUNS.

| *Masculine.* | *Neuter.* |
|---|---|
| **amīcus,** *friend.* | **bracchium,** *arm.* (79.) |
| **cibus,** *food.* | **dōnum,** *gift.* |
| **discipulus,** *pupil.* | **ōvum,** *egg.* |
| **dominus,** *lord, master.* | **pīlum,** *javelin.* |
| **equus,** *horse.* | **pōculum,** *cup.* |
| **servus,** *slave* or *servant.* | **vīnum,** *wine.* |

| ADJECTIVES. | VERBS. |
|---|---|
| **dēfessus, -a, -um,** *tired.* | **laudat,** (*he, she, it*) *praises.*[1] |
| **dūrus, -a, -um,** *hard.* | **laudant,** (*they*) *praise.* |
| **grātus, -a, -um,** *pleasing.* | **portat,** (*he, she, it*) *carries.* |
| **novus, -a, -um,** *new.* | **portant,** (*they*) *carry.* |

**44.** Adjectives of the first and second declensions have three terminations to mark the different genders: **bonus,** masculine; **bona,** feminine; **bonum,** neuter. The feminine of the adjective is declined like **tuba,** the masculine like **hortus,** and the neuter like **bellum.** The full declension of **bonus** is given on page 24.[2]

**45.** Form the masculine and neuter of all the adjectives in **19** and **29.**

### Nominative and Accusative.

**46.** EXERCISES.

I. 1. Amīcī bonī. 2. Amīcus bonus. 3. Amīcōs bonōs. 4. Amīcum bonum. 5. Pōculum novum. 6. Pōcula nova. 7. Equus dēfessus. 8. Equum dēfessum. 9. Equōs dēfessōs. 10. Equī dēfessī. 11. Pōcula māgna. 12. Servōs malōs.

---

[1] **Laudat** may be translated *praises, is praising,* or *does praise.* So of the other verb-forms.

[2] In declining adjectives, it will be found advantageous to decline each gender separately.

II. 1. In like manner form the nominative and accusative in both numbers of the words meaning *long*[1] *javelin, hard master, small horse, good wine*. Decline together **bonus cibus, servus malus, vīnum novum.**

2. Examine the following sentences: —

**Galba est amīcus**, *Galba is a friend.*
**Galba et Cornēlia sunt amīcī**, *Galba and Cornelia are friends.*

3. Observe in these examples that the subject and predicate nouns are in the same case, just as in English.

**47.** Rule of Syntax. — **A noun in the predicate referring to the same person or thing as the subject is in the same case.**

### 3.

**48.** EXERCISES.

I. 1. Dōnum est grātum. 2. Servus bonus est dēfessus. 3. Amīcus pīlum portat. 4. Discipulus ōvum dūrum habet. 5. Equus dēfessus cibum portat. 6. Dōna sunt pōcula parva. 7. Discipulus bracchia longa habet. 8. Dominī servōs laudant. 9. Dominus servum laudat. 10. Servī pōcula parva portant. 11. Novum equum laudat. 12. Equōs novōs laudant.

II. 1. The servant has the cup. 2. The servants have the cups. 3. The pupil has wine and eggs. 4. The master has good food. 5. The gifts are long javelins. 6. The master and the slave are good friends. 7. The little horses are tired. 8. The new pupil has a big[2] cup. 9. They praise the second horse. 10. He is praising the good master. 11. They have some[3] good friends. 12. The slave carries the cups and wine.

---

[1] The adjective must be of the same gender as the noun.

[2] See page 19, note 1.

[3] Omit.

## 4.

## Genitive and Dative.

**49.** EXERCISES.

I. 1. Amīcīs bonīs. 2. Amīcō bonō. 3. Amīcī bonī. 4. Amīcōrum bonōrum. 5. Pōculō novō. 6. Pōculōrum novōrum. 7. Pōculīs novīs. 8. Equī dēfessī. 9. Equīs dēfessīs. 10. Equōrum dēfessōrum. 11. Equō dēfessō. 12. Servīs bonīs.

II. In like manner, form the genitive and dative in both numbers of the words meaning *long javelin, hard master, small horse, good wine*. Decline together **bonus amīcus, discipulus malus, dōnum grātum.**

## 5.

**50.** EXERCISES.

I. 1. Dōnum amīcī bonī est grātum. 2. Servī bonī dominōrum malōrum sunt dēfessī. 3. Amīcīs discipulī dat[1] pīla multa. 4. Amīcō bonō discipulī sunt pīla multa. 5. Amīcī bonōrum discipulōrum pīla multa habent. 6. Equus dēfessus cibum dominī portat. 7. Longa sunt bracchia servī bonī. 8. Dōna dominī servīs sunt grāta. 9. Puellīs parvīs ōva alba dant.[1] 10. Servī rēgīnīs ōva aquilārum dant.

II. 1. The gift is pleasing to the good friend. 2.[2] The slave has the master's cup. 3.[2] The servants have the masters' cups. 4. The master gives the slave[3] a hard egg. 5. The food of the master is wine and eggs. 6. The master praises the little pupil's cup. 7. The tired horses are carrying gifts for the friend. 8. The girl has many new[4] friends. 9. The broad cup is pleasing to the new pupil. 10. The eagle's eggs are gifts of the good servant.

---

[1] When there is no subject expressed in the sentence, how is the verb to be rendered?

[2] Translate in two ways. See **32**.

[3] Not accusative.

[4] *Many and new.*

## 6.

**51.** *Answer the following in Latin:*[1] —

1. Quid portat Jacōbus (*James*)? 2. Portatne dominō[2] vīnum et ōva? 3. Nōnne[3] portat ōva columbae albae? 4. Laudatne caudam longam equī albī? 5. Quid, Jacōbe, habet dominī fīlia in (*in*) pōculō?

Form and answer five other questions in Latin.

# CHAPTER IV. 1.

## FIRST AND SECOND DECLENSIONS.

**52.** VOCABULARY.

NOUNS.

*Masculine.*[4]

**agricola, -ae,** *farmer.*
**nauta, -ae,** *sailor.*
**poēta, -ae,** *poet.*
**carrus, -ī,** *wagon.*
**rēmus, -ī,** *oar.*
**ventus, -ī,** *wind.*

*Neuter.*

**frūmentum, -ī,** *grain.*
**pābulum, -ī,** *fodder.*

ADJECTIVES.

**clārus, -a, -um,** *famous.*
**peritus, -a, -um,** *skilful.*
**quartus, -a, -um,** *fourth.*
**quīntus, -a, -um,** *fifth.*
**tertius, -a, -um,** *third.*
**validus, -a, -um,** *strong, sturdy.*

PREPOSITION.

**in** (with ablative), *in, on.*
**in** (with accusative), *into, to.*

**53.** In the preceding exercises an adjective qualifying a noun has had the same termination as the noun. Now observe the following examples: **agricola bonus,** *a good farmer;* **agricolae bonī,** *of a good farmer;* **agricolae bonō,** *to* or *for a good farmer,* etc. Here the adjective has a different termination from the noun. Since **agricola** is masculine, the adjective that goes with it must have the masculine form, as well as the same number and case.

[1] See note 1, p. 10.
[2] *for,* not *to, the master.*
[3] When **ne** is appended to **nōn,** the answer *yes* is expected. See note 2, p. 10. So in English, a question asked with *not* expects the answer *yes.*
[4] See **11.** 1.

**54.** Rule of Syntax.—**Adjectives agree with their nouns in gender, number, and case.**

**55.** EXERCISES.

I. 1. Agricolae validī. 2. Agricolam validum. 3. Agricolās validōs. 4. Agricola validus. 5. Agricolae validō. 6. Agricolārum validōrum. 7. Agricola valide.

II. 1. A skilful sailor (*nom. and acc.*). 2. Skilful sailors (*nom. and acc.*). 3. Of a skilful sailor. 4. For a skilful sailor. 5. Skilful sailor (*voc.*). 6. For skilful sailors. 7. Of a famous poet. 8. Of famous poets. 9. Pleasing poets. 10. A pleasing poet (*nom. and acc.*).

## 2.

**56.** EXERCISES.

I. 1. Hortus agricolae māgnus est. 2. Agricola validus hortum māgnum habet. 3.[1] Agricolae (*dat.*) est hortus māgnus. 4. Nautae rēmus longus est. 5. Poēta vīnum bonum agricolae perītī laudat. 6. Hōra est quarta. 7.[2] Lūna est plēna. 8. Pābulum equī albī est frūmentum. 9. Dominus servum perītum laudat. 10.[3] Nautae (*dat.*) grāta sunt ōva et vīnum agricolae bonī.

II. 1. Ō[4] agricola valide, carrus est plēnus frūmentī. 2. Domine bone, secunda hōra est, et discipulus est dēfessus. 3. Hortōs agricolārum perītōrum laudant. 4. Pōculum māgnum est vīnī plēnum. 5. Agricola bonus equō validō dat pābulum.

---

[1] See **32**.

[2] We may translate, *there is a full moon, it is a full moon*, or *the moon is full*. There is nothing in Latin answering to our *it* and *there* used in this way at the beginning of a sentence.

[3] Translate this sentence without changing the order of the words, and you will feel the emphasis imparted to **nautae** from its position.

[4] Ō sometimes accompanies the vocative.

## 3.

**57.** EXERCISES.

I. 1. The poet likes[1] the farmer's wine. 2.[2] Farmers have large wagons and strong horses. 3. Skilful sailors like a good breeze. 4. In the garden there[3] are many roses. 5. The poet and his[3] daughter are in the wagon. 6. The horse carries the farmer's grain. 7. There is wine in the little girl's cup. 8. There are many[4] small girls in the street. 9. Galba carries fodder for the horses. 10. The food of the little dove is grain.

II. 1. My (Ō) good friend, the master's cup is full. 2. The servant gives the queen[5] a large cup. 3. The strong sailors are carrying javelins in their[3] arms. 4. In the strong wagon is good fodder for the farmer's horses. 5. In the poet's gardens there are many friends. 6. Farmers have horses, wagons, doves, eggs, and[3] wine.

## 4.

**58.** COLLOQUIUM.

Datne[6] Carolus (*Charles*) amīcō cymbam (*boat*)?
Carolus amīcō cymbam et rēmōs dat.
Quid in cymbā habet Carolus?
Carolus rēmum et pīlum in cymbā habet.
Quota (*what*) hōra est?[7] Hōra est quīnta.
Quid in carrō habet rūsticus (*countryman*) validus?
Quid in pōculō dēsīderat (*wants*) rūsticus dēfessus?

---

[1] Occasionally words occur in the English exercises which are purposely not given as definitions in the vocabularies, but by a little thought the pupil will understand what Latin word is meant.

[2] Translate in two ways.

[3] Omit.

[4] *Many and small.*

[5] Not accusative.

[6] Remember that ne is appended as the sign of a question.

[7] *What time is it?* or, *What is the time of day?*

# CHAPTER V. 1.

## SECOND DECLENSION.

**59.** PARADIGM.

**Puer**, *boy*.

| SINGULAR. | | PLURAL. | TERMINATIONS. SING. | PLUR. |
|---|---|---|---|---|
| N.V. | puer | puer**ī** | — | **ī** |
| G. | puer**ī** | puer**ōrum** | **ī** | **ōrum** |
| D. | puer**ō** | puer**īs** | **ō** | **īs** |
| Ac. | puer**um** | puer**ōs** | **um** | **ōs** |
| Ab. | puer**ō** [1] | puer**īs** | **ō** | **īs** |

**60.** VOCABULARY.

**gener, -erī,** M., *son-in-law.*
**līberī, -ōrum,** (pl.) M., *children.*
**socer, -erī,** M., *father-in-law.*
**vir, virī,** M., *man, hero.*

**asper, -era, -erum,** *rough.*
**līber, -era, -erum,**[2] *free.*
**miser, -era, -erum,** *poor, wretched.*

**tener, -era, -erum,** *tender.*
**sextus, -a, -um,** *sixth.*

**ā (ab),** prep. w. abl., *by, away from.*

**amātur,** (*he, she, it*) *is loved.*
**amantur,** (*they*) *are loved.*
**laudātur,** (*he, she, it*) *is praised.*
**laudantur,** (*they*) *are praised.*

**puerī,** general word for *children.*
**līberī,** *children of free parents.*

**61.** *The farmer is praised by the queen* would be expressed in Latin thus: **Agricola ā** (or **ab**) **rēgīnā laudātur**; and *The queen is praised by the farmer*, thus: **Rēgīna ab** (not **ā**) **agricolā laudātur.**

Observe that in the first sentence, **rēgīnā**, and in the second, **agricolā**, denotes the person by whom the thing is done (the agent); also, that these words are in the ablative, and are preceded by **ā** or **ab**. The ablative thus used, together with the preposition, answers the question *by whom?*

[1] To translate **puerō**, "*with, from, by a boy,*" as is commonly done, is wholly wrong. *With a boy* would be **cum puerō**; *from*, or *by a boy*, **ā puerō**. See p. 7, note 2.

[2] Decline the masculine of adjectives in *er* in this lesson like **puer**. The full declension is given on p. 24.

**62.** Rule of Syntax.—**The agent is expressed by the ablative with *ā* or *ab*,—*ab* before vowels or *h*, *ā* or *ab* before consonants.**

**63.** Read again **53** and **54**, then add the proper terminations of the adjectives, and translate the following:—

I. 1. Generī bon-, gener bon- (*nom. and voc.*). 2. Vir māgn-, ā virō māgn-. 3. Ab agricolā dēfess-, agricolae miser-. 4. Ā rēgīnā tener-. 5. Puerī asper-.

II. 1. By the bad father-in-law. 2. By the rough sailor. 3. By the children of the hero. 4. The free men (*nom. and acc.*). 5. Of the wretched sons-in-law.

2.

**64.** EXERCISES.

I. 1. Gener virī servus est. 2. Puer bonus ab amīcō laudātur. 3. Līberī ā nautā asperō amantur. 4. Puella tenera columbās parvās amat. 5. Columbae parvae ā puellā tenerā amantur. 6. Miserī servī ā dominō bonō laudantur. 7.[1] Lātā in viā sunt puerī multī et asperī. 8. Equī validī agricolae ā līberīs laudantur. 9. Fīlia socerī est misera. 10. Virī fīliās poētae laudant.

II. 1. The sons-in-law of the men are farmers. 2. Good men are praised by their[2] friends. 3. The boy is loved by the rough sailors. 4. The sixth boy is a new one.[2] 5. The tired children are in the farmer's wagon. 6. The tender dove is loved by the little girl. 7. Poor slaves are not praised by their rough masters. 8. The strong man is in the poet's garden. 9. The heroes are praised by the pupils. 10. They love the daughter of the poor sailor.

[1] Adjective, preposition, noun, is often the order where, as here, the three are combined. What is the English order?

[2] Omit.

# CHAPTER VI. 1.

## SECOND DECLENSION.

**65.** PARADIGM.

| **Ager,** *field.* | | Terminations. | |
|---|---|---|---|
| SINGULAR. | PLURAL. | SING. | PLUR. |
| N.V. ager | agr**ī** | — | **ī** |
| G. agr**ī** | agr**ōrum** | **ī** | **ōrum** |
| D. agr**ō** | agr**īs** | **ō** | **īs** |
| Ac. agr**um** | agr**ōs** | **um** | **ōs** |
| Ab. agr**ō** | agr**īs** | **ō** | **īs** |

Observe that the above terminations are the same as those on page 20. Wherein does the declension of **ager** differ from that of **puer**?

**66.** VOCABULARY.

**aper, aprī,** M., *boar.*
**culter, cultrī,** M., *knife.*
**faber, -brī,** M., *smith.*
**līber,**[1] **-brī,** M., *book.*
**magister, -trī,** M., *master.*
**minister, -trī,** M., *servant.*
**aeger, aegra, aegrum,**[2] *sick.*
**niger, nigra, nigrum,** *black.*
**pulcher, pulchra, pulchrum,** *beautiful, handsome.*
**ruber, rubra, rubrum,** *red.*
**septimus, -a, -um,** *seventh.*

**magister,** *a superior, director;* hence, *master* of a school, etc.
**dominus (43),** *master of a household, slaves,* etc.
**minister,** *an inferior, attendant, servant.*
**servus (43),** *a serving man, slave.*

**67.** Most nouns in *er* are declined like **ager,** and most adjectives in *er* like **aeger.** The most important nouns and adjectives that keep the *e* before *r* in all the cases were given in the vocabulary, **60,** and should now be committed to memory.

**68.** Decline together **equus niger, bonus faber, aper asper, vir aeger.**

[1] Distinguish **līber,** *free,* from **liber,** *book.* [2] See p. 24.

## 2.

**69.** EXERCISES.

I. 1. Socer est faber. 2. Magister est discipulī amīcus. 3. Generī virī sunt ministrī. 4. Culter puerō est grātus. 5. Librī magistrī discipulīs sunt grātī. 6. Vīnum rubrum ā fabrō dēfessō amātur. 7. Librī poētae ā magistrō amantur. 8. Puellae pulchrae virīs rosās rubrās dant. 9. Nauta cultrum longum habet. 10.[1] Librōs multōs in bracchiīs portat puer.

II. 1. The fathers-in-law are smiths.[2] 2. The masters are loved by their pupils. 3. The man's son-in-law is a servant. 4. The knives are pleasing to the little boy. 5. The pretty[3] cups are liked by the boys and girls. 6. A girl gives a man[4] a beautiful rose. 7. The sailors have many long knives. 8. The children of the master are carrying[5] the books in their arms. 9. The smith's son-in-law has children. 10. There is a rough boar in the farmer's field.

**70.** *Answer the following in Latin:*—

1. Quis (*who*) est amīcus poētae? 2. Quis est socer Carolī? 3. Ubi (*where*) sunt discipulī magistrī? 4. Amantne hodiē (*to-day*) pēnsum (*task*)? 5. Nōnne Carolus columbae frūmentum hodiē dat? 6. Quae (*who, fem.*) rosās rubrās habet? 7. Quis bracchia longa habet? 8. Quis est vir līber? 9. Ubi est equus rūsticī? 10. Quae puellās pulchrās habet? 11. Rēgīnane puellās pulchrās habet? 12. Ubi sunt Jacōbī amīcī?

---

[1] What is peculiar in the order of the words? Translate as the words stand, and see what word is made emphatic by its position.

[2] What case is used after est and sunt? Compare the first three sentences in I. See rule, **47**.

[3] See p. 19, note 1.

[4] Not accusative.

[5] Not passive. See p. 14, note 1.

## ADJECTIVES: FIRST AND SECOND DECLENSIONS.

**71.** PARADIGMS.

**Bonus**, *good.*

| | | MASCULINE. | FEMININE. | NEUTER. |
|---|---|---|---|---|
| Sing. | N.V. | bon **us, ĕ** | bon **a** | bon **um** |
| | G. | bon **ī** | bon **ae** | bon **ī** |
| | D. | bon **ō** | bon **ae** | bon **ō** |
| | Ac. | bon **um** | bon **am** | bon **um** |
| | Ab. | bon **ō** | bon **ā** | bon **ō** |
| Plur. | N.V. | bon **ī** | bon **ae** | bon **a** |
| | G. | bon **ōrum** | bon **ārum** | bon **ōrum** |
| | D. | bon **īs** | bon **īs** | bon **īs** |
| | Ac. | bon **ōs** | bon **ās** | bon **a** |
| | Ab. | bon **īs** | bon **īs** | bon **īs** |

**Līber**, *free.*

| | | | | |
|---|---|---|---|---|
| Sing. | N.V. | līber | līber **a** | līber **um** |
| | G. | līber **ī** | līber **ae** | līber **ī** |
| | D. | līber **ō** | līber **ae** | līber **ō** |
| | Ac. | līber **um** | līber **am** | līber **um** |
| | Ab. | līber **ō** | līber **ā** | līber **ō** |
| Plur. | N.V. | līber **ī** | līber **ae** | līber **a** |
| | G. | līber **ōrum** | līber **ārum** | līber **ōrum** |
| | D. | līber **īs** | līber **īs** | līber **īs** |
| | Ac. | līber **ōs** | līber **ās** | līber **a** |
| | Ab. | līber **īs** | līber **īs** | līber **īs** |

**Aeger**, *sick.*

| | | | | |
|---|---|---|---|---|
| Sing. | N.V. | aeger | aegr **a** | aegr **um** |
| | G. | aegr **ī** | aegr **ae** | aegr **ī** |
| | D. | aegr **ō** | aegr **ae** | aegr **ō** |
| | Ac. | aegr **um** | aegr **am** | aegr **um** |
| | Ab. | aegr **ō** | aegr **ā** | aegr **ō** |
| Plur. | N.V. | aegr **ī** | aegr **ae** | aegr **a** |
| | G. | aegr **ōrum** | aegr **ārum** | aegr **ōrum** |
| | D. | aegr **īs** | aegr **īs** | aegr **īs** |
| | Ac. | aegr **ōs** | aegr **ās** | aegr **a** |
| | Ab. | aegr **īs** | aegr **īs** | aegr **īs** |

# CHAPTER VII.

## THE IRREGULAR VERB **Sum,** *I am.*

**72.** Stems *es* and *fu.*

**73.** For convenience the inflection of **sum** is given in full. Directions will be given from time to time as to what parts are to be learned.

### INDICATIVE MOOD.

PRESENT TENSE.

| | SINGULAR. | PLURAL. |
|---|---|---|
| 1. | s**um**,[1] *I am.* | s**umus**, *we are.* |
| 2. | es, *thou art.*[2] | es**tis**, *you are.* |
| 3. | es**t**, *he (she, it) is.* | s**unt**, *they are.* |

IMPERFECT.

| | | |
|---|---|---|
| 1. | er**am**,[3] *I was.* | er**āmus**, *we were.* |
| 2. | er**ās**, *thou wast.* | er**ātis**, *you were.* |
| 3. | er**at**, *he was.* | er**ant**, *they were.* |

FUTURE.

| | | |
|---|---|---|
| 1. | er**ō**,[4] *I shall be.* | er**imus**, *we shall be.* |
| 2. | er**is**, *thou wilt be.* | er**itis**, *you will be.* |
| 3. | er**it**, *he will be.* | er**unt**, *they will be.* |

PERFECT.

| | | |
|---|---|---|
| 1. | fu**ī**, *I have been, was.* | fu**imus**, *we have been, were.* |
| 2. | fu**istī**, *thou hast been, wast.* | fu**istis**, *you have been, were.* |
| 3. | fu**it**, *he has been, was.* | fu**ērunt**, or fu**ēre**, *they have been, were.* |

PLUPERFECT.

| | | |
|---|---|---|
| 1. | fu**eram**, *I had been.* | fu**erāmus**, *we had been.* |
| 2. | fu**erās**, *thou hadst been.* | fu**erātis**, *you had been.* |
| 3. | fu**erat**, *he had been.* | fu**erant**, *they had been.* |

[1] **Sum** for **esum.**

[2] Or, *you are*, as in the plural. But in translating into Latin be careful to use the singular form of the verb, if by *you* one person only is meant.

[3] **Eram** for **esam.**

[4] **Erō** for **esō.**

### Future Perfect.

| | SINGULAR. | PLURAL. |
|---|---|---|
| 1. | fu**erō**, *I shall have been.* | fu**erimus**, *we shall have been.* |
| 2. | fu**eris**, *thou wilt have been.* | fu**eritis**, *you will have been.* |
| 3. | fu**erit**, *he will have been.* | fu**erint**, *they will have been.* |

## SUBJUNCTIVE.[1]

| | Present. | | Imperfect. | |
|---|---|---|---|---|
| | SING. | PLUR. | SING. | PLUR. |
| 1. | s**im** | s**īmus** | es**sem** | es**sēmus** |
| 2. | s**īs** | s**ītis** | es**sēs** | es**sētis** |
| 3. | s**it** | s**int** | es**set** | es**sent** |

| | Perfect. | | Pluperfect. | |
|---|---|---|---|---|
| 1. | fu**erim** | fu**erimus** | fu**issem** | fu**issēmus** |
| 2. | fu**eris** | fu**eritis** | fu**issēs** | fu**issētis** |
| 3. | fu**erit** | fu**erint** | fu**isset** | fu**issent** |

## IMPERATIVE.

### Present.

| | SINGULAR. | PLURAL. |
|---|---|---|
| 2. | es, *be thou.* | es**te**, *be ye.* |

### Future.

| | | |
|---|---|---|
| 2. | es**tō**, *thou shalt be.* | es**tōte**, *ye shall be.* |
| 3. | es**tō**, *he shall be.* | s**untō**, *they shall be.* |

## INFINITIVE.

Present, es**se**, *to be.*
Perfect, fu**isse**, *to have been.*
Future, fu**tūrus** es**se**, *to be about to be.*

## PARTICIPLE.

fu**tūrus**, -a, -um, *about to be.*

[1] No meanings can be given to the subjunctive that are not misleading. Its forms are therefore better left untranslated until its use has been illustrated. The subjunctive is treated on pp. 164–186.

# CHAPTER VIII. 1.

## THE VERB Sum.

**74.** Learn the present, imperfect, and future indicative, and the present imperative and infinitive.

**75.** EXERCISES.

I. 1. Est, erat, erit. 2. Sunt, erant, erunt. 3. Sumus, erāmus, erimus. 4. Erō, eram, sum. 5. Erās, es, eris. 6. Estis, eritis, erātis. 7. Es, este. 8. Esse.

II. 1. I am, we are, I was, we were, I shall be, we shall be. 2. He was, they were, he is, they are, he will be, they will be. 3. You (*sing.*) will be, are, were. 4. You (*plur.*) will be, are, were. 5. Be ye, be thou. 6. To be.

## 2.

From this point the vocabularies follow the exercises, and it is recommended that the pupil go through the exercises mentally, referring to the vocabularies for the meanings of words. Before *writing* the translations into Latin the vocabularies should be reviewed, but the task of committing to memory will then be found an easy one.

**76.** EXERCISES.

I. 1. Inimīcus pīlum habet. 2. Inimīcō est pīlum. 3. Somnus puerō erit grātus. 4. Līberī agricolae erunt dēfessī. 5. Minerva āram in oppidō habēbat. 6. Minervae in oppidō erat āra. 7. In terrā virī, in aquā rānae sunt. 8. Inimīcī erāmus incolārum malōrum. 9. Oculī dominī dūrī erant māgnī et nigrī. 10.[1] Dominō dūrō erant oculī māgnī et nigrī. 11.[1] Dominus dūrus oculōs māgnōs et nigrōs habēbat. 12. Cōnsilium fabrī perītī bonum erat.

[1] What word is better left untranslated, though needed in the Latin?

II. 1.[1] The farmer had a wagon. 2. I shall be the man's friend. 3. There[2] is a large town on[3] the island. 4. There was a red egg on the table. 5. Children were carrying the food of the men. 6. A boy gave a smith[4] some[2] javelins. 7. In the town are enemies of the inhabitants. 8. They were praising the words of the sturdy farmer. 9. The poet's gifts will be pleasing to Minerva. 10. Boys, be ye strong and skilful.

## 3.

**77.** EXERCISES.

I. 1. Eritis validō in carrō agricolae perītī. 2. Erās nōnus discipulus et fīlius poētae erat octāvus. 3. Ō miser serve, tū (*thou*) es inimīcus pulchrae Minervae. 4. Amīcus erō Minervae māgnae. 5.[5] Agricolīs arātra dūra et valida dabant virī. 6. In Britanniā sunt oppida multa et māgna. 7. Puer bone, es amīcus equī miserī.

II. 1. A girl gave a sick sailor[6] some wine and water. 2. The wine she carried in a pretty[7] cup. 3. He praised the maiden's[7] pretty cup and the ruddy wine. 4. The maiden and the sailor were inhabitants of Britain. 5. Britain is a large island, and has handsome towns.

**78.** VOCABULARY.

**aqua, -ae,** F., *water.*
**āra, -ae,** F., *altar.*
**arātrum, -ī,** N., *plough.*
**cōnsilium, -ī,** N., *advice* (**79**).
**incola, -ae,** M. & F., *inhabitant.*
**inimīcus, -ī,** M., *enemy.*
**īnsula, -ae,** F., *island.*
**mēnsa, -ae,** F., *table.*

---

[1] Translate in two ways.
[2] Omit. See p. 18, note 2.
[3] See vocabulary, **52**.
[4] Indirect object, see **33** & **34**. What name is given to the dative **agricolis**?
[5] Compare the order with that of **69**. I. 10, and see the note there.
[6] See **69**. II. 6, and note.
[7] See p. 19, note 1.

**Minerva, -ae,** F., *Minerva, goddess of wisdom.*
**nōnus, -a, -um,** adj., *ninth.*
**octāvus, -a, -um,** adj., *eighth.*
**oculus, -ī,** M., *eye.*
**oppidum, -ī,** N., *town.*
**rāna, -ae,** F., *frog.*
**somnus, -ī,** M., *sleep.*
**verbum, -ī,** N., *word.*

**amābat,** *(he she it) was loving, loved.*
**dabat,** *(he, she, it) was giving, gave.*
**habēbat,** *(he, she, it) was having, had.*
**laudābat,** *(he, she, it) was praising, praised.*
**portābat,** *(he, she, it) was carrying, carried.*

**amābant,** *they were loving, loved.*
**dabant,** *they were giving, gave.*
**habēbant,** *they were having, had.*
**laudābant,** *they were praising, praised.*
**portābant,** *they were carrying, carried.*

**79.** Nouns in *ius* and *ium* contract the genitive ending *iī* to ī: **cōnsilī.** **Fīlius** (*son*) and **genius** (*guardian deity*), and proper nouns in *ius*, drop the *e* of the vocative: **fīlī, Mercurī,** *Mercury.* But the word is accented as if the longer form were used.

## 4.

**80.** COLLOQUIUM.

Nōnne aquam in pōculō habet faber?

Minimē. Faber in pōculō habet novum vīnum.
no

Dēsīderatne Galba somnum grātum?
wishes

Certē, nam hodiē est Galba dēfessus.
certainly for to-day

Ubi est amīcus agricolae pigrī?
lazy

Est in oppidō, nam nōn amābat amīcī cōnsilium.

Ubi sunt arma agricolārum validōrum?
tools

Agricolārum equī, carrī, arātra sunt in agrō.

## CHAPTER IX. 1.

### THE VERB Sum.

**81.** Learn the perfect, pluperfect, and future perfect indicative, and the perfect infinitive. See pp. 25 and 26.

**82.** EXERCISES.

I. 1. Fuit, fuerat, fuerit. 2. Fuērunt, fuerant, fuerint. 3. Fuimus, fuerāmus, fuerimus. 4. Fuerō, fueram, fuī. 5. Fuerās, fueris, fuistī. 6. Fuistis, fueritis, fuerātis. 7. Fuisse.

II. 1. I have been, we have been, I had been, we had been, I shall have been, we shall have been. 2. He has been, they have been, he had been, they had been, he will have been, they will have been. 3. You (*sing.*) will have been, had been, have been. 4. You (*plur.*) will have been, had been, have been. 5. To have been.

### 2.

**83.** EXERCISES.

I. 1. In Graeciā erant templa multa. 2. In Graeciā erant templa deōrum et deārum. 3. Aurum erat in statuā Minervae. 4. Minervae fuit statua māgna et clāra. 5. Minerva statuam māgnam et clāram habēbat. 6. Multae et pulchrae erant Graeciae statuae. 7. Nōn alta erant pulchra Graeciae templa. 8. Fluviī Graeciae nōn lātī et altī erant. 9. Clārī fuērunt multī Graecī. 10. Graecōrum antīquōrum erit glōria sempiterna.

II. 1. They had been in the towns of the Greeks. 2. The monuments of Greece were temples and statues. 3. The statue of Minerva had a shield and spear. 4. The arms of the Greeks were shields and spears. 5. The gods had many statues in Greece. 6. The red roses will be pleasing to the queen. 7. The man's children are in the street. 8. He has been on the farmer's horse. 9. The children are carried in the poet's arms. 10. Many inhabitants of Britain have been skilful sailors.

**84.** VOCABULARY.

**altus, -a, -um,** adj., *deep, high.*
**antīquus, -a, -um,** adj., *ancient.*
**arma, -ōrum,** N. (plur.), *arms.*
**aureus, -a, -um,** adj., *of gold, golden.*
**aurum, -ī,** N., *gold.*
**dea, -ae,** F., *goddess.* p. 8, n. 1.
**decimus, -a, -um,** adj., *tenth.*
**deus, -ī,** M., *god* (**262**).
**fluvius, -ī,** M., *river* (**79**).
**glōria, -ae,** F., *glory.*
**Graecia, -ae,** F., *Greece.*
**Graecus, -ī,** M., *a Greek.*
**hasta, -ae,** F., *spear.*
**monumentum, -ī,** N., *monument.*
**scūtum, -ī,** N., *shield.*
**sempiternus, -a, -um,** adj., *everlasting.*
**statua, -ae,** F., *statue.*
**templum, -ī,** N., *temple.*

3.

**85.** COLLOQUIUM.

Duo Puerī.
two

Ubi est Carolus hodiē? Nōnne est in scholā?
Charles school

Minimē. Est in fluviō; nam habet cymbam parvam, et libenter nāvigat.
likes sailing

Unde Carolō est cymba? Where did C. get a boat?
whence to Charles is a boat.

Ab avunculō, nam Carolus ab avunculō amātur.
from uncle

Quid in cymbā portat Carolus?

Nesciō; procul dubiō prandium; etenim in animō habet . . .
I don't know doubtless luncheon for mind

Quid in animō habet?

Valē, bone amīce, crās patēbit.
good by to-morrow it will be open = the secret will be out.

# CHAPTER X.

## FIRST CONJUGATION.

**86.** VERBS IN *ā*.

**Amō** (stem **amā**), *love*.

PRINCIPAL PARTS:[1] **amō, amāre, amāvī, amātum.**

### INDICATIVE.

| ACTIVE VOICE. | | PASSIVE VOICE. | |
|---|---|---|---|
| | PRESENT. | | |
| *I love, am loving, do love, etc.* | | *I am loved, etc.* | |
| am **ō** | am **āmus** | am **or** | am **āmur** |
| am **ās** | am **ātis** | am **āris**, *or* **-re** | am **āminī** |
| am **at** | am **ant** | am **ātur** | am **antur** |
| | IMPERFECT. | | |
| *I loved, was loving, did love, etc.* | | *I was loved, etc.* | |
| am **ābam** | am **ābāmus** | am **ābar** | am **ābāmur** |
| am **ābās** | am **ābātis** | am **ābāris**, *or* **-re** | am **ābāminī** |
| am **ābat** | am **ābant** | am **ābātur** | am **ābantur** |
| | FUTURE. | | |
| *I shall love, etc.* | | *I shall be loved, etc.* | |
| am **ābō** | am **ābimus** | am **ābor** | am **ābimur** |
| am **ābis** | am **ābitis** | am **āberis**, *or* **-re** | am **ābiminī** |
| am **ābit** | am **ābunt** | am **ābitur** | am **ābuntur** |
| | PERFECT. | | |
| *I have loved, I loved, etc.* | | *I have been (was) loved, etc.* | |
| amāv **ī** | amāv **imus** | amāt **us** { **sum** | amāt **ī** { **sumus** |
| amāv **istī** | amāv **istis** | **es** | **estis** |
| amāv **it** | amāv **ērunt**, *or* **-re** | **est** | **sunt** |

[1] Certain forms of the verb are called, from their importance, *principal parts*. These forms are the first person of the present indicative, showing the *present stem*; the present infinitive, showing the *conjugation*; the first person of the perfect indicative, showing the *perfect stem*; and the perfect participle, showing the *participle stem*. The neuter of the participle is given, as intransitive verbs have the perfect participle only in that gender.

| ACTIVE VOICE. | | PASSIVE VOICE. | |
|---|---|---|---|

### PLUPERFECT.

| *I had loved, etc.* | | *I had been loved, etc.* | |
|---|---|---|---|
| amāv **eram** | amāv **erāmus** | amāt **us** { **eram** | amāt **ī** { **erāmus** |
| amāv **erās** | amāv **erātis** | **erās** | **erātis** |
| amāv **erat** | amāv **erant** | **erat** | **erant** |

### FUTURE PERFECT.

| *I shall have loved, etc.* | | *I shall have been loved, etc.* | |
|---|---|---|---|
| amāv **erō** | amāv **erimus** | amāt **us** { **erō** | amāt **ī** { **erimus** |
| amāv **eris** | amāv **eritis** | **eris** | **eritis** |
| amāv **erit** | amāv **erint** | **erit** | **erunt** |

## SUBJUNCTIVE.[1]

### PRESENT.

| | | | |
|---|---|---|---|
| am **em** | am **ēmus** | am **er** | am **ēmur** |
| am **ēs** | am **ētis** | am **ēris**, *or* -**re** | am **ēminī** |
| am **et** | am **ent** | am **ētur** | am **entur** |

### IMPERFECT.

| | | | |
|---|---|---|---|
| am **ārem** | am **ārēmus** | am **ārer** | am **ārēmur** |
| am **ārēs** | am **ārētis** | am **ārēris**, *or* -**re** | am **ārēminī** |
| am **āret** | am **ārent** | am **ārētur** | am **ārentur** |

### PERFECT.

| | | | |
|---|---|---|---|
| amāv **erim** | amāv **erimus** | amāt us { **sim** | amāt **ī** { **sīmus** |
| amāv **eris** | amāv **eritis** | **sīs** | **sītis** |
| amāv **erit** | amāv **erint** | **sit** | **sint** |

### PLUPERFECT.

| | | | |
|---|---|---|---|
| amāv **issem** | amāv **issēmus** | amāt **us** { **essem** | amāt **ī** { **essēmus** |
| amāv **issēs** | amāv **issētis** | **essēs** | **essētis** |
| amāv **isset** | amāv **issent** | **esset** | **essent** |

[1] See p. 26, note.

## IMPERATIVE.

| ACTIVE VOICE. | PASSIVE VOICE. |
|---|---|
| PRESENT. | |
| am**ā**, *love thou.* | am**āre**, *be thou loved.* |
| am**āte**, *love ye.* | am**āminī**, *be ye loved.* |
| FUTURE. | |
| am**ātō**, *thou shalt love.* | am**ātor**, *thou shalt be loved.* |
| am**ātō**, *he shall love.* | am**ātor**, *he shall be loved.* |
| am**ātōte**, *you shall love.* | |
| am**antō**, *they shall love.* | am**antor**, *they shall be loved.* |

## INFINITIVE.

| | |
|---|---|
| PRES. am**āre**, *to love.* | am**ārī**, *to be loved.* |
| PERF. amāv**isse**, *to have loved.* | amāt**us esse**, *to have been loved.* |
| FUT. amāt**ūrus esse**, *to be about to love.* | amāt**um īrī**, *to be about to be loved.* |

## PARTICIPLE.

| | |
|---|---|
| PRES. am**āns**, **-antis**, *loving.* | ——————[1] |
| FUT. amāt**ūrus**, **-a**, **-um**, *about to love.* | GER.[2] am**andus**, **-a**, **-um**, *to be loved.* |
| ——————[1] | PERF. amāt**us**, **-a**, **-um**, *having been loved.* |

## GERUND.

G. am**andī**, *of loving.*
D. am**andō**, *for loving.*
Ac. am**andum**, *loving.*
Ab. am**andō**, *by loving.*

## SUPINE.

| | |
|---|---|
| Ac. amāt**um**, *to love.* | Ab. amāt**ū**, *to love, to be loved.* |

[1] Observe that the Latin has neither a perfect active nor a present passive participle.

[2] Gerundive, sometimes less correctly called *future passive participle.*

# CHAPTER XI. 1.

## FIRST CONJUGATION.

**87.** Learn the present, imperfect, and future indicative, and the present imperative and infinitive, active and passive, of **amō**.[1]

**88.** EXERCISES.

I. 1. Amātis, amābātis, amābitis. 2. Amātur, amābātur, amābitur. 3. Amat, amābat, amābit. 4. Amantur, amābantur, amābuntur. 5. Amō, amor. 6. Amās, amāris. 7. Amāmus, amāmur. 8. Amābitis, amābiminī. 9. Amābat, amābātur. 10. Amāre, amārī.

II. 1. He loves, he is loved. 2. He will love, he will be loved. 3. They were loved, they were loving. 4. I shall love, I shall be loved. 5. You (*sing.*) love, you are loved. 6. They loved, they were loving, they will love. 7. You (*plur.*) are loving, you were loving, you will be loving. 8. Love (*sing.*), be loved. 9. To be loved, to love.

## 2.

**89.** EXERCISES.

**Laudō**, *praise;* **portō**, *carry;* **superō**, *conquer.*

I. 1. Laudat, portat, superat. 2. Laudātur, portātur, superātur. 3. Laudābitur, portābitur, superābitur. 4. Laudāsne? portābāsne? superābisne? 5. Laudāmur, portābāmur, superābimur. 6. Laudā, portā, superā. 7. Superāre, portāre, laudārī. 8. Nōn superāminī, nōn portābāminī, nōn laudābiminī. 9. Laudāre, portāminī, superāte. 10. Laudor, portābar, superābor.

II. 1. Thou praisest, you carry, he conquers. 2. He is praised, they are carried, they will be conquered. 3. I praise, I was carrying, I shall conquer. 4. Thou art praised, thou

[1] Notice how frequently the letter *r* marks a form as passive. Where is it absent in the first three tenses?

art carried, thou art conquered. 5. Praise (thou), carry, conquer. 6. He will be conquered, he was praised, it is carried. 7. To conquer, to be carried, to be praised. 8. Do we carry? are we conquered? are we praised? 9. I am not carried, he was not conquered, they are not praised. 10. Thou wilt praise, he will be praised, they were carried.

**90.** *Examine the following sentences:* —

1. **Agricola ā rēgīnā laudātur,** *the farmer is praised by the queen.*
2. **Agricola rēgīnae verbīs laudātur,** *the farmer is praised by the words of the queen.*
3. **Servī gladiīs armantur,** *the slaves are being armed with swords.*

On the first example see **61** and **62**. In the second and third, observe that there is no **ā** or **ab** used with **verbīs** and **gladiīs**.

These ablatives, **verbīs** and **gladiīs**, answer the questions *by what? with what? by means of what?* The ablative thus used is called the **Ablative of Means or Instrument.**

**91.** Rule of Syntax. — **Means and Instrument are expressed by the ablative without a preposition.**

## 3.

**92.** EXERCISES.

I. 1. Puellae rosās amant. 2. Rosae albae ā puellīs amantur. 3. Homērus virōs Graecōs laudābat. 4. Ab[1] Homērō laudābantur virī Graecī. 5. Oppidum nōminābant Rōmam.[2] 6. Oppidum Rōma[3] nōminābātur. 7. Servōs gladiīs armābimus. 8. Inimīcus gladiō vulneratur. 9. Inimīcus ā Galbā vulnerātur. 10. Ō Rōmānī, servōs hastīs armāte.

II. 1. Sing, good boy. 2. Many goddesses were loved by the Greeks. 3. The boy will put the doves to flight.

[1] Before words beginning with *h* use **ab**, not **ā**.

[2] Predicate accusative.

[3] Predicate nominative. See **47**.

4. The doves will be put to flight by the boy. 5. We shall invite friends and enemies. 6. Friends and enemies will be invited. 7. The Romans were not loved by the Greeks. 8. You will be summoned by a golden[1] trumpet. 9. The slaves will be armed with javelins. 10. The black horse was wounded by a spear.

4.

**93.** EXERCISES.

I. 1. Dum nōs (*we*) labōrāmus, cantat caecus poēta. 2. Quid (*what*) cantābat caecus poēta dum labōrābāmus? 3. Dum in oppidō ambulant dominī, servī labōrant in agrō. 4. Puerī vigilābunt dum somnus grātus virōs dēfessōs recreābit. 5. Nauta dēfessus aquā frīgidā recreābitur. 6. Equī dēfessī pābulō bonō recreābuntur. 7. Verba bona discipulī ā magistrō laudābantur. 8. Mūrī altī ab oppidānīs aedificābantur. 9.[2] Multōs et altōs mūrōs aedificābunt oppidānī. 10. Nōn ā pigrīs virīs oppidum aedificābātur.

II. 1. While the man was working, the boy was singing. 2. While the master is being refreshed with sleep, the servant is watching. 3. Pleasant sleep refreshes the weary boy. 4. By pleasant sleep the boy will be refreshed. 5. A high wall is being built by the townsmen. 6. A famous Roman was called the Sword[3] of Italy. 7. They called a famous Roman the Sword[4] of Italy. 8. The tired farmer is refreshed by food and sleep.[5] 9. We will walk in the streets of the town, while the farmers are working[6] in the fields. 10. Sing, O blind poet, while we toil.

[1] *Golden*, **aureā** or **ex aurō**. The material of which a thing is made is expressed in Latin either by an adjective or by ē (ex) with the ablative. How is it in English?

[2] Compare, for order, **77**. I. 5, and **69**. I. 10, and note.

[3] *Sword*, in the nominative case, just as if *was* took the place of *was called*. See **92**. I. 6, and note.

[4] *Sword*, in the accusative case. See **92**. I. 5, and note.

[5] Cf. 5 and 6 in I.

[6] Imitate 4 in I.

**94.** VOCABULARY.

**aedificō**, 1, *build.*
**ambulō**, 1, *walk.*
**armō**, 1, *arm.*
**cantō**, 1, *sing.*
**fugō**, 1, *put to flight.*
**invītō**, 1, *invite, summon.*
**labōrō**, 1, *work, toil.*
**laudō**, 1, *praise.*
**nōminō**, 1, *name, call.*
**portō**, 1, *carry.*
**recreō**, 1, *refresh.*
**superō**, 1, *surpass, conquer.*
**vigilō**, 1, *watch.*
**vulnerō**, 1, *wound.*
**aqua**,[1] **-ae**, F., *water.*
**aureus**, **-a**, **-um**, adj., *golden.*
**caecus**, **-a**, **-um**, adj., *blind.*
**dum**, adv., *while.*
**ē** (**ex**), prep. w. abl., *out of, from.*
**frīgidus**, **-a**, **-um**, adj., *cold.*
**gladius**, **-ī**, M., *sword* (**79**).
**Homērus**, **-ī**, M., *Homer.*
**Ītalia**, **-ae**, F., *Italy.*
**mūrus**, **-ī**, M., *wall.*
**oppidānus**, **-ī**, M., *townsman.*
**piger**, **-gra**, **-grum**, adj., *lazy.*
**Rōma**, **-ae**, F., *Rome.*
**Rōmānus**, **-ī**, M., *a Roman.*

5.

**95.** COLLOQUIUM.

PATER ET FĪLIOLUS.
Father and little son.

*P.* Quae, mī fīliole, in pēnsō hodiernō tractābantur?
what — my little son — lesson — to-day's — treat *or* discuss

*F.* Tractābantur cāsus ablātīvus atque verbum *amō*.
case — and

*P.* Quid sīgnificat Anglicē verbum *amō*?
means — in English

*F.* *Amō* sīgnificat "love."

*P.* Dē ablātīvō quoque mihi nārrā.
about — also — me — tell

*F.* Rēgulam dē ablātīvō tibi nārrābō.
rule — you

*P.* Rēgulamne tibi dabat magister?

*F.* Certē, rēgulam dē ablātīvō īnstrūmentī. Cum ablātīvō īnstrūmentī nunquam pōnitur praepositiō; ante ablātīvum agentis semper pōnitur praepositiō *ā* vel *ab*.
certainly — instrument — with — never — is put — preposition — before — of agent — always — or

*P.* Optimē, mī puer; tibi erit mālum rubrum.
well done — apple

[1] Words are sometimes purposely repeated in the vocabularies.

# CHAPTER XII. 1.

## FIRST CONJUGATION.

**96.** Learn the perfect, pluperfect, and future perfect indicative, and perfect infinitive, active and passive, of **amō**.

**97.** The compound tenses are formed by combining forms of the verb **sum** with the perfect passive participle. The participle (declined like **bonus**) agrees in gender and number with the subject: **amāta est**, *she was loved;* **amātī sunt**, *they were loved.*

**98.** EXERCISES.

I. 1. Amāvit, amāverat, amāverit. 2. Amātus est, amātus erat, amātus erit. 3. Amāvērunt, amāverant, amāverint. 4. Amāvī, amātus sum. 5. Amāverāmus, amātī erāmus. 6. Amāveritis, amātī eritis. 7. Amāvisse, amātus esse.

II. 1. You loved, you have been loved. 2. You had loved, you had been loved. 3. You will have loved, you will have been loved. 4. He has loved, he has been loved. 5. We had loved, we had been loved. 6. To have been loved, to have loved.

## 2.

**99.** EXERCISES.

I. 1. Laudātus est, portātus est, superātus est. 2. Laudāvitne? portāveratne? superāveritne? 3. Portāvistī, laudāvistis, superāvit. 4. Superāverās, portāveris, laudāveritis. 5. Laudātī estis, portāta sunt, superātus es. 6. Nōnne laudātae sunt? nōnne portātae estis? nōnne superātae sumus? 7. Portāvī, laudātus sum, superātus eram. 8. Nōn laudāvimus, nōn portāverimus, nōn superāverō. 9. Laudāvisse, portāvisse, superāvisse. 10. Portātus esse, superātus esse, laudātus esse.

II. 1. They have carried, we have been praised, you have been conquered. 2. Have I praised? have you been carried? had they conquered? 3. We had been carried, I shall have praised, they will have been conquered. 4. You had not carried, thou hadst not praised, thou hadst not been conquered. 5. To have been conquered, to have praised, to have carried. 6. I had praised, I had been conquered, I (*fem.*) had been carried. 7. Has it not been praised? will it not have been carried? have they not been conquered? 8. We (*fem.*) had been carried, thou wilt have praised, he conquered. 9. They praised, you carried, we conquered. 10. I was praised, thou wast conquered, it was carried.

### 3.

**100.** In Latin, the words for *my*, *thy*, *your*, *our*, *his*, *her*, *its*, and *their*, are very often omitted when they are not emphatic. Accordingly, in the exercises to be turned into Latin, for the present, leave these words untranslated.

**101.** EXERCISES.

I. 1. Pūgna fortūnā mūtāta est. 2. Fortūna pūgnam mūtāvit. 3. Rōmānī Graecōs superāverant. 4. Graecī ā Rōmānīs superātī erant. 5. Virī multī et ēgregiī agrōs arāvērunt. 6. Ministrī scūtīs armātī sunt. 7. Agricola ēgregius ā ministrō miserō vituperātus est. 8. Agrī lātī ab agricolīs arātrō māgnō arātī sunt. 9. Magister malōs discipulōs vituperāvit. 10. Poēta pūgnās et victōriās virōrum clārōrum cantāvit.

Read again the explanations and rules on pp. 20, 21, and 36.

II. 1. An eagle changed the fortune of the battle. 2. We shall witness a battle on the broad river. 3. Many good men will have been blamed by their enemies. 4. The boys will have recited to their master. 5. The land in Italy has been ploughed with iron ploughs. 6. The master freed his pupils from their hard tasks (*abl.*). 7. The goddess Minerva has been praised by many poets. 8. The victories of famous men have been sung by the poets. 9. The tyrant armed a great number of slaves with swords.

**102.** VOCABULARY.

**arō**, 1, *plough*.
**līberō**, 1, *free, set free*.
**mūtō**, 1, *change*.
**recitō**, 1, *read aloud, recite*.
**spectō**, 1, *look at, witness*.
**superō**, 1, *surpass, conquer*.
**vituperō**, 1, *blame, censure*.

**ēgregius, -a, -um**, adj., *excellent*.
**ferreus, -a, -um**, adj., *of iron, iron*.
**fortūna, -ae**, F., *fortune*.
**numerus, -ī**, M., *number*.
**pēnsum, -ī**, N., *task, lesson*.
**pūgna, -ae**, F., *battle*.
**scūtum, -ī**, N., *shield*.
**terra, -ae**, F., *earth, land*.
**tyrannus, -ī**, M., *tyrant*.
**victōria, -ae**, F., *victory*.

# CHAPTER XIII. 1.

## THIRD DECLENSION.

**103.** The stem ends in a consonant or in *i*.

**104.** Consonant stems are named, according to their final letter, *mute stems, liquid stems, sibilant stems*. See 3.

### Mute Stems.

**105.** PARADIGMS.

| | **Prīnceps**, M., *chief.* Stem **prīncip-** | **Rēx**, M., *king.* St. **rēg-** | **Jūdex**, M., *judge.* St. **jūdic-** | **Aetās**, F., *age.* St. **aetāt-** | **Caput**, N., *head.* St. **capit-** |
|---|---|---|---|---|---|
| | | | SINGULAR. | | |
| N.V. | prīncep**s** | rēx | jūdex | aetā**s** | caput |
| G. | prīncip**is** | rēg**is** | jūdic**is** | aetāt**is** | capit**is** |
| D. | prīncip**ī** | rēg**ī** | jūdic**ī** | aetāt**ī** | capit**ī** |
| Ac. | prīncip**em** | rēg**em** | jūdic**em** | aetāt**em** | caput |
| Ab. | prīncip**e** | rēg**e** | jūdic**e** | aetāt**e** | capit**e** |
| | | | PLURAL. | | |
| N.V. | prīncip**ēs** | rēg**ēs** | jūdic**ēs** | aetāt**ēs** | capit**a** |
| G. | prīncip**um** | rēg**um** | jūdic**um** | aetāt**um** | capit**um** |
| D. | prīncip**ibus** | rēg**ibus** | jūdic**ibus** | aetāt**ibus** | capit**ibus** |
| Ac. | prīncip**ēs** | rēg**ēs** | jūdic**ēs** | aetāt**ēs** | capit**a** |
| Ab. | prīncip**ibus** | rēg**ibus** | jūdic**ibus** | aetāt**ibus** | capit**ibus** |

| | **Pēs**, M., *foot*. St. **ped-** | **Mīlĕs**, M., *soldier*. St. **mīlit-** | TERMINATIONS. MASC. & FEM. *Sing.* | *Plur.* |
|---|---|---|---|---|
| | SINGULAR. | | | |
| N.V. | pē**s** | mīle**s** | **s** | **ēs** |
| G. | ped**is** | mīlit**is** | **is** | **um** |
| D. | ped**ī** | mīlit**ī** | **ī** | **ibus** |
| Ac. | ped**em** | mīlit**em** | **em** | **ēs** |
| Ab. | ped**e** | mīlit**e** | **e** | **ibus** |
| | PLURAL. | | NEUTER. | |
| N.V. | ped**ēs** | mīlit**ēs** | — | **a** |
| G. | ped**um** | mīlit**um** | **is** | **um** |
| D. | ped**ibus** | mīlit**ibus** | **ī** | **ibus** |
| Ac. | ped**ēs** | mīlit**ēs** | — | **a** |
| Ab. | ped**ibus** | mīlit**ibus** | **e** | **ibus** |

**106.** Observe that the vowel before the final consonant of the stem is not always the same in the nominative as in the other cases.

**107.** Consonant stems may be found by dropping the termination of the genitive singular. But there are some exceptions.

**108.** Decline **grex, poēma, servitūs**. Decline together **lapis asper, fīdus comĕs**, and **mīlĕs aeger**. For the nouns, see **110**.

## 2.

**109.** EXERCISES.

I. 1. Poēta comitī aegrō poēma grātum recitāvit. 2. Comĕs poētae poēmate grātō līberātus est cūrā.[1] 3. Māgnus erat equitum numerus. 4. Mīlitēs multī ā servō dominī invītātī sunt. 5. Gregēs albōs habent agricolae[2] īnsulae vīcīnae. 6. Ager vīcīnus lapidēs multōs et asperōs habet. 7. In agrō vīcīnō sunt lapidēs multī et asperī. 8. Servitūs ā virīs nōn est amāta. 9. Pēs puerī lapide asperō vulnerātus est. 10. Rēgis amīcī ā mīlitibus gladiīs et pīlīs sunt fugātī.

II. 1. The king has changed the fortune of the war. 2. The fortune of the war was changed by the king. 3. The

[1] *from care.* See **101**. II. 6. [2] The subject.

soldiers will free the king. 4. The king will be freed by the soldiers. 5. The king had armed the soldiers with shields and spears. 6. Dædalus fitted wings to his son. 7. Wings were fitted to his son by Dædalus. 8. We shall read aloud the poems of Homer. 9. The girl sings for the weary soldier and is praised.

**110.** VOCABULARY.

**comĕs, -itis,** M. & F., *companion.*
**equĕs, -itis,** M., *horseman.*
**grex, gregis,** M., *flock, herd.*
**lapis, -idis,** M., *stone.*
**mīlĕs, -itis,** M., *soldier.*
**pēs, pĕdis,** M., *foot.*
**poēma, -ătis,** N., *poem.*
**rēx, rēgis,** M., *king.*
**servitūs, -ūtis,** F., *slavery.*
**voluptās, -ātis,** F., *pleasure.*

**aptō,** 1, *fit.*
**Daedalus, -ī,** M., *Dædalus,* builder of the Labyrinth.
**fīlius, -ī,** M., *son* (**79**).
**vīcīnus, -a, -um,** adj., *neighboring.*

3.

**111.** COLLOQUIUM.

FRĀTER ET SORŌRCULA.
brother — little sister

*S.* Quid hodiē nārrāvit magister in scholā? (to-day; school)

*F.* Nārrāvit dē Īcarō, Daedalī fīliō.

*S.* Mihi quoque dē Īcarō Latīnē nārrā. Fuitne Īcarus puer malus? (me; also; in Latin)

*F.* Minimē malus sed miserrimus. Habēbat ālās; ālās cērā aptāverat Daedalus; Īcarus ēvolāvit et cēra sōle liquefacta est. Tum . . . (not; unfortunate; wings; wax; flew away; sun; was melted; then)

*S.* Tum . . . quid?

*F.* Mihi nōn sunt verba Latīna. Itaque haesitō. (words; that is why; hesitate)

*S.* Ergō nārrā Anglicē. Nam linguam Anglicam intellegō. (well, then; language; understand)

*F.* Minimē. Latīnē tibi nārrō, nōn Anglicē. (by no means)

# CHAPTER XIV.

## SECOND CONJUGATION.

**112.** VERBS IN *ē*.

**Moneō** (stem **monē**), *advise*.

PRINCIPAL PARTS: **moneō, monēre, monuī, monitum.**

### INDICATIVE.

ACTIVE. PASSIVE.

PRESENT.

| *I advise, etc.* | | *I am advised, etc.* | |
|---|---|---|---|
| mon **eō** | mon **ēmus** | mon **eor** | mon **ēmur** |
| mon **ēs** | mon **ētis** | mon **ēris**, *or* **-re** | mon **ēminī** |
| mon **et** | mon **ent** | mon **ētur** | mon **entur** |

IMPERFECT.

| *I was advising, etc.* | | *I was advised, etc.* | |
|---|---|---|---|
| mon **ēbam** | mon **ēbāmus** | mon **ēbar** | mon **ēbāmur** |
| mon **ēbās** | mon **ēbātis** | mon **ēbāris**, *or* **-re** | mon **ēbāminī** |
| mon **ēbat** | mon **ēbant** | mon **ēbātur** | mon **ēbantur** |

FUTURE.

| *I shall advise, etc.* | | *I shall be advised, etc.* | |
|---|---|---|---|
| mon **ēbō** | mon **ēbimus** | mon **ēbor** | mon **ēbimur** |
| mon **ēbis** | mon **ēbitis** | mon **ēberis**, *or* **-re** | mon **ēbiminī** |
| mon **ēbit** | mon **ēbunt** | mon **ēbitur** | mon **ēbuntur** |

PERFECT.

| *I have advised, I advised, etc.* | | *I have been (was) advised, etc.* | |
|---|---|---|---|
| monu **ī** | monu **imus** | monit **us** { **sum** | monit **ī** { **sumus** |
| monu **istī** | monu **istis** | **es** | **estis** |
| monu **it** | monu **ērunt**, *or* **-re** | **est** | **sunt** |

PLUPERFECT.

| *I had advised, etc.* | | *I had been advised, etc.* | |
|---|---|---|---|
| monu **eram** | monu **erāmus** | monit **us** { **eram** | monit **ī** { **erāmus** |
| monu **erās** | monu **erātis** | **erās** | **erātis** |
| monu **erat** | monu **erant** | **erat** | **erant** |

| ACTIVE. | | PASSIVE. | |
|---|---|---|---|

FUTURE PERFECT.

*I shall have advised, etc.* — *I shall have been advised, etc.*

| | | | |
|---|---|---|---|
| monu **erō** | monu **erimus** | monit **us** { **erō** | monit **ī** { **erimus** |
| monu **eris** | monu **eritis** | **eris** | **eritis** |
| monu **erit** | monu **erint** | **erit** | **erunt** |

## SUBJUNCTIVE.

PRESENT.

| | | | |
|---|---|---|---|
| mon **eam** | mon **eāmus** | mon **ear** | mon **eāmur** |
| mon **eās** | mon **eātis** | mon **eāris,** *or* -re | mon **eāminī** |
| mon **eat** | mon **eant** | mon **eātur** | mon **eantur** |

IMPERFECT.

| | | | |
|---|---|---|---|
| mon **ērem** | mon **ērēmus** | mon **ērer** | mon **ērēmur** |
| mon **ērēs** | mon **ērētis** | mon **ērēris,** *or* -re | mon **ērēminī** |
| mon **ēret** | mon **ērent** | mon **ērētur** | mon **ērentur** |

PERFECT.

| | | | |
|---|---|---|---|
| monu **erim** | monu **erimus** | monit **us** { **sim** | monit **ī** { **sīmus** |
| monu **eris** | monu **eritis** | **sīs** | **sītis** |
| monu **erit** | monu **erint** | **sit** | **sint** |

PLUPERFECT.

| | | | |
|---|---|---|---|
| monu **issem** | monu **issēmus** | monit **us** { **essem** | monit **ī** { **essēmus** |
| monu **issēs** | monu **issētis** | **essēs** | **essētis** |
| monu **isset** | monu **issent** | **esset** | **essent** |

## IMPERATIVE.

PRESENT.

| | |
|---|---|
| mon **ē,** *advise thou.* | mon **ēre,** *be thou advised.* |
| mon **ēte,** *advise ye.* | mon **ēminī,** *be ye advised.* |

FUTURE.

| | |
|---|---|
| mon **ētō,** *thou shalt advise.* | mon **ētor,** *thou shalt be advised.* |
| mon **ētō,** *he shall advise.* | mon **ētor,** *he shall be advised.* |
| mon **ētōte,** *you shall advise.* | |
| mon **ento,** *they shall advise.* | mon **entor,** *they shall be advised.* |

### INFINITIVE.

| ACTIVE. | PASSIVE. |
|---|---|
| PRES. mon**ēre**, *to advise.* | mon**ērī**, *to be advised.* |
| PERF. monu**isse**, *to have advised.* | monit**us esse**, *to have been adv'd.* |
| FUT. monit**ūrus esse**, *to be about to advise.* | monit**um īrī**, *to be about to be advised.* |

### PARTICIPLE.

| | |
|---|---|
| PRES. mon**ēns**, **-entis**, *advising.* | ——— |
| FUT. monit**ūrus**, **-a**, **-um**, *about to advise.* | GER. mon**endus**, **-a**, **-um**, *to be advised.* |
| ——— | PERF. monit**us**, **-a**, **-um**, *having been advised.* |

### GERUND.

G. mon**endī**, *of advising.*
D. mon**endō**, *for advising.*
Ac. mon**endum**, *advising.*
Ab. mon**endō**, *by advising.*

### SUPINE.

Ac. monit**um**, *to advise.* Ab. monit**ū**, *to advise, to be advised.*

---

# CHAPTER XV. 1.

## SECOND CONJUGATION.

**113.** Learn the present, imperfect, and future indicative, and present imperative and infinitive, active and passive, of **moneō**.

**114.** EXERCISES.

I. 1. Monet, monētur. 2. Monēbat, monēbātur. 3. Monēbit, monēbitur. 4. Monē, monēre. 5. Monēte, monēminī. 6. Monēbimus, monēbimur. 7. Monēmus, monēmur. 8. Monēbās, monēs. 9. Monēbis, monēris. 10. Monērī, monēre.

II. 1. You are advising, you will be advised, you were advised. 2. Advise ye, be ye advised. 3. We do advise, we are advising, we shall be advising. 4. We were advising, we were advised. 5. They are advised, they advised, they were advising. 6. They will advise, they will be advised.

## 2.

**115.** EXERCISES.

**Habeō,** *have,* or *hold;* **dēleō,**[1] *destroy;* **terreō,** *frighten.*

I. 1. Habet, dēlēbat, terrēbit. 2. Nōnne habēmus? nōnne dēlēbāmus? nōnne terrēbimus? 3. Dēlēs, habēbās, terrēbunt. 4. Habēte, terrēte, dēlēte. 5. Dēlētur,[2] habēbātur, terrēbātur.[2] 6. Terrēre, dēlērī, habērī. 7. Habetne? dēlēturne? terrēbatne? 8. Dēlēbitur, habēbantur, terrēbiminī. 9. Nōn terrēmus, nōn dēlēbunt, nōn habent. 10. Habēbuntur, terrentur, dēlēbantur.

II. 1. We are held, they will be destroyed, he was frightened. 2. I frighten, thou hast (you have), he destroys. 3. To have, to destroy, to be frightened. 4. Is he frightened? are they destroyed? were you held? 5. Destroy (thou), have (ye), frighten (ye). 6. Have we not? does he not frighten? did not they destroy? 7. You will be frightened, it is held, we were frightened. 8. I was holding, he was destroying, you were frightening. 9. I shall destroy, we shall frighten, they have.

## 3.

**116.** EXERCISES.

Before translating the following exercises, review the tables of declensions and terminations, pp. 41 and 42.

I. 1. Poenam merēbis, sī memoriam nōn exercēbis.[3]

[1] For principal parts of **dēleō**, see vocabulary, **119**.

[2] The present, which denotes continued action, means *it is being (destroyed)*; the imperfect, *he was being (frightened)*.

[3] Translate as if it were the present tense; but in Latin the future is necessary, because future time is meant. Cf. **93**. I. 4. Observe the difference between the Latin and English idioms.

2. Exercē memoriam, comēs. 3. Studium memoriam auget. 4. Mīlitēs ā ducibus exercentur et docentur. 5. Perīcula mīlitēs nōn terrēbunt. 6. Perīculum nōn timēbit mīlēs. 7. Oppidum ā mīlitibus tenētur. 8. Jūdicēs poenīs malōs coercent. 9. Quid vidēs? 10. Multa videō.

II. 1. The tyrant is restrained. 2. The water of the river was increased. 3. The leader will have a statue. 4. The faithful comrade advises his friend. 5. The friend is advised by his faithful companion. 6. Lazy slaves fear a hard master. 7. A hard master is feared by lazy slaves. 8. Italy is the land of famous poets. 9. The soldiers will not be terrified by dangers. 10. The boy remembered the master's words.

**117.** **Malōs** (I. 8), *bad men*, and **multa** (I. 10), *many things*, are examples of the frequent use in Latin of an adjective without a noun. Compare, in English, *the good*, *the wise*.

## 4.

**118.** EXERCISES.

I. 1. Equōs et equitēs multōs in viā videō. 2. Cȳrus, prīmus Persārum rēx,[1] nōmina[2] mīlitum memoriā tenēbat. 3. Sī oppidum dēlēbunt, poenam merēbunt. 4. Prīncipēs ā templō deī prohibēbimus. 5. Voluptātēs memoriae augēbantur. 6. Studiō augētur memoria. 7. Mīlitēs ā prīncipe monēbantur. 8. Rēx māgnum mīlitum numerum tenēbat. 9. Prīnceps equitēs pigrōs exercēbat.

II. 1. In ancient states there were many slaves. 2. Why had the ancient Romans many slaves? 3. We saw the great number of horsemen in the road and were frightened. 4. Roman boys were often taught by Greek slaves. 5. Greek slaves often taught Roman boys. 6. The horsemen were trained by the king's son. 7. Many horses and horsemen are seen in the town. 8. The chief will deserve a great victory.

---

[1] **Rēx**, in apposition with **Cȳrus**. See **157**. [2] *names.*

**119.** VOCABULARY.

**coerceō**, 2, **-uī**, **-itum**, *check, restrain.*
**exerceō**, 2, **-uī**, **-itum**, *train, exercise.*
**habeō**, 2, **-uī**, **-itum**, *have, hold.*
**mereō**, 2, **-uī**, **-itum**, *deserve, merit.*
**prohibeō**, 2, **-uī**, **-itum**, *prevent, keep off.*
**terreō**, 2, **-uī**, **-itum**, *frighten.*
**timeō**, 2, **-uī**, ——, *fear.*

**augeō**, 2, **auxī**,[1] **auctum**, *increase.*
**dēleō**, 2, **-ēvī**,[2] **-ētum**, *destroy.*
**doceō**, 2, **-uī**, **doctum**,[3] *teach.*
**teneō**, 2, **-uī**, **tentum**,[4] *keep, hold.*
**videō**, 2, **vīdī**,[5] **vīsum**, *see*; passive, *seem.*

**antīquus**, **-a**, **-um**, adj., *old, ancient.*
**cīvitās**, **-ātis**, F., *state.*
**cūr**, adv., *why?*
**custōs**, **-ōdis**, M. & F., *keeper.*
**Cȳrus**, **-ī**, M., *Cyrus.*
**dux**, **ducis**, M. & F., *leader, general.*
**memoria**, **-ae**, F., *memory.*
**memoriā teneō**, *remember.*
**poena**, **-ae**, F., *punishment.*
**quid**, interrog. pron., *what?*
**Rōmānus**, **-a**, **-um**, *Roman;* noun, *a Roman.*
**saepe**, adv., *often.*
**sī**, conj., *if.*
**studium**, **-ī**, N., *zeal, study.*
**templum**, **-ī**, N., *temple.*

## CHAPTER XVI. 1.

## SECOND CONJUGATION.

**120.** Learn the perfect, pluperfect, and future perfect indicative, and perfect infinitive, active and passive, of **moneō**.

**121.** EXERCISES.

I. 1. Monuit, monuerat, monuerit. 2. Monuērunt, monuerant, monuerint. 3. Monuī, monitus sum. 4. Monuerit, monitus erit. 5. Monuistī, monuerās, monueris. 6. Monitus est, monitus erat, monitus erit. 7. Monuisse, monitus esse.

II. 1. You have advised, you had advised, you will have advised. 2. They have been advised, they had been advised,

[1] **Auxī** for **aug-sī**. See p. 1, n. 2.

[2] Only **fleō**, *weep*, **neō**, *spin*, and the compounds of the obsolete **pleō**, *fill*, are conjugated like **dēleō**, with the perfect in *ēvī*.

[3] Observe, not **docitum**.

[4] Observe, not **tenitum**.

[5] **Vīdī**. Perfect stem formed by lengthening the vowel of the present stem, **vĭd** to **vīd**.

they will have been advised. 3. I had advised, I had been advised. 4. He has advised, he has been advised. 5. We have advised, we have been advised. 6. To have been advised, to have advised.

## 2.

**122.** EXERCISES.

I. 1. Habuit, dēlēvit, terruit. 2. Habuistī, dēlēvistī, terruistī. 3. Nōn dēlēvimus, nōn dēlēverāmus, nōn dēlēverimus. 4. Dēlētum est, territus erat, habita sunt. 5. Habuerōne? estne territa? suntne dēlētae? 6. Nōnne habuerātis? nōnne dēlētum erat? nōnne terruērunt? 7. Terruisse, dēlēvisse, habitus esse. 8. Dēlēverās, territus erās, habuistis. 9. Habuerint, dēlētum erit, habuērunt. 10. Dēlēta sunt, habitī sumus, territae estis.

II. 1. They have had, they have frightened, they have destroyed. 2. I had had, I had been frightened, I had destroyed. 3. Have you had? had he destroyed? has he frightened? 4. We had not destroyed, they (*fem.*) had not been frightened, you had not destroyed. 5. We have had, we shall have destroyed, we had been frightened. 6. To have destroyed, to have been held, to have been frightened. 7. Have you been frightened? had they (*neut.*) been destroyed? has she had? 8. I have destroyed, I have not had, I shall not have been frightened. 9. They will have had, they will have been frightened, they (*neut.*) will have been destroyed. 10. Have you not had? did they not destroy? have not you (*fem.*) been frightened?

## 3.

**123.** EXERCISES.

I. 1. Rēx Rōmam obsēderat. 2. Rōma ā rēge obsēssa erat. 3. Scrība cum (*with*) rēge sedēbat. 4. Īra ferōcem (*fierce*) animum virī mōvit. 5. Rēgulī conjugī et līberīs alimenta praebuērunt Rōmānī. 6. Captīvī retentī sunt. 7. Novamne lūnam vīdistī? 8. Aquila in (*on*) templō sēdit. 9. Māter flēvit quia fīlius captīvus erat. 10. Caesar oppidum Galliae obsēdit.

II. 1. The town was besieged by the general. 2. Why did the general besiege the town? 3. The king is sitting[1] with his clerk. 4. The minds of the men were moved with anger. 5. Regulus was retained (as) a prisoner.[2] 6. Regulus deserved great glory. 7. The new moon has been seen. 8. The commander's daughter was a prisoner. 9. We wept because we were prisoners. 10. The town had been besieged by Pyrrhus.

4.

**124.** EXERCISES.

I. 1. Mīlitibus māgna praemia ā rēge praebita sunt. 2. Mīlitēs timuērunt quia elephantōs vīdērunt. 3. Numerum verbōrum auximus. 4. Caesar mīlitēs in oppidō retinuerat. 5. Jūdicum bonōrum memoria nunquam dēlēbitur. 6. Multa Rōmānōrum monumenta[3] dēlēta sunt. 7. Dux castra ab oppidō mōverat. 8. Dominus servōs in servitūte tenuit. 9. Multa verba in memoriā mānsērunt. 10. Mīlitis conjunx in Minervae templō sedēbat.

II. 1. The king furnished food for his weary soldiers. 2. Elephants had frightened the horses of the Romans. 3. Have you increased the number of your friends? 4. Cæsar's soldiers were besieged in the town. 5. The sword of the tyrant has restrained the judge. 6. War has destroyed many monuments[3] of great men. 7. The camp had been moved away from the town. 8. We weep if our children are held in slavery. 9. Shall you remain in Italy?

[1] Not passive.

[2] Predicate nom.; see **47**.

[3] When a noun is limited both by an adjective and a genitive, the order often is: *adjective, genitive, noun.* Cf. **118**. I. 2 and 8.

**125.** VOCABULARY.

**fleō**, 2, **flēvi**, **flētum**, *weep, bewail.*
**maneō**, 2, **mānsi**, **mānsum**, *remain, await.*
**moveō**, 2, **mōvi**,[1] **mōtum**, *move.*
**ob-sideō**, 2, **-sēdi**,[1] **-sēssum**, *besiege.*
**praebeō**, 2, **-uī**, **-itum**, *furnish.*
**re-tineō**, 2, **-tinui**, **-tentum**, *keep back, retain.*
**sedeō**, 2, **sēdi**,[1] **sēssum**, *sit.*

**ā (ab)**, prep. w. abl., *away from, by.*
**alimentum**, **-ī**, N., *food, support.*
**captīvus**,[2] **-ī**, M., *prisoner, captive.*
**castra**, **-ōrum**, (pl.) N., *camp.*
**conjunx**, **conjugis**, F., *wife.*
**elephantus**, **-ī**, M., *elephant.*
**īra**, **-ae**, F., *anger.*
**lūna**, **-ae**, F., *moon.*
**novus**, **-a**, **-um**, adj., *new.*
**nunquam**, adv., *never.*
**praemium**, **-ī**, N., *reward.*
**Pyrrhus**, **-ī**, M., *Pyrrhus*, king of Epirus.
**quia**, conj., *because.*
**Rēgulus**, **-ī**, M., *Regulus*, a Roman.
**scrība**, **-ae**, M., *clerk.* (**11.** 1.)

5.

**126.** COLLOQUIUM.

PRAECEPTOR ET DISCIPULUS.

*P.* Latīnē mihi (to me) interrogantī (asking) respondē (answer) sī possīs (you can). Quae (what) īnsula Graeciae est parva quidem (to be sure) sed clāra?

*D.* Admodum (very) clāra est Ithaca īnsula, ubi (where) habitābat Ulixēs (Ulysses).

*P.* Rēctē (right), mī puer, Ulixēs Ithacae rēx fuit et dux (leader) in bellō ēgregius. Quis cantāvit dē Ulixe ēgregiō?

*D.* Homērus, poēta caecus (blind), quī (who) autem (however) Ulixem nunquam (never) vīderat.

*P.* Tenēsne memoriā nōmen (name) fīdī servī Ulixis?

*D.* Servus Ulixis fīdus erat Eumaeus.

---

[1] See p. 49, note 5. [2] Also **captīva**, **-ae**, F.

# CHAPTER XVII. 1.

## REVIEW.

**127.** EXERCISES.

I. 1. Magister discipulōs invītāvit. 2. Nōnne ā magistrō discipulī invītātī sunt? 3. Vīdistīne agricolārum arātra ferrea? 4. Mīlitēs lapidēs māgnōs portābant. 5. Rēx ab oppidō castra mōvit. 6. Gregis custōdēs lapidibus fugātī sunt. 7. Mī[1] fīlī, poēmata Homērī recitāvistīne? 8. Sī oppidum tenuerimus, vīctōriam merēbimus. 9. Conjugēs mīlitum pūgnam spectābant et flēbant. 10. In Ītaliā antīquā ā Pyrrhō Ēpīrī rēge superātī sunt Rōmānī.

II. 1. We shall see the flocks in the fields. 2. The king was not frightened by the elephant. 3. Horses are frightened by elephants. 4. The townsmen were sitting on the wall. 5. The prisoners were wounded by the soldiers with their swords. 6. My boy, what are you looking at? 7. Do you not see the horsemen's swords? 8. Do you remember the poems of the Roman poet? 9. The king's sons were finding fault with fortune. 10. Why are the townsmen armed with swords?

**128.** *Examine the two following groups of sentences:* —

1. **Iter ab Arare Helvētiī āverterant,** *the Helvetii had turned their course from the Arar.*
2. **Arāneās dēiciam dē pariete,** *I will brush down the cobwebs from the wall.*
3. **Hannibal ex Ītaliā excēssit,** *Hannibal withdrew from Italy.*

1. **Nōs cūrā līberābis,** *you will free us from care.*
2. **Oculīs sē prīvāvit,** *he deprived himself of his sight (eyes).*
3. **Homo cibō caret,** *the man is in want of food.*

**129.** The verbs have the general idea of *separation;* and in the first group the ablative with a preposition, in the second the ablative

[1] Vocative singular of **meus,** *my.*

alone, answers the question *from what? of what?* Observe further, that the verbs of the first group are compounds of **ā, dē, ex**, and the "separation" is *literal*, or *physical;* in the second group the "separation" is *figurative*, or less literal.

**130.** Rule of Syntax.—**Separation is expressed by the ablative with *ā* (*ab*), *dē*, *ē* (*ex*), in connection with verbs compounded with these prepositions,[1] or by the ablative alone with simple verbs meaning *to set free, deprive,* or *want.***

## 2.

**131.** EXERCISES.

I. 1. Hunc (*him*) ā tuīs ārīs arcēbis. 2. Fīlius rēgis Rōmānōs cūrā līberāvit. 3. Rōmānī ā fīliō rēgis cūrā līberātī sunt. 4. Vir aeger aquā prīvātus est. 5. Servī servitūte līberābuntur. 6. Dux Rōmānus Corinthum multīs statuīs prīvāvit. 7. Servī, equīs dēfessīs aquam praebēte. 8.[2] Sāturnus Italōs agrī cultūram docuit. 9. Līber vīnī erat deus et in Ītaliā templa multa habēbat. 10. Avārī mīlitēs ārās dōnīs spoliant. 11. Mī puer, equus pābulō et aquā caret.

Before translating the following sentences, read over the explanations and rules on pp. 20, 21, and 36, and consider what expressions are equivalent to the Latin ablative of *agent* with *ā* or *ab*, the ablative of *means*, and the ablative of *separation*.

II. 1. They deprived the sick man of water. 2. The state was freed from the tyrant by Brutus. 3. The Italians were taught by Saturn. 4. The leader adorned the town with statues. 5. The horsemen are in want of swords and horses. 6. Corinth was robbed of many statues by a Roman general. 7. The goddess will keep off the Romans

1 With other verbs than those indicated in **129** and **130**, of similar meaning, the preposition is sometimes used and sometimes omitted.

2 Observe the two accusatives, one of the *person*, the other of the *thing*, with **doceō**.

from her temple. 8. The town was destroyed by the plans of the general. 9. Will not the Romans be kept off from the temple? 10. They thrust forth the leaders from the town. 11. The leaders are hustled out of town.

**132.** VOCABULARY.

**agrī cultūra, -ae,** F., *agriculture.*
**avārus, -a, -um,** adj., *greedy.*
**arceō,** 2, **-uī, -tum,** *keep off.*
**Brūtus, -ī,** M., *Brutus,* a Roman.
**careō,** 2, **-uī, -itum,** *want, lack.*
**causa, -ae,** F., *cause.*
**Corinthus, -ī,** F., *Corinth* (**11.** 4).
**Ēpīrus, -ī,** F., *Epirus* (**11.** 4).
**exturbō,** 1, *thrust out.*
**Italus, -ī,** M., *an Italian.*
**Līber, -erī,** M., *Bacchus,* god of wine.
**meus, -a, -um,** poss. adj., *my, mine* (voc. sing. masc. **mī**).
**ōrnō,** 1, *adorn.*
**prīvō,** 1, *deprive.*
**Sāturnus, -ī,** M., *Saturn,* god of agriculture.
**tuus, -a, -um,** poss. adj., *thy, your.*

3.

**133.** COLLOQUIUM.

PRAECEPTOR ET DISCIPULUS.

*P.* Dīc mihi, puer, elephantōsne aliquandō vīdistī?
tell ever

*D.* Certē, praeceptor, elephantōs māgnōs et parvōs vīdī.

*P.* In agrīsne?

*D.* Minimē vērō; in circō et interdum in viīs.
indeed circus sometimes

*P.* Quis rēx clārus elephantōrum auxiliō pūgnābat?
what aid

*D.* Pyrrhus, rēx Ēpīrī, ita pūgnābat.

*P.* Nōnne elephantī equōs Rōmānōrum terrēbant?

*D.* Terrēbant. Mīlitēs quoque terrēbantur.
yes also

*P.* Superāvitne Pyrrhus Rōmānōs?

*D.* Saepe superāvit.
often

*P.* Quibus armīs pūgnant elephantī?
with what

*D.* Dentibus, proboscide, pedibus, capite pūgnant.
tusks trunk feet

# CHAPTER XVIII. 1.

## THIRD DECLENSION.

### Liquid Stems.

**134.** PARADIGMS.

| | **Cōnsul**, M., *consul.* St. **cōnsul-** | **Pater**, M., *father.* St. **patr-** | **Pāstor**, M., *shepherd.* St. **pāstōr-** | **Leō**, M., *lion.* St. **leōn-** |
|---|---|---|---|---|
| | | Singular. | | |
| N.V. | cōnsul | pater | pāstor | leō |
| G. | cōnsul **is** | patr **is** | pāstōr **is** | leōn **is** |
| D. | cōnsul **ī** | patr **ī** | pāstōr **ī** | leōn **ī** |
| Ac. | cōnsul **em** | patr **em** | pāstōr **em** | leōn **em** |
| Ab. | cōnsul **e** | patr **e** | pāstōr **e** | leōn **e** |
| | | Plural. | | |
| N.V. | cōnsul **ēs** | patr **ēs** | pāstōr **ēs** | leōn **ēs** |
| G. | cōnsul **um** | patr **um** | pāstōr **um** | leōn **um** |
| D. | cōnsul **ibus** | patr **ibus** | pāstōr **ibus** | leōn **ibus** |
| Ac. | cōnsul **ēs** | patr **ēs** | pāstōr **ēs** | leōn **ēs** |
| Ab. | cōnsul **ibus** | patr **ibus** | pāstōr **ibus** | leōn **ibus** |

| | **Imāgō**, F., *image.* St. **imāgin-** | **Nōmen**, N., *name.* St. **nōmin-** | Terminations. Masc. & Fem. *Sing.* | *Plur.* |
|---|---|---|---|---|
| | Singular. | | | |
| N.V. | imāgō | nōmen | — | **ēs** |
| G. | imāgin **is** | nōmin **is** | **is** | **um** |
| D. | imāgin **ī** | nōmin **ī** | **ī** | **ibus** |
| Ac. | imāgin **em** | nōmen | **em** | **ēs** |
| Ab. | imāgin **e** | nōmin **e** | **e** | **ibus** |
| | Plural. | | Neuter. | |
| N.V. | imāgin **ēs** | nōmin **a** | — | **a** |
| G. | imāgin **um** | nōmin **um** | **is** | **um** |
| D. | imāgin **ibus** | nōmin **ibus** | **ī** | **ibus** |
| Ac. | imāgin **ēs** | nōmin **a** | — | **a** |
| Ab. | imāgin **ibus** | nōmin **ibus** | **e** | **ibus** |

**135.** *Examine the following:* —

1. **Hieme et aestāte,** *in winter and summer.*
2. **Sōlis occāsū,**[1] *at the setting of the sun.*
3. **Prīmā lūce,** *at daybreak (first light).*
4. **Hīs vīgintī annīs,** *within these twenty years.*

It will be seen that the above phrases are expressions of *time*, and answer the question *when?* or, *within what time?*

**136.** RULE OF SYNTAX. — ***Time when* is expressed by the ablative without a preposition; *time within which*, by the ablative alone, or by the ablative with *in*.**

## 2.

**137.** EXERCISES.

I. 1. Tertiā hōrā mīlitēs fugātī sunt. 2. Prīmō annō Brūtum cōnsulem creāvērunt Rōmānī. 3. Oppidum mīlitibus ab imperātōre implētum est. 4. Imperātor oppidum mīlitibus implēbit. 5. Terror clāmōre hominum augētur. 6. Clāmōrēs dēfēnsōrum omnēs puerōs[2] terrēbunt. 7. Nōmen et imāginem amīcī semper in memoriā habēbat. 8. Semper erit clārum imperātōris ēgregiī nōmen. 9. Nōnne Hannibal Rōmānīs fuit terror? 10. Hannibal fortitūdinem māgnam semper habēbat.

II. 1. Europe has no[3] lions. 2. A slave had a great lion. 3. The name of the slave was Androclus. 4. There are many lions in Africa. 5. The friend of my brothers has seen a lion. 6. A lion has been seen by my father and my brother. 7. The shouts of the soldiers scared the men in the town. 8. The defenders of the town were scared by the shouts of the men. 9. Why are many men miserable in time[4] of war? 10. Do we not see by the sun's light? 11. At daybreak they saw Hannibal's horsemen.

---

[1] Ablative of the fourth declension. See **245**.

[2] *Children.* See **60**.

[3] *Not.*

[4] *Tempore.*

## 138. VOCABULARY.

**clāmor, -ōris,** M., *shout.*
**dēfēnsor, -ōris,** M., *defender.*
**fortitūdō, -inis,** F., *bravery.*
**frāter, -tris,** M., *brother.*
**Hannibal, -ălis,** M., *Hannibal,* a Carthaginian general.
**homo, -inis,** M., *man.*
**imperātor, -ōris,** M., *general.*
**lūmen, -inis,** N., *light.*
**sōl, sōlis,** M. (no gen. pl.), *sun.*
**terror, -ōris,** M., *terror.*
**timor, -ōris,** M., *fear.*
**Āfrica, -ae,** F., *Africa.*
**Androclus, -ī,** M., *Androclus.*
**annus, -ī,** M., *year.*
**creō,** 1, *elect, choose.*
**Eurōpa, -ae,** F., *Europe.*
**Horātius, -ī,** M., *Horace,* a Roman poet (**79**).
**impleō,** 2, **-ēvī, -ētum,** *fill.*
**juventūs, -ūtis,** F., *youth.*
**semper,** adv., *always.*
**voluptās, -ātis,** F., *pleasure.*

**homo,** *man,* as distinguished from lower animals; general word for man, *mankind.*

**vir** (**60**), *man,* as distinguished from woman; man in an honorable sense, *hero.*

## 3.

## 139. COLLOQUIUM.

### MAGISTER ET DISCIPULUS.

*M.* Quae, mī puer, sunt in pēnsō hodiernō?
(Quae = what things; hodiernō = to-day's)

*D.* Multa sunt in pēnsō, ut nōmina, adjectīva, dēclīnātiōnēs, rēgulae.
(Multa = many things; ut = as; nōmina = nouns; dēclīnātiōnēs = declensions)

*M.* Quot genera sunt nōminibus Latīnīs?
(Quot genera = how many genders)

*D.* Genera sunt tria: masculīnum, fēminīnum, neutrum.
(Genera = genders; tria = three)

*M.* Dē quibus nōminibus est rēgula prīma?
(quibus = what)

*D.* Prīma rēgula est dē nōminibus generis masculīnī. Secunda rēgula est dē nōminibus generis fēminīnī.

*M.* Verbōrum quot sunt conjugātiōnēs?
(Verbōrum = verbs; quot = how many)

*D.* Quattuor sunt conjugātiōnēs, dēclīnātiōnēs autem quīnque.
(Quattuor = four; autem = but; quīnque = five)

# CHAPTER XIX. 1.

## THIRD DECLENSION.

### Sibilant Stems.[1]

**140.** PARADIGMS.

| | **Mōs**, M., *custom.* St. **mōs-** | **Jūs**, N., *right.* St. **jūs-** | **Opus**, N., *work.* St. **opes-** | **Corpus**, N., *body.* St. **corpos-** |
|---|---|---|---|---|
| | SINGULAR. | | | |
| N.V. | mōs | jūs | opus | corpus |
| G. | mōr**is** | jūr**is** | oper**is** | corpor**is** |
| D. | mōr**ī** | jūr**ī** | oper**ī** | corpor**ī** |
| Ac. | mōr**em** | jūs | opus | corpus |
| Ab. | mōr**e** | jūr**e** | oper**e** | corpor**e** |
| | PLURAL. | | | |
| N.V. | mōr**ēs** | jūr**a** | oper**a** | corpor**a** |
| G. | mōr**um** | jūr**um** | oper**um** | corpor**um** |
| D. | mōr**ibus** | jūr**ibus** | oper**ibus** | corpor**ibus** |
| Ac. | mōr**ēs** | jūr**a** | oper**a** | corpor**a** |
| Ab. | mōr**ibus** | jūr**ibus** | oper**ibus** | corpor**ibus** |

**141.** ADJECTIVE.

**Vetus**, *old.* Stem **vetes-**

| | SINGULAR. M. & F. | SINGULAR. NEUT. | PLURAL. M. & F. | PLURAL. NEUT. |
|---|---|---|---|---|
| N.V. | vetus | vetus | veter**ēs** | veter**a** |
| G. | veter**is** | veter**is** | veter**um** | veter**um** |
| D. | veter**ī** | veter**ī** | veter**ibus** | veter**ibus** |
| Ac. | veter**em** | vetus | veter**ēs** | veter**a** |
| Ab. | veter**e** | veter**e** | veter**ibus** | veter**ibus** |

**142.** The above were originally sibilant stems, the *s* having been changed to *r* between two vowels. Compare **eram** for **esam**, **erō** for **esō**, p. 25. But for practical purposes they may be regarded as stems in **r**.

[1] For table of terminations, see **134**.

**143.** EXERCISES.

I. 1. Cerēs agrī cultūrae erat dea. 2. Cererī multa erant templa in Siciliā. 3. Cerēs multa templa in Siciliā habēbat. 4. Cerēs agrī cultūram docēbat. 5. Aestāte est pulvis molestus. 6. Servīs temporibus antīquīs nōn erant jūra. 7. Servī temporum veterum jūra nōn habēbant. 8. Equus perītō ab equite exercitus erat. 9. Equitī perītō praebitus erit equus niger.

II. 1. The statue of Minerva has been seen. 2. The statue of Minerva had often been praised. 3. The works of the Greeks were pleasing to the Romans. 4. Our pleasures have been increased by work[1] and zeal. 5. What[2] were seen in the temples of Greece? 6. In ancient times men saw statues of gods and goddesses. 7. Statues of gods and goddesses were seen by men in ancient times.

## 2.

**144.** *Examine the following:* —

1. **Cum virtūte vīxit,** *he lived with virtue (virtuously).*
2. **Agricola agrum cum cūrā arat,** *the farmer ploughs his field with care (carefully).*
3. **Agricola agrum māgnā cum cūrā arat,** *the farmer ploughs his field with great care.*
4. **Summā vī proelium commīsērunt,** *they joined battle with the greatest violence.*

Manner is usually expressed by adverbs: **benĕ,** *well;* **līberē,** *freely.* So the phrases **cum virtūte, cum cūrā, māgnā cum cūrā,** and **summā vī,** plainly denote manner, — *how* a thing is done, — like adverbs of manner.

**145.** Rule of Syntax. — **Manner is sometimes expressed by the ablative with *cum;* but if the ablative has an adjective, *cum* is often omitted.**

[1] Read again explanations and rule, p. 36. [2] **Quae** = *what things.*

**146.** EXERCISES.

I. 1. Captīvī lūmen sōlis māgnō gaudiō vīdērunt. 2.[1] Sī in agrīs tempore flōrum eritis,[2] libenter eōs (*them*) vidēbitis. 3. Māgnā voluptāte aestāte videntur pulchrī flōrēs. 4. Librōs cum studiō et voluptāte recitāmus. 5. Puerī corpora cum studiō et cūrā exercent. 6. Multa Rōmānōrum opera tempore[3] nōn dēlēta sunt.

II. 1. They look at the lion with great fear. 2. If he blames (is blaming) the boy angrily,[4] he deserves punishment. 3. Dædalus had fitted wings to Icarus with care. 4. They remember the words of the good judge with joy. 5. The words of the good judge will be carefully[4] remembered. 6. How many works of the Romans time has not destroyed!

**147.** VOCABULARY.

**Cerēs, -eris,** F., *Ceres,* goddess of agriculture.
**flōs, flōris,** M., *flower.*
**pulvis, -eris,** M., *dust.*
**tempus, -oris,** N., *time.*

**aestās, -ātis,** F., *summer.*
**cum,** prep. w. abl., *with.*
**cūra, -ae,** F., *care.*
**gaudium, -ī,** N., *joy.*
**Īcarus, -ī,** M., *Icarus.*
**īra, -ae,** F., *anger.*
**libenter,** adv., *gladly, with pleasure.*
**molestus, -a, -um,** adj., *troublesome.*
**quam,** adv., *how, than.*
**sacer, -cra, -crum,** adj., *sacred.*
**Sicilia, -ae,** F., *Sicily.*

3.

**148.** COLLOQUIUM.

DUO PUERĪ.

Hodiē dūrum pēnsum habuī.

Studuistīne cum cūrā et dīligentiā?
(did you study ... diligence)

Certē cum dīligentiā, nōn cum voluptāte studuī.

[1] Notice that *in the fields* = **in agrīs**; *in the time* = **tempore**.

[2] See p. 47, note 3.

[3] Why would it be wrong to write **ā tempore**?

[4] Compare **144**. 1.

Cūr nōn cum voluptāte studuistī? Eratne magister mōrōsus an pēnsum longum?
cross or

Mehercule! longum erat pēnsum neque memoriā tenēbam.
truly and not

Aspice. Nōnne vidēs multa vocābula in vocābulāriō et verbum *moneō* et dēclīnātiōnis tertiae substantīva et adjectīva?
look words vocabulary

Heu amīcum miserum, quam studēs!
ah have to study

## CHAPTER XX. 1.

### THIRD DECLENSION.

### Stems in *i*.

**149.** PARADIGMS.

| **Hostis**, M. & F., *enemy.* St. **hosti-** | **Nūbēs**, F., *cloud.* St. **nūbi-** | **Turris**, F., *tower.* St. **turri-** | **Īgnis**, M., *fire.* St. **īgni-** |
|---|---|---|---|
| | SINGULAR. | | |
| N.V. host**is** | nūb**ēs** | turr**is** | īgn**is** |
| G. host**is** | nūb**is** | turr**is** | īgn**is** |
| D. host**ī** | nūb**ī** | turr**ī** | īgn**ī** |
| Ac. host**em** | nūb**em** | turr**im, em** | īgn**em** |
| Ab. host**e** | nūb**e** | turr**ī, e** | īgn**ī, e** |
| | PLURAL. | | |
| N.V. host**ēs** | nūb**ēs** | turr**ēs** | īgn**ēs** |
| G. host**ium** | nūb**ium** | turr**ium** | īgn**ium** |
| D. host**ibus** | nūb**ibus** | turr**ibus** | īgn**ibus** |
| Ac. host**ēs, īs** | nūb**ēs, īs** | turr**ēs, īs** | īgn**ēs, īs** |
| Ab. host**ibus** | nūb**ibus** | turr**ibus** | īgn**ibus** |

| | **Animal**, N., *animal.* St. **animāli-** | **Mare**, N., *sea.* St. **mari-** | **Calcar**, N., *spur.* St. **calcāri-** | TERMINATIONS. MASC. & FEM. *Sing.* | *Plur.* |
|---|---|---|---|---|---|
| | SINGULAR. | | | | |
| N.V. | animal | mar**e** | calcar | **is, ēs** | **ēs** |
| G. | animāl**is** | mar**is** | calcār**is** | **is** | **ium** |
| D. | animāl**ī** | mar**ī** | calcār**ī** | **ī** | **ibus** |
| Ac. | animal | mar**e** | calcar | **em, im** | **ēs, īs** |
| Ab. | animāl**ī** | mar**ī** | calcār**ī** | **e, ī** | **ibus** |
| | PLURAL. | | | NEUTER. | |
| N.V. | animāl**ia** | mar**ia** | calcār**ia** | **e** *or* — | **ia** |
| G. | animāl**ium** | mar**ium** | calcār**ium** | **is** | **ium** |
| D. | animāl**ibus** | mar**ibus** | calcār**ibus** | **ī** | **ibus** |
| Ac. | animāl**ia** | mar**ia** | calcār**ia** | **e** *or* — | **ia** |
| Ab. | animāl**ibus** | mar**ibus** | calcār**ibus** | **ī** | **ibus** |

**150.** ADJECTIVES.

**Ācer**, *keen, eager.* St. **ācri-**

| | SINGULAR. MASC. | FEM. | NEUT. | PLURAL. MASC. | FEM. | NEUT. |
|---|---|---|---|---|---|---|
| N.V. | ācer | ācr**is** | ācr**e** | ācr**ēs** | ācr**ēs** | ācr**ia** |
| G. | ācr**is** | ācr**is** | ācr**is** | ācr**ium** | ācr**ium** | ācr**ium** |
| D. | ācr**ī** | ācr**ī** | ācr**ī** | ācr**ibus** | ācr**ibus** | ācr**ibus** |
| Ac. | ācr**em** | ācr**em** | ācr**e** | ācr**ēs, īs** | ācr**ēs, īs** | ācr**ia** |
| Ab. | ācr**ī** | ācr**ī** | ācr**ī** | ācr**ibus** | ācr**ibus** | ācr**ibus** |

**Levis**, *light, nimble.* St. **levi-**

| | SINGULAR. M. & F. | NEUT. | PLURAL. M. & F. | NEUT. |
|---|---|---|---|---|
| N.V. | lev**is** | lev**e** | lev**ēs** | lev**ia** |
| G. | lev**is** | lev**is** | lev**ium** | lev**ium** |
| D. | lev**ī** | lev**ī** | lev**ibus** | lev**ibus** |
| Ac. | lev**em** | lev**e** | lev**ēs, īs** | lev**ia** |
| Ab. | lev**ī** | lev**ī** | lev**ibus** | lev**ibus** |

**Memor**, *mindful*. St. **memori-**

| | SINGULAR. M. & F. | NEUT. | PLURAL. |
|---|---|---|---|
| N.V. | memor | memor | memor**ēs** |
| G. | memor**is** | memor**is** | memor**um** |
| D. | memor**ī** | memor**ī** | memor**ibus** |
| Ac. | memor**em** | memor | memor**ēs, īs** |
| Ab. | memor**ī** | memor**ī** | memor**ibus** |

**151.** An inspection of the tables shows: —

1. That the *i* of the stem is sometimes lost, and sometimes changed to *e*. It appears in the terminations *im*, *īs* (acc. plur.), *ī* (abl. sing.), *ia*, and *ium*.

2. That the ablative singular has in some nouns *ī*, in some *e*, and in some *ī* or *e*; in adjectives, always *ī*.

3. That the genitive plural has *ium*, and the nominative and accusative plural neuter *ia*. Compare these endings with the nominative and genitive plural of consonant stems (**105, 134, 140**).

4. **Memor** has *um* in the genitive plural, masculine and feminine. It has no neuter plural. Like **memor** decline **vigil**, *watchful*, which has neuter plural **vigilia, vigilium**, etc.

**152.** To stems in *i* belong: —

1. Nouns in *is* and *ēs* not increasing in the genitive.[1]
2. Neuters in *e*, *al*, and *ar*.
3. Adjectives of two terminations.
4. Adjectives of the third declension of three terminations.

**153.** Nouns in *ēs* (gen. *is*) are declined like **nūbēs**. Most nouns in *is* are declined like **hostis**. **Canis**, *dog*, has genitive plural **canum**.

**154.** The principal nouns declined like **turris** are: **clāvis**, *key*; **nāvis**, *ship*; **puppis**, *stern of a ship*; **secūris**, *axe*.

Like **ignis** are: **amnis**, *river*; **anguis**, *snake*; **avis**, *bird*; **cīvis**, *citizen*; **clāssis**, *fleet*; **collis**, *hill*; **fīnis**, *end*; **orbis**, *circle*; **postis**, *post*.

[1] That is, having no more syllables than in the nominative.

**155.** Adjectives declined like **ācer** are called adjectives of three terminations; those declined like **levis**, adjectives of two terminations; while those declined like **vetus (141)**, **audāx** and **prūdēns (164)**, are called adjectives of one termination.

**156.** Decline together **nāvis longa**, *ship of war*; **vallis profunda**, *deep valley*; **Alpēs altae**, *high Alps*. See **161**.

## 2.

**157.** *Paradigm illustrating apposition:* —

N.V. **Cicerō cōnsul**, *Cicero, the consul.*
G. **Cicerōnis cōnsulis**, *of Cicero, the consul.*
D. **Cicerōnī cōnsulī**, *to* or *for Cicero, the consul.*
Ac. **Cicerōnem cōnsulem**, *Cicero, the consul.*
Ab. **ā Cicerōne cōnsule**, *by Cicero, the consul.*

**158.** Rule of Syntax. — **An appositive is in the same case as the noun or pronoun which it qualifies.**

**159.** EXERCISES.

I. 1. In vallibus Alpium sunt fluviī pulchrī. 2. Quae (*what*) animālia aquilam timent? 3. Nāvēs Gallōrum erant longae et altae. 4. Gallī longās nāvēs habēbant. 5. Fuimus in nāvī altā. 6. Rōbur tuum levī labōre augēbitur. 7. Somnus hominibus voluptātem praebet. 8. Habentne mīlitēs dēfessī cibum et aquam? 9. Hominēs cibum īgnī coquunt (*cook*). 10. Leōnēs et elephantī sunt animālia fera.

II. 1. In the tower there were many men. 2. The towers of the ships were high. 3. From the high tower we saw the broad sea. 4. The broad sea was seen by men in the high tower. 5. The flight of the horsemen was seen by brave soldiers. 6. Robbers fear a brave man. 7. A brave man is feared by robbers. 8. On the shore they built a tower for the king. 9. Numa, king of the Romans, changed the number of the months. 10. The number of the months was changed by Numa, a Roman king.

## 3.

**160.** EXERCISES.

I. 1. Turrim altam vidēbant rēgis comitēs. 2. Corpora hominum nōn animī sunt mortālia. 3. Capita animālium multōrum vidēbantur. 4. Ācrī animō nāvem latrōnum submovent nautae. 5. Nāvis latrōnum ab ācribus nautīs submovētur. 6. Vīctōriam dēbēmus turribus nostrīs validīs. 7. Multa animālia sunt levia et vigilia. 8. Avium nōn multa genera in ruīnīs turrium antīquārum habitant. 9. Servī Graecī fīliōs Rōmānōrum nōbilium ēducābant. 10. Fīliī Rōmānōrum nōbilium ā servīs Graecīs saepe ēducābantur.

II. 1. Polyphemus, son of Neptune, had a huge body. 2. Cyrus, the first king of the Persians, remembered all the names of his soldiers. 3. The names of all his soldiers were remembered by Cyrus, king of the Persians. 4. How many ships of the Gauls were driven off? 5. The number of fires in the town was great.

**161.** VOCABULARY.

**Alpēs, -ium,** F., *Alps.*
**avis, -is,** F., *bird* (**154**).
**fortis, -e,** adj., *brave.*
**mēnsis, -is,** M., *month.*
**mortālis, -e,** adj., *mortal.*
**nāvis, -is,** F., *ship* (**154**).
**nōbilis, -e,** adj., *noble.*
**omnis, -e,** adj., *all, every.*
**vallis** (or **-ēs**), **-is,** F., *valley.*
**vigil,** adj., *watchful* (**151.** 4).

**animus, -ī,** M., *mind, soul.*
**ēducō,** 1, *train, educate.*
**ferus, -a, -um,** adj., *wild.*
**fuga, -ae,** F., *flight.*
**genus, -eris,** N., *kind, race.*
**habitō,** 1, *dwell, inhabit.*
**latrō, -ōnis,** M., *robber.*
**lītus, -ōris,** N., *shore.*
**multitūdō, -inis,** F., *multitude.*
**Neptūnus, -ī,** M., *Neptune,* god of the sea.
**noster, -tra, -trum,** poss. adj., *our, ours.*
**Numa, -ae,** M., *Numa,* a Roman king.
**Persae, -ārum,** M., *the Persians.*

**Polyphēmus, -ī**, M., *Polyphemus.*
**quot**, adj. indecl., *how many?*
**rōbur, -ŏris**, N., *strength.*
**ruīna, -ae**, F., *ruin.*
**sub-moveō**, 2, **-mōvī, -mōtum**, (*move from beneath*) *remove, drive away.*
**vītō**, 1, *avoid, shun.*

## 4.

**162.** COLLOQUIUM.

### Frāter et Sorōrcula.

*S.* Nārrā mihi, frāter, dē Polyphēmō; quis fuit et ubi habitābat?
where

*F.* Polyphēmus fīlius Neptūnī fuit et cum frātribus in īnsulā habitābat.

*S.* Fuitne arātor et agrōs arābat?

*F.* Minimē. Neque fuit arātor neque agrōs arābat Polyphēmus.
neither ploughman nor

*S.* Nauta igitur sine dubiō fuit, et maria nāvibus nāvigābat.
therefore

*F.* Errāvistī, mea sorōrcula, Polyphēmus fuit pāstor atque māgnās ovium gregēs habēbat. Fuit autem ingentis corporis et ūnum tantum oculum habuit. Ulixēs dolōsus eī ūnum oculum stīpite perforāvit.
and; sheep; moreover; huge; only; crafty; for him; his one; stake; dug out

*S.* Ēheu! miserrimum Polyphēmum!
Oh dear! poor

## CHAPTER XXI. 1.

## THIRD DECLENSION.

### Mixed Stems.[1]

**163.** PARADIGMS.

| | **Cliēns**, M. & F., *client.* | **Urbs**, F., *city.* | **Arx**, F., *citadel.* | TERMINATIONS. |
|---|---|---|---|---|
| | | SINGULAR. | | |
| N.V. | cliēn**s** | urb**s** | arx | **s** |
| G. | client**is** | urb**is** | arc**is** | **is** |
| D. | client**ī** | urb**ī** | arc**ī** | **ī** |
| Ac. | client**em** | urb**em** | arc**em** | **em** |
| Ab. | client**e** | urb**e** | arc**e** | **e** |
| | | PLURAL. | | |
| N.V. | client**ēs** | urb**ēs** | arc**ēs** | **ēs** |
| G. | client**ium** | urb**ium** | arc**ium** | **ium** |
| D. | client**ibus** | urb**ibus** | arc**ibus** | **ibus** |
| Ac. | client**ēs, īs** | urb**ēs, īs** | arc**ēs, īs** | **ēs, īs** |
| Ab. | client**ibus** | urb**ibus** | arc**ibus** | **ibus** |

**164.** ADJECTIVES.

**Audāx**, *bold;* **prūdēns**, *sagacious.*

| | M. & F. | NEUT. | M. & F. | NEUT. |
|---|---|---|---|---|
| | | SINGULAR. | | |
| N.V. | audāx | audāx | prūdēns | prūdēns |
| G. | audāc**is** | audāc**is** | prūdent**is** | prūdent**is** |
| D. | audāc**ī** | audāc**ī** | prūdent**ī** | prūdent**ī** |
| Ac. | audāc**em** | audāx | prūdent**em** | prūdēns |
| Ab. | audāc**ī, e** | audāc**ī, e** | prūdent**ī, e** | prūdent**ī, e** |
| | | PLURAL. | | |
| N.V. | audāc**ēs** | audāc**ia** | prūdent**ēs** | prūdent**ia** |
| G. | audāc**ium** | audāc**ium** | prūdent**ium** | prūdent**ium** |
| D. | audāc**ibus** | audāc**ibus** | prūdent**ibus** | prūdent**ibus** |
| Ac. | audāc**ēs, īs** | audāc**ia** | prūdent**ēs, īs** | prūdent**ia** |
| Ab. | audāc**ibus** | audāc**ibus** | prūdent**ibus** | prūdent**ibus** |

[1] Usually classed as *i* stems. See **166**.

**165.** PARTICIPLE.

**Amāns**, *loving.*

| | SINGULAR. | | PLURAL. | |
|---|---|---|---|---|
| | M. & F. | NEUT. | M. & F. | NEUT. |
| N.V. | **amāns** | **amāns** | **amantēs** | **amantia** |
| G. | **amantis** | **amantis** | **amantium** | **amantium** |
| D. | **amantī** | **amantī** | **amantibus** | **amantibus** |
| Ac. | **amantem** | **amāns** | **amantēs** | **amantia** |
| Ab. | **amante, ī** | **amante, ī** | **amantibus** | **amantibus** |

**166.** Note in the above tables:—

1. That the nouns are declined in the singular like consonant stems (**105, 134, 140**), and the adjectives also, except that, like *i* stems, they have an ablative in ī.

2. That the plural of both nouns and adjectives is like that of *i* stems (**149, 150**).

**167.** To the class of mixed stems belong:—

1. Nouns in *ns* and *rs*. But **parēns** has the genitive plural **parentum**.

2. Monosyllables in *s* and *x* following a consonant, together with **nix, nivis,** *snow;* **nox, noctis,** *night;* **os, ossis,** *bone;* **mūs, mūris,** *mouse.*

3. Adjectives of one ending, with some exceptions, of which the most important are: **dīves,** *rich;* **pauper,** *poor;* **particeps,** *sharing;* **prīnceps,** *chief;* and compounds of nouns that have consonant stems. These all have the genitive plural in *um.*

4. Present active participles.

**168.** RULES OF GENDER.—**1. Nouns ending in *ō, or, ōs, er, es* (gen. *ĭdis, ĭtis*), are masculine.**

But nouns ending in *dō* and *gō*, of more than two syllables, together with abstract[1] and collective[2] nouns in *iō*, are feminine.

**2. Nouns ending in *ās, ēs* not increasing in the genitive, *is, x,* and *s* following a consonant, are feminine.**

[1] Abstract nouns are such as denote a *thought* rather than a *thing:* **ratiō,** *method.*

[2] Collective nouns are such as in the singular imply a number of things or persons: **legiō,** *legion.*

**3. Nouns ending in *a, e, i, y, c, l, n, t, ar, ur*, and *us*, are neuter.**

There are many exceptions to these rules, which the learner should note as he advances.

**169.** Decline together **fōns profundus**, *deep spring;* **hostis audāx**, *bold enemy;* **māgna pars**, *great part*. See **172**.

## 2.

**170.** EXERCISES.

I. 1. Alpēs sunt montēs Eurōpae. 2. Saepe in lateribus montium sunt silvae. 3. Multōrum amnium fontēs sunt parvī. 4. In Alpibus sunt regiōnēs pulchrae et suāvēs. 5. Sunt vallēs profundae, rūpēs altae, silvae māgnae. 6. Ibi māgnam vidēbis multitūdinem vulpium. 7. Aestāte ovium gregēs videntur. 8. Mīlitem fortem nōn terrēbit perīculum. 9. Mīles fortis perīculō nōn terrēbitur. 10. Omnēs adulēscentēs erunt mīlitēs fortēs.

II. 1. There are mountains in Europe. 2. On the sides of the mountains are tall trees. 3. Many rivers have small sources. 4. Parts of the Alps are beautiful. 5. The Alps have deep valleys and high cliffs. 6. Wild beasts are seen on the sides of the Alps. 7. There you will see shepherds and sheep. 8. Brave soldiers do not fear dangers. 9. The fathers of the young men are soldiers. 10. We honor the brave soldier.

## 3.

**171.** EXERCISES.

I. 1. Quid vident hominēs in montibus altīs? 2. Aquilam, avem audācem, in rūpibus vident. 3. Nōnne in arboribus altīs habitat rēx avium? 4. Certē, et parvīs avibus est terror māgnus, nam inter avēs rēgnat. 5. Ācrēs sunt aquilārum oculī; longē vident vēnātōrem. 6. In marī clāssem hostium vidēmus. 7. Clāssis nāvium ā latrōnibus vidēbātur. 8. Magister mōrēs bonōs et dīligentiam discipulōrum laudābit. 9. Mōrēs bonī et dīligentia ā magistrō laudābuntur. 10. Omnis Galliae sunt partēs trēs (*three*).

II. 1. Men dwell in the deep valleys of the mountains. 2. In summer they have flocks on the mountains. 3. Why do men call the eagle the king[1] of birds? 4. Do not keen hunters see the eagle from afar? 5. The enemy's ships plough the deep sea. 6. The robbers saw the ships with great terror.[2] 7. Solon was the author of many good laws. 8. In ancient states there were free men and slaves. 9. The memory of the wise Solon has been honored.

**172.** VOCABULARY.

**adulēscēns, -entis**, M. & F., *youth, young man.*
**fōns, fontis**, M., *source, spring.*
**mōns, montis**, M., *mountain.*
**pars, partis**, F., *part.*
**sapiēns, -entis**, adj., *wise.*

**amnis, -is**, M., *river* (**154**).
**arbor, -ŏris**, F., *tree.*
**auctor, -ōris**, M., *author.*
**Belgae, -ārum**, M., *the Belgians.*
**clāssis, -is**, F., *fleet* (**154**).
**dīligentia, -ae**, F., *diligence.*
**fera, -ae**, F., *wild beast.*
**honōrō**, 1, *honor.*
**hostis, -is**, M. & F., *enemy.*
**ibi**, adv., *there.*
**inter**, prep. w. acc., *between, among.*
**latus, -eris**, N., *side.* Cf. **lātus**, *broad.*
**lēx, lēgis**, F., *law.*
**longē**, adv., *afar, at a distance.*
**mōs, mōris**, M., *manner, custom.*
**nam**, conj., *for.*
**ovis, -is**, F., *sheep.*
**pāstor, -ōris**, M., *shepherd.*
**perīculum, -ī**, N., *danger, peril.*
**profundus, -a, -um**, adj., *deep.*
**regiō, -ōnis**, F., *region.*
**rēgnō**, 1, *be king, rule, reign.*
**rūpēs, -is**, F., *rock, cliff.*
**silva, -ae**, F., *wood, forest.*
**Solōn, -ōnis**, M., *Solon*, an Athenian lawgiver.
**suāvis, -e**, adj., *sweet, pleasant.*
**vēnātor, -ōris**, M., *hunter.*
**vulpēs, -is**, F., *fox.*

**amnis**, *a large, deep river;* not the common prose word for *river.*
**flūmen** (**203**), general word for *river; flowing*, as opposed to *still water*, as a lake or pond.
**fluvius** (**84**), not different from **flūmen**, but much less used.

**hostis**, general word for *enemy: a public enemy, enemy in war.*
**inimīcus** (**78**), *a private or personal enemy;* opposed to **amīcus**.

[1] Predicate accusative. [2] See **144, 145**.

4.

COLLOQUIUM.

**173.** *Translate into Latin:* —

FATHER AND SON.

*F.* Tell me (*mihi*) about Solon, if you please (*sī placet*).

*S.* Solon was a wise Athenian (*Athēniēnsis*); his (*ējus*) laws were famous, and his memory will always be honored. He was the friend of poor men (*pauperum*). He saw many lands and many men. He did not fear Pisistratus the usurper (*tyrannum*).

*F.* Was Miltiades also (*quoque*) an Athenian?

*S.* Certainly; he overcame the Persians (*Persās*) in the battle of Marathon.[1] He was a brave and skilful leader. He had a brave son.

## CHAPTER XXII. 1.

### REVIEW.

**174.** Decline together **gladius ācer**, *sharp sword;* **cōnsilium ūtile**, *useful counsel;* **aquila celeris**, *swift eagle;* **animal vēlōx**, *fleet animal.* See **179**.

**175.** Examples of the locative case in the third declension are: **Carthāginī**, or **Carthāgine**, *at Carthage;* **rūrī**, *in the country.*

**176.** *Affix the proper terminations to the adjectives in the following, and translate:* —

1. Equō celer-, equōrum vēlōc-, equīs vēlōc-. 2. Puella trīst-, puellae trīst-, puellam trīst-, puellārum prūdent-. 3. Gladiīs ācr-, gladiōs ācr-, gladium ācr-. 4. Librō ūtil-, librōrum ūtil-, librum ūtil-. 5. Dōnum ūtil-, dōna ūtil-, dōnī ūtil-. 6. Servī fidēl-, servō fidēl-, servōs fidēl-, servīs fidēl-.

[1] *Of Marathon,* **Marathōnius, -a, -um.**

**177.** EXERCISES.

I. 1. Equī sunt celerēs. 2. Proelium equestre fuit. 3. Virī fortēs laudantur. 4. Virum fortem laudāmus. 5. Omne initium est difficile. 6. Bella sunt trīstia. 7. Cōnsilium ducis audāx fuit. 8. Vetus vīnum est bonum. 9. Ācris et vēlōx est aquila. 10. Multa animālia vītās brevēs habent.

II. 1. The soldiers have keen weapons. 2. I have a swift horse. 3. We praise brave men. 4. Do you like sweet food? 5. The lessons are not hard. 6. The plans of the commander are sagacious. 7. Life is short. 8. There are swift eagles in the mountains. 9. The king has bold sailors. 10. The wings of the swift eagle are long.

2.

**178.** EXERCISES.

Write out the whole of **177.** I. in Latin, changing singulars to plurals and plurals to singulars. Thus, 4 will be **virōs fortēs laudō.**

Turn II. into Latin, first changing the sentences as directed above in regard to I.

**179.** VOCABULARY.

**ācer, ācris, ācre,** adj., *sharp, eager.*
**brevis, -e,** adj., *short.*
**celer, celeris, celere,** adj., *quick, fleet, swift.*
**difficilis, -e,** adj., *difficult, hard.*
**equester, -tris, -tre,** adj., *equestrian.*
**fidēlis, -e,** adj., *faithful.*
**initium, -ī,** N., *beginning.*
**tēlum, -ī,** N., *weapon.*
**trīstis, -e,** adj., *sad.*
**ūtilis, -e,** adj., *useful.*
**vēlōx, -ōcis,** adj., *swift, fleet.*
**vīta, -ae,** F., *life.*

**celer,** *quick,* with the added notion of *eagerness* or *energy.*
**vēlōx,** *swift,* sometimes implying *nimbleness.*

# CHAPTER XXIII.

## THIRD CONJUGATION.

**180.** VERBS IN *ĕ*.

**Regō** (stem **rege**), *rule*.
PRINCIPAL PARTS: **regō, regĕre, rēxī,**[1] **rēctum.**[2]

### INDICATIVE.

| ACTIVE. | | PASSIVE. | |
|---|---|---|---|
| | | **PRESENT.** | |
| *I rule, etc.* | | *I am ruled, etc.* | |
| reg**ō** | reg**imus** | reg**or** | reg**imur** |
| reg**is** | reg**itis** | reg**eris,** *or* **-re** | reg**iminī** |
| reg**it** | reg**unt** | reg**itur** | reg**untur** |
| | | **IMPERFECT.** | |
| *I was ruling, etc.* | | *I was ruled, etc.* | |
| reg**ēbam** | reg**ēbāmus** | reg**ēbar** | reg**ēbāmur** |
| reg**ēbās** | reg**ēbātis** | reg**ēbāris,** *or* **-re** | reg**ēbāminī** |
| reg**ēbat** | reg**ēbant** | reg**ēbātur** | reg**ēbantur** |
| | | **FUTURE.** | |
| *I shall rule, etc.* | | *I shall be ruled, etc.* | |
| reg**am** | reg**ēmus** | reg**ar** | reg**ēmur** |
| reg**ēs** | reg**ētis** | reg**ēris,** *or* **-re** | reg**ēminī** |
| reg**et** | reg**ent** | reg**ētur** | reg**entur** |
| | | **PERFECT.** | |
| *I have ruled, etc.* | | *I have been ruled, etc.* | |
| rēx**ī** | rēx**imus** | rēct**us** **sum** | rēct**ī** **sumus** |
| rēx**istī** | rēx**istis** | rēct**us** **es** | rēct**ī** **estis** |
| rēx**it** | rēx**ērunt,** *or* **-re** | rēct**us** **est** | rēct**ī** **sunt** |
| | | **PLUPERFECT.** | |
| *I had ruled, etc.* | | *I had been ruled, etc.* | |
| rēx**eram** | rēx**erāmus** | rēct**us** **eram** | rēct**ī** **erāmus** |
| rēx**erās** | rēx**erātis** | rēct**us** **erās** | rēct**ī** **erātis** |
| rēx**erat** | rēx**erant** | rēct**us** **erat** | rēct**ī** **erant** |

[1] **Rēxī** for **reg-sī.** See p. 1, note 2. [2] **Rēctum** for **reg-tum.**

| **ACTIVE.** | | **PASSIVE.** | |
|---|---|---|---|
| | FUTURE PERFECT. | | |
| *I shall have ruled, etc.* | | *I shall have been ruled, etc.* | |
| rēx **erō** | rēx **erimus** | rēct **us erō** | rēct **ī erimus** |
| rēx **eris** | rēx **eritis** | rēct **us eris** | rēct **ī eritis** |
| rēx **erit** | rēx **erint** | rēct **us erit** | rēct **ī erunt** |

## SUBJUNCTIVE.[1]

| | | | |
|---|---|---|---|
| | PRESENT. | | |
| reg **am** | reg **āmus** | reg **ar** | reg **āmur** |
| reg **ās** | reg **ātis** | reg **āris**, *or* **-re** | reg **āminī** |
| reg **at** | reg **ant** | reg **ātur** | reg **antur** |
| | IMPERFECT. | | |
| reg **erem** | reg **erēmus** | reg **erer** | reg **erēmur** |
| reg **erēs** | reg **erētis** | reg **erēris**, *or* **-re** | reg **erēminī** |
| reg **eret** | reg **erent** | reg **erētur** | reg **erentur** |
| | PERFECT. | | |
| rēx **erim** | rēx **erimus** | rēct **us sim** | rēct **ī sīmus** |
| rēx **eris** | rēx **eritis** | rēct **us sīs** | rēct **ī sītis** |
| rēx **erit** | rēx **erint** | rēct **us sit** | rēct **ī sint** |
| | PLUPERFECT. | | |
| rēx **issem** | rēx **issēmus** | rēct **us essem** | rēct **ī essēmus** |
| rēx **issēs** | rēx **issētis** | rēct **us essēs** | rēct **ī essētis** |
| rēx **isset** | rēx **issent** | rēct **us esset** | rēct **ī essent** |

## IMPERATIVE.

PRESENT.

| | |
|---|---|
| reg **e**, *rule thou.* | reg **ere**, *be thou ruled.* |
| reg **ite**, *rule ye.* | reg **iminī**, *be ye ruled.* |

FUTURE.

| | |
|---|---|
| reg **itō**, *thou shalt rule.* | reg **itor**, *thou shalt be ruled.* |
| reg **itō**, *he shall rule.* | reg **itor**, *he shall be ruled.* |
| reg **itōte**, *ye shall rule.* | |
| reg **untō**, *they shall rule.* | reg **untor**, *they shall be ruled.* |

[1] See p. 26, note.

INFINITIVE.

| ACTIVE. | | PASSIVE. |
|---|---|---|
| PRES. | **regere**, *to rule.* | **regī**, *to be ruled.* |
| PERF. | **rēxisse**, *to have ruled.* | **rēctus esse**, *to have been ruled.* |
| FUT. | **rēctūrus esse**, *to be about to rule.* | **rēctum īrī**, *to be about to be ruled.* |

PARTICIPLE.

| | | |
|---|---|---|
| PRES. | **regēns, -entis**, *ruling.* | ——— |
| FUT. | **rēctūrus, -a, -um**, *about to rule.* | GER. **regendus, -a, -um**, *to be ruled.* |
| | ——— | PERF. **rēctus, -a, -um**, *having been ruled.* |

GERUND.

G. **regendī**, *of ruling.*
D. **regendō**, *for ruling.*
Ac. **regendum**, *ruling.*
Ab. **regendō**, *by ruling.*

SUPINE.

Ac. **rēctum**, *to rule.* Ab. **rēctū**, *to rule, to be ruled.*

## CHAPTER XXIV. 1.

### THIRD CONJUGATION.

**181.** Learn the present, imperfect, and future indicative, and present imperative and infinitive, active and passive, of **regō**.

**182.** EXERCISES.

I. 1. Regitis, regēbātis, regētis. 2. Regitur, regēbātur, regētur. 3. Regō, regēbam, regam. 4. Reguntur, regēbantur, regentur. 5. Regere, regī. 6. Regite, regere. 7. Regis, regeris. 8. Regimus, regimur. 9. Regit, regitur. 10. Regitis, regiminī.

II. 1. He rules, he was ruling, he will rule. 2. To be ruled, to rule. 3. They rule, they were ruling, they will rule. 4. We rule, we are ruled. 5. We shall rule, we shall be ruled. 6. You are ruling, you were ruling, you will rule. 7. Rule (thou), be (thou) ruled. 8. He is ruling, he is ruled. 9. They ruled, they were ruled. 10. I rule, I ruled, I shall rule.

## 2.

### 183. EXERCISES.

**Scrībō,**[1] *write;* **mittō,**[1] *send;* **emō,**[1] *buy.*

I. 1. Scrībis, mittis, emis. 2. Mittitur, scrībitur, emitur. 3. Nōnne mittēbās? nōnne scrībēbant? nōnne emēbam? 4. Scrībētur, mittēbantur, ementur. 5. Mitte, scrībite, emite. 6. Emere, scrībere, mittere. 7. Nōn mittunt, nōn scrībitis, nōn emet. 8. Scrībamne? emuntne? mittimusne? 9. Mitteris, mittēris, scrībētur. 10. Scrībī, mittī, emī.

II. 1. He writes, he is sent, they buy. 2. Is it written? does he send? are they bought? 3. I shall buy, thou wilt send, he will write. 4. It will not be written, we shall not be sent, thou wilt not be bought. 5. To write, to send, to buy. 6. Write, send, buy. 7. We are sent, they were bought, it is (being) written. 8. They write, they will buy, they were sending. 9. I was writing, we were sending, I shall buy. 10. You are sent, it was (being) written, they are bought.

### 184. EXERCISES.

I. 1. Imperātor multās urbēs vincet. 2. Multae terrae ab Rōmānīs regēbantur. 3. Omnem mundum regit Deus. 4. Dux Rōmānus ex Graeciā in Ītaliam portābat multās statuās. 5. Virī fortēs timōre nōn vincuntur. 6. Pābulum mīlitibus[2] emētur. 7. Hannibal mīlitēs trāns Alpēs dūcēbat.

---

[1] For principal parts, see **186**.

[2] What would be the meaning of **ā mīlitibus**?

8. Trāns fluvium erat parva urbs. 9. Urbs ā cīvibus dēfendēbātur. 10. Nautae, ē nāvī dēscendite.

II. 1. The commander writes a letter. 2. Letters are written by the commander. 3. Hannibal was leading his soldiers into Italy. 4. The citizens are defended by their[1] leaders. 5. Cæsar conquered all his enemies. 6. Rome will be defended by the citizens. 7. Drive the sheep into the fields. 8. There are many robbers in the city. 9. Near the town is a broad valley. 10. Come down out of the tower.

## 3.

**185.** EXERCISES.

I. 1. Omnis mundus ā Deō regitur. 2. Puerīs librōs emam. 3. Dēfēnsōrēs oppidī ā Caesaris mīlitibus vincentur. 4. In Āfricā servī emuntur. 5. Hieme multa animālia in vallēs dēscendunt. 6. Agricolae in urbem ovēs agent. 7. Omnēs canēs ex urbe agēmus. 8. Epistulam dē bellō scrībēbam. 9. Puer epistulam dē pēnsīs scrībēbat. 10. Poēta bonus poēmata bona scrībet.

II. 1. The king's brothers send soldiers into Greece. 2. I will send my brother's son into Africa. 3. You will be sent into Sicily. 4. Send men across the river. 5. The city was defended with[2] great bravery by all the citizens. 6. Pyrrhus led many men across the sea into Italy. 7. In[3] winter many animals are overcome by hunger. 8. The farmers are buying food for their sheep. 9. Strong men were driving the white horses into the river. 10. The good shepherd leads his sheep.

---

[1] See **100**.

[2] Is it necessary to translate *with* by **cum**? See examples and rule, **144**, **145**.

[3] Is *in* to be separately expressed in Latin? See fifth sentence above, and examples and rule, **135**, **136**.

**186.** VOCABULARY.

**agō**, 3, **ēgī**, **āctum**, *drive, lead.*
**dē-fendō**, 3, **-dī**, **-sum**, *defend.*
**dē-scendō**, 3, **-dī**, **-sum**, *descend, go down, come down.*
**dūcō**, 3, **dūxī**, **ductum**, *lead.*
**emō**, 3, **ēmī**, **ēmptum**, *buy.*
**mittō**, 3, **mīsī**, **missum**, *send.*
**scrībō**, 3, **scrīpsī**, **scrīptum**, *write.*
**sūmō**, 3, **sūmpsī**, **sūmptum**, *take.*
**vincō**, 3, **vīcī**, **victum**, *conquer.*
**Caesar**, **-āris**, M., *Cæsar.*
**canis**, **-is**, M. & F., *dog.* (**153**.)
**cīvis**, **-is**, M. & F., *citizen.*
**dē**, prep. w. abl., *concerning, about.*
**epistula**, **-ae**, F., *letter.*
**famēs**, **-is**, F., *hunger, famine.*
**hiems**, **hiemis**, F., *winter.*
**latrō**, **-ōnis**, M., *robber.*
**mundus**, **-ī**, M., *world, universe.*
**prope**, prep. w. acc., *near.*
**trāns**, prep. w. acc., *across, beyond.*

**superō** (**102**), *to have the upper hand, surpass, conquer.*
**vincō**, *to get the mastery, vanquish, conquer.*
What difference do you make out from a comparison of the meanings?

4.

**187.** COLLOQUIUM.

CHARŌN ET MERCURIUS.

*Ch.* Salvē, Ō Mercurī!
hail

*M.* Et tū, salvē, portitor.
ferryman

*Ch.* Mercurī, dūcisne hodiē multōs mānēs?
souls

*M.* Hodiē mānium dūcō numerum māgnum. Trīste est
sad
officium meum. Ithaca tibi procul dubiō nōta est atque Ulixēs.
duty without doubt known

*Ch.* Rēctē dīxistī. Ithaca est īnsula inter Graeciam et
you have said
Ītaliam sita; et mihi nōtus est Ulixēs, nam ipse ōlim hūc
situated himself formerly hither
vēnit.
came

*M.* Jam aspice mānēs procerum et servōrum īnfīdōrum.
now see chiefs unfaithful
Hī omnēs ab Ulixe necātī sunt.
these

*Ch.* Istud mihi placet. Mānēs in cymbā trānsveham.
that boat carry over
Valē, Mercurī.

*M.* Et tū valē, Charōn.

5.

**188.** FOR TRANSLATION.[1]

Pūblius Cornēlius Scīpiō.

Pūblius Cornēlius Scīpiō mājor,[2] adulēscēns[3] septendecim annōrum, ad Tīcīnum flūmen patrem vulnerātum servāvit. In pūgnā Cannēnsī fortiter dīmicāvit. Posteā Carthāginem Novam, urbem in Hispāniā Poenōrum firmissimam expūgnāvit. Obsidēs Hispānōrum benīgnē tractāvit et lībertāte dōnāvit.[4] Nōn minus fēlīciter Scīpiō in Āfricā bellāvit ibique Poenōs ita ursit[5] ut Hannibalem ex Ītaliā revocārent.[6] Ad Zamam Scīpiōnis et Hannibalis exercitūs[7] castra habuērunt; clārum est illud colloquium, quod Hannibal, dux Poenōrum, et Scīpiō, cōnsul Rōmānus, ante pūgnam habuērunt. Poenī ā Scīpiōne superātī fugātīque sunt. Scīpiō triumphum māgnificum ex Āfricā reportāvit et ā populō Āfricānus appellātus est.

## CHAPTER XXV. 1.

### THIRD CONJUGATION.

**189.** Learn the perfect, pluperfect, and future perfect indicative, and perfect infinitive, active and passive, of **regō**.

**190.** EXERCISES.

I. 1. Rēxit, rēxerat, rēxerit. 2. Rēxērunt, rēxerant, rēxerint. 3. Rēxisse, rēctus esse. 4. Rēctum est, rēctum erat, rēctum erit. 5. Rēxistī, rēxerās, rēxeris. 6. Rēximus,

[1] For meanings of words, see general vocabulary.

[2] *The elder.*

[3] *When a youth.*

[4] *Presented them with their liberty* = *set them free.*

[5] From **urgeō**; **ita ursit**, *pressed them so hard.*

[6] **Ut . . . revocārent**, *that they recalled.*

[7] Nom. plur., subject of **habuērunt.**

rēctī sumus. 7. Rēxistis, rēctī estis. 8. Rēxī, rēxeram, rēxerō. 9. Rēxerant, rēctī erant. 10. Rēcta est, rēcta erat, rēcta erit.

II. 1. I have ruled, I had ruled, I shall have ruled. 2. I have ruled, I have been ruled. 3. They have ruled, they have been ruled. 4. You ruled, you had ruled, you will have ruled. 5. He will have ruled, he will have been ruled. 6. To have been ruled, to have ruled. 7. They had ruled, they had been ruled. 8. She has ruled, she has been ruled. 9. It was ruled, it had been ruled, it will have been ruled. 10. They (*neut.*) were ruled, they had been ruled, they will have been ruled.

## 2.

**191.** EXERCISES.

I. 1. Dūxit, ēmerit, sūmpserit. 2. Ēmit,[1] dūxistī, sūmpsī. 3. Sūmptus est, ductae sumus, ēmpta sunt. 4. Eratne ductus? erantne ēmptae? eratne sūmptum? 5. Dūxerimus, sūmpseritis, ēmerint. 6. Nōnne dūximus? nōnne ēmerāmus? nōnne ēmerimus? 7. Dūxistī, ēmērunt, sūmpsimus. 8. Ducta est, ēmptum est, sūmpta erat. 9. Dūxisse, ēmisse, sūmpsisse. 10. Nōn dūxeram, nōn ēmerātis, nōn sūmpserō.

II. 1. She had been led, it has been bought, they (*neut.*) will have been taken. 2. I have taken, you have bought, he has led. 3. Has it not been taken? had he not been led? have they (*neut.*) not been bought? 4. I had led, you had bought, he had taken. 5. They will have taken, I shall have led, thou wilt have bought. 6. I was led, it was bought, it had been taken. 7. To have been led, to have been bought, to have been taken. 8. We shall have taken, I shall have bought, he will have led. 9. Did he take? didst thou buy? did you lead? 10. They did not lead, you had not bought, she will not have taken.

[1] How do you know whether this form is present or perfect?

**192.** EXERCISES.

I. 1. Hostēs vīcimus. 2. Hostēs territī vīctīque sunt. 3. Horātius oculum in proeliō āmīserat. 4. Ō patria, vīcistī īram meam. 5. Scīpiō in Hispāniam missus est. 6. Spartacus, dux gladiātōrum, cōnsulēs Rōmānōs vīcit. 7. Gallia inter Pȳrēnaeōs montēs et Rhēnum posita est.[1] 8. Metellus bellum in Hispāniā gessit. 9. Quid timēs? Caesarem vehis. 10. Bellum ā Pyrrhō in Ītaliā gestum est. 11. Ā Spartacō, duce gladiātōrum, cōnsulēs Rōmānī vīctī sunt.

II. 1. Have you lost your books? 2. My brother will sail[2] in a small ship. 3. Do men live in trees? 4. Neptune ruled (over) the deep sea. 5. A river flows out of the mountain. 6. The girl's head was encircled with flowers. 7. War has been waged in Italy. 8. A lazy boy is often despised. 9. The ancient Romans did not despise war. 10. The king had surrounded the city with walls. 11. Did not Pyrrhus, king of Epirus, wage war in Italy?

3.

**193.** EXERCISES.

I. 1. Avēs multae in arboribus vīvunt. 2. Virī fortēs urbem templaque deōrum dēfendērunt. 3. Dux trāns mare in nāvī vectus est. 4. Tyrannī ā virīs fortibus contemptī sunt. 5. Pōnite pedēs in rūpem. 6. Virgō ā templō tracta erat. 7. Hannibal ā Scīpiōne vīctus est. 8. Caesar mīlitēs in equōs posuit. 9. Oppidum mūrō altō cinctum erat. 10. Oppidānī oppidum mūrō altō cinxērunt. 11. Inter montem et oppidum fluēbat fluvius lātus. 12. Bellum in Hispāniā ā Metellō imperātōre Rōmānō gestum est.

II. 1. A large fleet was bought with gold by Cæsar. 2. The general's daughter had been carried in a wagon.

---

[1] **Posita est**, *is situated.* [2] Future passive of **vehō.**

3. The commander had carried on war against his enemies. 4. All the property[1] of the enemy has been lost. 5. Many men live by agriculture. 6. We went away from Italy to[2] Sicily. 7. My brother has departed from his native land. 8. Have they lost their books? 9. Have not men always despised tyrants? 10. The boys rode on horseback[3] with great pleasure.[4] 11. The farmer's cart is drawn by strong horses. 12. My books have been lost.

**194.** VOCABULARY.

**ā-mittō**, 3, **-mīsī**, **-missum**, *lose*.
**cingō**, 3, **cīnxī**, **cīnctum**, *bind, encircle, surround.*
**con-temnō**, 3, **-tempsī**, **-temptum**, *despise.*
**dis-cēdō**, 3, **-cēssī**, **-cēssum**, *depart.*
**fluō**, 3, **flūxī**, **flūxum**, *flow.*
**gerō**, 3, **gessī**, **gestum**, *carry on, wage (war).*
**pōnō**, 3, **posuī**, **positum**, *put, place.*
**trahō**, 3, **-xī**, **-ctum**, *drag, draw.*
**vehō**, 3, **vexī**, **vectum**, *carry, draw.*
**vīvō**, 3, **vīxī**, **vīctum**, *live.*

**contrā**, prep. w. acc., *against.*
**carrus**, **-ī**, M., *cart, wagon.*
**Gallia**, **-ae**, F., *Gaul.*
**gladiātor**, **-ōris**, M., *gladiator.*
**Hispānia**, **-ae**, F., *Spain.*
**Horātius**, **-ī**, M., *Horatius.* (**79**.)
**Metellus**, **-ī**, M., *Metellus*, a Roman general.
**patria**, **-ae**, F., *native land.*
**Pȳrēnaeus**, **-a**, **-um**, adj., *Pyrenean, Pyrenees.*
**-que** (enclitic),[5] conj., *and.*
**Rhēnus**, **-ī**, M., *the Rhine.*
**Scīpiō**, **-ōnis**, M., *Scipio*, a Roman general.
**Spartacus**, **-ī**, M., *Spartacus*, a gladiator.
**virgō**, **-inis**, F., *maiden, girl.*

**habitō** (**161**), trans. and intrans., *live*, in the sense of *dwell, inhabit*, with reference to place.

**vīvō**, intrans., *have life, live*, often with reference to some condition or circumstance other than place.

---

[1] *Goods.* See **117**.

[2] *Into.* See **52**.

[3] Ride on horseback = *be carried on a horse.*

[4] See **145**.

[5] *I.e.*, appended to some word, as in **192**. I. 2.

4.

**195.** COLLOQUIUM.

PRAECEPTOR ET DISCIPULUS.

*P.* Quis fuit Hannibal? Fuit Rōmānus an Carthāginiēnsis?
Carthaginian

*D.* Fuit Carthāginiēnsis et ā Scīpiōne vīctus est.

*P.* Ubi fuit Hannibalis patria?
where

*D.* Carthāgō, Hannibalis patria, fuit in Āfricā.

*P.* Cūr *fuit?* cūr nōn *est* in Āfricā?
why

*D.* Quia Carthāgō ā Scīpiōne dēlēta est.
was destroyed

*P.* Quot nōmina erant Scīpiōnī?
how many

*D.* Tria Scīpiōnī erant nōmina. Pūblius Cornēlius Scīpiō.
three

*P.* Rēctē, mī puer, praenōmen *Pūblius; Cornēlius* nōmen
first name
gentīle; *Scīpiō* cōgnōmen.
family cognomen

*D.* Nōnne interdum appellātus est Scīpiō *Āfricānus?*
sometimes was called

*P.* Certissimē. Hōc autem nōmen dīcēbant Rōmānī
this moreover
cōgnōmen secundum.

# CHAPTER XXVI. 1.

## REVIEW.

**196.** EXERCISES.

I. 1. Dēfendite, cīvēs, cīvitātem. 2. Cīvitās est māter nostra. 3. Cīvēs sunt frātrēs nostrī. 4. Puerī, frātrēs amāte. 5. Ōrnāte, cīvēs, urbem monumentīs statuīsque. 6. Urbēs pulchrae in Ītaliā videntur. 7. Habitāsne in urbe pulchrā? 8. Urbs Rōma[1] mūrō cincta est. 9. Rōma ā cīvibus cum fortitūdine dēfēnsa est. 10. Mīlitēs Rōmānī erant fortēs.

[1] See **157, 158**.

II. 1. The citizens are defenders of the state. 2. Roman mothers furnished brave heroes for the state. 3. Do you write letters to your brothers? 4. From[1] springs in the mountains the rivers flow. 5. The city will be adorned with golden[2] statues. 6. In Greece we do[3] not see many beautiful cities. 7. The city is defended by watchful guards. 8. A high wall encircles the farmer's field. 9. We shall remain near Cæsar's camp. 10. We teach our children by means of stories.[4]

## 2.

**197.** EXERCISES.

I. 1. Cōnsulēs ā Pyrrhō victī sunt. 2. Urbs ā cōnsulibus dēfendētur. 3. Fīliī rēgis audācis sunt cīvitātis dēfēnsōrēs. 4. Clāmōribus mīlitum nostrōrum territī sunt hostēs. 5. Mīlitēs in urbe nostrā nōn saepe vidēmus. 6. In montibus et silvīs vīvunt aprī. 7. Malī[5] poenae timōre coercentur. 8. Lēgibus patriae omnēs[6] coercēmur. 9. Fluvius oppidum cingit. 10. Mōrēs malī ab hominibus bonīs contemnuntur.

II. 1. Who defeated the Roman consuls? 2. The consul was besieging a city of Spain. 3. We all have seen the pleasant light of the moon. 4. The sad maidens were sitting near a deep river. 5. The maidens were weeping because they had lost their flowers. 6. The boars are descending headlong into the sea. 7. Soldiers are not often seen in our streets. 8. The ancient city of Rome[7] was ruled by kings. 9. The shepherd's son will weep if he loses (shall have lost) a sheep. 10. The teacher was teaching his pupils[8] the poems of Homer.

---

[1] ē rather than ā.
[2] See p. 37, note 1.
[3] See p. 14, note 1.
[4] See **90** and **91**.
[5] See **117**.
[6] **Omnēs** agrees with the understood subject of **coercēmur.**
[7] *The city of Rome* = *the city Rome.* See **157**, **158**.
[8] Accusative. See p. 54, note 2.

**198.** VOCABULARY.

**fābula, -ae,** F., *story, tale, fable.*
**frāter, -tris,** M., *brother.*
**māter, -tris,** F., *mother.*
**omnis, -e,** adj., *all, every, whole.*
**praeceps, -cipitis,** adj., *headlong.*
**trīstis, -e,** adj., *sad, gloomy.*

3.

**199.** FOR TRANSLATION.[1]

PRŌSERPĬNA.

Prōserpina, Cereris fīlia, aliquandō in Siciliā ad urbem Hennam in campīs flōrēs carpēbat, serta nectēbat lūdēbatque cum comitibus. Nam campī ibi flōribus pulchrīs sparsī[2] sunt. Subitō terra concussa[3] est atque Plūtō, īnferōrum deus, ē terrā ēmersit;[4] ējus currum equī ātrī vehēbant. Deus Prōserpinam abdūxit, ut uxor sua et īnferōrum rēgīna esset;[5] clāmōrem puellae compressit.[6] Jūppiter autem frātrī permīserat ut Prōserpinam abdūceret.[7] Māter cum[8] īgnōrāret, ubi fīlia esset,[9] tōtum orbem terrārum frūstrā peragrāvit.

[*Continued on p.* 92.]

# CHAPTER XXVII. 1.

## IRREGULAR ADJECTIVES.

**200.** The following adjectives have *īus* (rarely *ĭus*) in the genitive singular of all genders, and *ī* in the dative:

**alius, alia, aliud,** *another.*
**nūllus, -a, -um,** *no one, none, no.*
**sōlus, -a, -um,** *alone, sole.*
**tōtus, -a, -um,** *whole.*
**ūllus, -a, -um,** *any.*
**ūnus, -a, -um,** *one, alone.*

1 For meanings of words, see general vocabulary.
2 From **spargō.**
3 From **concutiō.**
4 From **ēmergō.**
5 **Ut . . . esset,** *that she might be.*
6 From **comprimō.**
7 **Ut . . . abdūceret,** *that he might lead away* = *to lead away.*
8 **Cum īgnōrāret,** *since she did not know.*
9 *Was.*

**alter, altera, alterum,** *the other of two.*
**neuter, neutra, neutrum,** *neither of two.*
**uter, utra, utrum,** *which of two?*
**uterque, utrăque, utrumque,** *each of two, both.*

**201.** PARADIGM.

| | Singular. | | | Plural. | | |
|---|---|---|---|---|---|---|
| | MASC. | FEM. | NEUT. | MASC. | FEM. | NEUT. |
| N. | ali**us** | ali**a** | ali**ud** | ali**ī** | ali**ae** | ali**a** |
| G. | ali**us** | ali**us** | ali**us** | ali**ōrum** | ali**ārum** | ali**ōrum** |
| D. | ali**ī** | ali**ī** | ali**ī** | ali**īs** | ali**īs** | ali**īs** |
| Ac. | ali**um** | ali**am** | ali**ud** | ali**ōs** | ali**ās** | ali**a** |
| Ab. | ali**ō** | ali**ā** | ali**ō** | ali**īs** | ali**īs** | ali**īs** |

**202.** EXERCISES.

I. 1. Virtūs sōla vēram dat voluptātem. 2. Alius[1] aliud dīxit. 3. In utram partem[2] fluit flūmen? 4. Alter[3] Graecus, alter[3] Rōmānus erat. 5. Utrī cōnsulī dat cīvitās tōtam laudem? Neutrī. 6. Aliī[4] virtūte, aliī[4] dolīs hostēs superant.[5] 7. Ūnīus hominis mors tōtam urbem servāvit. 8. Alterī discipulō laudem, alterī culpam dat[5] praeceptor. 9. Nūllīus precibus cēdēmus. 10. Ā Cicerōne ūnō urbs servāta est.

II. 1. The farmer was ploughing his field alone. 2. He is praised by one, blamed by another. 3. To which of the two does the teacher give the praise? 4. Some like[6] boys, others like girls. 5. Death is feared by no good man. 6. The consul conquered some of his enemies, by others he

[1] Literally, *another said another thing.* The English of it is, *one said one thing, another another.*

[2] *Into which part?* i.e., *in which direction?*

[3] **Alter . . . alter,** *the one . . . the other.*

[4] **Aliī . . . aliī,** *some . . . others;* **aliud . . . aliud,** *one thing . . . another thing.*

[5] This sentence illustrates a common usage of the Latin. A verb belonging to two groups of words is often placed only with the last, and must be mentally supplied with the first. With the English it is the reverse. Show the application of the remark.

[6] See note 5.

was conquered. 7. One leg is long, the other short. 8. Some praise one thing, others another. 9. The plan of the whole war was disclosed to the enemy. 10. The citizens praised Cicero alone.

### 203. VOCABULARY.

**brevis, -e,** adj., *short.*
**cēdō,** 3, **cēssī, cēssum,** *yield.*
**Cicerō, -ōnis,** M., *Cicero,* a Roman orator.
**crūs, crūris,** N., *leg.*
**culpa, -ae,** F., *blame, fault.*
**dolus, -ī,** M., *trick, deceit.*
**ē-nūntiō,** 1, *disclose, announce.*
**flūmen, -inis,** N., *river.* (**172.**)
**laus, laudis,** F., *praise.*
**mors, mortis,** F., *death.*
**praeceptor, -ōris,** M., *teacher.*
**precēs, -um,** F. (plur.), *prayers, entreaty.*
**ratiō, -ōnis,** F., *plan, method.*
**servō,** 1, *save, preserve.*
**vērus, -a, -um,** adj., *true.*
**virtūs, -ūtis,** F., *virtue, courage.*

## 2.

### 204. COLLOQUIUM.

PRAECEPTOR ET DISCIPULUS.

*D.* Quis fuit Cicerō?
*P.* Clārus cōnsul Rōmānus fuit.
*D.* Multane bella gessit?
*P.* Minimē. Ōrātor fuit; dux mīlitum semel.
once only
*D.* Nōnne ējus ōrātiōnēs in scholā legimus?
his read
*P.* Complūrēs. Multās epistulās quoque scrīpsit Cicerō.
several also
*D.* Ad quōs epistulās scrīpsit?
whom
*P.* Ad frātrem et amīcōs.
*D.* Fuitne *Cicerō* ējus "nōmen"?[1]
*P.* Nōn fuit "nōmen," sed "cōgnōmen."
*D.* Quid fuit ējus "nōmen"?
*P.* *Tullius.*

[1] See **195.**

*D.* Et praenōmen?

*P.* *Mārcus.*

*D.* Hōc dīcās mihi, praeceptor ērudītissime, sī placet; difficilēsne sunt Cicerōnis ōrātiōnēs?
tell most learned hard

*P.* Sine dubiō difficilēs sunt, puer autem ācer eās intellegere potest.
but them

## CHAPTER XXVIII. 1.

### COMPARISON OF ADJECTIVES.

**205.** Adjectives in Latin, as in English, change their terminations to express different degrees of quality: **altus, altior, altissimus,** *high, higher, highest.*

Adjectives may also be compared in Latin, as in English, by means of adverbs.

**206.** *Examine the following:—*

| POSITIVE. | COMPARATIVE. | SUPERLATIVE. |
|---|---|---|
| altus (alto) | alt**ior**, alt**ius** | alt**issimus**, etc. |
| levis (levi) | lev**ior**, lev**ius** | lev**issimus**, etc. |
| prūdēns (prūdent) | prūdent**ior**, prūdent**ius** | prūdent**issimus**, etc. |
| pulcher (pulchro) | pulchr**ior**, pulchr**ius** | pulcher**rimus**, etc. |
| miser (misero) | miser**ior**, miser**ius** | miser**rimus**, etc. |
| ācer (acri) | ācr**ior**, ācr**ius** | ācer**rimus**, etc. |

Observe (1) that the comparative is formed in both the above groups by dropping the final vowel of the stem, if the stem ends in a vowel, and adding *ior, ius.*

(2) That the superlative is formed in the first group from the shortened stem by adding *issimus, issima, issimum.*

(3) But if the adjective ends in *er*, the superlative is formed by adding *rimus, rima, rimum*, to the positive.

**207.** Six adjectives in *lis* drop the final vowel of the stem and add *limus* to form the superlative:

| | | |
|---|---|---|
| facilis, -e, *easy*. | facil**ior**, facil**ius** | facil**limus, -a, -um** |
| difficilis, -e, *hard*. | difficil**ior**, difficil**ius** | difficil**limus, -a, -um** |
| similis, -e, *like*. | simil**ior**, simil**ius** | simil**limus, -a, -um** |
| dissimilis, -e, *unlike*. | dissimil**ior**, dissimil**ius** | dissimil**limus, -a, -um** |
| humilis, -e, *low*. | humil**ior**, humil**ius** | humil**limus, -a, -um** |
| gracilis, -e, *slender*. | gracil**ior**, gracil**ius** | gracil**limus, -a, -um** |

**208.** IRREGULAR COMPARISON.

| | | |
|---|---|---|
| **bonus, -a, -um** | **melior, -ius** | **optimus, -a, -um** |
| **malus, -a, -um** | **pējor, -us** | **pessimus, -a, -um** |
| **māgnus, -a, -um** | **mājor, -us** | **māximus, -a, -um** |
| **multus, -a, -um** | **——, plūs**[1] | **plūrimus, -a, -um** |
| **vetus** | **vetustior, -ius** | **veterrimus, -a, -um** |

DECLENSION OF THE COMPARATIVE.

**209.** PARADIGM.

| | SINGULAR. | | PLURAL. | |
|---|---|---|---|---|
| | M. & F. | NEUT. | M. & F. | NEUT. |
| N.V. | altior | altius | altiōr**ēs** | altiōr**a** |
| G. | altiōr**is** | altiōr**is** | altiōr**um** | altiōr**um** |
| D. | altiōr**ī** | altiōr**ī** | altiōr**ibus** | altiōr**ibus** |
| Ac. | altiōr**em** | altius | altiōr**ēs, īs** | altiōr**a** |
| Ab. | altiōr**e, ī** | altiōr**e, ī** | altiōr**ibus** | altiōr**ibus** |

*Compare, and decline in the comparative:* —

| | |
|---|---|
| **atrōx, -ōcis,** *fierce*. | **līber, -era, -erum,** *free*. |
| **audāx, -ācis,** *bold*. | **piger, pigra, pigrum,** *lazy*. |
| **celer, -eris,** *swift*. | **placidus, -a, -um,** *calm*. |
| **fēlīx, -īcis,** *lucky*. | **sapiēns, -entis,** *wise*. |

[1] **Plūs** has in singular only nom., gen. (**plūris**), and acc.; in plural, nom. **plūrēs, plūra,** gen. **plūrium,** etc.

**210.** EXERCISES.

1. Of bolder soldiers. 2. For a bolder soldier. 3. On the highest tree. 4. The wisest king. 5. Of fiercer lions. 6. By a more lucky general. 7. With calmer joy. 8. Of a swifter horse. 9. For freer men. 10. Of wiser judges. 11. A deeper river. 12. Of deeper rivers. 13. In a deeper river. 14. For lazier boys.

## 2.

**211.** We can say in Latin without difference in meaning:

1. **Quis est ēloquentior quam Cicerō?**
2. **Quis est ēloquentior Cicerōne?**

} *Who is more eloquent than Cicero?*

**212.** Rule of Syntax. — **The comparative degree is followed by the ablative when *quam* (than) is omitted.**

But the ablative can only take the place of **quam** and the nominative, or **quam** and the accusative.

**213.** EXERCISES.

I. 1. Fluviī altiōrēs sunt rīvīs, maria altissima[1] sunt. 2. In Āfricā sunt animālia atrōciōra quam in Americā. 3. Leōnēs sunt audācissimae bēstiae. 4. Elephantī sunt prūdentiōrēs leōnibus. 5. Gentēs Āfricae et Eurōpae sunt dissimillimae. 6. Pēnsum tuum facillimum, meum difficillimum est. 7. Rōma est Ītaliae urbs veterrima,[1] sed vetustiōrēs sunt in lītoribus colōniae Graecōrum. 8. Templa Graeca erant humillima. 9. Nihil est pējus quam mendācium. 10. Mendācium autem pējus pigritiā et īgnāviā est.

II. 1. A river is longer than a brook. 2. Seas are deeper than rivers. 3. The sources of great rivers are not always in high mountains. 4. Elephants bear heavier burdens than

[1] The superlative must often be translated by *very* with the positive.

horses. 5. The horse and the dog are very faithful. 6. Your dog is better than mine. 7. Not many cities are more beautiful than Rome. 8. The elephant is bolder than the horse. 9. Your task is easier than mine; but mine is not very hard. 10. The bravest men are not always the wisest.

**214.** VOCABULARY.

**America, -ae,** F., *America.*
**autem,**[1] conj., *but, moreover.*
**bēstia, -ae,** F., *beast.*
**colōnia, -ae,** F., *colony.*
**gēns, gentis,** F., *nation, people.*
**īgnāvia, -ae,** F., *cowardice.*
**lītus, -oris,** N., *shore.*
**mendācium, -ī,** N., *lying.*
**nihil,** N. (indecl.), *nothing.*
**pigritia, -ae,** F., *laziness.*
**quam,** conj., *than.*
**rīvus, ī,** M., *brook.*

### 3.

*"Proserpin gathering flowrs,*
*Herself a fairer flowr, by gloomy Dis*
*Was gather'd, which cost Ceres all that pain*
*To seek her through the world."*

**215.** FOR TRANSLATION.[2]

Tandem Cerēs ā Sōle, quī omnia cōnspicit, audīvit quis fīliam abdūxisset.[3] Itaque statim iter ad Jovem[4] flexit[5] et precibus animum ējus īnflexit, ut fīlia ā Plūtōne remitterētur.[6] Jūppiter id permīsit, sī jējūna mānsisset.[7] Sed cum[8] Prōserpina mālī Pūnicī septem grāna gustāvisset,[9] nōn licuit. Tandem Prōserpinae permissum est,[10] ut per partem annī dīmidiam apud mātrem, per partem alteram apud īnferōs esset.[11]

[1] Always placed after the first or second word in the sentence.
[2] Continued from p. 86.
[3] *Had led away.*
[4] Nom. **Jūppiter.**
[5] From **flectō.**
[6] **Ut . . . remitterētur,** *that her daughter might be sent back.*
[7] *Had remained.*
[8] *Since.*
[9] *Had tasted.*
[10] *It was permitted = permission was given.*
[11] **Ut . . . esset,** *that she should be = to be.* For the order, see p. 87, note 5.

# CHAPTER XXIX. 1.

## FORMATION AND COMPARISON OF ADVERBS.

**216.** Most adverbs are formed from adjectives, and follow them in comparison.

**217.** *Examine the following:* —

| ADJECTIVE. | STEM. | ADVERB. |
|---|---|---|
| grātus, *thankful.* | grāto- | grāt **ē**, *thankfully.* |
| benīgnus, *kind.* | benīgno- | benīgn **ē**, *kindly.* |
| miser, *wretched.* | misero- | miser **ē**, *wretchedly.* |
| pulcher, *beautiful.* | pulchro- | pulchr **ē**, *beautifully.* |
| fortis, *brave.* | forti- | forti **ter**, *bravely.* |
| ācer, *eager.* | ācri- | ācri **ter**, *eagerly.* |
| prūdēns, *wise.* | prūdent- | prūden **ter**, *wisely.* |
| fēlīx, *lucky.* | fēlīci- | fēlīci **ter**, *luckily.* |

Observe (1) that the adjectives of the first group are of the *o* (or second) declension, and that the adverbs are formed from the stem of the adjectives by changing the final *o* of the stem to *ē*.

(2) That the adjectives of the second group are of the third declension, and that the adverbs are formed from the stem of the adjectives by adding *ter*.

(3) But stems in *nt* drop *t* before adding the suffix *ter*.

**218.** *Examine the following:* —

| ADJECTIVE. | ADVERB. |
|---|---|
| **multus**, *much.* | **multum**, *much.* |
| **facilis**, *easy.* | **facile**, *easily.* |
| **impūnis**, *unpunished.* | **impūne**, *with safety.* |
| **citus**, *quick.* | **citō**, *quickly.* |
| **subitus**, *sudden.* | **subitō**, *suddenly.* |
| **prīmus**, *first.* | **prīmō**, *at first.* |

Observe that in the first group the accusative singular neuter of the adjective is used as an adverb; in the second, the ablative.

**219.** *Examine the following:* —

| POSITIVE. | COMPARATIVE. | SUPERLATIVE. |
|---|---|---|
| **grātō** | **grātius** | **grātissimē** |
| **miserē** | **miserius** | **miserrimē** |
| **ācriter** | **ācrius** | **ācerrimē** |
| **fēlīciter** | **fēlīcius** | **fēlīcissimē** |
| **benĕ** [1] | **melius** | **optimē** |
| **malĕ** | **pējus** | **pessimē** |
| **multum** | **plūs** | **plūrimum** |
| ——— | **magis** | **māximē** |

Observe that the comparative of the adverb is the same as the neuter accusative singular of the adjective; and that the superlative is formed from the superlative of the adjective by changing, as in the positive, the final *o* of the stem to *ē*.

If the adjective is irregular in comparison, the adverb is likewise.

*Compare:* —

| | | |
|---|---|---|
| **placidē**, *calmly.* | **līberē**, *freely.* | **pulchrē**, *beautifully.* |
| **audācter**, *boldly.* | **celeriter**, *quickly.* | **prūdenter**, *wisely.* |

## 2.

**220.** EXERCISES.

I. 1. Ōlim fuit[2] Athēniēnsis clārissimus. 2. Fidēliter lēgibus[3] cīvitātis pārēbat. 3. Jūstē omnibus rēbus[4] agēbat. 4. Audācter pūgnāvit atque amīcum fortiter dēfendit. 5. Sapienter juvenēs aliōsque docēbat. 6. Falsō et turpiter accūsātus est; līberē sē[5] dēfendit neque timēbat. 7. Injūstissimē ad mortem damnātus est ā cīvibus. 8. Venēnum in carcere bibit placidē. 9. Ējus[6] memoria dēlēbitur nunquam. 10. Quis fuit Athēniēnsis?

II. 1. Was Socrates an illustrious Athenian? 2. Was he more illustrious than other citizens? 3. Did he not act most

[1] Formed irregularly from **bonus**.

[2] *There was.*

[3] Observe the dative with **pāreō.**

[4] *Things.* See **260.**

[5] *Himself.*

[6] *Of him.*

justly in all respects?[1] 4. Did he very[2] faithfully obey the laws of the Athenians? 5. Did he not teach the Athenians very wisely? 6. Did he not defend a young man in battle very bravely? 7. Why was he most basely accused and condemned to death? 8. We shall cherish his memory more diligently. 9. His memory will be cherished faithfully by the best men. 10. In vain shall we seek for a better man than Socrates.

III. 1. Julius Cæsar was a very famous man. 2. He was excellently brought up by his mother. 3. He learned the Greek language very well. 4. He was an illustrious general and fought many battles most successfully. 5. In Gaul he took towns, and cruelly slew many men. 6. He boldly sailed to Britain with many ships. 7. But the inhabitants did not basely beg for peace. 8. He quickly overcame all his enemies. 9. (As) consul he ruled the Roman state wisely and well. 10. He was foully slain by Brutus and other Romans.

**221.** VOCABULARY.

**crūdēliter** [**crūdēlis**], *cruelly.*
**dīligenter** [**dīligēns**], *diligently.*
**falsō** [**falsus**], *falsely.*
**fidēliter** [**fidēlis**], *faithfully.*
**frūstrā**, *in vain.*
**injūstē** [**injūstus**], *unjustly.*
**jūstē** [**jūstus**], *justly.*
**līberē** [**līber**], *freely, fearlessly.*
**ōlim**, *formerly.*
**optimē**, *very well, excellently.*
**sapienter** [**sapiēns**], *wisely.*
**turpiter** [**turpis**], *basely, foully.*

**accūsō**, 1 [**ad**, **causa**], *accuse.*
**Athēniēnsis**, **-e**, adj., *Athenian.*
**bibō**, 3, **bibī**, **pōtum**, *drink.*
**carcer**, **-eris**, M., *prison.*
**colō**, 3, **coluī**, **cultum**, *cultivate, cherish, care for.*
**damnō**, 1, *condemn.*
**discō**, 3, **didicī**, ——, *learn.*
**juvenis**, **-is**, M. & F., *youth.*
**lingua**, **-ae**, F., *tongue, language.*
**nāvigō**, 1 [**nāvis**, **agō**], *sail.*
**necō**, 1, *kill.* Cf. **interficiō**.
**pāreō**, 2, **-uī**, ——, *obey* (w. dat.).
**pāx**, **pācis**, F., *peace.*
**petō**, 3, **-īvī**, **-iī**, **-ītum**, *beg for, ask.*
**quaerō**, 3, **quaesīvī**, **-iī**, **quaesītum**, *seek for, ask, inquire.*
**sed**, conj., *but.* Cf. **autem** (**214**).
**Sōcratēs**, **-is**, M., *Socrates*, an Athenian philosopher.
**venēnum**, **-ī**, N., *poison.*

[1] Compare I. 3. [2] See p. 91, note.

### 3.

**222.** COLLOQUIUM.

PATER ET FĪLIOLUS.

*P.* Quid, mī fīliole, in scholā hodiē discēbās?
little son

*F.* Discēbam, mī pater, pēnsum de adverbiīs longissimum.

*P.* Cuī partī ōrātiōnis est adverbium simillimum?
to what speech

*F.* Simillimum, ut opīnor, est adverbium adjectīvō.
as I think

*P.* Rēctē, puer; sed illud mihi explicā, sī poteris: Sī,
this explain if you can
ut dīcis, adverbium adjectīvō est simile, unde nōmen traxit?
whence has derived

*F.* Fortasse propter hōc, quod saepissimē verbīs ad-
perhaps on account of this because very often verbs
jungitur.

*P.* Optimē, fīliole; ēn tibi āssem!
here is for you penny

## CHAPTER XXX.

### FOURTH CONJUGATION.

**223.** VERBS IN ī.

**Audiō** (stem **audī**), *hear.*

PRINCIPAL PARTS: **audiō, audīre, audīvī, audītum.**

INDICATIVE.

| ACTIVE. | | PASSIVE. | |
|---|---|---|---|
| | PRESENT. | | |
| *I hear, etc.* | | *I am heard, etc.* | |
| aud**iō** | aud**īmus** | aud**ior** | aud**īmur** |
| aud**īs** | aud**ītis** | aud**īris**, *or* **-re** | aud**īminī** |
| aud**it** | aud**iunt** | aud**ītur** | aud**iuntur** |
| | IMPERFECT. | | |
| *I was hearing, etc.* | | *I was heard, etc.* | |
| aud**iēbam** | aud**iēbāmus** | aud**iēbar** | aud**iēbāmur** |
| aud**iēbās** | aud**iēbātis** | aud**iēbāris**, *or* **-re** | aud**iēbāminī** |
| aud**iēbat** | aud**iēbant** | aud**iēbātur** | aud**iēbantur** |

| ACTIVE. | | PASSIVE. | |
|---|---|---|---|
| | **FUTURE.** | | |
| *I shall hear, etc.* | | *I shall be heard, etc.* | |
| aud**iam** | aud**iēmus** | aud**iar** | aud**iēmur** |
| aud**iēs** | aud**iētis** | aud**iēris**, *or* **-re** | aud**iēminī** |
| aud**iet** | aud**ient** | aud**iētur** | aud**ientur** |
| | **PERFECT.** | | |
| *I have heard, etc.* | | *I have been heard, etc.* | |
| audīv**ī** | audīv**imus** | audīt**us** { **sum** | audīt**ī** { **sumus** |
| audīv**istī** | audīv**istis** | audīt**us** { **es** | audīt**ī** { **estis** |
| audīv**it** | audīv**ērunt**, *or* **-re** | audīt**us** { **est** | audīt**ī** { **sunt** |
| | **PLUPERFECT.** | | |
| *I had heard, etc.* | | *I had been heard, etc.* | |
| audīv**eram** | audīv**erāmus** | audīt**us** { **eram** | audīt**ī** { **erāmus** |
| audīv**erās** | audīv**erātis** | audīt**us** { **erās** | audīt**ī** { **erātis** |
| audīv**erat** | audīv**erant** | audīt**us** { **erat** | audīt**ī** { **erant** |
| | **FUTURE PERFECT.** | | |
| *I shall have heard, etc.* | | *I shall have been heard, etc.* | |
| audīv**erō** | audīv**erĭmus** | audīt**us** { **erō** | audīt**ī** { **erimus** |
| audīv**erĭs** | audīv**erĭtis** | audīt**us** { **eris** | audīt**ī** { **eritis** |
| audīv**erit** | audīv**erint** | audīt**us** { **erit** | audīt**ī** { **erunt** |

## SUBJUNCTIVE.[1]

| | | | |
|---|---|---|---|
| | **PRESENT.** | | |
| aud**iam** | aud**iāmus** | aud**iar** | aud**iāmur** |
| aud**iās** | aud**iātis** | aud**iāris**, *or* **-re** | aud**iāminī** |
| aud**iat** | aud**iant** | aud**iātur** | aud**iantur** |
| | **IMPERFECT.** | | |
| aud**īrem** | aud**īrēmus** | aud**īrer** | aud**īrēmur** |
| aud**īrēs** | aud**īrētis** | aud**īrēris**, *or* **-re** | aud**īrēminī** |
| aud**īret** | aud**īrent** | aud**īrētur** | aud**īrentur** |
| | **PERFECT.** | | |
| audīv**erim** | audīv**erĭmus** | audīt**us** { **sim** | audīt**ī** { **sīmus** |
| audīv**erĭs** | audīv**erĭtis** | audīt**us** { **sīs** | audīt**ī** { **sītis** |
| audīv**erit** | audīv**erint** | audīt**us** { **sit** | audīt**ī** { **sint** |

[1] See p. 26, note.

| ACTIVE. | | PASSIVE. | |
|---|---|---|---|
| | PLUPERFECT. | | |
| audīv**issem** | audīv**issēmus** | audīt**us** essem | audīt**ī** essēmus |
| audīv**issēs** | audīv**issētis** | audīt**us** essēs | audīt**ī** essētis |
| audīv**isset** | audīv**issent** | audīt**us** esset | audīt**ī** essent |

## IMPERATIVE.

### Present.

| | |
|---|---|
| aud**ī**, *hear thou.* | aud**īre**, *be thou heard.* |
| aud**īte**, *hear ye.* | aud**īminī**, *be ye heard.* |

### Future.

| | |
|---|---|
| aud**ītō**, *thou shalt hear.* | aud**ītor**, *thou shalt be heard.* |
| aud**ītō**, *he shall hear.* | aud**ītor**, *he shall be heard.* |
| aud**ītōte**, *ye shall hear.* | |
| aud**iuntō**, *they shall hear.* | aud**iuntor**, *they shall be heard.* |

## INFINITIVE.

| | |
|---|---|
| Pres. aud**īre**, *to hear.* | aud**īrī**, *to be heard.* |
| Perf. audīv**isse**, *to have heard.* | audīt**us esse**, *to have been heard.* |
| Fut. audīt**ūrus esse**, *to be about to hear.* | audīt**um īrī**, *to be about to be heard.* |

## PARTICIPLE.

| | |
|---|---|
| Pres. aud**iēns, -entis**, *hearing.* | ———— |
| Fut. audīt**ūrus, -a, -um**, *about to hear.* | Ger. aud**iendus, -a, -um**, *to be heard.* |
| ———— | Perf. audīt**us, -a, -um**, *heard, having been heard.* |

## GERUND.

G. aud**iendī**, *of hearing.*
D. aud**iendō**, *for hearing.*
Ac. aud**iendum**, *hearing.*
Ab. aud**iendō**, *by hearing.*

## SUPINE.

| | |
|---|---|
| Ac. audīt**um**, *to hear.* | Ab. audīt**ū**, *to hear, to be heard.* |

# CHAPTER XXXI. 1.

## FOURTH CONJUGATION.

**224.** Learn the present, imperfect, and future indicative, and present imperative and infinitive, active and passive, of **audiō**.

**225.** EXERCISES.

I. 1. Audiō, audiēbam, audiam. 2. Audit, audiēbat, audiet. 3. Audītur, audiēbātur, audiētur. 4. Audī, audīre. 5. Audīmur, audiēbāmur, audiēmur. 6. Audīre, audīrī. 7. Audītis, audiēbātis, audiētis. 8. Audīs, audīris. 9. Audiunt, audiuntur. 10. Audient, audientur.

II. 1. Thou hearest, thou wast hearing, thou wilt hear. 2. I hear, I am heard. 3. He is hearing, he was hearing, he will hear. 4. To be heard, to hear. 5. We were hearing, we were (being) heard. 6. We hear, we heard, we shall hear. 7. They will hear, they will be heard. 8. You heard, you were heard. 9. Hear (ye), be ye heard. 10. I hear, I heard, I shall be heard.

## 2.

**226.** EXERCISES.

**Pūniō**, *punish;* **mūniō**, *fortify;* **vestiō**, *clothe.*

I. 1. Pūniēbam, mūniēbam, vestiēbam. 2. Mūnītur, pūnītur, vestītur. 3. Pūniet, vestiet, mūniet. 4. Pūnī, mūnīte, vestīminī. 5. Vestiētur, pūniētur, mūniētur. 6. Nōnne pūnīmus? nōnne vestīmur? nōnne mūniuntur? 7. Vestiamne? pūnietne? mūniēturne? 8. Mūniēbant, pūniēbāminī, vestior. 9. Nōn vestīris, nōn pūnit, nōn mūniēmus. 10. Pūniar, mūniam, vestiēbāris.

II. 1. He was clothing, he was punishing, he was fortifying. 2. They will be clothed, they will be fortified, they will be punished. 3. Be thou clothed, punish (thou), fortify. 4. I fortify, he punishes, we are clothing. 5. Are you not being clothed? was it not fortified? will he not be punished? 6. They are being punished, it is being fortified, thou wilt be clothed. 7. We punish, we were fortifying, they will clothe. 8. Were you being clothed? will it be fortified? shall I be punished? 9. I shall not fortify, you are not being clothed, they will not be punished. 10. I punished, you will fortify, they clothe.

### 3.

**227.** EXERCISES.

I. 1. Vēre terra grāmine et flōribus vestītur. 2. Vēre avium carmina audīmus. 3. Mors vītam nostram fīniet. 4. Puerī in grāmine dormiēbant. 5. Somnō mollīmus cūrās. 6. Canēs agricolārum ovēs custōdiunt. 7. Mīlitēs urbem custōdient. 8. Bellum ā Scīpiōne fīniētur. 9. Audīte verba sapientium. 10. Injūstē puer pūnītur.

II. 1. A good father will nurture, clothe, and[1] instruct his children. 2. It is very[2] pleasant[3] to hear the sweet voice of the nightingale. 3. All our[1] pains are ended by death. 4. The general justly punishes a cowardly soldier. 5. The sheep are carefully[4] guarded by the dog. 6. Scipio finished the war in Africa. 7. The pupils are very faithfully instructed by their teachers. 8. My son, soothe your mother's cares. 9. The city is fortified by strong walls. 10. In summer the trees are clothed with leaves.

**228.** VOCABULARY.

**custōdiō**, 4 [**custōs**], *guard.*
**dormiō**, 4, *sleep.*
**ē-rudiō**, 4 [**rudis**], *teach, instruct.*
**fīniō**, 4 [**fīnis**], *end, finish.*
**molliō**, 4 [**mollis**], *soften, soothe.*
**mūniō**, 4, *fortify, defend.*
**nūtriō**, 4, *nurture, nourish.*
**pūniō**, 4, *punish.*
**vestiō**, 4, *clothe.*
**carmen, -inis**, N., *song.*
**dolor, -ōris**, M., *pain.*
**folium, -ī**, N., *leaf.*
**grāmen, -inis**, N., *grass.*
**ignāvus, -a, -um**, adj., *cowardly.*
**jūcundus, -a, -um**, adj., *pleasant.*
**luscinia, -ae**, F., *nightingale.*
**vēr, vēris**, N., *spring.*
**vōx, vōcis**, F., *voice.*

[1] Omit. [2] See p. 91, note. [3] Neuter gender. [4] See **144, 145.**

# CHAPTER XXXII. 1.

## FOURTH CONJUGATION.

**229.** Learn the perfect, pluperfect, and future perfect indicative, and perfect infinitive, active and passive, of **audiō**.

**230.** EXERCISES.

I. 1. Audīvī, audīveram, audīverō. 2. Audītus est, audītus erat, audītus erit. 3. Audīvimus, audīverāmus, audīverimus. 4. Audīverant, audītī erant. 5. Audīvistī, audīverās, audīveris. 6. audīvisse, audītus esse. 7. Audīverātis, audītī erātis. 8. Audīvit, audīverat, audīverit.

II. 1. Thou hast heard, thou hadst heard, thou wilt have heard. 2. They have been heard, they had been heard, they will have been heard. 3. I have heard, I have been heard. 4. To have been heard, to have heard. 5. We have heard, we had heard, we shall have heard. 6. We have been heard, we had been heard, we shall have been heard. 7. You have heard, you have been heard. 8. He had heard, he had been heard.

## 2.

**231.** EXERCISES.

I. 1. Fīnīveram, ērudīveram, vestīveram. 2. Fīnītum est, ērudītus sum, vestītus sum. 3. Nōnne fīnīta sunt? nōnne vestītus eram? nōnne ērudītus erō? 4. Vestīverās, ērudīverās, fīnīverās. 5. Fīnīveris, ērudītus eris, vestīverimus. 6. Vestītae erant, fīnīta erant, ērudītī erant. 7. Ērudīverātis, fīnīveram, vestīverint. 8. Vestītīne sumus? estne ērudītus? estne fīnītum? 9. Ērudīta es, fīnīstī,[1] vestierās.[2] 10. Nōn ērudīstis, nōn fīnīverātis, nōn vestīverit.

[1] For **fīnīvistī**. Perfects in *īvī* often drop *v* and contract *iī* to *ī*.

[2] For **vestīverās**.

II. 1. Have they not been clothed? have they (*neut.*) not been finished? were they not taught? 2. We have finished, we have clothed, we have taught. 3. She had been taught, they (*neut.*) had been finished, we (*fem.*) had been clothed. 4. Didst thou teach? have you finished? has she clothed? 5. They had clothed, they will have taught, I have finished. 6. I had clothed, thou hadst taught, he had finished. 7. We shall not have finished, they will not have clothed, you will not have taught. 8. It was not finished, we had not been taught, you will not have been clothed. 9. You have taught, you had finished, you will have clothed. 10. I shall have clothed, I had taught, I finished.

## 3.

**232.** EXERCISES.

I. 1. Medicus rēgis nocte ad Fabricium vēnit.[1] 2. Fabricius medicum vinxit et ad dominum mīsit. 3. Urbs virtūte et fortitūdine mīlitum mūnīta erit. 4. Rōmānī artibus[2] et lītterīs[2] ā Graecīs ērudītī sunt. 5. Octō hōrās dormīre puerīs satis est. 6. Lūce sōlis calōreque aperiuntur flōrēs. 7. Omnēs terrās fortibus virīs aperuit nātūra. 8. Mīlitēs arcem fidēliter custōdīvērunt. 9. Brūtus in castra Caesaris vēnerat. 10. Nihil scīre turpissimum est.

II. 1. The king's physician was bound by Fabricius' slave. 2. The valor and endurance (*fortitūdō*) of the soldiers fortified the city. 3. The Greeks instructed the Romans in the arts.[3] 4. Is it enough for a boy to sleep two hours?[4] 5. The light and heat of the sun had opened the flowers. 6. The citadel was very[5] carefully guarded by

---

[1] How do you know whether this form is present or perfect?

[2] *In the arts and literature.*

[3] Compare I. 4.

[4] **Duās hōrās.**

[5] See p. 91, note.

the soldiers. 7. To know many things[1] is very useful. 8. To be ignorant of many things is not disgraceful. 9. The general's camp[2] had not been fortified. 10. Did you not hear the voice of your father?

**233.** VOCABULARY.

**aperiō**, 4, **-uī, -tum,** *open, disclose.*
**ne-sciō**, 4, *know not, be ignorant of.*
**sciō**, 4, *know, know how.*
**veniō**, 4, **vēnī, ventum,** *come.*
**vinciō**, 4, **vinxī, vinctum,** *bind.*

**ad**, prep. w. acc., *to, towards.*
**ars, artis,** F., *art.* (**167**. 2.)
**calor, -ōris,** M., *heat.*
**Fabricius, -ī,** M., *Fabricius,* a Roman general.
**litterae, -ārum,** F., *letters, literature;* often = **epistula.**
**lūx, lūcis,** F., *light, daylight.*
**medicus, -ī,** M., *physician.*
**nox, noctis,** F., *night.* (**167**. 2.)
**octō**, num. adj., indecl., *eight.*
**turpis, -e,** adj., *base, disgraceful.*

4.

**234.** COLLOQUIUM.

PRAECEPTOR ET DISCIPULUS.

*P.* Dē quā rē est pēnsum hodiernum?

*D.* Pēnsum hodiernum est iterum dē conjugātiōne quartā.

*P.* Herī quartam conjugātiōnem nesciēbās; scīsne hodiē?

*D.* Partim (partly) sciō, modum (mood) autem subjunctīvum nesciō.

*P.* Mox (soon) subjunctīvum quoque (also) discēs.

*D.* Estne ūtilius indicātīvum scīre quam subjunctīvum?

*P.* Utrumque dēbēmus scīre; indicātīvus autem saepius invenītur.

*D.* Adhūc (thus far) conjugātiōnēs didicī quattuor. Suntne plūrēs?

*P.* Nōn plūrēs; sed multa verba sunt anōmala (irregular).

---

[1] See **117**.

[2] Remember that the Latin word for *camp* is plural, **castra, -ōrum.** What must be the number of the verb of which **castra** is subject?

# CHAPTER XXXIII.

## THIRD CONJUGATION.

**235.** VERBS IN *iō*.[1]

**Capiō** (stem **cape**), *take*.
PRINCIPAL PARTS: **capiō, capĕre, cēpī, captum.**

### INDICATIVE MOOD.

| ACTIVE. | | PASSIVE. | |
|---|---|---|---|
| | | | |
| PRESENT. | | | |
| *I take, etc.* | | *I am taken, etc.* | |
| cap**iō** | cap**imus** | cap**ior** | cap**imur** |
| cap**is** | cap**itis** | cap**eris**, *or* **-re** | cap**iminī** |
| cap**it** | cap**iunt** | cap**itur** | cap**iuntur** |
| IMPERFECT. | | | |
| *I was taking, etc.* | | *I was taken, etc.* | |
| cap**iēbam** | cap**iēbāmus** | cap**iēbar** | cap**iēbāmur** |
| cap**iēbās** | cap**iēbātis** | cap**iēbāris**, *or* **-re** | cap**iēbāminī** |
| cap**iēbat** | cap**iēbant** | cap**iēbātur** | cap**iēbantur** |
| FUTURE. | | | |
| *I shall take, etc.* | | *I shall be taken, etc.* | |
| cap**iam** | cap**iēmus** | cap**iar** | cap**iēmur** |
| cap**iēs** | cap**iētis** | cap**iēris**, *or* **-re** | cap**iēminī** |
| cap**iet** | cap**ient** | cap**iētur** | cap**ientur** |
| PERFECT. | | | |
| cēp**ī**, cēp**istī**, cēp**it**, etc. | | cap**tus sum, es, est**, etc. | |
| PLUPERFECT. | | | |
| cēp**eram**, cēp**erās**, cēp**erat**, etc. | | cap**tus eram, erās, erat**, etc. | |
| FUTURE PERFECT. | | | |
| cēp**erō**, cēp**eris**, cēp**erit**, etc. | | cap**tus erō, eris, erit**, etc. | |

[1] Verbs in *iō* of the third conjugation are distinguished from those of the fourth by the active infinitive present. What forms of capiō are like those of **audiō**? Make a general statement.

## SUBJUNCTIVE.

| ACTIVE. | PASSIVE. |
|---|---|
| *Present.* | |
| **capiam, capiās, capiat,** etc. | **capiar, -iāris** *or* **-re, -iātur,** etc. |
| *Imperfect.* | |
| **caperem, caperēs, caperet,** etc. | **caperer, -erēris** *or* **-re, -erētur.** |
| *Perfect.* | |
| **cēperim, cēperīs, cēperit,** etc. | **captus sim, sīs, sit,** etc. |
| *Pluperfect.* | |
| **cēpissem, cēpissēs, cēpisset,** etc. | **captus essem, essēs, esset,** etc. |

## IMPERATIVE.

| | | |
|---|---|---|
| Pres. | **cape,** *take thou.* | **capere,** *be thou taken.* |
| | **capite,** *take ye.* | **capiminī,** *be ye taken.* |
| Fut. | **capito,** *thou shalt take,* etc. | **capitor,** *thou shalt be taken,* etc. |

## INFINITIVE.

| | | |
|---|---|---|
| Pres. | **capere,** *to take.* | **capī,** *to be taken.* |
| Perf. | **cēpisse,** *to have taken.* | **captus esse,** *to have been taken.* |
| Fut. | **captūrus esse,** *to be about to take.* | **captum īrī,** *to be about to be taken.* |

## PARTICIPLE.

| | | | |
|---|---|---|---|
| Pres. | **capiēns,** *taking.* | | |
| Fut. | **captūrus,** *about to take.* | Ger. | **capiendus,** *to be taken.* |
| | | Perf. | **captus,** *having been taken.* |

## GERUND.

**capiendī,** *of taking,* etc.

## SUPINE.

| | | | |
|---|---|---|---|
| Ac. | **captum,** *to take.* | Ab. | **captū,** *to take, to be taken.* |

# CHAPTER XXXIV. 1.

## THIRD CONJUGATION.

**236.** VERBS IN *iō*.

Learn all the tenses of the indicative, the present imperative, and the present and perfect infinitive, active and passive, of **capiō**.

**237.** EXERCISES.

I. 1. Capiunt, capiēbant. 2. Capior, capiēbar, capiar. 3. Capimur, capiēbāmur, capiēmur. 4. Capis, caperis. 5. Cēpī, captus sum. 6. Cēpimus, cēperāmus, cēperimus. 7. Capta sunt, capta erant, capta erunt. 8. Cape, capere. 9. Capere, capī. 10. Cēpisse, captus esse.

II. 1. We are taking, we were taking, we shall be taking. 2. Take, be taken. 3. Thou art taking, thou wast taking, thou wilt take. 4. You have taken, you had taken, you will have taken. 5. It is taken, it was taken, it will be taken. 6. I was taking, I was taken. 7. To take, to have taken. 8. To be taken, to have been taken. 9. It (*fem.*) has been taken, it had been taken, it will have been taken. 10. We have taken, we have been taken.

# 2.

**238.** EXERCISES.

I. 1. Tarentīnī lēgātīs Rōmānōrum injūriam fēcērunt. 2. Pyrrhus, Ēpīrī rēx, ad Tarentīnōs vēnit. 3. Contrā Pyrrhum missus est Laevīnus cōnsul. 4. Pyrrhus elephantīs vīcit, nam Rōmānōrum equī territī sunt et fugiēbant. 5. Nox proelī fīnem fēcit; Laevīnus per noctem fūgit. 6. Multī et fortēs Rōmānī in pūgnā interfectī sunt. 7. Captīvōs Rōmānōs summō in honōre habuit Pyrrhus. 8. Deinde[1] in Campāniam sē recēpit. 9. Lēgātī, ā Rōmānīs missī,[2]

[1] Pronounced **de-in'-de.** [2] *Sent.*

honōrificē ā Pyrrhō exceptī sunt. 10. Pāx cum Pyrrhō nōn facta est.

II. 1. A wrong was done to the Romans by the Tarentines. 2. Against Pyrrhus, king of Epirus, the Romans sent the consul Lævinus. 3. The spies of Pyrrhus were taken by Lævinus and led through his camp. 4. The Romans did not make peace with King Pyrrhus. 5. Fabricius saw through the design of the king and was not[1] frightened. 6. You will welcome your friend to-day. 7. I welcome my best friend with great pleasure.[2] 8. The enemy threw their spears and fled into the woods. 9. Did not Cæsar either conquer or slay all his enemies? 10. Finally he was himself (*ipse*) slain by Brutus his friend, and others.

**239.** VOCABULARY.

**ex-cipiō,** 3, **-cēpī, -ceptum** [**capiō**], *catch, accept, welcome.*
**faciō,** 3, **fēcī, factum,** *make, do.*
**fugiō,** 3, **fūgī, fugitum,** *flee.*
**inter-ficiō,** 3, **-fēcī, -fectum** [**faciō**], *kill, slay.* Cf. **necō** (**221**).
**jaciō,** 3, **jēcī, jactum,** *throw.*
**per-spiciō,** 3, **-spexī, -spectum** [**speciō**], *see through, into.*
**re-cipiō,** 3, **-cēpī, -ceptum** [**capiō**], *take back, get again, receive.*
**sē recipere,** *withdraw, retreat.*

**aut . . . aut,** conj., *either . . . or.*
**Campānia, -ae,** F., *Campania,* a division of Italy.
**contrā,** prep. w. acc., *against.*
**de-inde,** adv., *then, next.*
**dēnique,** adv., *finally.*
**explōrātor, -ōris,** M., *scout, spy.*
**fīnis, -is,** M., *end.*
**honōrificē,** adv., *honorably.*
**injūria, -ae,** F., *wrong, injury.*
**Laevīnus, -ī,** M., *Lævinus,* a Roman consul.
**lēgātus, -ī,** M., *ambassador, lieutenant.*
**per,** prep. w. acc., *through.*
**proelium, -ī,** N., *battle.* Cf. **pūgna** (**102**).
**summus, -a, -um** (sup. of **superus**), adj., *highest.*
**Tarentīnus, -ī,** M., *an inhabitant of Tarentum, a Tarentine.*

[1] *And . . . not,* **neque.** [2] See **144, 145.**

# CHAPTER XXXV. 1.

## REVIEW OF THE FOUR CONJUGATIONS.

**240.** EXERCISES.

I. 1. Amāmus, monēmus, regimus, audīmus. 2. Laudant, dēlent, agunt, custōdiunt. 3. Ōrnābam, dēlēbam, vincēbam, mūniēbam. 4. Cantāvistī, habuistī, posuistī, vinxistī. 5. Mūtāvērunt, tenuērunt, ēgērunt, cēpērunt, mūnīvērunt. 6. Portāverātis, dēlēverātis, praebuerātis, dūxerātis, dormīverātis.

II. 1. Fugātur, terrētur, pōnitur, vincītur. 2. Servāberis, tenēberis, mittēre, vestiēre. 3. Laudātī sumus, prohibitī sumus, ductī sumus, ērudītī sumus. 4. Ōrnāre, monēre, trahere, pūnīre. 5. Amārī, docērī, contemnī, jacī, aperīrī. 6. Amātae sunt, monitae sunt, exceptae sunt, audītae sunt.

III. 1. Dormīte, superāte, facite, vincite, vincīte, praebēte. 2. Vulnerāvisse, jēcisse, vēnisse, docuisse, flūxisse. 3. Recipimur, spectāmur, agimur, vestīmur, docēmur. 4. Docēbitis, pūniētis, trahētis, fugiētis, creābitis. 5. Mīsit, habuit, armāvit, jēcit, fūgit. 6. Vinciminī, vituperāminī, terrēminī, vincīminī, capiminī.

## 2.

**241.** EXERCISES.

I. 1. Thou lovest, thou advisest, thou rulest, thou hearest. 2. I shall praise, I shall destroy, I shall drive, I shall guard. 3. You were adorning, you were seeing, you were conquering, you were fortifying. 4. We have sung, we have had, we have placed, we have bound. 5. You have changed, you have held, you have driven, you have taken, you have fortified. 6. I had carried, I had destroyed, I had furnished, I had led, I had slept.

II. 1. We are put to flight, we are frightened, we are placed, we are bound. 2. He will be saved, he will be held, he will be sent, he will be clothed. 3. They have been praised, they have been prevented, they have been led, they have been instructed. 4. They shall be adorned, they shall be advised, they shall be drawn, they shall be punished. 5. To be loved, to be taught, to be despised, to be thrown, to be opened. 6. Thou hast been loved, thou hast been advised, thou hast been welcomed, thou hast been heard.

III. 1. Sleep, surpass, do (*fac*), bind, conquer, furnish. 2. To wound, to throw, to come, to teach, to flow. 3. They are received, they are witnessed, they are driven, they are clothed, they are taught. 4. I shall teach, I shall punish, I shall draw, I shall flee, I shall create. 5. They have sent, they have had, they have armed, they have thrown, they have fled. 6. Thou art conquered, thou art blamed, thou art frightened, thou art bound, thou art taken.

### 3.

**242.** COLLOQUIUM.

JACŌBUS ET AUGUSTUS.

*J.* Dēnique ad fīnem pēnsī pervēnimus; quid jam incipiēmus?
(dēnique: finally; fīnem: end; jam: now; incipiēmus: begin)

*A.* Tū quidquid vidēbitur incipiēs: ego incipiam nihil.
(tū: you; quidquid: whatever; vidēbitur: seems good)

*J.* Quārē? esne dēfessus?
(quārē: why)

*A.* Certē, admodum dēfessus; pēnsum recōgnōscendum mē quidem paene fīnīvit.
(certē: certainly; admodum: downright; recōgnōscendum: review; quidem: at least; paene: almost)

*J.* Mox recreāberis, sī mēcum ad natandum veniēs.
(mox: soon; recreāberis: will be rested; mēcum: with me; natandum: swim)

*A.* Profectō tēcum veniam, nam natāre mihi est jūcun-
surely with you for
dissimum et semper et praecipuē cum,
both especially when

"*Sōle sub ardentī resonant arbusta cicādīs.*"
under glowing resound groves the *cicadae*

*J.* Quam lautē poētam aliquem laudās!
how elegantly some quote

*A.* Hunc Vergilī versiculum mē docuit praeceptor.
this Vergil line

## CHAPTER XXXVI. 1.

### FOURTH DECLENSION.

**243.** The stem ends in *u*.

**244.** Rule of Gender.—**Nouns in *us* are masculine; those in *ū* are neuter.**

1. The following nouns, and a few others, are feminine: **acus,** *needle;* **domus,** *house;* **Īdūs** (plur.), *Ides;* **manus,** *hand;* **porticus,** *portico;* **tribus,** *tribe.*

**245.** PARADIGMS.

| | **Gradus,** M., *step.* | | **Genū,** N., *knee.* | |
|---|---|---|---|---|
| | SING. | PLUR. | SING. | PLUR. |
| N.V. | grad**us** | grad**ūs** | gen**ū** | gen**ua** |
| G. | grad**ūs** | grad**uum** | gen**ūs** | gen**uum** |
| D. | grad**uī** (**ū**) | grad**ibus** | gen**ū** | gen**ibus** |
| Ac. | grad**um** | grad**ūs** | gen**ū** | gen**ua** |
| Ab. | grad**ū** | grad**ibus** | gen**ū** | gen**ibus** |

| | MASC. | TERMINATIONS. | NEUT. | |
|---|---|---|---|---|
| N.V. | **us** | **ūs** | **ū** | **ua** |
| G. | **ūs** | **uum** | **ūs** | **uum** |
| D. | **uī (ū)** | **ibus (ubus)** | **ū** | **ibus (ubus)** |
| Ac. | **um** | **ūs** | **ū** | **ua** |
| Ab. | **ū** | **ibus (ubus)** | **ū** | **ibus (ubus)** |

**246.** The fourth declension is a modification of the third. Thus, **gradūs** is for **graduis**, **gradum** for **graduem**, **gradū** for **gradue**, etc.

**247.** **Artus**, *joint*, **partus**, *birth*, **tribus**, *tribe*, sometimes **portus**, *harbor*, **verū**, *a spit;* also dissyllables in *cus*, have the termination *ubus* in the dative and ablative plural.

**248.** **Domus**, *house*, has also forms of the second declension. See special paradigms, **262**.

**249.** Decline together **domus mea**, *my house;* **exercitus māgnus**, *large army;* **Īdūs Mārtiae**, *Ides of March*.

## 2.

**250.** EXERCISES.

I. 1. Vēre adventus avium hominibus est jūcundissimus. 2. Sēnsūs avium ācrēs sunt, mōtūs celerēs. 3. In lacubus et in palūdibus māgna avium est multitūdō. 4. Avēs multae in porticibus altīs domicilium habent. 5. Quercus Jovī sacra erat. 6. Quercūs frōns est vīctōris ōrnāmentum. 7. Cōnsulātus erat Rōmānōrum magistrātus amplus. 8. Salūs cīvitātis in manibus cōnsulum erat. 9. Cōnsulēs exercituum erant imperātōrēs. 10. Erant in portibus nāvēs[1] longae.

II. 1. The enemy (*plur.*) were conquered on the arrival[2] of Cæsar. 2. Many animals fight with their horns. 3. Many lakes are seen in the Alps. 4. The ancients honored the oak (as) the tree[3] of Jupiter. 5. The songs of birds are heard among the oaks. 6. In ancient times men fought with bows and arrows. 7. The consulship of Cicero was very renowned. 8. Cæsar came into Italy with a large army. 9. The arrival of the army freed the citizens from fear.[4] 10. Between school and home we take (make) many steps.

[1] **Nāvēs longae**, *ships of war.*
[2] See **136**.
[3] Predicate accusative.
[4] See **128, 129, 130**.

**251.** VOCABULARY.

**adventus, -ūs,** M. **[adveniō]**, *arrival, approach.*
**arcus, -ūs,** M., *bow.*
**cōnsulātus, -ūs,** M. **[cōnsul]**, *consulship.*
**cornū, -ūs,** N., *horn.*
**exercitus, -ūs,** M. **[exerceō]**, *army.*
**lacus, -ūs,** M., *lake.*
**magistrātus, -ūs,** M. **[magister]**, *office, magistrate.*
**manus, -ūs,** F., *hand.*
**metus, -ūs,** M., *fear.*
**mōtus, -ūs,** M. **[moveō]**, *movement, motion.*
**portus, -ūs,** M., *harbor.*
**quercus, -ūs,** F., *oak.* (**11. 4.**)
**sēnsus, -ūs,** M. **[sentiō]**, *sense, feeling.*

**amplus, -a, -um,** adj., *great, renowned, honorable.*
**domicilium, -ī,** N., *home.* (**79.**)
**frōns, frondis,** F., *chaplet of leaves.*
**Jūppiter, Jovis,** M., *Jupiter,* the supreme god. (**262.**)
**sagitta, -ae,** F., *arrow.*
**salūs, -ūtis,** F., *safety.*
**schola, -ae,** F., *school.*
**victor, -ōris,** M. **[vincō]**, *conqueror.*

## CHAPTER XXXVII. 1.

### FIFTH DECLENSION.

**252.** The stem ends in *ē*.

**253.** Rule of Gender. — **Nouns of the fifth declension are feminine, except** ***diēs, day,*** **which is commonly masculine in the singular, and always in the plural.**

**254.** PARADIGMS.

| | **Diēs,** *day.* | | **Rēs,** *thing, affair.* | | Terminations. | |
|---|---|---|---|---|---|---|
| | SING. | PLUR. | SING. | PLUR. | SING. | PLUR. |
| N.V. | di**ēs** | di**ēs** | r**ēs** | r**ēs** | **ēs** | **ēs** |
| G. | di**ēī** | di**ērum** | r**eī** | r**ērum** | **ēī** | **ērum** |
| D. | di**ēī** | di**ēbus** | r**eī** | r**ēbus** | **ēī** | **ēbus** |
| Ac. | di**em** | di**ēs** | r**em** | r**ēs** | **em** | **ēs** |
| Ab. | di**ē** | di**ēbus** | r**ē** | r**ēbus** | **ē** | **ēbus** |

**255.** Only **diēs** and **rēs** are complete in the plural. A few other nouns have nominative and accusative plural.

**256.** Decline together **rēs pūblica**, *state;* in sing., **bona fidēs**, *good faith;* **māgna spēs**, *great hope;* **diēs quīntus**, *fifth day.*

**257.** EXERCISES.

I. 1. In omnibus rēbus certus ōrdō est. 2. Domina rērum hūmānārum est fortūna. 3. Tertiō diē cōnsul in urbem veniet. 4. Dux exercitum in plānitiem dūxit. 5. Ibi aciem īnstrūxit et hostēs exspectābat. 6. Māgnam victōriae spem habuit. 7. Nam māximae erant mīlitum fidēs et virtūs. 8. Prō salūte reī pūblicae pūgnābant. 9. Posterō diē hostēs in pūgnam prōcessērunt. 10. Ad diēī fīnem victī sunt et fugātī.

II. 1. God is the creator of all things. 2. The commonwealth is dear to all good citizens. 3. In all human affairs there is much uncertainty.[1] 4. The army was marshalled in a large plain. 5. The enemy advanced against[2] the Romans' line of battle. 6. The general praised the soldiers for[3] their[4] fidelity. 7. In the line of battle were many foot-soldiers. 8. They had great hopes of victory. 9. In[5] a few days the arrangement of things will be changed. 10. The consul gave a pledge to the state.

**258.** VOCABULARY.

**aciēs, -ēī,** F., *line of battle.*
**fidēs, -ěī,** F., *faith, fidelity, pledge.*
**plānitiēs, -ēī,** F., *plain.*
**rēs pūblica,** F., *commonwealth, state.*
**spēs, spěī,** F., *hope.*

**certus, -a, -um,** adj., *fixed, certain.*
**creātor, -ōris,** M., *creator.*
**domina, -ae,** F., *mistress.*
**ex-spectō,** 1, *await, expect.*
**hūmānus, -a, -um,** adj., *human.*
**in-certus, -a, -um,** adj., *uncertain.*
**in-struō,** 3, **-strūxī, -strūctum,** *draw up, marshal.*
**ōrdō, -inis,** M., *order, arrangement.*
**paucus,**[6] **-a, -um,** adj., *few, little.*
**pedes, -itis,** M. [**pēs**], *foot-soldier.*
**posterus, -a, -um,** adj., *following, next.*
**prō,** prep. w. abl., *for, in behalf of.*
**prō-cēdō,** 3, **-cēssī, -cēssum,** *advance.*

[1] *Many things are uncertain.*
[2] **In** with accusative.
[3] **Dē** with ablative.
[4] Omit.
[5] See **135**, **136**.
[6] Mostly used in the plural.

**259.** *Examine the following:* —

1. **Claudus alterō pede,** *lame in one foot.*
2. **Mōribus similēs,** *similar in character.*
3. **Virtūte praecēdunt,** *they excel in courage.*
4. **Numerō ad duodecim,** *about twelve in number.*

Observe that the ablatives **pede, mōribus, virtūte,** and **numerō,** answer the question *in what respect?* This ablative is called the **Ablative of Specification.**

**260.** RULE OF SYNTAX. — **The ablative is used to denote that in respect to which anything is said to be, or to be done.**

## 2.

**261.** COLLOQUIUM.

PRAECEPTOR ET DISCIPULUS.

*P.* Omnium dēclīnātiōnum quae est difficillima?
which

*D.* Tertia mihi vidētur difficillima.

*P.* Quārē ita cēnsēs?
why think

*D.* Varietātis causā terminātiōnum in nōminātīvō singulārī.
variety on account

Genus quoque est mihi molestissimum, praesertim nōminum
gender also especially nouns

in *is* dēsinentium.
ending

*P.* Tenēsne memoriā quae nōmina plūrālem genetīvum in *ium* habeant?
have

*D.* Prīmum nōmina in *is* et *ēs* dēsinentia, sī in genetīvō
first

singulārī nōn crēscunt; ut *hostis* et *nūbēs.*

Deinde monosyllaba in *s* vel *x* dēsinentia, sī ante *s* et *x* stat cōnsonāns; ut *urbs* et *arx.*
consonant

Tum nōmina in *ns* et *rs* dēsinentia; ut *cliēns* et *cohors.*

Dēnique neutra in *e*, *al*, *ar* dēsinentia; ut *mare*, *animal*,
neuters

*calcar.*

*P.* Optimē, mī puer; bene studuistī et bene memoriā tenēs. Jam tibi licet īre ad lūdendum.
you may play

# CHAPTER XXXVIII. 1.

## 262. SPECIAL PARADIGMS.

| | **Vir**, M., *man.* | **Vīs**, F., *strength.* | **Deus**, M., *god.* | **Senex**, M., *old man.* |
|---|---|---|---|---|
| | | SINGULAR. | | |
| N.V. | vir | vīs | deus | senex |
| G. | virī | vīs [1] | deī | senis |
| D. | virō | vī [1] | deō | senī |
| Ac. | virum | vim | deum | senem |
| Ab. | virō | vī | deō | sene |
| | | PLURAL. | | |
| N.V. | virī | vīrēs | deī, diī, dī | senēs |
| G. | virōrum | vīrium | deōrum, deūm | senum |
| D. | virīs | vīribus | deīs, diīs, dīs | senibus |
| Ac. | virōs | vīrēs | deōs | senēs |
| Ab. | virīs | vīribus | deīs, diīs, dīs | senibus |

| | **Iter**, N., *way.* | **Jūppiter**, *Jupiter.* | **Bōs**, M. & F., *ox, cow.* | **Domus**, F., *house.* |
|---|---|---|---|---|
| | | SINGULAR. | | |
| N.V. | iter | Jūppiter | bōs | domus |
| G. | itineris | Jovis | bovis | domūs |
| D. | itinerī | Jovī | bovī | domuī, ō |
| Ac. | iter | Jovem | bovem | domum |
| Ab. | itinere | Jove | bove | domō, ū |
| | | PLURAL. | | |
| N.V. | itinera | | bovēs | domūs |
| G. | itinerum | | bovum, boum | domuum, ōrum |
| D. | itineribus | | bōbus, būbus | domibus |
| Ac. | itinera | | bovēs | domōs, ūs |
| Ab. | itineribus | | bōbus, būbus | domibus |

[1] The genitive and dative singular are rare.

## 2.

**263.** FOR TRANSLATION.

### PROSERPINA IS CARRIED OFF BY PLUTO.

[*Review* **199** *and* **215.**]

Dum Proserpina luco
Ludit, et aut violas aut candida lilia carpit,
Dumque puellari studio[1] calathosque[2] sinumque[2]
Implet, et aequales[3] certat superare legendo,[4]
Paene simul visa est dilectaque[5] raptaque[6] Diti.[7]

### HER CHANCE OF RETURN IS LOST.

Dixerat.[8] At Cereri certum est[9] educere[10] natam.[11]
Non ita fata sinunt, quoniam jejunia virgo
Solverat et, cultis[12] dum simplex errat[13] in hortis,
Poeniceum[14] curva[15] decerpserat arbore pomum,
Sumptaque callenti septem de cortice grana
Presserat[16] ore suo: solusque ex omnibus illud
Ascalaphus vidit. . . .
Vidit, et indicio reditum crudelis ademit.

---

1 **Puellārī studiō** = **puellārī cum studiō.** See **144** and **145.**

2 **Que . . . que,** *both . . . and.*

3 **Aequālēs** = **comitēs.**

4 **Legendō,** *in gathering* (*flowers*).

5 **Dīlecta,** from **dīligō.**

6 **Rapta,** from **rapiō.** With **dīlecta** and **rapta** supply **est.**

7 **Dītī.** Translate as if, instead of the dative, it were **ā Dīte.**

8 **Dixerat,** *i.e.* **Jūppiter.**

9 **Cererī certum est,** *to Ceres it is determined* = *Ceres is resolved.*

10 **Ēdūcere,** that is, from the lower world.

11 **Nātam** = **fīliam.**

12 **Cultīs,** with **hortīs.**

13 **Errat.** Translate as if it were **errābat.** The present is very often used after **dum,** referring to past time. So **lūdit,** l. **2.**

14 **Poenīceum,** with **pōmum.**

15 **Curvā,** *bending.* The tree is loaded with fruit.

16 **Presserat,** from **premō.**

# CHAPTER XXXIX. 1.

## PRONOUNS.

Pronouns may be divided into eight classes, and arranged in three groups:

| | | |
|---|---|---|
| I. 1. Personal. 2. Reflexive. 3. Possessive. | II. 4. Determinative. 5. Demonstrative. | III. 6. Relative. 7. Interrogative. 8. Indefinite. |

### Personal Pronouns.

**264.** PARADIGMS.

First Person.

**Egŏ**, *I.*

| | SINGULAR. | PLURAL. |
|---|---|---|
| N. | **egŏ**, *I.* | **nōs**, *we.* |
| G. | **meī**, *of me.* | **nostrum**, or **nostrī**, *of us.* |
| D. | **mihĭ** (**mī**), *to, for me.* | **nōbīs**, *to, for us.* |
| Ac. | **mē**, *me.* | **nōs**, *us.* |
| Ab. | (**ā**) **mē**, *by me.* | (**ā**) **nōbīs**, *by us.* |

Second Person.

**Tū**, *thou.*

| | | |
|---|---|---|
| N. | **tū**, *thou.* | **vōs**, *you, ye.* |
| G. | **tuī**, *of thee.* | **vestrum**, or **vestrī**, *of you.* |
| D. | **tibĭ**, *to, for thee.* | **vōbīs**, *to, for you.* |
| Ac. | **tē**, *thee.* | **vōs**, *you.* |
| Ab. | (**ā**) **tē**, *by thee.* | (**ā**) **vōbīs**, *by you.* |

### Reflexive Pronoun.

**Suī**, *of himself, etc.*

| | SINGULAR. | PLURAL. |
|---|---|---|
| N. | ——— | ——— |
| G. | **suī**, *of himself, herself, itself.* | **suī**, *of themselves.* |
| D. | **sibĭ**, *to, for himself, etc.* | **sibĭ**, *to, for themselves.* |
| Ac. | **sē** (**sēsē**), *himself, etc.* | **sē** (**sēsē**), *themselves.* |
| Ab. | (**ā**) **sē** (**sēsē**), *by himself, etc.* | (**ā**) **sē** (**sēsē**), *by themselves.* |

**265.** 1. The personal pronoun of the third person is **is, ea, id,** *he, she, it.* But when reference is made in the oblique cases to the subject of the sentence, the reflexive **suī** is used: **Omnēs hominēs sē** (or **sēsē**) **amant,** *all men love themselves.*

2. The nominatives of the personal pronouns are much less frequently used in Latin than their equivalents in English. Why is this? In general, they are used only for emphasis or contrast: **Ego sum aegrōtus, tū valēs,** *I am sick, you are well.*

3. "*With me, with you,*" etc., are not expressed, as you would expect, by **cum mē, cum tē,** etc., but always by **mēcum, tēcum, sēcum, nōbīscum, vōbīscum.** So **quibuscum (279).**

4. The personal pronouns of the first and second person are often used with reflexive sense: **Tū tē amās,** *thou lovest thyself;* **ego mihi noceō,** *I injure myself.*

### Possessive Adjective Pronouns.

**266.** Possessive adjective pronouns are formed from the stems of personal and reflexive pronouns:

| | |
|---|---|
| **meus, -a, -um,** *my, mine* (voc. sing. masc. **mī**). | **suus, -a, -um,** *his, her, its, their (own).* |
| | **noster, -tra, -trum,** *our, ours.* |
| **tuus, -a, -um,** *thy, thine.* | **vester, -tra, -trum,** *your, yours.* |

## 2.

**267.** EXERCISES.

I. 1. Pater mē amat et patrem ego amō. 2. Tū quoque patrem meum amās. 3. Patrem tuum ego quoque amō. 4. Puella nimium sē culpat. 5. Fīlium tuum amāmus nōs omnēs. 6. Vōs (*acc.*) agitātis. 7. Nōn ut aliī nōs (*acc.*) vidēmus. 8. Brūtus sē suō gladiō perfōdit. 9. Nōs sumus miserī, beātī estis vōs. 10. Sine tē et tēcum pariter sumus miserī. 11. Mēcum eris miserrimus. 12. Dē tē erat mea ōrātiō. 13. Vōbīscum trīstis erō nunquam. 14. Mihi mea vīta, tibi tua est cāra. 15. Amīcus noster est memor vestrī.

II. 1. Thy mother is dear to thee, mine to me. 2. All your plans are known to us. 3. The boy loves himself too much. 4. The burden will be carried by me, by you, by us, by thee. 5. With you and without you we shall be equally happy. 6. Thee I love, but not thy dog. 7. O, how I shall miss you, my friend! 8. We[1] are poor, you[1] are rich. 9. Our life is very short. 10. The boy carried a wooden cup with him(self).

**268.** VOCABULARY.

**agitō,** 1 [**agō,** *put in motion*], *disturb, vex, chase.*
**beātus, -a, -um,** adj., *happy.*
**culpō,** 1 [**culpa**], *blame, censure, reproach.*
**dēsiderō,** 1, *desire, long for, miss.*
**ligneus, -a, -um,** adj. [**lignum,** *wood*], *of wood, wooden.*
**nimium,** adv., *too, too much.*
**nōtus, -a, -um,** adj., *known.*
**onus, -eris,** N., *burden.*
**ōrātiō, -ōnis,** F. [**ōrō**], *speech, talk, address.*
**pariter,** adv. [**pār,** *equal*], *equally.*
**pauper, -eris,** adj., *poor.* (**167**. 3.)
**per-fodiō,** 3, **-fōdī, -fossum,** *dig through, stab, pierce.*
**quoque,** conj., *also, too.*
**sine,** prep. w. abl., *without.*
**ut,** adv. and conj., *as.*

3.

**269.** COLLOQUIUM.

FRĀTER ET SORŌRCULA.

*F.* Age, sorōrcula mea, sī tibi placet, ambulābimus.
come little sister walk

*S.* Quō est tibi in animō, cāre frāter, ambulāre? Nōnne in agrōs?
whither

*F.* Ita est, in agrōs et in umbrā silvārum.
yes shade

*S.* Libenter tēcum ambulō, tamen . . .
gladly but

*F.* Quid? cūr tantum dubitās, sī, ut dīcis, mēcum ambulās libenter?
so much hesitate

*S.* Nōlī mē rīdēre. Metuō anguēs. "Frīgidus latet anguis in herbā," ut cantat Vergilius.
don't laugh at snakes cold lurks

*F.* Nōlī metuere. Venī; ubi frāga mātūra sunt repperī.
where strawberries ripe are have found

*S.* Ō quam suāve! In mē nōn jam est mora.
delightful now delay

[1] Why should the pronouns be expressed in Latin?

# CHAPTER XL. 1.

## DETERMINATIVE PRONOUNS.

**270.** PARADIGMS: **Is, Idem, ipse.**

**Is**, *that, this;* also, *he, she, it.*

| | SINGULAR. | | | PLURAL. | | |
|---|---|---|---|---|---|---|
| N. | **is** | **ea** | **id** | **eī, iī** | **eae** | **ea** |
| G. | **ējus** | **ējus** | **ējus** | **eōrum** | **eārum** | **eōrum** |
| D. | **eī** | **eī** | **eī** | **eīs, iīs** | **eīs, iīs** | **eīs, iīs** |
| Ac. | **eum** | **eam** | **id** | **eōs** | **eās** | **ea** |
| Ab. | **eō** | **eā** | **eō** | **eīs, iīs** | **eīs, iīs** | **eīs, iīs** |

**Īdem**, *same.*

| | SINGULAR. | | | PLURAL. | | |
|---|---|---|---|---|---|---|
| N. | **īdem** | **eădem** | **idem** | **eīdem**<br>**iīdem** | **eaedem** | **eădem** |
| G. | **ējusdem** | **ējusdem** | **ējusdem** | **eōrundem** | **eārundem** | **eōrundem** |
| D. | **eīdem** | **eīdem** | **eīdem** | **eīsdem**<br>**iīsdem** | **eīsdem**<br>**iīsdem** | **eīsdem**<br>**iīsdem** |
| Ac. | **eundem** | **eandem** | **idem** | **eōsdem** | **eāsdem** | **eădem** |
| Ab. | **eōdem** | **eādem** | **eōdem** | **eīsdem**<br>**iīsdem** | **eīsdem**<br>**iīsdem** | **eīsdem**<br>**iīsdem** |

**Ipse**, *self* (*himself, etc.*).

| | SINGULAR. | | | PLURAL. | | |
|---|---|---|---|---|---|---|
| N. | **ipse** | **ipsa** | **ipsum** | **ipsī** | **ipsae** | **ipsa** |
| G. | **ipsīus** | **ipsīus** | **ipsīus** | **ipsōrum** | **ipsārum** | **ipsōrum** |
| D. | **ipsī** | **ipsī** | **ipsī** | **ipsīs** | **ipsīs** | **ipsīs** |
| Ac. | **ipsum** | **ipsam** | **ipsum** | **ipsōs** | **ipsās** | **ipsa** |
| Ab. | **ipsō** | **ipsā** | **ipsō** | **ipsīs** | **ipsīs** | **ipsīs** |

1. Determinative pronouns, like adjectives, agree with nouns expressed or understood; **īdem** and **ipse** also with pronouns.

2. **Is** is very often used as a personal pronoun, meaning *he, she, it, they.* Also as the antecedent of **quī**, *who;* **is quī**, *he who.*

3. **Īdem** is compounded of *is* and the suffix *dem.* **Īdem** is for **isdem**; **idem** for **iddem**; **eundem**, etc., for **eumdem**, etc; **eōrundem**, etc., for **eōrumdem**, etc.

4. **Ipse**, *self* (intensive) is used to emphasize a noun or pronoun expressed or understood, and must be distinguished from **sē**, *self* (reflexive):

(1) **Homo ipse veniet**, *the man himself* (and not another) *will come.*
(2) **Hominem ipsum vīdī**, *I saw the man himself.*
(3) **Homo sē culpat nimium**, *the man blames himself too much.*
(4) **Mīles frātrem, dein sē ipsum interfēcit**, *the soldier killed his brother, then himself.*

5. How do we indicate in English in speech, and how in writing, when we use *self* (*himself*, etc.) whether we intend the intensive or the reflexive *self?*

6. **Ipse** may be variously translated: **ipse fēcī**, *I* MYSELF *did it, I did it* ALONE, *I did it* OF MY OWN ACCORD.

**271.** Decline together **is homo**, *that man;* **ea nāvis**, *that ship;* **id bellum**, *that war;* **īdem diēs**, *the same day;* **eadem manus**, *the same hand;* **idem onus**, *the same burden;* **vir ipse**, *the man himself.*

## 2.

**272.** EXERCISES.

I. 1. Cicerō est scrīptor ēlegantissimus; ējus librōs legimus. 2. Fīdum amīcum habeō; eum ego magis quam tū amās. 3. Eum magis quam tē amō. 4. Nōn semper eundem hominem laudāmus. 5. Magister ipse tē laudābit. 6. Sunt sex partēs orbis terrārum; māxima eārum est Asia. 7. Fortūna nunc mihi,[1] nunc eī[1] favet. 8. Interdum amīcīs[1] ipsīs, interdum inimīcīs[1] nocet. 9. Semper īdem erat Sōcratis vultus. 10. In eōdem specū habitābant Androclus et leō.

II. 1. Sallust is an elegant author; have you read his writings? 2. I have not read those, but Cicero's. 3. Fortune favored now you,[2] now them.[2] 4. Even (*ipse*) your own friend will blame you. 5. The minds of men are not always the same. 6. We were sailing[3] with you in the same ship. 7. He gave me the book of his own accord.[4] 8. The master

[1] Indirect object, though translated as a direct object. See **343**.
[2] Dative. Cf. I. 7.
[3] Use passive of **vehō.**
[4] See **270**. 6.

offers the same rewards to the boys. 9. The same rewards are offered by the master himself.

**273.** VOCABULARY.

**Androclus, -ī**, M., *Androclus.*
**auctor, -ōris**, M. [**augeō**, *increase*], *maker, author.*
**ēlegāns, -ntis**, adj., *choice, elegant.*
**faveō**, 2, **fāvī, fautum**, *be favorable to, befriend* (with dat.).
**interdum**, adv., *sometimes.*
**mēns, mentis**, F., *mind, purpose.*
**noceō**, 2, **nocuī, nocitum**, *do harm to, hurt, injure* (with dat.).
**orbis, -is**, M., *circle.*
**orbis terrārum,** *the earth, the world.*
**Sallustius, -ī**, M., *Sallust*, a historian. (**79.**)
**scrīptor, -ōris**, M. [**scrībō**], *writer, author.*
**scrīptum, -ī**, N. [**scrībō**], *writing, written work.*
**sex**, num. adj., indecl., *six.*
**specus, -ūs**, M., *cave.*
**suāviter**, adv. [**suāvis**], *sweetly, delightfully.*
**vultus, -ūs**, M., *countenance, features, looks.*

**animus (161)**, *mind, soul, heart;* the general word for *mind.*
**mēns**, *mind*, as that which thinks, *intellect;* more limited in meaning.

3.

COLLOQUIUM.

**274.** *Translate into Latin:* —

BROTHER AND LITTLE SISTER. — *Continued.*

*B.* Let us carry[1] with us two[2] little-baskets.[3]

*S.* See![4] I have them in my hand already.[5]

*B.* The sun is hot,[6] but there is a cool[7] breeze.

*S.* Oh, how the trees and flowers delight me!

*B.* To stay in the house is downright[8] stupid.[9]

*S.* Yes, indeed,[10] and I don't mean to any more.[11]

*B.* Here are[12] the strawberries. Now we will fill our baskets. Isn't it jolly?[13]

---

1 *Let us carry*, **portēmus.**
2 **Duās.** See **311. 4.**
3 **Corbula, -ae.**
4 **Ecce.**
5 **Jam.**
6 **Ardēns.**
7 **Frīgidus.**
8 **Admodum.**
9 **Molestus.**
10 *Yes, indeed*, **ista sunt**, *those things are (true).*
11 *Neither is it in mind to me more.* See **269**, 1. 2.
12 *Here are* = **ēn!** or **ecce!**
13 **suāvissimum.**

# CHAPTER XLI. 1.

## DEMONSTRATIVE PRONOUNS.

**275.** PARADIGMS: **Hīc, iste, ille.**

**Hīc,** *this (near), this of mine.*

| | SINGULAR. | | | PLURAL. | | |
|---|---|---|---|---|---|---|
| N. | **hīc** | **haec** | **hōc** | **hī** | **hae** | **haec** |
| G. | **hūjus** | **hūjus** | **hūjus** | **hōrum** | **hārum** | **hōrum** |
| D. | **huīc** | **huīc** | **huīc** | **hīs** | **hīs** | **hīs** |
| Ac. | **hunc** | **hanc** | **hōc** | **hōs** | **hās** | **haec** |
| Ab. | **hōc** | **hāc** | **hōc** | **hīs** | **hīs** | **hīs** |

**Iste,** *that, that of yours.*

| | | | | | | |
|---|---|---|---|---|---|---|
| N. | **iste** | **ista** | **istud** | **istī** | **istae** | **ista** |
| G. | **istīus** | **istīus** | **istīus** | **istōrum** | **istārum** | **istōrum** |
| D. | **istī** | **istī** | **istī** | **istīs** | **istīs** | **istīs** |
| Ac. | **istum** | **istam** | **istud** | **istōs** | **istās** | **ista** |
| Ab. | **istō** | **istā** | **istō** | **istīs** | **istīs** | **istīs** |

**Ille,** *that (yonder).*

| | | | | | | |
|---|---|---|---|---|---|---|
| N. | **ille** | **illa** | **illud** | **illī** | **illae** | **illa** |
| G. | **illīus** | **illīus** | **illīus** | **illōrum** | **illārum** | **illōrum** |
| D. | **illī** | **illī** | **illī** | **illīs** | **illīs** | **illīs** |
| Ac. | **illum** | **illam** | **illud** | **illōs** | **illās** | **illa** |
| Ab. | **illō** | **illā** | **illō** | **illīs** | **illīs** | **illīs** |

1. **Hīc** is used of that which is near the speaker in *place, time,* or *thought,* and hence is called the Demonstrative of the First Person: **Hīc equus,** *this horse (near me,* or *belonging to me).*

2. **Iste** is used of that which has some relation to the person addressed, and hence is called the Demonstrative of the Second Person: **Iste equus,** *that horse (near you,* or *belonging to you).*

3. **Ille** is used of that which is relatively remote from the speaker, or person addressed, in *place, time,* or *thought,* and hence is called the Demonstrative of the Third Person: **Ille equus,** *that horse (yonder).*

4. **Ille** often means *that well-known, that famous.*

5. **Hīc** and **ille** are sometimes used in contrast: **Hīc**, *the latter;* **ille**, *the former.*

6. **Is**, as a determinative pronoun, sometimes approaches **hīc** in meaning, sometimes **ille**. Hence it is to be translated *this* or *that*, according to the connection.

**276.** EXERCISES.

I. 1. Illīus hominis fīlium laudābant omnēs. 2. Iste canis semper lātrat. 3. Hūjus scholae semper memorēs erimus. 4. Dabō tibi illud carmen pulcherrimum. 5. Illī lapidēs dūrī sunt. 6. Multī virī dīvitēs in hāc urbe habitant. 7. Variī sunt colōrēs hūjus flōris. 8. Nōmen illīus poētae est clārissimum. 9. Hārum avium cantus nōs dēlectat. 10. Ista tua studia amō et laudō. 11. Hās terrās silvīs pulcherrimīs ōrnāvit Deus. 12. Illud ducis cōnsilium nōbīs ūtile fuit.

II. 1. These mountains are very[1] high. 2. I shall always be mindful of that friend of yours.[2] 3. This thing will be hurtful to you. 4. Demosthenes and Cicero were famous[3] orators; the former[4] was a Greek, the latter[4] a Roman. 5. The citizens of yonder city are most wretched. 6. The air in these mountains is lighter than in those valleys. 7. He gave me this pretty bird. 8. That old farmer's wine is good. 9. I have read that book of yours. 10. That book of yours has been read by me, by you, by us, by us ourselves.

2.

**277.** EXERCISES.

I. 1. Hannibal, clārissimus ille imperātor, Alpēs montēs superāvit. 2. Mīlitum animōs hāc ōrātiōne firmāvit. 3. Vidētis, mīlitēs fortissimī, Ītaliam illam. 4. Illud est domicilium hostium nostrōrum. 5. Gallī, incolae hārum regiōnum, sociī amīcīque nostrī erunt. 6. Hī nōbīs omnēs rēs necessāriās praebēbunt. 7. Hī erunt hostēs illōrum Rōmānōrum

[1] See p. 91, note.
[2] *That of yours* = **iste**.
[3] Superlative.
[4] See **275**. 5.

improbōrum. 8. Rōma illa praeda vestra erit. 9. Vōs ipsī expūgnāvistis Saguntum, oppidum illud firmissimum. 10. Hās Alpēs, illōs Pȳrēnaeōs montēs superāvistis; Rōmānōs mox vincētis.

II. 1. Hannibal increased the courage of the soldiers by these words. 2. Again, soldiers, have you defeated those famous Romans. 3. The gods and your own courage have given us the victory. 4. This fair Italy will soon be ours. 5. Rome itself, that proud city, shall be taken. 6. Those arms of yours shall be stained with the best blood of Rome. 7. Those famous legions are defeated. 8. Cross with me yonder mountains. 9. Those fierce enemies of the Romans, the Samnites, will welcome us. 10. Rome shall be the reward of valor. Forward![1]

**278.** VOCABULARY.

**āēr, āeris,** M., *air.*
**cantus, -ūs,** M., *singing, song.*
**dēlectō,** 1, *delight.*
**Dēmosthenēs, -is,** M., *Demosthenes,* an Athenian orator.
**dīvěs, -itis,** adj., *rich.* (**167**. 3.)
**dō, dare, dědī, datum,** *give.*
**ex-pūgnō,** 1, *take by storm, take.*
**firmō,** 1 [**firmus**], *make firm or steadfast, fortify, strengthen.*
**firmus, -a, -um,** adj., *strong, firm.*
**improbus, -a, -um,** adj., *bad.*
**iterum,** adv., *a second time, again.*
**lātrō,** 1, *bark, bark at.*
**legiō, -ōnis,** F., *legion.*
**maculō,** 1, *stain.*
**mox,** adv., *soon.*
**necessārius, -a, -um,** adj., *necessary.*
**praeda, -ae,** F., *booty, spoil.*
**Saguntum, -ī,** N., *Saguntum,* town in Spain.
**Samnīs, -ītis,** M. & F., *a Samnite.*
**sanguis, -inis,** M., *blood.*
**silva, -ae,** F., *wood, forest.*
**socius, -ī,** M., *ally, associate.*
**superbus, -a, -um,** adj., *proud.*
**tenuis, -e,** adj., *thin, light.*
**trānscendō, 3, -ī, -sum,** *cross.*

**cantus,** *song, melody,* whether of the voice of man, of birds, or of musical instruments.
**carmen,** *song,* as *melody,* and also in a wider sense; often with reference to the composition. Hence, *a poem.*[2]

[1] **Prōcēdite.**
[2] It must not be supposed that distinctions in synonymous words are always observed in usage.

# CHAPTER XLII. 1.

## PRONOUNS: RELATIVE, INTERROGATIVE, AND INDEFINITE.

**279.** PARADIGMS: **Quī, quis, aliquis.**

RELATIVE: **Quī**, *who, which, that.*

| | SINGULAR. | | | PLURAL. | | |
|---|---|---|---|---|---|---|
| N. | **quī** | **quae** | **quod** | **quī** | **quae** | **quae** |
| G. | **cūjus** | **cūjus** | **cūjus** | **quōrum** | **quārum** | **quōrum** |
| D. | **cuī** | **cuī** | **cuī** | **quibus** | **quibus** | **quibus** |
| Ac. | **quem** | **quam** | **quod** | **quōs** | **quās** | **quae** |
| Ab. | **quō** | **quā** | **quō** | **quibus** | **quibus** | **quibus** |

INTERROGATIVE: **Quis**, *who, which, what?*

| | | | | | | |
|---|---|---|---|---|---|---|
| N. | **quis** | **quae** | **quid** | **quī** | **quae** | **quae** |
| G. | **cūjus** | **cūjus** | **cūjus** | **quōrum** | **quārum** | **quōrum** |
| D. | **cuī** | **cuī** | **cuī** | **quibus** | **quibus** | **quibus** |
| Ac. | **quem** | **quam** | **quid** | **quōs** | **quās** | **quae** |
| Ab. | **quō** | **quā** | **quō** | **quibus** | **quibus** | **quibus** |

INDEFINITE: **Aliquis**, *some one, some, any one.*

| | SINGULAR. | | |
|---|---|---|---|
| N. | **aliquis** | **aliqua** | **aliquid** *or* **-quod** |
| G. | **alicūjus** | **alicūjus** | **alicūjus** |
| D. | **alicuī** | **alicuī** | **alicuī** |
| Ac. | **aliquem** | **aliquam** | **aliquid** *or* **-quod** |
| Ab. | **aliquō** | **aliquā** | **aliquō** |
| | PLURAL. | | |
| N. | **aliquī** | **aliquae** | **aliqua** |
| G. | **aliquōrum** | **aliquārum** | **aliquōrum** |
| D. | **aliquibus** | **aliquibus** | **aliquibus** |
| Ac. | **aliquōs** | **aliquās** | **aliqua** |
| Ab. | **aliquibus** | **aliquibus** | **aliquibus** |

1. Observe the feminine nominative singular, and the neuter nominative plural of **aliquis**, and compare them with corresponding forms of **quis**.

2. **Aliquis** is used adjectively in the neuter form **aliquod**, and sometimes in the masculine and feminine forms. The same is true of **quīdam** and **quisque** (4).

3. Besides the interrogative **quis** and its compounds, there is an interrogative adjective **quī** (*which, what?*) declined like the relative **quī**.

4. Besides **aliquis**, the most important indefinites are:

| | | |
|---|---|---|
| **quīdam** | **quaedam** | **quiddam,** or **quoddam,** *certain one, certain.* |
| **quisquam** | (*wanting*) | **quidquam,** *any one* (*at all*), no plural. |
| **quisque** | **quaeque** | **quidque,** or **quodque,** *each one, every.* |

5. **Quīdam, quisquam,** and **quisque** are declined like the simple pronouns. **Quīdam** changes *m* to *n* before *d*; **quendam,** etc., **quōrundam,** etc.

6. **Aliquis,** *some one, any one* (without emphasis); **quisquam,** *any one at all* (emphatic), also in negative and interrogative sentences.

7. **Aliquis** means *some man,* I don't know who; **quīdam,** *a certain man,* whom I know, but don't mean to describe.

**280.** *Examine the following:* —

1. **Puer quī vēnit,** *the boy who came.*
2. **Puella quae vēnit,** *the girl who came.*
3. **Librī quōs legis,** *the books which you read.*
4. **Puellae quās vīdistī,** *the girls whom you saw.*

Compare the relative in each of the above examples with the noun to which it refers (called the *antecedent*) in respect, first to gender, and then to number.

Look now at the case of the relative in each of the examples, and compare the English with the Latin. Plainly, the case of the relative has nothing to do with that of the antecedent. It may be the same or different.

**281.** Rule of Syntax.[1] — **A relative pronoun agrees with its antecedent in *gender* and *number*.**

[1] As the *person* of the antecedent has no effect on the relative, it is wrong, though customary, to say "the relative agrees with its antecedent in gender, number, and person."

**282.** *Examine the following:* —

1. **Ego quī vēnī,** *I who came.*
2. **Vōs quī vēnistis,** *you who came.*

Observe now the person and number of the verb in these two examples, and in the first two given in **280**.

**283.** Rule of Syntax. — **The verb of which a relative pronoun is the subject agrees in *person* and *number* with the antecedent of the relative.**

## 2.

**284.** EXERCISES.

I. 1. Quis forum Rōmānōrum rōstrīs ōrnāvit? 2. Gājus Duīlius, quī māgnam praedam ā Carthāginiēnsibus reportāvit. 3. Quae amīcitia potest esse[1] inter improbōs? 4. Quis clārior fuit in Graeciā Themistocle?[2] 5. Quem timēs in meā domō? 6. Quae animālia sunt celerrima et ferōcissima? 7. Omne animal quod sanguinem habet cor habet. 8. Dīvitēs sunt iī quī suīs rēbus contentī sunt. 9. Erant quōque[3] annō duo cōnsulēs in cīvitāte Rōmānā. 10. Sunt animālia quaedam in quibus est aliquid simile ratiōnī.

II. 1. What have you in your hand? 2. By whom was the Roman forum adorned with the prows of ships? 3. We see the general whom you praise. 4. He is rich who is contented. 5. He will be praised whose[4] courage saved our country. 6. We love those whose manners are pleasing. 7. The boy has something in his hand. 8. Certain labors are pleasant to us. 9. We are the same[5] to-day that[5] we were yesterday. 10. What things are brought to us from Africa?

---

[1] **Potest esse,** *can be.*
[2] See **212**.
[3] Ablative of **quisque**.
[4] *Of whom.*
[5] *The same . . . that,* or *same . . . as,* **idem . . . quī.**

## 3.

**285.** EXERCISES.

Before trying to do the following exercises, review the declension of irregular adjectives (**200, 201**), and write out the declension of **quīdam, quisquam,** and **quisque.**

I. 1. Est quisquam tibi cārior quam parentēs tuī? 2. Propriī līberī cārissimī cuīque sunt. 3. Erant duo fīliī Rhēae Silviae, quōrum alterī erat nōmen Rōmulus, alterī Rēmus; uterque fortis erat. 4. Estne in ūllō animālī mājor prūdentia quam in cane? 5. Vidēsne illa duo sīdera? utrīus lūx clārior est? 6. Virtūs eōrum quī patriam nostram servāvērunt semper laudābitur. 7. In istīs arboribus quae hortum ōrnant avēs variae cantant. 8. Rīsus aliōrum saepe causa īrae nostrae est. 9. Nūllum malum sine aliquō bonō est. 10. Nēmō nostrum īdem est in senectūte quī[1] fuit in juventūte. 11. Urbēs illae, quārum glōria māgna est, ā mīlitibus nostrīs expūgnātae sunt.

II. 1. All animals that have blood have hearts. 2. We shall be the same[1] to-morrow as[1] we are to-day. 3. Is any[2] animal more sagacious than the elephant?[3] 4. We have five fingers on each hand. 5. Those have hope who have nothing else.[4] 6. Many men build houses which they will never inhabit. 7. The moon sends upon the earth the light which she has received from the sun. 8. Cornelia had two sons, both of whom[5] were killed. 9. Hector, by whose bravery many Greeks were slain, was himself killed. 10. Will not some friend relieve me of this burden?[6]

**286.** VOCABULARY.

**accipiō,** 3, **-cēpī, -ceptum** [**ad-capiō**], *take to, receive, accept.*
**bonum, -ī,** N., *good thing, blessing.*
**Carthāginiēnsis, -e,** adj. [**Carthāgō**], *of Carthage, Carthaginian.*
**clārus, -a, -um,** *bright, famous.*

[1] See p. 128, note 5.
[2] See I. 4.
[3] See **211, 212.**
[4] **Aliud.**
[5] *Of whom each.*
[6] See **128, 129.**

**contentus, -a, -um**, adj., *contented.*
**cor, cordis**, N., *heart.*
**crās**, adv., *to-morrow.*
**digitus, -ī**, M., *finger.*
**duo, -ae, -o**, num. adj., *two* (**311.** 4).
**ex-pūgnō, 1** [**pūgna**], *take, capture.*
**forum, -ī**, N., *market-place, forum.*
**Gājus Duilius, -ī**, M., *Caius Duilius.*
**Hector, -oris**, M., *Hector*, chief of the Trojan heroes.
**herī**, adv., *yesterday.*
**hodiē**, adv., *to-day.*
**labor, -ōris**, M., *labor.*
**malum, -ī**, N., *bad thing, evil.*
**nēmō (-inis)**, M. & F. [**nē, homo**], *no one.* For genitive and ablative use **nūllius, nūllō.**
**parēns, -entis**, M. & F., *parent.* (**167.** 1.)
**proprius, -a, -um**, adj., *one's own.*
**prūdentia, -ae**, F. [**prūdēns**], *foresight, sagacity, wisdom.*
**Remus, -ī**, M., *Remus*, brother of Romulus.
**re-portō**, 1, *bring back.*
**Rhēa Silvia, -ae**, F., *Rhea Silvia.*
**rīsus, -ūs**, M. [**rīdeō**], *laughter.*
**Rōmulus, -ī**, M., *Romulus*, first king of Rome.
**rōstrum, -ī**, N., *prow of a vessel.*
**sīdus, -eris**, N., *star, constellation.*
**Themistoclēs, -is**, M., *Themistocles*, a famous Greek.
**varius, -a, -um**, adj., *different, changeable, various.*

# CHAPTER XLIII. 1.

## REVIEW OF PRONOUNS.

*Review the paradigms.*

**287.** EXERCISES.

I. 1. Īdem es quī[1] semper fuistī. 2. Hodiē eadem dictitat quae[1] herī. 3. Ecce domum quam aedificāvit Jōhanniculus. 4. Quīdam puer cachinnābat. 5. Iste homo, quī tē laudābat, est stultissimus. 6. Sua cuīque[2] cārissima sunt. 7. Suī cuīque[2] cārissimī sunt. 8. Cōram mē aliquis illam fābulam nārrābat. 9. Egēns est et is quī nōn satis habet, et is cuī nihil satis est. 10. Beātus est quī[3] nōn cupit quae[3] nōn habet.

[1] See p. 128, note 5.

[2] Notice the order; **quisque** likes to stand after the reflexives.

[3] The antecedent of the relative is often omitted when it is some form of **is**.

II. 1. She is the same that[1] she always has been. 2. He will say the same things to-morrow as[1] to-day. 3. Certain boys laughed out loud in school. 4. That friend of yours is a very wise man. 5. Those trees yonder are covered with leaves. 6. This man is praised by the citizens, that one is blamed. 7. The general himself led his brave soldiers. 8. The soldiers were led by the brave general himself. 9. Danger itself is pleasing to the brave.[2] 10. Those who are most faithful to their friends are most dear to us.

## 2.

**288.** EXERCISES.

I. 1. Quod[3] nōn dedit fortūna, nōn ēripit. 2. Līber est quī[3] nūllī turpitūdinī servit. 3. Quis est amīcior frātrī quam frāter? 4. Saepe nihil est inimīcius hominī quam ipse sibi. 5. Saepe iī nōbīs nocent[4] quī nōs amant. 6. Eōs quī aliōrum rēbus adversīs nōn moventur, omnēs contemnunt. 7. Eōs vincere difficile est, quī nihil timent. 8. Dēforme est dē sē ipsō praedicāre. 9. Aliud[5] bonum, aliud[5] malum est. 10. Alterī[6] laudem, alterī[6] culpam dabat.

II. 1. Some one has done this. 2. Yesterday a story was read to us by some one. 3. The slave killed himself together with his master. 4. My friend will migrate with me into Gaul. 5. The inhabitants of the city were frightened by the coming of the enemy. 6. Some[7] bear[8] thirst easily, others[7] hunger. 7. The fruits of this tree are pleasing to me, for they are sweet. 8. Those[9] trees are higher than these[9] houses. 9. These towers are high, those are low. 10. Those[10] maidens, whose modesty is known, are praised by all.

[1] See p. 128, note 5.
[2] Plural. See **117**.
[3] See p. 130, note 3.
[4] See **343**.
[5] See p. 87, note 4.
[6] See p. 87, note 3.
[7] See p. 87, note 4.
[8] See p. 87, note 5.
[9] See **275**. 1 and 3.
[10] A form of **is**.

**289.** VOCABULARY.

**ad-versus, -a, -um,** adj., *unfavorable.*

**cachinnō,** 1, *laugh aloud.* Cf. **rīdeō.**

**cōram,** prep. w. abl., *in presence of.*

**cupiō,** 3, **-īvī, -ītum,** *desire.*

**dē-fōrmis, -e,** adj. [**forma**], *misshapen, ugly, base, disgraceful.*

**dictitō,** 1 [**dīcō**], *keep saying.*

**ecce,** interj., *lo! see! see there!*

**egēns, -entis,** adj., *in want, needy.*

**ē-ripiō,** 3, **-uī, ēreptum** [**rapiō**], *snatch away; seize and bear off.*

**famēs, -is,** F., *hunger, famine.*

**frondōsus, -a, -um,** adj. [**frōns**], *covered with leaves, leafy.*

**frūctus, -ūs,** M., *fruit.*

**Jōhanniculus, -ī,** M., *little John, Johnny, Jack.*

**migrō,** 1, *move from one place to another, migrate.*

**modestia, -ae,** F., *modesty.*

**nārrō,** 1, *tell, relate, report.*

**prae-dicō,** 1 [**prae,** *before;* **dīcō, -āre,** *make known*], *proclaim, boast.* Cf. **praedīcō,** *predict.*

**satis,** adv., *enough.*

**serviō,** 4 [**servus**], *be a slave to, serve* (w. dat.).

**sitis, -is,** F., *thirst.*

**tolerō,** 1, *bear, endure.*

**turpitūdō, -inis,** F. [**turpis**], *ugliness, baseness.*

## 3.

**290.** COLLOQUIUM.

### Sōcratēs et Rhadamanthus.

*R.* Tū, nisi fallor, es Sōcratēs, ille Athēniēnsis.
(nisi fallor: unless I am mistaken)

*S.* Rēctē dīcis. Ego sum Sōcratēs, fīlius, ut ferunt, Sōphroniscī.
(ut: as; ferunt: say)

*R.* Cūr dīcis *ut ferunt?* Nōnne rē vērā es fīlius illīus?
(rē vērā: in truth)

*S.* Ipse quidem nesciō, Ō Rhadamanthe, cūjus sim fīlius.
(quidem: indeed; nesciō: not know; sim: am)

*R.* Num[1] mē lūdis, Sōcratēs? Cavētō. Nōnne tē sapientem dīxit ōrāculum?
(lūdis: mock; cavētō: beware; ōrāculum: oracle)

*S.* Ita est; sed quā rē nōn intellegō, nisi quia mē ipse īnscium perspiciō.
(ita est: yes; quā rē: why; intellegō: understand; īnscium: ignorant; perspiciō: see plainly)

[1] This word is used in asking questions when the answer *no* is expected. It is not to be translated.

*R.* Quō modo aetātem dēgistī?
how pass

*S.* Māgnā ex parte loquēbar māximēque dē virtūte
for the most part I used to talk especially
quaerēbam.
inquired

*R.* Mihi dē virtūte explicātō, Sōcratēs; per breve tempus tibi aurēs praebēbō.

*S.* Ēheu! Rhadamanthe, dē istā rē sum īnscius, nam mihi
alas!
explicāre poterat nēmō.
was able no one

*R.* Minimē sapiēns, Sōcratēs, tū mihi vidēris. At quid
seem but
hōc locō tibi est in animō facere?

*S.* Ante omnia, sī vidēbitur, cum Homērō velim et Ulixe
seem good I should like
et aliīs clārissimīs Graeciae prīncipibus loquī.
to talk

*R.* Apage igitur ad istās mānēs.
be off then shades

4.

**291.** FOR TRANSLATION.

THE BATTLE OF MARATHON, B.C. 490.

Hōc in tempore nūlla cīvitās Athēniēnsibus auxiliō[1] fuit praeter Plataeēnsēs. Ea[2] mīlle mīsit mīlitum. Itaque hōrum adventū decem mīlia armātōrum[3] complēta sunt, quae manus mīrābilī flagrābat pūgnandī cupiditāte. Quō factum est[4] ut plūs quam collēgae Miltiādēs valēret.[5] Ējus ergō auctōritāte impulsī[6] Athēniēnsēs cōpiās ex urbe ēdūxērunt locōque[7] idōneō castra fēcērunt. Deinde posterō diē proelium commīsērunt. Dātis, etsi nōn aequum[8] locum vidēbat suīs,[9]

[1] **Auxiliō fuit,** *was for assistance* = *assisted.* See **344.**

[2] Supply **cīvitās.**

[3] **Armātōrum** (participle as noun), *of armed men.*

[4] **Quō factum est,** *by which it was brought about* = *the result was.*

[5] **Plūs valēret,** *had more influence.*

[6] **Impulsī** (participle from **impellō**) *prompted.*

[7] **Locō** = **in locō.**

[8] **Aequum,** *favorable.*

[9] Supply **mīlitibus.**

tamen frētus numerō cōpiārum suārum cōnflīgere cupiēbat, eōque[1] magis, quod, priusquam Lacedaemoniī subsidiō[2] venīrent,[3] dīmicāre ūtile arbitrābātur. Itaque in aciem peditum centum,[4] equitum decem mīlia prōdūxit proeliumque commīsit. In quō tantō[5] plūs virtūte[6] valuērunt Athēniēnsēs, ut decemplicem numerum hostium prōflīgārint,[7] adeōque eōs perterruērunt, ut Persae nōn castra, sed nāvēs petierint.[8] Quā pūgnā[9] nihil adhūc exstitit nōbilius: nūlla enim unquam tam exigua manus tantās opēs prōstrāvit.[10]—*Nepos. Milt.* v.

## CHAPTER XLIV. 1.

### COMPOUNDS OF **Sum.**

**292. Possum, posse, potuī, ——,** *be able, can.*

**Possum** is compounded of **potis,** *able,* and **sum.** **Potis** is everywhere shortened to **pot**; then *t* is changed to *s* before *s*, and *f* is dropped after *t*.

| | INDICATIVE. | | SUBJUNCTIVE. | |
|---|---|---|---|---|
| | SINGULAR. | PLURAL. | SINGULAR. | PLURAL. |
| PRES. *I am able, can, etc.* | | | | |
| | **possum** | **possumus** | **possim** | **possīmus** |
| | **potes** | **potestis** | **possīs** | **possītis** |
| | **potest** | **possunt** | **possit** | **possint** |
| IMPER. *I was able, could, etc.* | | | | |
| | **poteram** | **poterāmus** | **possem** | **possēmus** |
| FUT. *I shall be able, etc.* | | | | |
| | **poterō** | **poterimus** | | |

[1] **Eōque magis,** *and the more.*

[2] **Subsidiō**: cf. **auxiliō,** first line, and note.

[3] **Venīrent,** *should come.*

[4] **Centum**: supply **mīlia.**

[5] **Tantō plūs valuērunt,** *were so much superior.*

[6] **Virtūte.** See **259, 260.**

[7] **Prōflīgārint,** *they routed.*

[8] **Petierint,** *fled to.* See p. 101, note 1.

[9] **Pūgnā**: ablative after the comparative **nōbilius.** (**212.**)

[10] From **prōsternō.**

| | | | | |
|---|---|---|---|---|
| PERF. *I have been able, could, etc.* | | | | |
| | **potuī** | **potuimus** | **potuerim** | **potuerīmus** |
| PLUP. *I had been able, could have, etc.* | | | | |
| | **potueram** | **potuerāmus** | **potuissem** | **potuissēmus** |
| FUT. PERF. *I shall have been able, etc.* | | | | |
| | **potuerō** | **potuerīmus** | | |

INFINITIVE.

PRES. **posse,** *to be able.* PERF. **potuisse,** *to have been able.*

**293. Prōsum, prōdesse, prōfuī, ——,** *benefit.*

**Prōsum** is compounded of **prōd** (old form of **prō**), *for,* and **sum.** The *d* of **prōd** is retained before *e.*

| | INDICATIVE. | | SUBJUNCTIVE. | |
|---|---|---|---|---|
| | SINGULAR. | PLURAL. | SINGULAR. | PLURAL. |
| PRES. *I benefit, etc.* | | | | |
| | **prō-sum** | **prō-sumus** | **prō-sim** | **prō-sīmus** |
| | **prōd-es** | **prōd-estis** | **prō-sīs** | **prō-sītis** |
| | **prōd-est** | **prō-sunt** | **prō-sit** | **prō-sint** |
| IMP. | **prōd-eram** | **prōd-erāmus** | **prōd-essem** | **prōd-essēmus** |
| FUT. | **prōd-erō** | **prōd-erimus** | | |
| PERF. | **prō-fuī** | **prō-fuimus** | **prō-fuerim** | **prō-fuerimus** |
| PLUP. | **prō-fueram** | **prō-fuerāmus** | **prō-fuissem** | **prō-fuissēmus** |
| F. P. | **prō-fuerō** | **prō-fuerīmus** | | |

IMPERATIVE.

PRES. **prōd-es, prōd-este** FUT. **prōd-estō, prōd-estōte**

INFINITIVE.

PRES. **prōd-esse** PERF. **prō-fuisse**
Fut. **prō-futūrus esse**

PARTICIPLE.

FUT. **prō-futūrus**

The other compounds of **sum** are inflected like the simple verb.

**294.** Learn the tenses of the indicative, imperative, and infinitive of **possum** and **prōsum.**

**295.** RULE OF SYNTAX.—**The compounds of *sum*, except *possum* and *absum*, all take the dative; but *insum* is often followed by *in* with the ablative, and *intersum* by *inter* with the accusative.**

## 2.

**296.** EXERCISES.

I. 1. In vērā amīcitiā māgnum inest praesidium. 2. Amīcus vērus adest amīcō, neque deerit in perīculō. 3. Amīcō prōdesse dulce est, amīcō deesse turpe. 4. Amīcus fīdus nōn aberit ab amīcō in cāsibus fortūnae. 5. Mōrēs malī amīcitiae obsunt; inter hominēs malōs vēra amīcitia nōn interest. 6. Cicerō cōnsul reī pūblicae praefuit. 7. Multae epistulae Cicerōnis et ējus amīcōrum supersunt. 8. Virī praestantēs Athēniēnsibus nūllō tempore dēfuērunt. 9. Mōrēs tyrannī sibi[1] amīcōs parāre nōn poterant. 10. Nōn omnēs hominēs rēgēs esse possunt.

II. 1. Cornelia was able to train her sons wisely. 2. All can be good citizens.[2] 3. Hannibal was not able to take the city. 4. In Hannibal there was great cunning and bravery. 5. Hannibal was long absent from his own country. 6. He commanded armies in Spain and Italy. 7. He was present at many battles, and was the terror[3] of the Romans. 8. He benefited his country in many ways.[4] 9. But his enemies in his own land injured him. 10. Scipio defeated him in battle[5] in Africa. 11. He survived this defeat many years.[6] 12. His name will never lack renown.[7]

---

[1] *For him.*

[2] See **47.**

[3] Compare **auxiliō, 291,** first line, and note.

[4] *Ways* = *things.* See **259, 260.**

[5] Ablative without **in.**

[6] Accusative.

[7] *Renown will never be wanting to his name.*

**297.** VOCABULARY.

**ab-sum, -esse, āfuī,** *be away, absent* (**ā** or **ab** w. abl.).
**ad-sum, -esse, -fuī** (also **affuī**), *be present, stand by, side with.*
**dē-sum, -esse, -fuī,** *be wanting, lack.*
**in-sum, -esse, -fuī,** *be in, among.*
**inter-sum, -esse, -fuī,** *be present at, among.*
**ob-sum, -esse, -fuī,** *be against, opposed to, injure.*
**possum, posse, potuī,** *be able, can.*
**prae-sum, -esse, -fuī,** *be before, at the head of, command.*
**prō-sum, prōd-esse, prō-fuī,** *be useful, benefit.*
**super-sum, -esse, -fuī,** *remain over, survive, exist.*

**calliditās, -ātis,** F. [**callidus**], *shrewdness, cunning.*
**cāsus, -ūs,** M. [**cadō,** *fall*], *falling down, mischance, misfortune.*
**clādēs, -is,** F., *destruction, defeat.*
**diū,** adv., *long, a long time.*
**dulcis, -e,** adj., *sweet, pleasant.* Cf. **suāvis.**
**fāma, -ae,** F., *rumor, fame, renown.*
**ne-que,** conj., *and not, nor;* **neque . . . neque,** *neither . . . nor.*
**parō,** 1, *make ready, prepare, get.*
**patria, -ae,** F., *native land, country.*
**praesidium, -ī,** N. [**prae, sedeō**], *defence, help, garrison.*
**praestāns, -tis,** adj. [**prae-stō,** *stand before*], *pre-eminent, distinguished.*

# CHAPTER XLV. 1.

## DEPONENT VERBS.

### First and Second Conjugations.

**298.** Deponent verbs have the forms of the passive voice with the meaning of the active. There are deponents of each of the four regular conjugations:

**Admīrāmur opera Deī,** *we admire the works of God.*
**Miserōs tuēbimur,** *we shall protect the wretched.*
**Audī multa, loquere pauca,** *listen much, say little.*
**Caesar prōvinciam sortītus est,** *Cæsar obtained* (*by lot*) *a province.*

**299.** Review the passive indicative, imperative, and infinitive of **amō** and **moneō**.

The principal parts of deponent verbs are thus given:

**admīror, admīrārī, admīrātus** (**sum**).
**tueor, tuērī, tuitus** (**sum**).
**loquor, loquī, locūtus** (**sum**).
**sortior, sortīrī, sortītus** (**sum**).

**300.** EXERCISES.

I. 1. Admīrāmur māgnitūdinem caelī. Quis nōn admīrābitur? 2. Nocte contemplāmur sīdera. 3. Pars vagātur certīs cursibus, plūrima nōn vagantur. 4. Sōl dominātur inter stellās. 5. Terram lūna comitātur ūna, Jovis stellam lūnae comitantur quattuor. 6. Dārēus Alexandrō māgnam Asiae partem pollicitus est. 7. Improbī sunt iī quī nēminem verentur. 8. Homo facinus cōnfessus est. 9. Comitēs quī salūtem rēgis tuitī erant, māximum praemium accēpērunt.

II. 1. Who does not admire the beauty of the stars? 2. Other nations accompanied the Cimbri across the Rhine. 3. They wandered far[1] and wide[1] through Gaul and Spain. 4. The Romans wondered at the great bodies of the Germans. 5. Certain animals imitate human voices. 6. We were contemplating that beautiful likeness. 7. The general promised the soldiers[2] a great reward. 8. He[3] is a bad man who does not respect any one.[4] 9. Children respect their parents, slaves fear their master.

**301.** VOCABULARY.

**ad-mīror,** 1, *wonder at, admire.*
**Alexander, -drī,** M., *Alexander,* king of Macedon.
**beneficium, -ī,** N., *benefit, favor.*
**caelum, -ī,** N., *sky, heavens.*
**Cimbrī, -ōrum,** M., *Cimbri,* a German tribe.
**comitor,** 1 [**comes, -itis**], *accompany, attend.*
**cōn-fiteor,** 2, **-fessus,** *confess.*

---

[1] **Longē lātēque.**
[2] Not accusative.
[3] **Is.**
[4] *Not any one = no one.*

**contemplor,** 1, *look at, observe.*
**cursus, -ūs,** M. [**currō,** *run*], *running, course.*
**Dārēus, -ī,** M., *Darius,* Persian king.
**dominor,** 1 [**dominus**], *be a lord and master, rule.*
**facinus, -ŏris,** N. [**faciō**], *deed, crime.* Cf. **scelus.**
**Germānus, -a, -um,** adj., *German.*
**imitor,** 1, *imitate.*
**māgnitūdō, -inis,** F. [**māgnus**], *greatness.*
**mereor,** 2, *be worthy of, deserve.*
**per,** prep. w. acc., *through, by.*
**polliceor,** 2, *promise.*
**pulchritūdō, -inis,** F. [**pulcher**], *beauty.*
**stella, -ae,** F., *star.*
**tueor,** 2, **tuitus** and **tūtus,** *watch, defend.* Cf. **dēfendō.**
**vagor,** 1, *go to and fro, wander.*
**vastō,** 1, *lay waste, ravage.*
**vereor,** 2, *reverence, respect.*

**sīdus (286),** *a star, a great star, a constellation.*
**stella,** *a star* as a bright heavenly body.

## 2.

**302.** COLLOQUIUM.

### Pater et Fīliolus.

*P.* Ades, mī fīliole, et mihi libellum ostentā.
(Ades: come here; libellum: little book; ostentā: show)

*F.* Eccum, cāre pater, sī libellum Latīnum vidēre cupis.
(Eccum: here it is; cupis: wish)

*P.* Quod pēnsum tibi hodiē imperāvit praeceptor?
(imperāvit: impose)

*F.* Pēnsum verbōrum dēpōnentium quae ad conjugātiōnem prīmam atque secundam pertinent.
(dēpōnentium: deponent; pertinent: belong)

*P.* Quam ob rem sīc appellantur ista verba?
(appellantur: name)

*F.* Quia formam actīvam et sīgnificātiōnem passīvam plērumque dēposuērunt. Sīc nōs praeceptor docuit.
(formam: form; sīgnificātiōnem: meaning; plērumque: generally; dēposuērunt: lay aside)

*P.* Quod autem pēnsum in crāstinum diem imperāvit praeceptor?
(in: for; crāstinum: to-morrow)

*F.* Ad haec addidit praeceptor alia dēpōnentia. At tū, mī pater, Latīnae linguae jam puer studēbās?
(addidit: add; At: but)

*P.* Certē, fīliole, idque vehementer.
right hard

*F.* Num ego, sī dīligenter didicerō, ērudītus, ut tū, fīam?
learn learned as become

*P.* Procul dubiō. At jam tibi eundum est dormītum.
you must go to bed

## CHAPTER XLVI. 1.

### DEPONENT VERBS.

### THIRD AND FOURTH CONJUGATIONS.

**303.** *Examine the following:—*

1. **Ūtor vestrā benīgnitāte,** *I avail myself of (use) your kindness.*
2. **Abūtitur patientiā nostrā,** *he abuses our patience.*
3. **Lūx quā fruimur ā Deō nōbīs datur,** *the light which we enjoy is given us by God.*
4. **Fungor vice cōtis,** *I serve as (discharge the office of) a whetstone.*
5. **Māgnā praedā potītus est,** *he got great booty.*
6. **Lacte et carne vescēbantur,** *they lived upon milk and flesh.*

Compare the translation of the examples with the Latin. Observe that the direct object of the verb, or of the preposition closely connected with the verb in English, is represented in Latin by the ablative case.

**304.** RULE OF SYNTAX.—**The deponents *ūtor, fruor, fungor, potior, vescor,* and their compounds, take the ablative.**

**305.** *Examine the following:—*

1. **Meminit praeteritōrum,** *he remembers the past.*
2. **Haec ōlim meminisse juvābit,** *to remember these things will one day give pleasure.*

3. **Tōtam causam oblītus est,** *he forgot the whole case.*
4. **Tōtīus causae oblītus est,** *he forgot the whole case.*

Observe that in the above examples the genitive is used in 1 and 4, the accusative in 2 and 3.

**306.** RULE OF SYNTAX. — **Verbs of *remembering* and *forgetting* take the genitive or accusative.**

1. Neuter pronouns and adjectives are commonly put in the accusative. **Recordor** regularly takes the accusative.

**307.** Review the passive indicative, imperative, and infinitive of **regō** and **audiō**.

**308.** EXERCISES.

I. 1. Sūlla urbem Rōmam armātus ingressus est. 2. Athēniēnsium dux māximam adeptus est glōriam. 3. Alexander Māgnus in Asiam profectus est. 4. Eum multī et nōbilēs virī secūtī sunt. 5. Quās injūriās passus es oblīviscere.[1] 6. Beneficia quae accēpimus nōn oblīviscēmur. 7. Quod beneficium accēpit id oblīviscitur. 8. Omnia patī[2] discimus. 9. Cicerō māgnā cum glōriā cōnsulātū fūnctus est. 10. Lūx quā fruimur dōnum est Deī.

II. 1. Alexander and his companions entered Asia. 2. They suffered both[3] hunger and thirst. 3. He obtained great glory by his victories. 4. He did not forget the words of his master. 5. For he had been the pupil of a wise man. 6. The soldiers follow their general. 7. They[4] are bad men who forget benefits. 8. We can learn to endure all things. 9. Who does not enjoy the light which is given us by God? 10. The boys faithfully discharged their duty.

2.

**309.** EXERCISES.

I. 1. Caesar, Pompējus, Crassus, imperium inter sē partītī sunt. 2. Caesar Galliam prōvinciam sortītus est. 3. Sae-

[1] Imperative.
[2] Present infinitive of **patior**.
[3] **Et.**
[4] **Iī.** See **270**. 2.

pissimē bellī fortūnam expertus est. 4. Posteā tōtā Ītaliā potītus est. 5. Patrēs bona sua cum līberīs partiuntur. 6. Multa in Ītaliā bella orta sunt. 7. Frōns, oculī, vultus, saepe mentiuntur. 8. Quī post mortem Alexandrī rēgnō illīus potītī sunt? 9. Optimē scīmus quod expertī sumus.

II. 1. Soldiers often try the fortune of war. 2. The leaders had divided among themselves the property[1] of the enemy. 3. The Rhone rises not far from the sources of the Rhine. 4. The Rhine, which rises in the Alps, flows into the ocean. 5. The best friends share perils with friends. 6. Who possessed the kingdom after Alexander? 7. We will make trial of our valor. 8. They got possession of the camp of the enemy. 9. Who gets by lot Sicily (as) his province?[2]

**310.** VOCABULARY.

**adipiscor**, 3, **adeptus**, *get, obtain.* Cf. **potior.**
**castra**, **-ōrum**, N. (pl.), *camp.*
**Crassus**, **-ī**, M., *Crassus*, a rich Roman, contemporary of Cæsar.
**ex-perior**, 4, **expertus**, *make trial of, test.*
**frōns**, **frontis**, F., *brow, forehead.*
**fruor**, 3, **fruitus** and **frūctus**, *enjoy.*
**fungor**, 3, **fūnctus**, *perform, discharge.*
**imperium**, **-ī**, N. [**imperō**], *command, authority, power.*
**in-gredior**, 3, **gressus** [**gradior**], *enter.*
**mentior**, 4, *lie, deceive.*
**oblīviscor**, 3, **oblītus**, *forget.*
**ōceanus**, **-ī**, M., *ocean.*
**officium**, **-ī**, N., *duty.*
**optimē**, adv., *most excellently, best.*
**orior**, 4, **ortus**, *rise, appear, begin.*
**partior**, 4 [**pars**], *divide, share.*
**patior**, 3, **passus**, *bear, suffer.*
**Pompējus**, **-ēi**, M., *Pompey*, a celebrated Roman general.
**posteā**, adv., *afterwards.*
**potior**, 4, *become master of, get.* Cf. **adipiscor.**
**proficiscor**, 3, **-fectus**, *set out, march.*
**prōvincia**, **-ae**, F., *province.*
**sequor**, 3, **secūtus**, *follow.*
**sortior**, 4, *draw lots, obtain by lot.*
**Sūlla**, **-ae**, M., *Sulla*, a Roman general and statesman.

[1] Compare I. 5. [2] Predicate accusative.

# CHAPTER XLVII. 1.

## 311. NUMERALS.

| | CARDINALS. | ORDINALS. |
|---|---|---|
| 1. | ūnus, -a, -um | prīmus, -a, -um |
| 2. | duo, duae, duo | secundus (*or* alter) |
| 3. | trēs, tria | tertius |
| 4. | quattuor | quartus |
| 5. | quīnque | quīntus |
| 6. | sex | sextus |
| 7. | septem | septimus |
| 8. | octō | octāvus |
| 9. | novem | nōnus |
| 10. | decem | decimus |
| 11. | ūndecim | ūndecimus |
| 12. | duodecim | duodecimus |
| 13. | tredecim | tertius decimus |
| 14. | quattuordecim | quartus decimus |
| 15. | quīndecim | quīntus decimus |
| 16. | sēdecim, *or* sexdecim | sextus decimus |
| 17. | septendecim | septimus decimus |
| 18. | duodēvīgintī [1] | duodēvīcēsimus |
| 19. | ūndēvīgintī [1] | ūndēvīcēsimus |
| 20. | vīgintī | vīcēsimus |
| 21. | vīgintī ūnus, *or* ūnus et vīgintī | vīcēsimus prīmus, *or* ūnus et vīcēsimus |
| 22. | vīgintī duo, *or* duo et vīgintī | vīcēsimus secundus, *or* alter et vīcēsimus |
| 28. | duodētrīgintā [1] | duodētrīcēsimus |
| 29. | ūndētrīgintā [1] | ūndētrīcēsimus |
| 30. | trīgintā | trīcēsimus |
| 40. | quadrāgintā | quadrāgēsimus |
| 50. | quīnquāgintā | quīnquāgēsimus |
| 60. | sexāgintā | sexāgēsimus |
| 70. | septuāgintā | septuāgēsimus |

[1] **Duodēvīgintī** = *two from twenty*; **ūndēvīgintī** = **ūnus dē vīgintī**, *one from twenty*. Similarly are formed 28, 29, 38, 39, etc.

| | CARDINALS. | ORDINALS. |
| --- | --- | --- |
| 80. | octōgintā | octōgēsimus |
| 90. | nōnāgintā | nōnāgēsimus |
| 100. | centum | centēsimus |
| 101. | centum ūnus, *or* centum et ūnus | centēsimus prīmus, *or* centēsimus et prīmus |
| 200. | ducentī, -ae, -a | ducentēsimus |
| 300. | trecentī | trecentēsimus |
| 400. | quadringentī | quadringentēsimus |
| 500. | quīngentī | quīngentēsimus |
| 600. | sēscentī | sēscentēsimus |
| 700. | septingentī | septingentēsimus |
| 800. | octingentī | octingentēsimus |
| 900. | nōngentī | nōngentēsimus |
| 1,000. | mīlle | mīllēsimus |
| 2,000. | duo mīlia | bis mīllēsimus |
| 100,000. | centum mīlia | centiēs mīllēsimus |

1. Cardinal numbers answer the question *how many?* Ordinals, *which in order?*

2. The cardinals from **quattuor** to **centum**, inclusive, are indeclinable: **quattuor hominēs**, *four men;* **quattuor hominum**, *of four men.*

3. **Ūnus** is declined like **bonus**, except that it has genitive and dative singular **ūnīus**, **ūnī**, like **alius** (**201**).

4. **Duo** and **trēs** are thus declined:

| | MASC. | FEM. | NEUT. | M. & F. | NEUT. |
| --- | --- | --- | --- | --- | --- |
| N. | **duo** | **duae** | **duo** | **trēs** | **tria** |
| G. | **duōrum** | **duārum** | **duōrum** | **trium** | **trium** |
| D. | **duōbus** | **duābus** | **duōbus** | **tribus** | **tribus** |
| Ac. | **duōs, duo** | **duās** | **duo** | **trēs** | **tria** |
| Ab. | **duōbus** | **duābus** | **duōbus** | **tribus** | **tribus** |

5. The hundreds, **ducentī**, etc., are declined like the plural of **bonus**.

6. **Mīlle** is indeclinable in the singular, and is sometimes an adjective and sometimes a noun: **mīlle hominēs**, *a thousand men;* **mīlle hominum**, *a thousand (of) men.* The plural has the forms **mīlia**, **mīlium**, **mīlibus**, and is always a noun: **tria mīlia hominum**, *three thousand men (three thousands of men).*

7. The ordinals are declined like **bonus.**

8. Other kinds of numerals are the distributives: **singulī, -ae, -a,** *one each,* **bīnī, -ae, -a,** *two each,* etc.; and the numeral adverbs: **semel,** *once,* **bis,** *twice,* etc.

**312.** *Examine the following:* —

1. **Decem annōs Trōja oppūgnābātur,** *Troy was besieged for ten years.*
2. **Turris alta est centum pedēs,** *the tower is a hundred feet high.*

The accusative **annōs** denotes duration or extent of *time;* **pedēs,** extent of *space.* The accusative, then, is used to answer the question *how long?* or *how far?* (in *time* or *space*), and may be called the **Accusative of Extent.**

**313.** RULE OF SYNTAX. — **Extent of *time* or *space* is expressed by the accusative.**

2.

**314.** EXERCISES.

I. 1. Homo ūnum ōs, duās aurēs, duōs oculōs habet. 2. Alexander Māgnus tredecim annōs rēgnāvit. 3. Templum Diānae quadringentōs quīnquāgintā pedēs longum et ducentōs vīgintī pedēs lātum erat. 4. Annus spatium trecentōrum sexāgintā quīnque diērum est. 5. Duodecim sunt mēnsēs. 6. Mēnsis trīgintā diēs habet, Februārius duodētrīgintā. 7. Diēs vīgintī quattuor hōrās habet. 8. Rōmānōrum veterum annus decem mēnsēs habēbat; Mārtius erat prīmus, December decimus. 9. Aut tertius decimus aut quīntus decimus diēs mēnsis Īdūs nōminābātur.

II. 1. Romulus, the first king of Rome, reigned thirty-seven years. 2. This house is fifty-nine[1] feet long and forty-eight feet wide. 3. The river is fourteen feet deep and ninety-two feet wide. 4. With[2] the ancient Romans September was the seventh month; with us September is the ninth month. 5. The Roman consuls held power for one year.

[1] See p. 143, note. [2] **Apud,** with accusative.

6. In the five hundred and fiftieth year of the city Scipio was consul. 7. Five and twenty languages were known to King Mithridates. 8. In the first month of the year there are thirty-one days. 9. A Roman legion had five thousand foot-soldiers and three hundred horse-soldiers.

**315.** VOCABULARY.

**annus, -ī,** M., *year.*
**auris, -is,** F., *ear.*
**December, -bris,** M. [**decem**], *December.* Often as adj.
**Diāna, -ae,** F., *Diana,* goddess of the chase. [as adj.
**Februārius, -ī,** M., *February.* Oft.
**Īdūs, -uum,** F., plur., *the Ides of the month.* (**244**. 1.)
**lingua, -ae,** F., *tongue, language.*
**Mārtius, -ī,** M. [**Mārs**], *March.* Often as adj.
**Mithridātēs, -is,** M., *Mithridates,* king of Pontus.
**ōs, ōris,** N., *mouth, face.*
**September, -bris,** M. [**septem**], *September.* Often as adj.
**spatium, -ī,** N., *room, space, period.*

## CHAPTER XLVIII. 1.

**316.** IRREGULAR VERBS.

**Volō, velle, voluī,** ——, *be willing, will, wish.*
**Nōlō, nōlle, nōluī,** ——, *be unwilling, will not.*
**Mālō, mālle, māluī,** ——, *be more willing, prefer.*

INDICATIVE.

| | | | |
|---|---|---|---|
| Pres. | **volō** | **nōlō** | **mālō** |
| | **vīs** | **nōn vīs** | **māvīs** |
| | **vult** | **nōn vult** | **māvult** |
| | **volumus** | **nōlumus** | **mālumus** |
| | **vultis** | **nōn vultis** | **māvultis** |
| | **volunt** | **nōlunt** | **mālunt** |
| Imper. | **volēbam** | **nōlēbam** | **mālēbam** |
| Fut. | **volam** | **nōlam** | **mālam** |
| Perf. | **voluī** | **nōluī** | **māluī** |
| Plup. | **volueram** | **nōlueram** | **mālueram** |
| F. P. | **voluerō** | **nōluerō** | **māluerō** |

SUBJUNCTIVE.

| | | | |
|---|---|---|---|
| Pres. | **velim** | **nōlim** | **mālim** |
| | **velīs** | **nōlīs** | **mālīs** |
| | **velit** | **nōlit** | **mālit** |
| | **velīmus** | **nōlīmus** | **mālīmus** |
| | **velītis** | **nōlītis** | **mālītis** |
| | **velint** | **nōlint** | **mālint** |
| Imper. | **vellem** | **nōllem** | **māllem** |
| | **vellēs** | **nōllēs** | **māllēs** |
| | **vellet** | **nōllet** | **māllet** |
| | **vellēmus** | **nōllēmus** | **māllēmus** |
| | **vellētis** | **nōllētis** | **māllētis** |
| | **vellent** | **nōllent** | **māllent** |
| Perf. | **voluerim** | **nōluerim** | **māluerim** |
| Plup. | **voluissem** | **nōluissem** | **māluissem** |

IMPERATIVE.

| | | | |
|---|---|---|---|
| Pres. | (*Wanting*) | **nōlī**<br>**nōlīte** | (*Wanting*) |
| Fut. | (*Wanting*) | [**nōlītō**, etc.] | (*Wanting*) |

INFINITIVE.

| | | | |
|---|---|---|---|
| Pres. | **velle** | **nōlle** | **mālle** |
| Perf. | **voluisse** | **nōluisse** | **māluisse** |

PARTICIPLE.

| | | | |
|---|---|---|---|
| Pres. | **volēns** | **nōlēns** | (*Wanting*) |

**317.** Learn the tenses of the indicative and infinitive of **volō**, **ōlō**, and **mālō**, and the present imperative of **nōlō**.

## 2.

**318.** EXERCISES.

I. 1. Nōs scrībere volumus, tū vīs legere, ille puer lūdere ult. 2. Cūr in hortō ambulāre volunt? 3. In hortō ambuire mālunt quod ibi sunt fontēs et arborēs. 4. Volēbantne itia sua excūsāre? 5. Nōlī excūsāre vitia tua. 6. Nōlīte oblīviscī praeceptōrum[1] parentum. 7. Tīmoleōn māluit dīligī quam metuī. 8. Valēre māluerat quam dīves esse. 9. Aliēna quisque vitia reprehendere māvult quam sua corrigere. 10. Volumus ad fīnem itineris prōgredī.

II. 1. Why would you rather read than write? 2. We would rather walk in the fields with you. 3. Who would not rather be praised than blamed? 4. They will be unwilling to accept your gift. 5. Do not forget,[2] boys, the precepts of your teacher. 6. Do not forget, my boy, the lesson which I have explained. 7. He listened because he wished to learn. 8. He would not[3] blame another's fault; he greatly desired to correct his own. 9. We wish the same (things) as[4] you. 10. Our friends will wish the same (thing) as ourselves.

**319.** VOCABULARY.

**aliēnus, -a, -um,** adj. [**alius**], *belonging to another, another's.*
**ambulō,** 1, *walk, take a walk.*
**corrigō,** 3, **-rēxi, -rēctum** [**com, regō,** *keep straight*], *make straight, reform, correct.*
**dīligō,** 3, **-lēxi, -lēctum** [**dis,** *apart,* **legō,** *choose*], *esteem, love.* Cf. **amō.**
**ex-cūsō,** 1 [**causa**], *excuse.*
**ex-plicō,** 1, **-āvī, -ātum,** and **-uī, -itum** [**plicō**], *unfold, explain.*
**ibi,** adv., *there.* Cf. **ubi,** *where.*
**iter, itineris,** N. [**eō, 327.** 1], *journey.* (**262.**)
**lūdō,** 3, **lūsī, lūsum,** *play.*
**mālō, mālle, māluī,** —— [**magis, volō**], *wish rather, prefer, would rather.*
**māximē,** adv. (sup. of **magis,** *more*), *most, especially, greatly.*
**metuō,** 3, **-uī, -ūtum** [**metus**], *fear.* Cf. **timeō.**
**nōlō, nōlle, nōluī,** —— [**nōn, volō**], *be unwilling, will not, not wish.*
**praeceptum, -ī,** N. [**praecipiō**], *maxim, precept.*
**prō-gredior,** 3, **-gressus** [**gradior**], *go forward.*
**quod,** conj., *because.* Cf. **quia.**
**re-prehendō,** 3, **-dī, -hēnsum,** *hold back, restrain, reprove.*
**Tīmoleōn, -ontis,** M., *Timoleon,* a Corinthian.
**valeō,** 2, **-uī, -itum,** *be strong* or *well.*
**vitium, -ī,** N., *fault, blemish, vice.*
**volō, velle, voluī,** ——, *be willing, will, wish, desire.* Cf. **dēsīderō.**

[1] From **praeceptum.**
[2] Cf. I. 6.
[3] *Was unwilling.*
[4] See p. 128, note 5.

**amō,** *love,* not implying and not excluding *esteem;* the common word.

**dīligō,** *love* unselfishly and with esteem; more restricted in meaning than **amō.**

**volō** means both less and more than *wish,* namely, *consent* and *will;* very much used.

**dēsīderō** means *wish ardently,* with the notion (which **volō** has not) of *lacking* or *missing* the thing much desired; more restricted in meaning than **volō.**

3.

**320.** FOR TRANSLATION.

Multī hominēs volunt quidem rēctē facere, sed nōn faciunt; nam velle et facere nōn idem est. Saepe homo rēctē agere vult, sed vīrēs dēsunt. Multī peccāta sua excūsāre quam dēpōnere mālunt. Saepe aliēna peccāta vituperāre quam nostra corrigere mālumus. Multī suā sorte nōn sunt contentī, sed aliēna appetere mālunt. At cūr nōn fēlīciter vīvere māvīs? Fēlīx is est quī rēctē agere vult rēctēque agit.

## CHAPTER XLIX. 1.

### 321. THE IRREGULAR VERB **Ferō.**

**Ferō, ferre, tulī, lātum:** *bear, carry, endure.*

INDICATIVE.

| | ACTIVE. | | PASSIVE. | |
|---|---|---|---|---|
| PRES. | **ferō** | **ferimus** | **feror** | **ferimur** |
| | **fers** | **fertis** | **ferris,** *or* **-re** | **feriminī** |
| | **fert** | **ferunt** | **fertur** | **feruntur** |
| IMPER. | **ferēbam** | | **ferēbar** | |
| FUT. | **feram** | | **ferar** | |
| PERF. | **tulī** | | **lātus sum** | |
| PLUP. | **tuleram** | | **lātus eram** | |
| F. P. | **tulerō** | | **lātus erō** | |

SUBJUNCTIVE.

| | ACTIVE. | PASSIVE. |
|---|---|---|
| PRES. | **feram** | **ferar** |
| IMPER. | **ferrem** | **ferrer** |
| PERF. | **tulerim** | **lātus sim** |
| PLUP. | **tulissem** | **lātus essem** |

### IMPERATIVE.

| | ACTIVE. | | PASSIVE. | |
|---|---|---|---|---|
| PRES. | **fer**[1] | **ferte** | **[ferre]** | **feriminī** |
| FUT. | **fertō** | **fertōte** | **fertor** | |
| | **fertō** | **feruntō** | **fertor** | **feruntor** |

### INFINITIVE.

| | | |
|---|---|---|
| PRES. | **ferre** | **ferrī** |
| PERF. | **tulisse** | **lātus esse** |
| FUT. | **lātūrus esse** | **lātum īrī** |

### PARTICIPLES.

| | | | |
|---|---|---|---|
| PRES. | **ferēns** | | ——— |
| FUT. | **lātūrus** | GER. | **ferendus** |
| | ——— | PERF. | **lātus** |

### GERUND.

G. **ferendī**
D. **ferendō**
Ac. **ferendum**
Ab. **ferendō**

### SUPINE.

Ac. **lātum** Ab. **lātū**

**322.** Compounds of **ferō** are conjugated like the simple verb. Observe the changes suffered by certain of the prepositions in the following:

| | |
|---|---|
| **ab-** | **auferō, auferre, abstulī, ablātum.** |
| **ad-** | **adferō, adferre, attulī, allātum (adl).** |
| **com-** | **cōnferō, cōnferre, contulī, collātum (conl).** |
| **dis-** | **differō, differre, distulī, dīlātum.** |
| **ex-** | **efferō, efferre, extulī, ēlātum.** |
| **in-** | **īnferō, īnferre, intulī, illātum (inl).** |
| **ob-** | **offerō, offerre, obtulī, oblātum.** |
| **sub-** | **sufferō, sufferre, sustulī, sublātum.** |

**323.** Learn the tenses of the indicative, the imperative, and the present and perfect infinitive, active and passive, of **ferō.**

[1] For **fere; dīcō, dūcō, faciō, ferō,** have imperative present second singular **dīc, dūc, fac, fer.**

**324.** EXERCISES.

I. 1. Aufert, aufertur. 2. Auferet, auferētur. 3. Abstulit, ablātus est. 4. Cōnferre, cōnferrī. 5. Cōnferunt, cōnferuntur. 6. Cōnferent, cōnferentur. 7. Contulerant, collātī erant. 8. Distulērunt, dīlātī sunt. 9. Distulerit, dīlātus erit. 10. Distulisse, dīlātus esse. 11. Differēbant, differēbantur.

II. 1. We bear, we are borne. 2. We were bearing, we were borne. 3. We have borne, we have been borne. 4. We shall bear, we shall be borne. 5. We had borne, we had been borne. 6. Bear thou, bear ye. 7. To offer, to be offered. 8. Ye shall offer, ye shall be offered. 9. To have offered, to have been offered. 10. Ye offer, ye will offer. 11. Ye are offered, ye will be offered.

2.

**325.** EXERCISES.

I. 1. Ferte patienter[1] labōrēs. 2. Bene ferre māgnam fortūnam disce. 3. Ferte patienter quae[2] mūtārī nōn possunt. 4. Nōn omnis ager quī seritur fert frūgēs. 5. Benīgnum rēgem nōn tulistis; jam ferum et barbarum fertōte. 6. Nōlīte differre pēnsum quod hodiē facere potestis. 7. Imperātor mīlitibus dēfessīs auxilium attulit. 8. In ūnum locum collātum est ex agrīs omne frūmentum. 9. Longa[3] nōbīs est omnis mora quae gaudia differt. 10. Caesar omnibus quī contrā sē arma tulerant veniam dedit.

II. 1. They bore labor with patience. 2. They did not endure a good king; now they are enduring a bad one.[4] 3. We cannot put off our tasks. 4. We shall learn to bear our good fortune well. 5. They bore with patience that[5] which they could not change. 6. The robbers bore off the

[1] What might be substituted for the adverb? See **144**, **145**.
[2] See p. 130, note 3. [3] *Tedious.* [4] Omit. [5] Id.

booty which they had seized. 7. Do not[1] bring me that which I do not want. 8. Delays which postpone our joy are always tedious. 9. The townsmen carried their all[2] with them out of the town.

**326.** VOCABULARY.

**ad-ferō (afferō), adferre, attulī, adlātum,** *bear to, bring.*
**au-ferō, auferre, abstulī, ablātum [ab(s)],** *bear off, carry away.*
**auxilium, -ī,** N., *help, aid.*
**barbarus, -a, -um,** adj., *foreign, barbarous.*
**benignus,-a,-um,** adj., *kind, good.*
**cōn-ferō, cōnferre, contulī, collātum (conlātum),** *bring together, collect;* **sē cōnferre,** *betake one's self.*
**dif-ferō, differre, distulī, dīlātum [dis,** *apart*], *bear apart, scatter, put off, postpone.*
**ef-ferō, efferre, extulī, ēlātum [ex],** *bear out, bring forth.*
**ferus, -a, -um,** adj., *wild, cruel.*
**frūgēs, -um,** F., plur., *fruits.*
**gaudium, -ī,** N. [**gaudeō,** *rejoice*], *joy, delight.*
**in-ferō, inferre, intulī, illātum (inlātum),** *bear in, cause;* **bellum inferre,** *to make war,* w. dat.
**jam,** adv., *already, now, at last.*
**mora, -ae,** F., *delay.*
**of-ferō, offerre, obtulī, oblātum [ob,** *before*], *present, offer.*
**patienter,** adv. [**patiēns**], *patiently, with patience.*
**serō,** 3, **sēvī, satum,** *sow, plant.*
**suf-fero, sufferre, sustulī, sublātum [sub],** *undergo, endure.*
**venia, -ae,** F., *indulgence, kindness, mercy.*

## CHAPTER L. 1.

### 327. IRREGULAR VERBS.

**Eō, īre, iī [īvī], itum,** *go.*
**Fīō, fierī, factus sum** (supplies pass. to **faciō**), *be made, become.*

INDICATIVE.

| | Eō. | | Fīō. | |
|---|---|---|---|---|
| PRES. | **eō** | **īmus** | **fīō** | **fīmus** |
| | **īs** | **ītis** | **fīs** | **fītis** |
| | **it** | **eunt** | **fit** | **fīunt** |

[1] Compare I. 6. [2] *Their all,* **omnia sua.**

| | Eō. | | Fīō. |
|---|---|---|---|
| IMPER. | **ībam** | | **fīēbam** |
| FUT. | **ībō** | | **fīam** |
| PERF. | **iī** | | **factus sum** |
| PLUP. | **ieram** | | **factus eram** |
| F. P. | **ierō** | | **factus erō** |

SUBJUNCTIVE.

| | | |
|---|---|---|
| PRES. | **eam** | **fīam** |
| IMPER. | **īrem** | **fierem** |
| PERF. | **ierim** | **factus sim** |
| PLUP. | **iissem** | **factus essem** |

IMPERATIVE.

| | | | | |
|---|---|---|---|---|
| PRES. | **ī** | **īte** | **fī** | **fīte** |
| FUT. | **ītō** | **ītōte** | | |
| | **ītō** | **euntō** | | |

INFINITIVE.

| | | |
|---|---|---|
| PRES. | **īre** | **fierī** |
| PERF. | **iisse** | **factus esse** |
| FUT. | **itūrus esse** | **factum īrī** |

PARTICIPLES.

| | | | |
|---|---|---|---|
| PRES. | **iēns**, Gen. **euntis** | | ——— |
| FUT. | **itūrus** | GER. | **faciendus** |
| | ——— | PERF. | **factus** |

GERUND.

G. **eundī**
D. **eundō**
Ac. **eundum**
Ab. **eundō**

SUPINE.

Ac. **itum** Ab. **itū**

1. The root of **eō**, namely *i*, is changed to *e* before a vowel, except in perf. plup. and fut. perf., and in nom. sing. of pres. part.
2. Compounds of **eō** generally form the perfect in *iī* instead of *īvī*. The simple verb rarely, if ever, has *īvī*, *īveram*, etc.
3. The *i* of **fīō** is long except when followed by *er*, and in **fit**.

**328.** Learn the tenses of the indicative, the imperative, and the present and perfect infinitive of **eō** and **fīō**.

**329.** EXERCISES.

I. 1. Nōlīte velle id quod fierī nōn potest. 2. Amīcī Alexandrī rēgēs factī sunt. 3. Nēmō nāscitur sapiēns, nēmō cāsū fit bonus. 4. Leve fīēbat onus, quod bene ferēbātur. 5. Apud veterēs Rōmānōs ex agricolīs fīēbant cōnsulēs. 6. Omnēs ferē[1] hominēs senectūte fīunt prūdentiōrēs. 7. Quīdam amnēs subeunt terram rūrsusque in terram redeunt. 8. Alpēs nēmō ante Hannibalem cum exercitū trānsiit. 9. Miltiadēs Parum īnsulam expūgnāre nōn potuit et in patriam rediit. 10. Populus solet nōn nunquam[2] dīgnōs praeterīre.

II. 1. That has been done which you wished. 2. My friends, you become wiser by old age. 3. Men never become good by chance. 4. Who will cross the river with me?[3] 5. The generals crossed the mountains with a large part[4] of their forces. 6. Light become the burdens that are patiently borne. 7. Our friends have gone away, but they will return. 8. The people passed by many worthy men. 9. The inhabitants of the city went out with their horses and wagons. 10. The generals return to[5] their country with prisoners and booty. 11. Do not[6] cross the very deep river.

2.

**330.** EXERCISES.

I. 1. Septiēs Marius, quī Cimbrōs et Teutonēs duōbus ācerrimīs proeliīs vīcit, cōnsul factus est. 2. Sōcratēs aequō animō diem suprēmum obiit. 3. Ariovistī cōpiae intrā annōs quattuordecim tectum nōn subierant. 4. Autumnō multae avēs in aliās terrās proficīscuntur, at vēre novō

[1] **Ferē** is often thus placed between an adjective and its noun.

[2] **Nōn nunquam,** *not never* = *sometimes.*

[3] See **265**. 3.

[4] See p. 21, note 1.

[5] *To* = *into.*

[6] See **318**. I. 5 and 6.

redeunt. 5. Abeunt omnia unde orta sunt. 6. Alexander cōnsiliō[1] fortitūdineque omnēs anteībat; omnēs labōrēs subībat.

II. 1. In winter[2] the days become shorter and the nights longer. 2. After the battle many perished of cold[3] and hunger. 3. Cicero was made consul[4] by the Romans. 4. By the prudence (*cōnsilium*) and valor of Scipio, Hannibal was compelled to return into Africa. 5. We ought to meet our last day with equanimity.[5] 6. Alexander came off victorious[6] from all his battles.

**331.** VOCABULARY.

**ab-eō, -īre, -iī, -itum,** *go off, come off, go away.* (**327.** 2.)

**aequus, -a, -um,** adj., *level, equal, calm.*

**ante-eō, -īre, -iī,** ——, *go before, surpass.*

**apud,** prep. with acc., *with, in, near, among.*

**Ariovistus, -ī,** M., *Ariovistus,* king of a German tribe.

**autumnus, -ī,** M., *autumn.*

**cōgō,** 3, **-ēgī, -āctum** [**com, agō**], *drive together; compel.*

**cōpia, -ae,** F., *power, abundance, wealth;* plur. *troops.*

**dēbeō,** 2, **-uī, -itum,** *owe, ought.*

**ex-eō, -īre, -iī, -itum,** *go out.*

**ferē,** adv., *nearly, for the most part.*

**intrā,** prep. with acc., *within.*

**Marius, -ī,** M., *Marius,* a famous Roman general.

**nāscor,** 3, **nātus,** *be born.*

**ob-eō, -īre, -iī, -itum,** *go towards, meet.*

**Parus, -ī,** F., *Paros,* an island in the Ægean Sea. (**11.** 4.)

**per-eō, -īre, -iī,** ——, *perish.*

**praeter-eō, -īre, -iī, -itum,** *go by, pass by, omit.*

**red-eō, -īre, -iī, -itum,** *go back.*

**re-ferō, -ferre, -tulī, -lātum,** *carry back.*

**rūrsus,** adv. [**re-vorsus, re-vertō**], *turned back, back, again.*

**septiēs,** num. adv. [**septem**], *seven times.*

**sub-eō, -īre, -iī, -itum,** *go under, enter, undergo.*

**tectum, -ī,** N. [**tegō,** *cover*], *covering, shelter, roof.*

**Teutonēs, -um,** M., *the Teutons,* a German tribe.

**trāns-eō, -īre, -iī, -itum,** *go over, cross.*

1 See **260.**

2 Compare I. 4.

3 Ablative.

4 Compare I. 1; also **47.**

5 Compare I. 2.

6 **Victor.**

3.

332. COLLOQUIUM.

TĪTYRUS ET MELIBOEUS.

*T.* Aliquis jānuam pulsat. Ī, puer, aperī jānuam.
door knock open

[*Meliboeus trīstī vultū passibus tardīs introit.*]
steps slow enter

Salvē, amīce, diū mē nōn adīstī. Cūr iste vultus trīstis?
how do you do

*M.* Ēheu! mī Tītyre, abeō ē meā patriā.

*T.* Cūr abīs? Quō abībis? Nōlī relinquere haec arva dulcia.
leave fields

*M.* Quid tibi vīs? Meōs agrōs mīlitibus impiīs dōnāvit
what would you have me do wicked has given
Octāviānus. Māgna pars gregum interiit. Ipse periī.
am undone

*T.* Minimē, amīce; adī ad Octāviānum; ille est benīgnus, neque vult tē perīre. Tū agrōs recipiēs.

*M.* Parvae spēs mihi sunt redeundī; tamen ībō, ut tū monēs; Octāviānō ad pedēs mē prōiciam.

*T.* Et redībis in agrōs tuōs; redībit pāx aurea. Valē, mī Meliboee, es bonō animō.
keep up your courage

*M.* Et tū valē, bone Tītyre.

## CHAPTER LI. 1.

### PREPOSITIONS.

**333.** Thus far several prepositions have been used in the exercises, some followed by the accusative and some by the ablative. These are the only cases in Latin that follow prepositions.

PREPOSITIONS FOLLOWED BY THE ABLATIVE.

| | |
|---|---|
| **ā (ab, abs)**, *away from, by.* | **ē (ex)**, *out of, from.* |
| **absque**, *without.* | **prae**, *before, in comparison with.* |
| **cōram**, *in presence of.* | **prō**, *before, for.* |
| **cum**, *with.* | **sine**, *without.* |
| **dē**, *from, concerning.* | **tenus**, *as far as, up to.* |

1. **In**, meaning *into, to, towards, for*, that is after verbs denoting *motion*, takes the accusative.

2. **In**, meaning *in, on, at*, that is after verbs denoting *rest*, takes the ablative. See **334**.

3. **Sub**, *under, up to*, after verbs of *motion*, takes the accusative; after verbs of *rest*, the ablative.

4. Remember that all prepositions except the ten mentioned, and **in** and **sub**, are followed by the accusative only.

## Expressions of Place.

**334.** *Examine the following:* —

1. **In oppidō**, *in the town.*
2. **In nāvī**, *on shipboard.*
3. **Ad montem**, *to the mountain.*
4. **Ex agrīs**, *from the fields.*
5. **In Ītaliā**, *in Italy.*
6. **In Ītaliam**, *to Italy.*
7. **Ex Ītaliā**, *from Italy.*
8. **Athēnīs**, *at (in) Athens.*
9. **Corinthī**, *at (in) Corinth.*
10. **Thūriīs**, *at (in) Thurii.*
11. **Carthāginī**, *at (in) Carthage.*
12. **Rōmae**, *at (in) Rome.*
13. **Rōmam**, *to Rome.*
14. **Rōmā**, *from Rome.*

Observe the ways of denoting the place *in, on, at, to, from* which. In English we always[1] use a preposition with the noun of *place*, as the examples show. So in Latin (see examples 1–7), except with names of towns.[2] For these a rule may be inferred from the examples 8–14.

**335.** Rule of Syntax. — **With names of towns —**

**1. The place *in* or *at* which is expressed by the locative.** (See **14. 2, 40, 175.**)

**2. The place *to* which, by the accusative without a preposition.**[3]

**3. The place *from* which, by the ablative without a preposition.**[4]

---

[1] Except in the case of the word *home*, after a verb of *motion.*

[2] Names of small islands are often treated like names of towns.

[3] This accusative may be called the **Accusative of Limit**, because it denotes the limit, or end, of motion.

[4] This ablative is the *ablative of separation.* (**128, 129, 130.**)

**336.** **Domus**, *home, house*, and **rūs**, *the country*, have the construction of names of towns:

| | |
|---|---|
| **domī**, *at home.* | **rūrī**, *in the country.* |
| **domum**, (*to*) *home.* | **rūs**, *to* (*into*) *the country.* |
| **domō**, *from home.* | **rūre**, *from the country.* |

## 2.

**337.** EXERCISES.

I. 1. Cōnsulēs in sēdem suam prōcēssēre.[1] 2. Porsena rēx īnfestō cum exercitū Rōmam vēnit. 3. Rōmānī ex agrīs in urbem dēmigrant. 4. Nova Rōmae dīgnitās creāta est, quae dictātūra appellāta est. 5. Tarquinius Cūmās sē contulit. 6. Missī sunt Rōmā ad Coriolānum ōrātōrēs dē pāce. 7. Is dē forō domum sē recipiēbat. 8. Erat quīdam Athēnīs quī sē sapientem profitēbātur. 9. Rēgulus in Āfricam trājēcit. 10. Deinde Rōmam missus est, sed mox Carthāginem rediit. 11. Rōmā missī sunt Carthāginem lēgātī. 12. Rōmānī duās clādēs in Hispāniā accēpērunt. 13. Tunc Scīpiō ex Siciliā in Āfricam profectus est. 14. Hannibal ex angustiīs ēvāsit.

II. 1. The consul set out from Rome with a large army. 2. We have removed from the city into the country. 3. Then the general retreated[2] into Campania. 4. I have lived in Athens three years.[3] 5. Tarquin remained at Cumæ a long time. 6. Scipio defeated Hannibal at Zama. 7. Regulus returned from Africa to Rome. 8. Afterwards he was sent back from Rome to Carthage. 9. Cæsar carried on war in Gaul eight years.[3] 10. Cicero was born at Arpinum. 11. The consul proceeded to Athens with his army. 12. From Athens he sailed[4] to Italy. 13. Do you remain (*imperative*) at home; I will return to the army. 14. Shall you come home soon?

[1] From **prōcēdō**, perfect tense.
[2] **Sē recipere.**
[3] See **313**.
[4] See **272**. II. 6.

**338.** VOCABULARY.

**angustiae, -ārum,** F., plur. [**angustus,** *narrow*], *narrow pass.* Cf. Eng. *narrows.*

**appellō,** 1, *address, call, name.*

**Arpīnum, -ī,** N., *Arpinum,* a town in Italy.

**Athēnae, -ārum,** F. plur., *Athens.*

**Carthāgō, -inis,** F., *Carthage,* a city in Africa.

**Coriolānus, -ī,** M., *a surname of C. Marcius,* a Roman consul.

**Cūmae, -ārum,** F. plur., *Cumæ,* a town in Campania.

**dē-migrō,** 1, *emigrate, remove.*

**dictātūra, -ae,** F. [**dictātor**], *office of dictator, dictatorship.*

**dignitās, -ātis,** F. [**dignus,** *worthy*], *worth, dignity, office.*

**ē-vādō,** 3, **ēvāsī, ēvāsum,** *go forth, escape.*

**īnfestus, -a, -um,** adj., *hostile, troublesome, dangerous.*

**ōrātor, -ōris,** M. [**ōrō,** *speak, plead*], *orator, ambassador.*

**Porsena, -ae,** M., *Porsena,* an Etruscan king.

**pro-fiteor,** 2, **-fessus** [**fateor**], *acknowledge, confess, declare.*

**re-mittō,** 3, **-mīsī, -missum,** *send back.*

**sēdēs, -is,** F. [**sedeō,** *sit*], *seat, abode.*

**Tarquinius, -ī,** M., *Tarquin,* a Roman king.

**trā-iciō,** 3, **-jēcī, -jectum** [**trāns, jaciō**], *throw across, pass over, cross.*

**tum,** adv., *then, at that time.*

**Zama, -ae,** F., *Zama,* a town in Africa.

3.

**339.** FOR TRANSLATION.

THE BATTLE OF CANNÆ, B.C. 216.

Hannibal in Āpūliam pervēnerat. Adversus eum Rōmā profectī sunt duo cōnsulēs, Aemilius Paullus et Terentius Varrō. Paullō[1] cunctātiō Fabī[2] magis placēbat; Varrō autem, ferōx[3] et temerārius, ācriōra sequēbātur cōnsilia. Ambō cōnsulēs ad vīcum, quī Cannae appellābātur, castra commūnīvērunt. Ibi deinde Varrō invītō collēgā[4] aciem īnstrūxit et sīgnum pūgnae dedit. Hannibal autem ita cōnstituerat aciem, ut Rōmānīs[5] et[6] sōlis radiī et ventus ab oriente

[1] For the case, see **343**.

[2] Fabius Maximus, whose policy had been one of prudence, or rather, of extreme caution.

[3] *Impetuous.*

[4] *His colleague unwilling* = *against the wishes of his colleague.* See **412**.

[5] *To the Romans,* dative with **adversī**.

[6] *Both.*

pulverem adflāns[1] adversī essent.[2] Vīctus caesusque est Rōmānus exercitus; nusquam graviōre vulnere afflīcta est rēs pūblica.

[*Continued on p.* 177.]

## CHAPTER LII.

### ADDITIONAL PRINCIPLES OF SYNTAX.

**340.** *Examine the following:* —

1. **Alter cōnsulum,** *one of the consuls.*
2. **Ūnus mīlitum,** *one of the soldiers.*
3. **Quis vestrum?** *who of you?*
4. **Nihil novī,** *nothing (of) new.*
5. **Satis pecūniae,** *enough (of) money.*
6. **Ūnus ex mīlitibus,** *one of the soldiers.*
7. **Minimus ex illīs,** *the youngest of them.*

The first five of the examples illustrate what is called the **Partitive Genitive,** the word in the genitive denoting a *whole,* and the word which it limits a *part* of that whole; 6 and 7 illustrate another way of expressing the partitive idea.

**341.** *Examine the following:* —

1. **Catilīna fuit ingeniō malō,** *Catiline was (a man) of bad disposition.*
2. **Iccius summā nōbilitāte fuit,** *Iccius was (a man) of the highest rank.*
3. **Puer sēdecim annōrum,** *a boy of sixteen years.*
4. **Vestis māgnī pretī,** *a garment of great value.*
5. **Vir summae virtūtis,** *a man of the highest courage.*

The above are examples of the **Descriptive Ablative** and the **Descriptive Genitive.** Observe that in each instance the ablative or genitive is limited by an adjective, and that the adjective and noun together denote a *quality* or *characteristic* of that which is described.

[1] Present participle of **adflō.** [2] *Were an annoyance.*

**342.** *Examine the following:* —

1. **Rēgī serviō,** *I serve the king.*
2. **Cīvitātī prōdest,** *he benefits the state.*
3. **Caesarī placuit,** *it pleased Cæsar.*
4. **Frātrī persuādet,** *he persuades his brother.*
5. **Crēde mihi,** *believe me.*
6. **Lēgibus cīvitātis pārēbat,** (**220.** I. 2).
7. **Interdum amīcīs nocet,** (**272.** I. 8).

Observe that the verbs, which in English have a direct object, are followed in Latin by the dative (the case of the indirect object). Such verbs should be carefully noted as they occur in the exercises. They may be summed up in the following —

**343.** RULE OF SYNTAX. — **Many verbs signifying to *please* or *displease*, *benefit* or *injure*, *command* or *obey*, *serve*, *resist*, *believe*, *threaten*, *persuade*, and the like, take the dative.**

**344.** *Examine the following:* —

1. **Māgnō ūsuī nostrīs fuit,** *it was of great service to our men.*
2. **Est mihi cūrae,** *it is (for) a care to me.*
3. **Equitātum auxiliō Caesarī mīserant,** *they had sent cavalry to aid Cæsar (for aid to Cæsar).*
4. **Quīnque cohōrtēs castrīs praesidiō relinquit,** *he leaves five cohorts to defend the camp (for defence to the camp).*

Observe in each of the above sentences two datives, one translated (literally) with *for*, the other with *to*. In 1 and 2, **ūsuī** and **cūrae** are like the predicate nominative, which is often used where we might expect this dative; in 3 and 4, **auxiliō** and **praesidiō** denote a purpose. This dative *for which* is sometimes called the **Dative of Service.** The two together are sometimes called the **Double Dative.**

Observe instances of the foregoing constructions as they occur in the exercises and reading lessons.

# CHAPTER LIII.

## DERIVATION.

**345.** Some derivations have been indicated in the vocabularies by separating the parts of compound words, and, beginning with **221**, by putting words in brackets. The bracketed words, however, are not to be understood as the primitives or originals of the words against which they stand, as is customarily the case in lexicons and special vocabularies, but that they are *connected with them in formation from a common root or stem.* The habit of observing such relationships is the important thing. The following list is selected from previous vocabularies for further study of the subject: —

1. **amō**, *love;* **amīcus**, *loving, friendly;* **amīcitia**, *friendship;* **inimīcus** (for **in-amīcus**), *unfriendly, hostile.*
2. **ager**, *field, land, soil;* **agri-cola** (**colō**, *cultivate*), *one who cultivates the soil, farmer;* **agri-cultūra**, *cultivation of the soil, agriculture.* **Colō** also means *dwell*, hence **incola**, *inhabitant.* Meaning of **incolō**?
3. **cīvis**, *citizen;* **cīvīlis**, *pertaining to a citizen;* **cīvitās**, *the condition of a citizen*, or *a body of citizens, state.* Like **cīvīlis**, form and define adjectives from the stems of **puer** and **hostis**.
4. **regō**, *rule;* **rēx** (**rēgs**), *ruler, king;* **rēgīna**, *ruler, queen;* **rēgnum**, *kingdom;* **rēgnō**, *be king, reign;* **rēgula**, *rule.*
5. **faciō**, *do;* **facinus**, *thing done, deed;* **facilis** (*that may be done*), *easy;* **difficilis** (for **dis-facilis**), *not to be done, difficult.*
6. **nōscō**, *know;* **nōmen** (*that by which a thing is known*), *name;* **nōminō**, v., *name;* **nōbilis** (*that can be known*), *well known, noble*, cf. **facilis**.
7. **fuga**, *flight;* **fugiō**, *flee.* **līber**, adj., *free;* **līberō**, v., *free.*
   **metus**, n., *fear;* **metuō**, v., *fear.* **laus**, n., *praise;* **laudō**, v., *praise.*
   **timor**, n., *fear;* **timeō**, v., *fear.* **discō**, *learn;* **discipulus**, *learner.*
   **dō**, *give;* **dōnum**, *gift.* **moveō**, *move;* **mōtus**, *motion.*
   **fluō**, *flow;* **fluvius**, **flūmen**, *stream, river.*
   **dominus**, *lord, master;* **domina**, *mistress;* **dominor**, *be master.*
8. **aurum**, *gold;* **aureus**, *of gold, golden.*
   **līgnum**, *wood;* **līgneus**, *of wood, wooden.*

**ferrum**, *iron;* **ferreus**, *of iron, iron.*
**argentum**, *silver.* Form an adjective from the stem of **argentum**, and define it.

9. **alō**, *nourish;* **alimentum** (*that which nourishes*), *food, provisions.*
**moneō**, *remind;* **monumentum** (*that which reminds*), *monument.*
**ōrnō**, *adorn;* meaning of **ōrnāmentum**?

10. **pulcher**, *beautiful;* **pulchritūdō**, *beauty.*
**fortis**, *brave;* **fortitūdō**, *bravery.*
**turpis**, *base;* **turpitūdō**, *baseness.*
**altus**, *high.* Form a noun from the stem of **altus**, and define it.

11. **īgnāvus** (*not busy*), *idle;* **īgnāvia**, *idleness.*
**memor**, *mindful;* **memoria** (*mindfulness*), *memory.*
**piger**, *lazy;* **pigritia**, *laziness.*
**prūdēns**, *wise, prudent;* **prūdentia**, *wisdom, prudence.*
**sapiēns**, *wise;* **sapientia**, *wisdom.*
**amīcus**, *friend;* **amīcitia**, *friendship.*
Form a noun from the stem of **inimīcus**, and define it.

12. **equus**, *horse;* **eques**, *horseman.*
**pēs** (stem **ped**), *foot;* **pedēs**, *foot-soldier.*

13. **arō**, v., *plough;* **arātrum**, n. (*thing to plough with*), *plough.*
(**rōdō**, *gnaw*); **rōstrum** (*that which gnaws*), *beak, snout,* hence *beak of a ship.*

14. **vir**, *man;* **virtūs**, *manliness, virtue.*
**servus**, *slave;* **servitūs**, *slavery.*
**cōnsul**, *consul;* **cōnsulātus**, *office of a consul, consulship.*
**magister**, *master;* **magistrātus**, *office of a* **magister**, *magistracy,* also *magistrate.*

15. **perīculum**, *danger;* **perīculōsus**, *full of danger, dangerous.*
**frōns**, *leaf;* **frondōsus**, *covered with leaves, leafy.*
**studium**, *zeal;* meaning of **studiōsus**?

16. **audeō**, *dare;* **audāx**, *daring.*
**rapiō**, *seize;* **rapāx**, *grasping.*
**teneō**, *hold;* meaning of **tenāx**?

17. **scrībō**, *write;* **scrīptor**, *writer.*
**vincō** (**victum**), *conquer;* **victor**, *conqueror.*
**dēfendō**, *defend;* **dēfēnsor**, *defender.*
From stem of **amō**, *love,* form a word meaning *lover;* from stem of **audiō**, *hear,* in the same way, a word meaning *hearer.*

18. **ūllus**, *any;* **nūllus**, *not any.*
**sciō**, *know;* **nesciō**, *know not.*
19. **homo**, *man;* **hūmānus** (*belonging to a man*), *human.*
**mors**, *death*; **mortālis** (*belonging to death*), *mortal.*
**alius**, *another;* **aliēnus** (*belonging to another*), *another's.*
20. Observe also the force of the various prefixes, **ā**, **ad**, **dē**, **dis**, **in**, **prae**, **prō**, **re**, **sub**, etc., as in **ā-mittō**, **ac-cēdō**, **dē-scendō**, **dī-mittō**, **īn-ferō**, **prae-sum**, **prō-cēdō**, **re-ferō**, **sub-eō**, etc.

# CHAPTER LIV. 1.

## THE SUBJUNCTIVE MOOD.

### Sequence of Tenses: Practice on Forms.

**346.** Learn the subjunctive of **sum** (**73**) and its compounds (**292**, **293**).

The chief use of the subjunctive is in subjoined, that is, dependent, clauses.

**347.** *Examine the following:* —

1. **Audiō ubi sit, fuerit, futūrus sit**, *I hear where he is, has been* or *was, is going to be.*
2. **Audīvī ubi sit, fuerit, futūrus sit**, *I have heard where he is, has been* or *was, is going to be.*
3. **Audiam ubi sit, fuerit, futūrus sit**, *I shall hear where he is, has been* or *was, is going to be.*
4. **Audīverō ubi sit, fuerit, futūrus sit**, *I shall have heard where he is, has been* or *was, is going to be.*

5. **Audiēbam ubi esset, fuisset, futūrus esset**, *I heard where he was, had been, was going to be.*
6. **Audīvī ubi esset, fuisset, futūrus esset**, *I heard where he was, had been, was going to be.*
7. **Audīveram ubi esset, fuisset, futūrus esset**, *I had heard where he was, had been, was going to be.*

Notice what tenses are used in the principal clauses of each of the preceding groups of examples. Those in the first group — the present, perfect definite,[1] future, and future perfect — are called *primary* or *principal* tenses. Those in the second group — the imperfect, perfect indefinite,[2] and the pluperfect — are called *secondary* or *historical* tenses.

Observe also that primary tenses of the subjunctive are used in the first four, secondary in the last three.

**348.** Rule of Syntax. — **Primary tenses of the subjunctive follow primary tenses of the indicative, and secondary follow secondary.**

Observe that the subjunctive in the foregoing examples is translated like the indicative.

**349.** *Examine the following:* —

1. **Nēmō adest quīn sit fortis,** *no one is present who is not brave.*
2. **Quis adest quīn sit fortis?** *who is present who is not brave?*
3. **Nēmō dubitat quīn sit fortis,** *no one doubts that he is brave,* or *his being brave.*
4. **Nōn dubium est quīn sit fortis,** *there is no doubt that he is brave,* or *of his being brave.*
5. **Nōn dubitō quīn sit fortis,** *I do not doubt that he is brave,* or *his being brave.*

Observe (1) that the subjunctive follows **quīn**; (2) that **quīn** is used after negative expressions and questions that expect a negative answer; (3) that the subjunctive clause with **quīn** (compounded of **quī**, *who*, and **nē**, *not*) may be variously rendered.

## 2.

**350.** EXERCISES.

I. 1. Quis dubitat quīn sint fortēs? 2. Nēmō dubitat quīn vīta sit brevis. 3. Nōn dubitō quīn adfuerint. 4. Nōn dubium erat quīn essent fortēs. 5. Quis dubitābat quīn

[1] That is, the perfect translated with *have* or *has*.

[2] That is, the perfect translated without *have* or *has*.

fuissent fortēs? 6. Nēmō dubitāverat quīn adfuisset; adfuissent. 7. Nōn est dubium quīn possit; possint; potuerit; potuerint. 8. Quis dubitābat quīn posset? possent? potuisset? potuissent? 9. Nōn est dubium quīn praesīs; praesītis; praefueris; praefueritis. 10. Quis dubitāverat quīn āfuisset? āfuissent?

II. 1. I do not doubt that he is present; has been present; is absent; has been absent. 2. Who doubted that he could? they could? we could? you could? 3. They do not doubt that he is at the head of (*praesum*); has been at the head of. 4. Who has doubted his surviving? their surviving? 5. Who doubted their injuring? having injured? 6. There is no doubt that he can; we can; you can; they can. 7. There was no doubt that he could; I could; they could.

## 3.

**351.** Learn the subjunctive, active and passive, of **amō (86)** and **moneō (112)**.

1. Observe that in the active voice the imperfect subjunctive can be formed readily from the present infinitive, and the pluperfect subjunctive from the perfect infinitive. Compare the perfect subjunctive with the future perfect indicative.

**352.** *Examine the following:* —

**Sē armant ut pūgnent,** *they arm themselves that they may fight, in order that they may fight, to fight, so as to fight, in order to fight, for the purpose of fighting.*

Observe that the various equivalents of **ut pūgnent** have a common notion or idea, that of *purpose*.

**353.** Rule of Syntax. — ***Ut* with the subjunctive may be used to denote a purpose, and may be variously translated.**

**354.** Review the indicative and imperative of **eō**, *go* **(327)**.

**355.** EXERCISES.

I. 1. It ut mōnstret et moneat. 2. Ībat ut mōnstrāret et monēret. 3. Iit ut mōnstret et moneat. 4. Iit ut mōnstrāret et monēret. 5. Ībunt ut mōnstrent et moneant. 6. Iērunt ut mōnstrārent et monērent. 7. Ierant ut mōnstrārent et monērent. 8. Nōn dubitāvī quīn mōnstrāvisset et monuisset. 9. Quis dubitāverat quīn mōnstrāvissent et monuissent? 10. Nēmō dubitāvit quīn mōnstrāvissēmus et monuissēmus. 11. Nōn est dubium quīn mōnstrēmus et moneāmus.

II. 1. He goes to see and praise. 2. They go for the purpose of seeing and praising. 3. We will go in order to see and praise. 4. Who will not go that he may see and praise? 5. You will go to see and praise. 6. They have gone to see and praise. 7. He has gone for the purpose of seeing and praising. 8. He went in order to see and praise. 9. Go (*plur.*) to see and praise. 10. He was going that he might see and praise. 11. Who doubts his having seen and praised? 12. No one doubted that they had seen and praised.

4.

**356.** EXERCISES.

I. 1. Eī (eīs, etc.) imperat ut[1] —
cōnētur, cōnentur, cōner, cōnēmur.
2. Eī (eīs, etc.) imperābat ut —
cōnārētur, cōnārentur, cōnārer, cōnārēmur.
3. Quis dubitat quīn —
cōnātus sit, cōnātī sint, cōnātus sim, cōnātī sīmus?
4. Nēmō dubitābat quīn —
cōnātus esset, cōnātī essent, cōnātus essem, cōnātī essēmus.

[1] Translate thus: *He orders him that he try,* or *him to try; them that they try,* or *them to try,* etc.

5. Eum (eōs, etc.) monet ut —
   tueātur, tueantur, tuear, tueāmur.
6. Eum (eōs, etc.) monēbat ut —
   tuērētur, tuērentur, tuērer, tuērēmur.
7. Quis dubitat quīn —
   tuitus sit, tuitī sint, tuitus sim, tuitī sīmus?
8. Nēmō dubitābat quīn —
   tuitus esset, tuitī essent, tuitus essem, tuitī essēmus.

II.[1] 1. They will order him[2] (them, me, us) to imitate. 2. They have ordered him (them, me, us) to imitate. 3. Who doubts his[3] (their, my, our) having imitated? 4. They ordered him (them, me, us) to imitate. 5. Nobody doubted his (their, my, our) having imitated. 6. They advise him (them, me, us) to promise. 7. They advised him (them, me, us) to promise. 8. There was no doubt that he (they, I, we) had promised.

## 5.

**357.** Learn the subjunctive, active and passive, of **regō (180)**, **audiō (223)**, **capiō (235)**.

**358.** The conjunction **nē**, *in order that not, that not, in order not to, so as not to, lest,* is used to denote a negative purpose, just as **ut** denotes a positive purpose. See **352, 353.**

**359.** EXERCISES.

I. 1. Eum (eōs) monet ut —

| | | | |
|---|---|---|---|
| regat, | regātur, | audiat, | audiātur, |
| regant, | regantur, | audiant, | audiantur. |

2. Eum (eōs) monuit ut —

| | | | |
|---|---|---|---|
| regat, | regātur, | audiat, | audiātur, |
| regant, | regantur, | audiant, | audiantur. |

3. Eum (eōs) monēbat ut —

| | | | |
|---|---|---|---|
| regeret, | regerētur, | audīret, | audīrētur, |
| regerent, | regerentur, | audīrent, | audīrentur. |

[1] Imitate the arrangement in I. [2] Dative.
[3] That is, *that he, they, I, we, have imitated.*

4. Eum (eōs) monuit ut —
regeret, regerētur, audīret, audīrētur,
regerent, regerentur, audīrent, audīrentur.

5. Tē (vōs) monet nē —
capiās, capiātis, capiāris, capiāminī.

6. Mē (nōs) monuit nē —
capiam, capiāmus, capiar, capiāmur.

7. Mē (nōs) monēbat nē —
caperem, caperēmus, caperer, caperēmur.

8. Mē (nōs) monuit nē —
caperem, caperēmus, caperer, caperēmur.

II. 1. They advise him (them) —
to lead, to be led, to find, to be found.

2. They warn him (them) —
not to receive, not to be received.

3. They will advise him (them) —
to lead, to be led, to find, to be found.

4. They were warning him (them) —
not to lead, find, receive,
not to be led, be found, be received.

5. Who doubted that he (they) —
had led, had found, had received,
had been led, been found, been received?

## 6.

**360.** Learn the subjunctive of **eō** (327), and **ferō** (321).

**361.** EXERCISES.

I. 1. Mē hortātur ut eam; feram. 2. Eōs hortāmur ut eant; ferantur. 3. Vōs hortantur ut eātis; ferātis. 4. Eum hortātī sunt ut īret; ferret. 5. Mē hortātī sunt nē eam; feram. 6. Tē hortābantur nē īrēs; ferrēs. 7. Eōs hortātī erant ut īrent; ferrent. 8. Nōn dubium erat quīn iissent; tulissent. 9. Nōn est dubium quīn ierit; tulerit. 10. Nēmō dubitābat quīn īret; ferrētur.

II. 1. He commands that he (they, I, we) go; bear; be borne. 2. He was commanding that he (they, I, we) should go; bear; be borne. 3. There is no doubt of his (their, my, our) having gone; borne; been borne. 4. There was no doubt that he (they, I, we) had gone; borne; been borne.

## 7.

**362.** EXERCISES.

I. 1. Imperātor exercitum in collem subdūxit, ut fortūnam bellī experīrētur. 2. Pater Horātī populum ōrābat nē sē orbum faceret. 3. Illud facit ut hostēs circumveniantur. 4. Cōnsul cūrāvit ut plēbs agrōs coleret. 5. Nōn dubium erat quīn Rōmānī auxilium ferrent. 6. Manlius ēdīcit nē quis[1] extrā ōrdinem pūgnet. 7. Omnēs occīdentur ut vīrēs hostium frangantur, aut omnēs dīmittentur ut beneficiō obligentur. 8. Nōn est dubium quīn terror animōs omnium cīvium occupāverit. 9. Incidit[2] ut eō tempore Hasdrubal ad eundem portum venīret. 10. Scīpiō uxōrem ōrāvit nē corpus suum Rōmam referrētur.

II. 1. The ambassadors beg the senate to render aid to their[3] kingdom. 2. The ambassador begged the senate to render aid to his[4] king. 3. Nobody doubts that Hannibal is brave. 4. Nobody doubted that Hannibal had fought bravely. 5. They did this that they might surround the enemy. 6. This they do in order to surround the enemy. 7. Scipio begs his wife not to carry his body back to Rome. 8. Scipio begged his wife not to carry his body back to Rome. 9. It turned out that the soldier received a wound on the head. 10. We will draw up the soldiers on a hill to try the fortune of war.

---

[1] **Nē quis,** *lest any one* = *that no one.*

[2] After verbs meaning *to happen, to turn out,* and the like, **ut** means *that,* but not *in order that.*

[3] **Suus,** because *their* means *their own,* and not *of them.*

[4] **Suus.**

**363.** VOCABULARY.

**circum-veniō**, 4, **-vēnī**, **-ventum**, *surround.*
**collis**, **-is**, M., *hill.* Cf. **mōns.**
**cōnor**, 1, *attempt.*
**cūrō**, 1 [**cūra**], *care for, take care.*
**dī-mittō**, 3, **-mīsī**, **-missum**, *send away, send off.*
**ē-dīcō**, 3, **-dīxī**, **-dictum**, *speak out, declare, proclaim.*
**ē-veniō**, 4, **-vēnī**, **-ventum**, *come forth, turn out, happen.* Cf. **accidō.**
**extrā**, prep. w. acc., *without, outside of.* Cf. **intrā.**
**frangō**, 3, **frēgī**, **fractum**, *break.*
**Hasdrubal**, **-alis**, M., *Hasdrubal*, brother of Hannibal.
**hortor**, 1, *urge, encourage.*
**in-cidō**, 3, **-cidī**, **-cāsum** [**cadō**], *fall into, happen, befall.*
**Manlius**, **-ī**, M., *Manlius*, a Roman general.
**mōnstrō**, 1, *show, point out.*
**ob-ligō**, 1, *bind, put under obligation, oblige.*
**oc-cīdō**, 3, **-cīdī**, **-cīsum** [**ob**, **caedō**, *cut*], *cut down, kill.*
**occupō**, 1 [**ob**, **capiō**], *take possession of, seize.*
**orbus**, **-a**, **-um**, adj., *bereaved, childless.*
**ōrō**, 1 [**ōs**, *mouth*], *pray, beg.*
**plēbs**, **-bis**, F., *the common people.*
**senātus**, **-ūs**, M. [**senex**], *council of elders, senate.* (**345.** 14.)
**sub-dūcō**, 3, **-dūxī**, **-ductum**, *draw from under, draw up.*
**uxor**, **-ōris**, F., *wife.* Cf. **conjunx.**
**vīs**, **vīs**, F., *strength, power.* (**262.**)

# CHAPTER LV.

## THE SUBJUNCTIVE: RELATIVE OF *PURPOSE.*

[It is suggested that the turning of English into Latin be now deferred till after the Reading Lessons, pp. 211–222, have been finished.]

**364.** In all the Latin sentences in the preceding lesson in which **ut** and **nē** are used with the subjunctive, except **362.** I. 9, the dependent clause expresses a purpose. And, on the other hand, in the English sentences all the dependent clauses expressing purpose ("*to render aid,*" "*not to carry,*" etc.) had to be turned into Latin by **ut** or **nē** with the subjunctive. But the Latin often expresses a purpose by means of a relative pronoun followed by the subjunctive. See the first six sentences below.

**365.** EXERCISES.

I. 1. Ancus lēgātum mittit ut rēs repetat. 2. Ancus lēgātum mittit quī rēs repetat. 3. Lēgātī vēnērunt ut pācem peterent. 4. Lēgātī vēnērunt quī pācem peterent. 5. Pater fīliō equum dabat ut equitāret. 6. Pater fīliō equum dabat quī eum veheret. 7. Ad singulās urbēs scrībēmus nē mūrōs dīruant. 8. Nōn dubium est quīn Catō ad urbēs scrīpserit. 9. Quis dubitāvit quīn Catō imperāvisset ut urbēs mūrōs dīruerent? 10. Rōmulus urbem fēcit quae asȳlum esset; Rōmulus urbem facit quae sit asȳlum.

II. 1. A horse was given to the boy by his father, for[1] him to ride. 2. A father sent a messenger to Rome to speak[2] to his son. 3. A father sends a messenger to Rome to speak[2] to his son. 4. Romulus makes proclamation that no one[3] shall leap[4] over his wall. 5. Romulus proclaimed that no one should leap over his wall. 6. We will warn them not to leap[5] over our walls. 7. Romulus sent messengers to invite[2] neighboring people to his games. 8. The father will give his son a horse for him to ride. 9. Who doubts that a kind father gives his son books? 10. Nobody doubted that the father had given his son many things.[6]

**366.** VOCABULARY.

**al-loquor,** 3, **-locūtus** [**ad**], *speak to, address.*

**Ancus, -ī,** M., *Ancus,* a Roman king.

**asȳlum, -ī,** N., *a place of refuge, asylum.*

**Catō, -ōnis,** M., *Cato,* a famous Roman censor.

**dī-ruō,** 3, **-ruī, -rutum,** *tear asunder, destroy.*

**equitō,** 1 [**eques**], *act the* **eques,** *ride.*

**fīnitimus, -a, -um,** adj. [**fīnis**], *bordering on, neighboring.*

**imperō,** 1, *order, command,* with dative. Cf. **jubeō** with acc.

**lūdus, -ī** [**lūdō**], *game, play.*

**nūntius, -ī,** M., *bearer of news, messenger.*

**re-petō,** 3, **-īvī, -iī, -ītum,** *seek again, demand back;* **rēs repetere,** *demand restitution.*

**trān-siliō,** 4, **-iī,** and **-uī,** —— [**saliō,** *leap*], *leap over* or *across.*

---

1 *Which he might ride.*
2 Translate in two ways.
3 See **362**. I. 6, and note.
4 Present subjunctive.
5 See **362**. I. 10.
6 *Many things,* **multa.**

## CHAPTER LVI.

### THE SUBJUNCTIVE: *Ut* and *Nē*.

**367.** The subjunctive with **ut** to denote *purpose* has been illustrated (**352**). But the subjunctive with **ut** has other uses.

**368.** *Examine the following:—*

1. **Tantus est mīlitum ardor ut ad bellum dūcantur,** *so great is the ardor of the soldiers that they are led to war.*
2. **Accidit ut nōn domī essem,** *it happened that I was not at home.*
3. **Fabricius adeō inops dēcēssit ut nihil relīquerit,**[1] *Fabricius died so poor as to leave nothing.*

In these examples the dependent clause denotes a *result*. Compare the translation of **ut** and the subjunctive in *purpose* clauses and in *result* clauses.

**369.** Still another use of the subjunctive with **ut** and **ne** is illustrated in the following sentences:—

1. **Timeō ut veniat,** *I fear that he is not coming,* or *will not come.*
2. **Timeō ut vēnerit,** *I fear that he has not come.*
3. **Timēbam ut vēnisset,** *I feared that he had not come.*
4. **Timeō nē veniat,** *I fear that he is coming,* or *will come*
5. **Timeō nē vēnerit,** *I fear that he has come.*
6. **Timēbam nē vēnisset,** *I feared that he had come.*

An inspection of the foregoing examples shows that **ut** and **nē** *seem* sometimes to exchange meanings.

After verbs of *fearing*, **ut** is translated *that not*, and **nē**, *that.*

Observe that in 1 and 4 the present subjunctive may be translated as a future.

**370.** EXERCISES.

I. 1. Pompējus ita ēgit ut ā Sūllā dīligerētur. 2. Is, ut Sūllae[2] subvenīret, mīlitēs collēgit. 3. Posteā in[3] Siciliam profectus est, ut eam prōvinciam ā Carbōne reciperet.

[1] An exception to **348**. [2] See **343**. [3] See **333**. 1.

4. Catilīnae exercitus adeō ācriter dīmicāvit, ut nēmō superesset. 5. Accidit ut esset plēna lūna. 6. Atticus sīc Graecē loquēbātur, ut Athēnīs nātus vidērētur. 7. Atticus Athēnīs ita vīxit, ut omnibus cīvibus esset cārissimus. 8. Nōn dubitō quīn nostrī mīlitēs hostēs superāverint. 9. Nōn est dubium quīn semper fidem servāveritis. 10. Timeō ut sustineās labōrēs. 11. Metuō nē malum cōnsilium capiās. 12. Metuō ut sustinueris labōrēs. 13. Quis metuit nē malum cōnsilium capiam?

Point out the *purpose* clauses in the above.

II. 1. The boy so acts that he is loved by all. 2. They so acted that they were loved by all. 3. He will so act as to be[1] loved by all. 4. He has so acted as to be loved by all. 5. They will not doubt our having come.[2] 6. They had not doubted our having come.[3] 7. I fear that you are not well. 8. I feared that you were not well. 9. I fear that you are sick. 10. I was afraid that you had been sick. 11. The enemy are fighting so spiritedly that no one will survive.[4] 12. They have fought so sharply that not one has survived. 13. We will set out for[5] Sicily in order to receive[6] that province.

**371.** VOCABULARY.

**ac-cidō,** 3, **-cidī,** —— [**ad, cadō**], *fall upon, fall out, happen.* Cf. **ēveniō** and **incidō.**

**ad-eō,** adv. (*to this*), *thus far, so, so very.*

**Atticus, -ī,** M., *Atticus,* a friend of Cicero.

**Carbō, -ōnis,** M., *Carbo,* a Roman.

**Catilīna, -ae,** M., *Catiline,* a famous Roman conspirator.

**col-ligō,** 3, **-lēgī, -lēctum** [**com, legō**], *collect.* Also **conligō.**

**dī-micō,** 1, *fight, contend.*

**Graecē,** adv. [**Graecus**], *in Greek.*

**loquor,** 3, **locūtus,** *speak, talk.*

**sub-veniō,** 4, **-vēnī, -ventum,** *come to the aid of, aid, assist,* with dative. Cf. **succurrō.**

**sustineō,** 2, **-tinuī, -tentum** [**sub, teneō**], *hold up, bear, endure.*

[1] *As to be,* **ut,** etc.
[2] *That we have come.*
[3] *That we had come.*
[4] Pres. subj.
[5] See I. 3, and note.
[6] Not infinitive.

## CHAPTER LVII. 1.

### THE SUBJUNCTIVE: *Cum.*

**372.** The subjunctive occurs very frequently in dependent clauses beginning with **cum**, meaning (1) *when, while, as*, of time; (2) *since, because, as*, of cause or reason; (3) *although*, of concession:

1. **Cum Servius in domō Tarquinī esset, mīrābile accidit,** *while Servius was in the house of Tarquin, a wonderful thing happened.*
2. **Cum Tarquinius occīsus esset, ējus fīlia populum allocūta est,** *when Tarquin had been killed, his daughter addressed the people.*
3. **Tullia, cum domum redīret, super corpus patris carpentum ēgit,** *Tullia, as she was returning home, drove her wagon over the body of her father.*

An inspection of the above examples shows that—

(1) The tenses of the subjunctive are the imperf. and pluperfect.

(2) The **cum** clause marks the time of the act of the principal clause, the verb of which is in the perfect.

(3) The sentences may be called *narrative sentences.*

**373.** Rule of Syntax.—***Cum*** **temporal, that is,** ***cum*** **in narrative clauses, is followed by the imperfect and pluperfect subjunctive to mark the time of the action in the principal clause.**

**374.** *Examine the following:*—

1. **Cum huīc lēgī senātus repūgnāret, Caesar rem ad populum dētulit,** *since the senate opposed this law, Cæsar referred the matter to the people.*
2. **Cum dē imprōvīsō vēnisset, Rēmī lēgātōs mīsērunt,** *since he had come unexpectedly, the Remi sent ambassadors.*
3. **Cum vīta metūs plēna sit, amīcitiās parāte,** *since life is full of fear, form friendships.*
4. **Cum mē interrogāveris, respondēbō,** *as you have asked me, I will answer.*

5. **Nihil mē adjūvit cum posset,** *he gave me no aid (aided me in nothing), although it was in his power.*

Notice that—

(1) All the four tenses of the subjunctive are used.

(2) The **cum** clause states the cause or reason of the act of the principal clause; or denotes a concession, indicated in English by *though, admitting that,* etc.

**375.** Rule of Syntax.—***Cum* causal or concessive is followed by the subjunctive in all its tenses.**

1. **Cum** followed by the present or perfect subjunctive is almost always causal, and may be translated *since* or *as;* followed by the imperfect or pluperfect it is very often temporal.

2. **Cum** temporal and the subjunctive can often be translated in some other way better than by *when* or *as* with the indicative. Thus, in **372.** 2, we might translate, *After the killing of Tarquin,* etc.; and in 3, *Tullia, returning home,* or *Tullia, on her way home.*

**376.** EXERCISES.

I. 1. Cum jūssī essent invicem dīcere, ūnus orsus est. 2. Pyrrhus, cum tot Rōmānōs mortuōs vidēret, manūs ad caelum sustulit. 3. Cum explōrātōrēs cēpisset, eōs per castra circumdūxit. 4. Quae cum ita sint,[1] perge. 5. Cum sit in nōbīs cōnsilium, cūr dubitāmus? 6. Cum dē imprōvīsō vēnerit Caesar, ad eum lēgātōs mittēmus. 7. Cum amīcī adsint, gaudēmus. 8. Cum[2] nox appropīnquāret, abiērunt. 9. Cum nox appropīnquāvisset, abiērunt. 10. Caesar, cum frūstrā mīsisset, sōlus nāviculam cōnscendit nē āgnōscerētur.

II. 1. When one had begun,[3] the rest became (*were*) silent. 2. Pyrrhus, having seen[4] the bravery of the Romans, spoke these words. 3. Since he has seen the bravery of the Romans, he raises his hands to heaven. 4. Since night is

[1] *Since these things are so = such being the case.*

[2] **Cum** may be translated as temporal or causal: *on the approach of night;* or, *since night was approaching.*

[3] See **373.**

[4] *Pyrrhus, when he had seen.*

approaching, we will go off. 5. When our friends had arrived, we went to Boston. 6. On the arrival of our friends we went to Boston. 7. While Cæsar was embarking in a boat, no one recognized him. 8. As[1] Cæsar was alone, he was not recognized. 9. As[1] I was telling him a story, he suddenly laughed. 10. As[1] they had prudence, we did not hesitate.

### 377. VOCABULARY.

**ā-gnōscō,** 3, **-nōvī, -nitum,** [**ad,** (**g**)**nōscō,** *know*], *recognize.*
**ap-propinquō,** 1 [**ad**], *approach.*
**Bostonia,** -ae, F., *Boston.*
**cēterī, -ae, -a,** adj., *the rest.*
**circum-dūcō,** 3, **-xī, -ductum,** *lead around.*
**cōn-scendō,** 3, **-dī, -scēnsum** [**scandō,** *climb*], *ascend, embark, go on board.*
**dubitō,** 1 [**dubius**], *doubt, hesitate.*
**dubius, -a, -um,** adj., *doubtful.*
**gaudeō,**[2] 2, **gāvīsus sum,** *be glad, rejoice.*
**im-prō-vīsō,** adv. [**videō**], *unexpectedly.*
**in-vicem,** adv., *by turns, in turn.*
**jubeō,** 2, **jūssī, jūssum,** *bid, order.* Cf. **imperō.**
**mortuus, -a, -um** [P. of **morior**], *dead.*
**nāvicula, -ae,** F. [**nāvis**], *little vessel, boat.*
**ordior,** 4, **orsus,** *begin, undertake.*
**pergō,** 3, **perrēxī, perrēctum** [**per, regō**], *go on, continue.*
**taceō,** 2, **tacuī, tacitum,** *be silent, say nothing about.*
**tollō,** 3, **sustulī, sublātum,** *raise, lift up.*
**tot,** adj., indecl., *so many.* Cf. **quot.**

## 2.

### 378. FOR TRANSLATION.

THE BATTLE OF CANNÆ.—*Continued.*

Aemilius Paullus tēlīs obrutus cecidit. Quem[3] cum mediā in pūgnā sedentem in saxō opplētum cruōre cōnspexisset quī-

---

[1] The *as* of *reason*, or of *time?*

[2] Four common verbs, **audeō,** *dare,* **gaudeō,** *rejoice,* **soleō,** *be accustomed,* **fīdō,** *trust,* have the passive form in the perfect, and hence are called *semi-deponents.*

[3] Translate first mentally, taking the words as they stand, rendering **cum,** *when;* then recast this preliminary translation, beginning with **cum quīdam tribūnus,** and rendering **quem,** *him.*

Follow this method, when a Latin sentence appears difficult; but keep a sharp eye on the terminations of the words.

dam tribūnus mīlitum: "Cape," inquit, "hunc equum et fuge, Aemilī. Etiam sine tuā morte lacrimārum[1] satis lūctūsque est." Ad ea cōnsul:[2] "Tū quidem macte virtūte estō.[3] Sed cavē,[4] exiguum tempus ē manibus hostium ēvādendī perdās.[4] Abī, nūntiā patribus, ut urbem mūniant āc,[5] prius quam hostis victor adveniat, praesidiīs firment. Mē in hāc strāge meōrum mīlitum patere[6] exspīrāre." Alter cōnsul cum paucīs equitibus Venusiam[7] perfūgit. Cōnsulārēs aut praetōriī occidērunt[8] vīgintī, senātōrēs captī aut occīsī sunt trīgintā, nōbilēs virī trecentī, mīlitum quadrāgintā mīlia, equitum tria mīlia et quīngentī. Hannibal in[9] testimōnium victōriae suae trēs modiōs aureōrum ānulōrum Carthāginem mīsit, quōs dē manibus equitum Rōmānōrum et senātōrum dētraxerat.

## CHAPTER LVIII.

### THE SUBJUNCTIVE: INDIRECT QUESTIONS.

**379.** *Examine the following:* —

| DIRECT. | INDIRECT. |
|---|---|
| 1. **Quis est?** *who is he?* | **Sciō quis sit,** *I know who he is.* |
| 2. **Ubi sumus?** *where are we?* | **Sciō ubi sīmus,** *I know where we are.* |
| 3. **Cūr rīdēs?** *why do you laugh?* | **Sciō cūr rīdeās,** *I know why you laugh.* |
| 4. **Quem vīdistī?** *whom have you seen?* | **Sciō quem vīderis,** *I know whom you have seen.* |

[1] See **340.** 5.

[2] Supply **dīxit** or **respondit.** But it is livelier without a verb.

[3] Perhaps the literal translation of this phrase is, *be thou blessed in* (or *for*) *thy courage;* **macte** for **mactus,** because **tū** is here almost more of a vocative than a nominative.

[4] Supply **nē** after **cavē,** *beware lest you lose = beware of losing.*

[5] Connects **mūniant** and **firment.**

[6] Imperative from **patior.**

[7] Account for the case.

[8] From **occidō.** But **occīsī,** in the next clause, from **occīdō.**

[9] *For;* **in** expresses purpose.

Compare each of the foregoing examples in the left hand column with the corresponding one on the right. Observe that each dependent clause in the right hand column begins with an interrogative word, and contains the substance of a question, though not a question in form. Such dependent clauses are called **Indirect Questions**. Observe the mood, and how it is translated.

**380.** RULE OF SYNTAX. — **Indirect questions take the subjunctive.**

1. The commonest interrogative words introducing indirect questions are **quis**, *who?* **cūr**, *why?* **num**, *whether?* **ubi**, *where?* **quō**, *whither?* **unde**, *whence?* **quot**, *how many?*

**381.** EXERCISES.

[Read again the remarks and rule, p. 165.]

I. 1. Scit quid agās. 2. Scit quid ēgeris. 3. Sciēbat quid agerēs. 4. Sciēbat quid ēgissēs. 5. Audīvī quid agat. 6. Audīvī quid ēgerit. 7. Audīvī quid ageret. 8. Audīvī quid ēgisset. 9. Audīveram quid ageret. 10. Audīveram quid ēgisset.

II. 1. Volō scīre unde vēneris. 2. Dīc[1] mihi num meam sorōrem vīderis. 3. Nesciō unde veniant tot mīlitēs. 4. Quaeram num omnia fēlīciter ēvēnerint. 5. Speculābimur quot hominēs in urbem ineant et quot exeant. 6. Nāsīca hominem interrogāvit num manibus ambulāre solitus esset. 7. Quaerēbat quae[2] cīvitātēs in armīs essent. 8. Quīdam homo interrogātus est quae nāvēs essent tūtissimae. 9. Dīc mihi quid in manū habeās. 10. Caesar omnem equitātum mittit, quī videat[3] quās in partēs[4] hostēs iter faciant.

III. 1. He sees who is walking; has walked. 2. They see who are walking; have walked. 3. We shall see who walk; have walked. 4. We knew why he was laughing; had laughed. 5. You knew why I was laughing; had laughed.

---

[1] See p. 150, note.

[2] See **279**. 3.

[3] Compare **365**. I. 2 and 4.

[4] *Into what parts = in what direction.*

6. They wondered why he was praised; had been praised. 7. They will wonder why I am praised; have been praised. 8. Do you not wonder why we are praised; have been praised? 9. I wonder whether he had been admonished; is being admonished. 10. They wondered whether we were admonished; had been admonished.

**382.** VOCABULARY.

**interrogō,** 1, *ask, inquire.*
**Nāsica, -ae,** M., *Nasica,* surname of one of the Scipios.
**num,**[1] interrog. adv., *whether,* introducing indirect questions.
**rogō,** 1, *ask, question.*
**sciō,** 4, **scīvī, scītum,** *know.*
**soleō,**[2] 2, **solitus,** *be accustomed.*
**speculor,** 1, *spy out, watch.*
**tūtus, -a, -um,** adj., *safe.*

**interrogō,** *ask a question, inquire,* and nearly limited to that sense.
**rogō,** *ask a question,* but much more commonly *ask a favor, make a request.*
**quaerō,** *ask a question,* but much used in the sense of *seeking to gain* or *to know, searching into.*

# CHAPTER LIX. 1.

## THE SUBJUNCTIVE: WISHES AND CONDITIONS.

**383.** *Examine the following:* —

1. **Utinam pater veniat!** *would that father would come! I wish father would come! O that father would come!*
2. **Sī pater veniat, laetus sim,** *if father should come, I should be glad.*
3. **Utinam pater adesset!** *would that father were here!*
4. **Sī pater adesset, laetus essem,** *if father were here, I should be glad.*
5. **Utinam pater adfuisset!** *would that father had been here!*
6. **Sī pater adfuisset, laetus fuissem,** *if father had been here, I should have been glad.*

---

[1] Introducing direct questions, it indicates that the answer *no* is expected, but does not usually admit of translation. [2] See p. 177, n. 2.

(1) In 1 and 2 what time do the words *would come*, *should come*, *should be*, point to? Plainly not to the past, nor to the instant present, but vaguely to the future; and this vague future is expressed in Latin by the present subjunctive. The wish and the condition referring to the future *may be* fulfilled; the father *may* come.

(2) In 3 and 4 the wish and condition refer to the present; and this present is expressed by the imperfect subjunctive. The wish and condition are plainly *contrary to what is the fact;* the father *is*, in fact, *not present*.

(3) In 5 and 6 the tense of the subjunctive offers no difficulty. The wish and condition are plainly *contrary to what was the fact;* the father *was*, in fact, *not present*.

**384.** Rule of Syntax.—**In wishes and conditions the present subjunctive is used of what *may be* fulfilled, the imperfect subjunctive of what *is not* true, the pluperfect subjunctive of what *was not* true. The same mood is regularly employed in the conclusion of such conditional sentences.**

The indicative is not used in wishes. The use of the indicative in conditional sentences is easily understood.

**385.** *Examine the following:*—

1. **Sī pater adest, bene est,** *if father is present, it is well.*
2. **Sī pater aderat, bene erat,** *if father was present, it was well.*
3. **Sī pater aderit, bene erit,** *if father shall be present,*[1] *it will be well.*

Observe that in examples 1 and 2 a condition is stated without implying anything. In example 3, as the time is future, that which is supposed *may be* fulfilled. This form, then, of stating a supposition is almost exactly equivalent to that of the present subjunctive in **383**; it is only a livelier way of putting it.

---

[1] In English we commonly use a present form in such conditions that refer to the future. Thus we say, *If he is* (*to-morrow, next week, etc.*) *present, it will be well.* Do not be deceived, when translating into Latin, by this apparent present. See if the conclusion contains a future.

**386.** EXERCISES.[1]

I. 1. Sī vīctōriam certam videam, nunquam pūgnem. 2. Sī mē virum bonum jūdicārēs,[2] nōn mē corrumpere vellēs.[2] 3. Dictātor,[3] sī adfuisset, rem nōn melius gessisset. 4. Varrō, sī Carthāginiēnsium dux fuisset, temeritātis poenās dedisset.[4] 5. Sī patrem tuum crās videam, quid dīcat? 6. Nōn profectus essem, nisi Caesar jūssisset. 7. Sī rēctē faciās, laudēris. 8. Sī maneat Mārcus, gaudeāmus; sīn autem eat, tamen eum laudēmus. 9. Sī leō accēderet,[5] omnēs fugerent. 10. Utinam frāter meus vīveret clāssemque iterum dūceret! 11. Utinam māter nōbīs fābulam nārret! 12. Utinam tēcum[6] in agrīs ambulāvissem!

II.[7] 1. Would that I were walking in the fields with you to-day! 2. I wish you had been walking[8] with me[6] yesterday. 3. O take[9] a walk with us in the fields to-morrow! 4. If you should see victory certain, my friend, should you not fight? 5. I should not now be setting out if Cæsar did not order it. 6. If you were acting rightly, you would be praised. 7. If you had acted rightly, you would have been praised. 8. I wish[9] you would act rightly, so as to[10] be praised. 9. If we should see a lion, we should flee.

---

[1] In translating these sentences, render the present subjunctive in such a way as to indicate vaguely future time; thus, **videam** ... **pūgnem,** *should see ... should fight.*

[2] Compare **383**. 4, and read again **383** (2).

[3] Notice the position of this word, which is the subject of **gessisset.** It may be translated as it stands, first.

[4] *Given punishments of* = *paid the penalty for.*

[5] If a lion *were coming,* not *were to come,* which would be expressed by the present subjunctive.

[6] See **265**. 3.

[7] In turning these sentences into Latin, do not be misled as to the real time of the verbs; *were walking,* in the first sentence, denotes present time. Read again the examples, **383**, and the remarks. See also the varied translation of the first example.

[8] Compare I. 12.

[9] Compare **383**. 1.

[10] **Ut.** See **352.**

10. I wish I had seen a huge lion. 11. If my brother[1] were living, he would now be commanding the fleet. 12. Would that your brother were alive!

**387.** VOCABULARY.

**ac-cēdō**, 3, **-cēssī, -cēssum** [**ad**], *go* or *come near, approach.*

**cor-rumpō**, 3, **-rūpī, -ruptum** [**com**], *break in pieces, destroy; corrupt, bribe.*

**dictātor, -ōris**, M. [**dictō, dīcō**], *chief magistrate, dictator.*

**immānis, -e**, adj., *huge, immense.*

**jūdicō**, 1 [**jūdex**], *judge, deem.*

**rēctē**, adv. [**rēctus**], *rightly.*

**sīn**, conj. [**sī, nē**], *but if, if however, if.*

**temeritās, -ātis**, F. [**temerē**], *chance; rashness.*

**uti-nam**, adv., *would that, O that, I wish that.*

2.

**388.** COLLOQUIUM.

JŌHANNĒS ET JACŌBUS.

*Jo.* Dīc mihi, Jacōbe, unde veniās, quid ēgeris.
have been doing

*Ja.* Rūre veniō, ubi fēriārum partem ēgī. Et tū?
vacation spent

*Jo.* Ego iter cum parentibus fēcī, neque sciō quandō domum revertar.
when return

*Ja.* Utinam ego quoque iter faciam! Sī parentēs adessent, iter mēcum facerent.

*Jo.* Ego itineris diūturnitāte sum dēfessus, et gaudērem sī in scholā essem.
length

*Ja.* Venī mēcum in scholam et ūnā ēdiscāmus.
together let us learn

*Jo.* Tēcum libenter in scholam ībō, sed cōgnōscere velim quī sit praeceptor.
know should like

*Ja.* Praeceptor est vir doctissimus. Vim Latīnī scit,
ever so much
atque semper est benīgnus, mōrōsus nunquam.
pleasant

*Jo.* Quid tē docet?

[1] Imitate the order in I. 3 and 4; the subject might, however, be placed after **sī**.

*Ja.* Docet nōs modum subjunctīvum. Herī, exemplī causā,
for example
nōbīs dē subjunctīvō in interrogātiōnibus indīrēctīs explicāvit.
questions

*Jo.* Multa dē interrogātiōnibus indīrēctīs audīvī, neque unquam intellegere potuī. Fēcitne praeceptor ut tū ista intellegerēs?

*Ja.* Sānē, mī amīce, et ego, ut opīnor, faciam ut tū quoque
yes indeed
eadem intellegās. Sī dīcam, *Ubi est frāter tuus?* interrogā-
question
tum sit dīrēctum; sīn autem, *Nesciō ubi sit frāter*, interrogātum sit indīrēctum. Intellegisne?

*Jo.* Satis intellegō. Sed in hunc diem hāctenus.
so-so for enough

## CHAPTER LX.

### THE SUBJUNCTIVE AND IMPERATIVE.

**389.** Learn the future imperative, active and passive, of the regular and irregular verbs, and review the present imperative.

**390.** In the last lesson occurred the first illustrations of the subjunctive not in dependent clauses, that is, in wishes and in the principal clauses of conditional sentences. The subjunctive is similarly used in commands and appeals, and when so used is called the **Hortatory Subjunctive.**

**391.** *Examine the following paradigms:* —

Commands and Appeals.

| Positive. | Negative. |
|---|---|
| **moneam,** *let me advise.* | **nē moneam,** *let me not advise.* |
| **monē,** or **moneās,** *advise.* | **nē monueris,** *do not advise.* |
| { **moneat,** / **monuerit,** } *let him advise,* or *he shall advise.* | { **nē moneat,** / **nē monuerit,** } *let him not,* or *he shall not, advise.* |
| **moneāmus,** *let us advise.* | **nē moneāmus,** *let us not advise.* |
| **monēte,** *advise.* | **nē monueritis,** *do not advise.* |
| { **moneant,** / **monuerint,** } *let them advise,* or *they shall advise.* | { **nē moneant,** / **nē monuerint,** } *let them not,* or *they shall not, advise.* |

(1) Observe that positive commands and appeals are expressed by the subjunctive only, except in the second person; and negative commands and appeals, by the subjunctive with **nē**.[1]

(2) Observe also that the present and perfect subjunctive, in the third person, are used without essential difference of meaning; and that in *negative commands and appeals in the second person* the perfect[2] only[3] is given.

(3) The future imperative is mostly confined to laws and maxims: **Hominem mortuum in urbe nē sepelītō,** *thou shalt not bury a dead man within the city.* **Percontātōrem fugitō, nam garrulus īdem est,** *avoid a questioner, for he is a babbler too.*

(4) The preceding paradigms, with the meanings, should be thoroughly committed to memory.

## 392. EXERCISES.

I. 1. Cotīdiē scrībe ad mē, mī fīlī, quid fēceris. 2. Puer ad patrem scrībit quid fēcerit. 3. Mittāmus nūntium ad Caesarem quī[4] eum moneat. 4. Nē mēcum in lītore hodiē ambulāveris. 5. Nē puerī incautī cultrōs habeant. 6. Imperātor cōnsilium cōnficiat. 7. Nōlīte, mīlitēs, hostium exercitum timēre. 8. Nē, mīlitēs, hostium exercitum timueritis. 9. Omnia sua[5] sēcum[6] incolae portāverint. 10. Mihi aurēs praebēte, discipulī, et dīligenter audīte quae dīcam. 11. Nē id quod est falsum dīxeris. 12. Leō dīxit: Restat pars quarta, at nē quisquam[7] audeat eam tangere.

II. 1. They shall not send[8] a messenger. 2. Let no one touch[9] the fourth part. 3. Touch not[10] the fourth part of the

---

[1] Prohibitions are more commonly expressed by **nōlī (nōlīte)** with the infinitive. See **318**. I. 5 and 6.

[2] This form of the subjunctive in this use is here called the *perfect*, in deference to custom; it is really the *subjunctive of the future perfect*.

[3] The imperative so used is not common, and not to be imitated.

[4] Compare **365**. I. 2 and 4.

[5] **Omnia sua,** *their all.*

[6] See **265**. 3.

[7] *Let no one.* See **279**. 6.

[8] **Nē** with perfect subjunctive

[9] See I. 12.

[10] Express in two ways.

booty. 4. Let the pupils listen attentively to the words of the master. 5. Do not listen,[1] boys, to the counsels of the bad. 6. Write daily to your parents what[2] you are doing. 7. Carry your books home[3] with you and study diligently. 8. Do not forget[1] what[4] has been said to you to-day. 9. Touch not[1] wine; let us not touch wine; they shall not touch wine. 10. Let us go out and carry our all with us.

**393.** VOCABULARY.

**at,** conj., *but.* Cf. **autem.** (**214.**)
**audeō,**[5] 2, **ausus sum,** *dare, be bold.*
**cōn-ficiō,** 3, **-fēcī, -fectum** [**com, faciō**], *make, accomplish, carry out.*
**cotīdiē,** adv. [**quot, diēs**], *daily.*
**falsus, -a, -um,** adj. [**fallō,** *deceive*], *deceptive, false.*
**in-cautus, -a, -um,** adj. [**caveō**], *incautious, heedless.*
**re-stō,** 1, **restitī,** ——, *stay behind, remain.*
**tangō,** 3, **tetigī, tactum,** *touch.*

**at,** *but on the contrary, but for all that.*
**sed,** *but,* without special emphasis.
**autem,** *but,* often to be rendered *however;* weaker than **at** or **sed.**

**394.** FOR TRANSLATION.

MĀRCUS PORCIUS CATŌ, PUER.

M. Porcius Catō jam puer[6] invīctum animī rōbur ostendit. Cum in domō Drūsī avunculī suī ēducārētur, Latīnī dē cīvitāte impetrandā[7] Rōmam vēnērunt. Popēdius, Latīnōrum prīnceps, quī Drūsī hospes erat, Catōnem puerum rogāvit, ut Latīnōs apud avunculum adjuvāret. Catō vultū cōnstantī

[1] Express in two ways.
[2] Compare I. 10.
[3] See **336.**
[4] **Id quod.**
[5] See p. 177, note 2.
[6] **Jam puer,** *already a boy = even in boyhood.*
[7] **Dē cīvitāte impetrandā,** *respecting the citizenship to be obtained = to obtain citizenship.*

negāvit id sē factūrum.[1] Iterum deinde āc saepius interpellātus[2] in prōpositō perstitit. Tunc Popēdius puerum in excelsam aedium partem levātum tenuit,[3] et sē abjectūrum[4] inde minātus est, nisi precibus obtemperāret; neque hōc metū[5] ā sententiā eum potuit dīmovēre. Tunc Popēdius exclāmāsse[6] fertur:[7] "Grātulēmur[8] nōbīs,[9] Latīnī, hunc esse tam parvum; sī enim senātor esset,[10] nē spērāre quidem[11] jūs[12] cīvitātis licēret.[10]

## CHAPTER LXI.

## THE INFINITIVE.

**395.** Learn the infinitives of the regular and irregular verbs. (**86**, **112**, **180**, **223**, **235**, etc.)

**396.** *Examine the following:*—

1. **Errāre est hūmānum,** *to err is human.*
2. **Possum vidēre,** *I am able to see.*
3. **Volō legere,** *I wish to read.*
4. **Eam sequī sē jubet,** *he orders her to follow him(self).*
5. **Sāturnus in Ītaliam vēnisse dīcitur,** *Saturn is said to have come into Italy.*

Observe that in each sentence the infinitive is used in Latin precisely as in English. This use of the infinitive, as offering no difficulty, has been tacitly illustrated in some of the foregoing exercises.

1 **Negāvit . . . factūrum,** *denied himself to be going to do it = refused to do it.*

2 Perf. part. See **amātus,** p. 34.

3 **Puerum . . . levātum tenuit,** *held the raised-up boy = raised up and held the boy.*

4 **Sē abjectūrum,** *that he would throw (him) down.*

5 **Hōc metū,** *by this fear = by fear of this.*

6 **Exclāmāsse** = **exclāmāvisse.**

7 **Fertur** = **dīcitur.**

8 **Grātulēmur,** *let us congratulate.* See **391**.

9 **Nōbīs.** See **343**.

10 **Esset . . . licēret.** See **383**.

11 **Nē . . . quidem,** *not even.*

12 **Jūs cīvitātis.** Cf. **cīvitāte,** line 2.

**397.** EXERCISES.

I. 1. Cūr mē vīs corrumpere? 2. Timēre incipiēbat. 3. Soror flēre incipiēbat. 4. Vincere scīs,[1] victōriā[2] ūtī nescīs. 5. Tarquinius Cūmās sē contulisse dīcitur. 6. Pontem jubet rescindī. 7. Dulce est prō patriā morī. 8. Catō esse quam vidērī bonus mālēbat. 9. Puerōs decet tacēre. 10. Tūne Marium audēbis occīdere? 11. Nōbīs est in animō[3] per prōvinciam iter facere. 12. Caesar ab urbe proficīscī matūrat.

II. 1. Pyrrhus wanted to bribe Fabricius. 2. Fabricius could not[4] be turned from (the path of) honor. 3. Why did you begin to weep? 4. Did Hannibal know how[5] to conquer? 5. Tarquin was said to have besieged Rome. 6. Rome is said to have been besieged. 7. Seeing is believing.[6] 8. The consul was ordered[7] to tear down the bridge. 9. The bridge is said to have been torn down. 10. It is pleasant[8] to live for (one's) friends. 11. We intend to tear down the bridge. 12. He is said to have departed from Italy.

**398.** VOCABULARY.

**ā-vertō,** 3, **-tī, -sum,** *turn away from, avert.*

**crēdō,** 3, **-didī, -ditum,** *trust, believe,* w. dat. (**343**.)

**decet,** 2, **decuit,** ——, impers. (p. 200), *it is becoming, fitting, proper.*

**honestās, -ātis,** F. [**honestus**], *honor, integrity, honesty.*

**in-cipiō,** 3, **-cēpī, -ceptum** [**capiō**] (*take in hand*), *begin.*

**matūrō,** 1 [**matūrus,** *ripe*], *hasten.*

**morior,**[9] 3, **mortuus,** *die.*

**pōns, pontis,** M., *bridge.*

**re-scindō,** 3, **-scidī, -scissum,** *tear away, tear down, break down.*

**soror, -ōris,** F., *sister.*

---

[1] *You know how.*

[2] See **304**.

[3] *It is in mind to us = we intend.*

[4] *Could not = was not able.*

[5] See I. 4.

[6] *To see is to believe.* Cf. I. 7.

[7] Use **jubeō.**

[8] Neuter. Cf. I. 7.

[9] **Morior** has future participle **moritūrus.**

## CHAPTER LXII. 1.

### ACCUSATIVE AND INFINITIVE.

#### Indirect Discourse.

**399.** *Examine the following:* —

Direct.

1. **Homo est,** *he is a man.*
2. **Īgnis calet,** *fire is hot.*
3. **Amīcus adest,** (*his*) *friend is present.*
4. **Mundus ā Deō regitur,** *the world is ruled by God.*

Indirect.

1. **Dīcit sē hominem esse,** *he says that he is a man.*
2. **Sentīmus īgnem calēre,** *we perceive that fire is hot.*
3. **Putat amīcum adesse,** *he thinks that his friend is present.*
4. **Scīmus mundum ā Deō regī,** *we know that the world is ruled by God.*

Notice the difference between the direct and indirect forms of statement.

In the second group, compare the English with the Latin. Observe (1) that after the leading verb there is nothing in the Latin corresponding to the conjunction *that;* (2) that, while the English retains the nominative and indicative of the direct form, the Latin has instead the accusative and infinitive.

The second group illustrates the *indirect discourse,* so called because what some one says, thinks, or knows, is stated in the dependent clause *indirectly.*

**400.** Rule of Syntax. — **The accusative and infinitive are regularly used after verbs of *saying, thinking, knowing, perceiving,* and the like.**

**401.** Rule of Syntax. — **The subject of the infinitive is in the accusative.**

## 402. Tenses of the Infinitive.

### Present.

| | | |
|---|---|---|
| **dīcit** | **tē scrībere,** | *he says that you are writing.* |
| **dīcet** | | *he will say that you are writing.* |
| **dīxit** | | *he said that you were writing.* |
| **dīcit** | **epistulam scrībī,** | *he says that the letter is being written.* |
| **dīcet** | | *he will say that the letter is being written.* |
| **dīxit** | | *he said that the letter was being written.* |

### Future.

| | | |
|---|---|---|
| **dīcit** | **tē scrīptūrum esse,** | *he says that you will write.* |
| **dīcet** | | *he will say that you will write.* |
| **dīxit** | | *he said that you would write.* |
| **dīcit** | **epistulam scrīptum īrī,**[1] | *he says that the letter will be written.* |
| **dīcet** | | *he will say that the letter will be written.* |
| **dīxit** | | *he said that the letter would be written.* |

### Perfect.

| | | |
|---|---|---|
| **dīcit** | **tē scrīpsisse,** | *he says that you wrote (have written).* |
| **dīcet** | | *he will say that you wrote (have written).* |
| **dīxit** | | *he said that you wrote (had written).* |
| **dīcit** | **epistulam scrīptam esse,** | *he says that the letter was (has been) written.* |
| **dīcet** | | *he will say that the letter was (has been) written.* |
| **dīxit** | | *he said that the letter was (had been) written.* |

A study of the above table will show that the present infinitive denotes the *same* time as that indicated by the tense of the leading verb; that the future infinitive denotes time *after* that indicated by the leading verb; and that the perfect infinitive denotes time *before* that indicated by the leading verb.

**403.** Rule of Syntax. — **The tenses of the infinitive refer to present, future, or past time, *relatively* to the time of the leading verb.**

[1] More commonly, **fore ut epistula** with subj. Also see p. 192, n. 1.

## 2.

**404.** EXERCISES.

[It will be best to translate each of the following sentences twice; first, literally, just as they stand, then into good English: thus, *History relates two sons to have been to Cornelia = history relates that Cornelia had two sons.* The eighth thus: *The ambassador said himself a public messenger to be of the Roman people = the ambassador said that he was,* etc.]

I. 1. Historia nārrat duōs fīliōs Cornēliae fuisse. 2. Cornēlia dīxit fīliōs suōs esse ōrnāmenta sua. 3. Scīmus mātrēs fīliōs amāre. 4. Trāditum[1] est Caesarem ā Brūtō et Cassiō occīsum esse. 5. Certum est cāsū bonum fierī nēminem.[2] 6. Sciō haec vēra esse. 7. Mārcellus Hannibalem vincī posse docuit. 8. Lēgātus dīxit sē pūblicum nūntium esse populī Rōmānī. 9. Thalēs aquam dīxit esse initium rērum. 10. Trāditum est Homērum fuisse caecum. 11. Lēgātus dīcit montem ab hostibus tenērī.

[Before translating into Latin, cast each sentence mentally into the Latin form; thus the first sentence will be, *It is said two sons to have been to Cornelia,* or *Cornelia two sons to have had;* and the seventh, *We know you the truth to be about to tell.* This practice is of capital importance.]

II. 1. It is said that Cornelia had two sons. 2. Have we not heard that Cornelia had jewels? 3. I think that you will have jewels. 4. We know that Cornelia loved her boys. 5. Do not[3] all mothers think that their sons are their jewels? 6. I think that the moon will be full to-morrow. 7. We know that you will tell the truth. 8. History relates that Hannibal was defeated by Marcellus. 9. It is related that Homer wrote poems. 10. I know that this has been done. 11. He said that the enemy held the mountain.

---

[1] In the compound tenses of the passive voice the perfect participle occasionally loses its idea of time and becomes virtually an adjective. Here **trāditum est** = *it is (a thing) related.*

[2] Subject of **fierī.**

[3] **Nōnne.**

## 3.

**405.** EXERCISES.

[Read the first paragraph, page 191.]

I. 1. Jūrāte vōs rem pūblicam nōn dēsertūrōs esse. 2. Vōx quondam audīta est Rōmam ā Gallīs captum[1] īrī. 3. Certum est Hannibalem ā Scīpiōne victum esse. 4. Ferunt[2] eō diē lūnam fuisse plēnam. 5. Cum Nāsīca ad Ennium vēnisset, servus dīxit Ennium domī nōn esse. 6. Nāsīca sēnsit illum[3] intus esse. 7. Posteā cum ad Nāsīcam vēnisset Ennius, exclāmāvit ipse Nāsīca sē[3] domī nōn esse. 8. Catō dīcere solēbat acerbōs inimīcōs saepe vērum dīcere. 9. Abī, nūntiā tē vīdisse Gājum Marium in Carthāginis ruīnīs sedentem (*sitting*). 10. Mātrōna quaedam dictitābat sē trīgintā tantum annōs habēre.[4]

[See second paragraph, p. 191. The first sentence expressed in the Latin idiom will be, *Ennius says himself at home not to be;* the third, *He thinks himself at home to be about to be;* the fourth, *Cato thought his friends the truth not always to speak* (compare I. 8).]

II. 1. Ennius says that he is not at home. 2. He said that he had not been at home. 3. He thinks that he shall be at home to-morrow. 4. Cato thought that his friends did not always tell him[5] the truth. 5. It is evident that the world was not made by chance. 6. We have sworn that we will not desert our leader. 7. The soldiers swore that they had not deserted the republic. 8. It was evident that the enemy was being defeated.[6] 9. Do you not know that the enemy are near? 10. It is certain that they are advancing towards the town.

---

[1] **Captum,** being a supine (**433**), does not change its form to agree with **Rōmam.**

[2] **Ferunt** = **dīcunt.**

[3] Observe the difference between **illum** in 6 and **sē** in 7.

[4] *To have thirty years* = *to be thirty years old.*

[5] *Him* = *himself;* not accusative.

[6] Notice that the time of the dependent verb is present, with reference to that of the leading verb.

**406.** VOCABULARY.

**acerbus, -a, -um,** adj. [**ācer**], *harsh, bitter.*
**arbitror,** 1, *think, suppose, believe.*
**cōn-stat,** 1, **-stitit,** ——, impers. (**415**), *it is evident, clear.*
**dē-serō,** 3, **-uī, -tum,** *desert, abandon.*
**Ennius, -ī,** M., *Ennius,* a Roman poet.
**ex-clāmō,** 1, *cry out, exclaim.*
**Gallus, -ī,** M., *a Gaul.*
**historia, -ae,** F., *history.*
**in-imīcus,-a,-um,**adj.[**amīcus**], *unfriendly, hostile;* noun, *an enemy.* (**172.**)
**intus,** adv. [**in**], *inside, within.*
**jūrō,** 1 [**jūs**], *swear, take an oath.*
**Mārcellus, -ī,** M., *Marcellus,* a Roman general.
**mātrōna, -ae,** F. [**māter**], *wife, lady, matron.*
**nūntiō,** 1 [**nūntius**], *announce, report.*
**ōrnāmentum, -ī,** N. [**ōrnō**], *ornament, jewel.* (**345.** 9.)
**populus, -ī,** M., *people.*
**pūblicus, -a, -um,** adj. [**populus**] (*pertaining to the people*), *public.* (**345.** 19.)
**quondam,** adv., *once, formerly.*
**sentiō,** 4, **sēnsī, sēnsum,** *feel, know (by the senses), see, perceive.*
**tantum,** adv. [**tantus**], *only.*
**Thalēs, -is,** M., *Thales,* a Greek philosopher.
**trā-dō,** 3, **-didī, -ditum** [**trāns**], *give over, deliver; relate, recount.*
**vērum, -ī,** N. [**vērus**], *the truth.*

## 4.

**407.** FOR TRANSLATION.

### Nāsīca and Ennius.

Nāsīca,[1] cum ad poētam Ennium vēnisset,[2] eīque[3] ab ōstiō quaerentī[4] Ennium ancilla dīxisset eum domī[5] nōn esse, sēnsit illam[6] dominī jūssū dīxisse, et illum[7] intus esse. Paucīs post diēbus, cum ad Nāsīcam vēnisset Ennius et eum ā[8] jānuā quaereret, exclāmat Nāsīca sē domī nōn esse. Tum Ennius, "Quid? ego nōn cōgnōscō vōcem," inquit,[9] "tuam?"

[1] Subject of **sēnsit.**

[2] **Ad . . . vēnisset,** *had come to,* that is, *to call on.*

[3] *To him,* dat. of **is.** See **270.** 2.

[4] Pres. part. of **quaerō,** in the dat. with **eī,** *to him asking for.*

[5] See **336.**

[6] Refers to **ancilla,** and is the subject acc. of **dīxisse.**

[7] That is, **Ennius.**

[8] **Ā jānuā,** *at the door.*

[9] Observe the position of **inquit.**

Hīc[1] Nāsīca: "Homo es impudēns. Ego, cum tē quaererem, ancillae[2] tuae crēdidī tē[3] domī nōn esse; tū mihi nōn crēdis ipsī?"[4]

## CHAPTER LXIII. 1.

### PARTICIPLES.

**408.** Learn the participles of the regular and irregular verbs.

1. For declension of a present active participle, see **165**. The ablative singular generally ends in *e*, but in *ī* when the participle is used as an adjective.

2. The other participles, ending in *us, a, um*, are declined like **bonus** (**71**).

**409.** *Examine the following:* —

1. **Fortissimē dīmicāns** { **cadit**, *he falls* / **cadet**, *he will fall* / **cecidit**, *he fell* } *fighting most bravely.*
2. **Hostēs adortus prōflīgāvit**, *he attacked and routed* (*having attacked, he routed*) *the enemy.*
3. **Eī advenientī aquila pilleum sustulit**, *an eagle took off his cap as he was approaching* (*to him approaching*).
4. **Leōnidās superātus cēdere nōluit**, *Leonidas*, (*though*) *overpowered, would not yield.*
5. **Rōmā expulsus Athēnās ībit**, (*if*) *expelled from Rome, he will go to Athens.*
6. **Epistulam sibi commissam dētulit**, *he delivered the letter* (*which had been*) *intrusted to him.*
7. **Eā rē commōtus in Ītaliam rediit**, *he returned into Italy* (*because he was*) *alarmed at this event.*
8. **Nōs moritūrī salūtāmus**, *we*, (*who are*) *about to die, salute you.*
9. **Ob virginēs raptās**, *on account of the seizure of the maidens* (*maidens seized*).

---

[1] An adverb, *hereupon*.
[2] Dat. after **crēdidī**. See **343**.
[3] Subject acc. of **esse**. See **401**.
[4] Emphasizes **mihi**. (**270. 4.**)

Study the above examples with reference first to the tenses of the participles, and observe that the time of the participles is present, past, or future, relatively to the time of the leading verb.

Notice how the participle is translated in each example; only in the first is it best translated literally. What the Latin expresses by a participle we very often express by a clause beginning *as*, *though*, *if*, *because*, etc., by a relative clause, or by a verb coördinate with one following.

## 2.

**410.** EXERCISES.

[It will be best to translate every sentence literally, then into good English.]

I. 1. Remus irrīdēns mūrum trānsiliit. 2. Abī hinc, oblīta[1] frātrum, oblīta[1] patriae. 3. Lēgātō rēs repetentī[2] superbē respōnsum est[3] ā Latīnīs. 4. Faliscī statim beneficiō victī portās Rōmānīs aperuērunt. 5. Fīlius Manlī Latīnum ex equō excussum trānsfīxit.[4] 6. Rōmānī necessitāte victī lēgātōs mittunt. 7. Hunc Fabricius vinctum redūcī jūssit. 8. Hannibal causam bellī quaerēns Saguntum ēvertit. 9. Eā rē commōtus in Ītaliam rediit armīs injūriam acceptam vindicātūrus.[5] 10. Missōs[6] ā senātū lēgātōs honōrificē excēpit.

[Cast each of the following sentences into the Latin idiom before attempting to translate. Thus, *Romulus killed Remus laughing at* (acc. in agreement with *Remus*); *Horatius stabbed his sister forgetful* (**oblītam**); *to the ambassadors demanding*, etc.]

II. 1. Romulus killed Remus because he laughed at his wall. 2. Horatius stabbed his sister with his sword because

[1] Feminine of the perf. part. **oblītus,** from **oblīviscor.** Translate, *Thou who hast forgotten* (lit., *having forgotten*).

[2] *To the ambassador demanding* = *to the ambassador who demanded*, or *when the ambassador demanded*.

[3] **Respōnsum est,** *it was replied* = *answer was made.*

[4] **Excussum trānsfīxit,** *struck off and stabbed.* See **409.** 2.

[5] *About to avenge*, i.e., *in order to avenge*.

[6] Compare **409.** 6.

she was forgetful of her country. 3. The Latins answered the ambassadors[1] haughtily, when they demanded restitution. 4. The Gauls entered the open houses. 5. To the Romans, as they came out of the pass, the light was sadder than death[2] itself. 6. The old men went forth to meet[3] Manlius[1] as he was returning to Rome. 7.[4] They bound the prisoner and brought him back to the city. 8. The letter which had been written by the boy was delivered. 9. The Romans never despaired, though they were often defeated.[5] 10. Cæsar received the senate sitting,[6] when they came[7] to him.

**411.** VOCABULARY.

**com-moveō**, 2, **-mōvī**, **-mōtum**, *shake, disturb, excite, alarm.*

**dē-ferō**, **-ferre**, **-tulī**, **-lātum**, (*bring down*), *deliver.*

**dē-spērō**, 1, *be hopeless, despair.*

**ē-vertō**, 3, **-tī**, **-sum**, *overturn, overthrow, destroy.*

**ex-cutiō**, 3, **-cussī**, **-cussum** [**quatiō**], *shake out, strike off, drive away, cast out.*

**Faliscī**, **-ōrum**, M., *the Faliscans*, a people of Etruria.

**hinc**, adv. [**hīc**], *from this place, hence.*

**ir-rīdeō**, 2, **-rīsī**, **-rīsum** [**in**], *laugh at, ridicule, jest, mock.*

**Latīnus**, **-a**, **-um** [**Latium**], *Latin;* noun, *a Latin.*

**necessitās**, **-ātis**, F. [**necesse**], *necessity, constraint.*

**ob-viam**, adv., *in the way;* with verb of motion, *meet;* w. dat.

**pateō**, 2, **-uī**, ——, *lie open, be open;* part. **patēns**, *open.*

**porta**, **-ae**, F., *gate, door.* Cf. **jānua.**

**re-dūcō**, 3, **-xī**, **-ductum**, *lead back, bring back.*

**senior**, **-ōris**, M. & F. (comp. of **senex**, *old*), *elder, old person.*

**statim**, adv. (**stō**), (*standing there*), *on the spot, immediately, at once.*

**superbē**, adv. [**superbus**], *proudly, haughtily.*

**trāns-fīgō**, 3, **-fīxī**, **-fīxum**, *pierce through, pierce, stab.*

**vindicō**, 1, *claim, avenge, punish.*

---

[1] Dative.

[2] See **211, 212**.

[3] *To meet*, **obviam.**

[4] Compare I. 7.

[5] Not the last word: *the Romans often defeated*, etc.

[6] In agreement with *Cæsar.*

[7] *Had come.* See **373.**

# CHAPTER LXIV.

## PARTICIPLES: ABLATIVE ABSOLUTE.

**412.** *Examine the following:—*

| | | |
|---|---|---|
| **Sōle oriente, fugiunt tenebrae,** | *the sun rising,*<br>*when the sun rises,*<br>*at the rising of the sun,* | *the shadows flee away.* |
| **Datō signō, virginēs raptae sunt,** | *the signal having been given,*<br>*when the signal was given,*<br>*at the given signal,* | *the maidens were seized.* |
| **Eō rēgnante, bellum exortum est,** | *he reigning,*<br>*in his reign,*<br>*while he was reigning,* | *a war arose.* |
| **Cōnsul, bellō cōnfectō, Rōmam rediit,** | *the war having been finished,*<br>*when the war was finished,*<br>*having finished the war,* | *the consul returned to Rome.* |
| **Tē duce, hostēs vincēmus,** | *you (being) leader,*<br>*if you are our leader,*<br>*with you for a leader,* | *we shall conquer the enemy.* |
| **Messāllā et Pīsōne cōnsulibus,** | *M. and P. (being) consuls.*<br>*when M. and P. were consuls.*<br>*in the consulship of M. and P.* | |
| **Serēnō caelō,** | *the sky (being) clear.*<br>*when the sky is clear.*<br>*in a clear sky.* | |

1. The foregoing examples illustrate the very common construction called the **Ablative Absolute.**

2. In the first four examples there is a noun (or pronoun) in the ablative, and a participle agreeing with it. In the last three there is no participle expressed, but instead, another noun or an adjective.

3. Carefully compare the Latin with the English translation, and observe that each ablative absolute may be rendered by a clause beginning with *when, while,* or *if* (in other instances *because, although,* etc.), the Latin noun in the ablative becoming the subject of the clause in English, and that this noun refers to a *different person or thing* from the subject of the leading verb.

4. We may also sometimes translate the participle in the ablative absolute by a verb coördinate with a following verb. Thus the fourth might be translated, *The consul finished the war and returned.*

5. If I wish to express in the Latin, *While he was reigning, he carried on war, he* being the subject of both the principal and subordinate clauses, I say, **Is rēgnāns bellum gessit**; but if I wish to express, *While he was reigning, war arose, he* being subject of the subordinate clause, and *war* of the principal, I use the ablative absolute, thus, **Eō rēgnante, bellum exortum est.**

6. In the fourth example notice the change of idiom. We might say, *The consul, having finished the war, returned to Rome;* but the Latin has no perfect active participle corresponding to *having finished;* therefore, in Latin the perfect passive participle must be used in the ablative with the noun **bellum**. The same idea may, of course, be expressed by a **cum** clause. See **372**.

7. From the nature of deponent verbs (passive form with active meaning), it will be seen that the English participle with *having* may be directly expressed in Latin, if there is a deponent verb of the right meaning; thus, *Cæsar having encouraged his men,* **Caesar mīlitēs hortātus.**

8. Most instances of the so-called ablative absolute may be resolved as the ablative of time, means, cause, etc.

**413.** EXERCISES.

[Translate each ablative absolute in as many ways as possible.]

I. 1. Strictō gladiō, trānsfīxit puellam. 2. Expulsīs rēgibus, duo cōnsulēs creātī sunt. 3. Quō factō,[1] mūtāta est proelī fortūna. 4. Occupātā Siciliā, quid posteā āctūrus es? 5. Hannibal, vīsō frātris occīsī capite, dīxit: "Āgnōscō fortūnam Carthāginis." 6. Hīs parātīs rēbus, Caesar mīlitēs nāvēs cōnscendere jubet. 7. Hōc factō, tūtus eris. 8. Alpibus superātīs, Hannibal in Ītaliam vēnit. 9. Caesar, mortuō Sūllā, Rhodum sēcēdere statuit. 10. Dēlētīs Teutonibus, C. Marius in Cimbrōs sē convertit.

[1] *When this had been done.* What is it literally?

[Before trying to translate the following sentences, consider well in each case what the probable Latin form of expression, or idiom, would be for the subordinate clause, adverbial phrase, etc.; thus, *When he had stabbed the girl* = *the girl (having been) stabbed; When Numa was king* = *Numa (being) king; By hurling their javelins* = *by the javelins hurled.*]

II. 1. When he had stabbed the girl, he put by his sword. 2. On the expulsion of King Tarquin, Brutus and Collatinus were made consuls. 3. When Numa was king, the temple of Janus was built. 4. Cæsar, after he had overcome the Gauls, waged war with Pompey. 5. On the death of Cato, there was no longer[1] a republic. 6. Having learned these facts (things), he hastened against the enemy. 7. The soldiers, by hurling their javelins, broke the enemy's line. 8. Having held a levy, the consul sets out immediately for (*ad*) the army. 9. O my country, thou hast overcome my anger by employing a mother's entreaties. 10. If we do[2] this, we shall all be safe.

**414.** VOCABULARY.

**ad-moveō**, 2, **-mōvi**, **-mōtum**, (*move up, towards*), *apply, employ.*

**cōgnōscō**, 3, **-gnōvi**, **-gnitum** [**com**, **(g)nōscō**], *learn, recognize, know.*

**Collātinus**, **-ī**, M., *Collatinus*, surname of L. Tarquinius.

**con-iciō**, 3, **-jēcī**, **-jectum** [**jaciō**] (*throw together*), *throw, hurl.*

**con-tendō**, 3, **-dī**, **-tum** (*draw tight*), *exert one's self, strive, hasten; contend.*

**con-vertō**, 3, **-tī**, **-sum**, *turn round, turn, change*; **sē convertere**, *turn one's self, turn.*

**dēlēctus**, **-ūs**, M. [**dēligō**, *choose out*], *selection, levy.*

**dē-pōnō**, 3, **-posuī**, **-positum**, *put down, put by, lay down.*

**ex-pellō**, 3, **-pulī**, **-pulsum**, *drive out* or *away, expel.*

**Jānus**, **-ī**, M., *Janus*, the two-faced god.

**per-fringō**, 3, **-frēgī**, **-fractum** [**frangō**, *break*], *break through, break.*

**Rhodus**, **-ī**, F., *Rhodes*, an island in the Ægean.

**sē-cēdō**, 3, **-cēssī**, **-cēssum**, *go apart, withdraw, retire.*

**statuō**, 3, **-uī**, **-ūtum**, *put, place; think, believe, determine.*

**stringō**, 3, **-nxī**, **strictum** (*draw tight*), *graze; draw, unsheathe.*

---

[1] *No longer* = **nūlla jam.** [2] *Shall have done.*

# CHAPTER LXV. 1.

## IMPERSONAL VERBS.

**415.** *Examine the following:* —

1. **Pluit,** *it rains.*
2. **Tonat,** *it thunders.*
3. **Mē pudet stultitiae meae,** *I am ashamed (it shames me) of my folly.*
4. **Eum paenitet sceleris,** *he repents (it repents him) of his crime.*
5. **Pūgnābātur,** *fighting was going on (it was being fought).*
6. **Caesarī**[1] **pārendum**[2] **est,** *Cæsar must be obeyed (it must be obeyed to Cæsar).*
7. **Tibi licet exīre,** *you may go out (it is permitted to you to go out).*
8. **Hōc nōs facere oportet,** *we ought to do this (it behooves us to do this).*
9. **Caesarī placuit ut lēgātōs mitteret,** *Cæsar determined (it pleased Cæsar) to send ambassadors.*

(1) Observe in each of the foregoing examples that the leading verb has no personal subject either expressed or implied. In 7, the subject of **licet** is the infinitive **exīre**; in 8, the phrase **hōc nōs facere** is the subject of **oportet**; in 9, the clause **ut lēgātōs mitteret** is the subject of **placuit**. In each of the first six the subject is contained in the verb itself.

(2) Some verbs, like **pluit, tonat, pudet, paenitet, licet,** the use of which is mostly confined to the third person singular, are called **Impersonal Verbs**; many others, as in the examples **pūgnābātur, oportet, placuit,** are sometimes *used impersonally.*

(3) Examples 7 and 8 show one way of rendering *may* and *must* into Latin.

(4) In 3 and 4 notice the use of the accusative and genitive after the verbs.

**416.** Rule of Syntax. — **The impersonal verbs *miseret, paenitet, piget, pudet, taedet* take the accusa-**

---

[1] See **417.** 2. [2] See **425.** (4).

**tive of the person and the genitive of the object or cause of the feeling.**

Some examples of verbs used impersonally have already been given. See **362.** I. 9; **370.** I. 5; **410.** I. 3.

**417.** *Examine the following:* —

| ACTIVE. | PASSIVE. |
|---|---|
| 1. **Frātrī persuādet,** *he persuades his brother.* | **Frātrī persuādētur,** *his brother is persuaded.* |
| 2. **Lēgibus pārēbant,** *they obeyed the laws.* | **Lēgibus pārēbātur,** *the laws were obeyed.* |
| 3. **Crēdit mihi,** *he believes me.* | **Mihi crēditur,** *I am believed.* |
| 4. **Amīcīs nocent,** *they injure their friends.* | **Amīcīs nocētur,** *their friends are injured.* |

Observe that the verbs are intransitive. Compare the active and passive in the examples one by one. Observe that in each case the passive is expressed by putting the verb in the third person singular, leaving the indirect object of the active unchanged.

**418.** RULE OF SYNTAX. — **Intransitive verbs are used impersonally in the passive, the person or thing affected (the subject in English) being expressed by the dative.**

**419.** EXERCISES.

I. 1. Omnēs decet rēctē agere. 2. Diū et ācriter pūgnātum est. 3. Sequitur ut falsum sit. 4. Eōrum nōs miseret.[1] 5. Taedet mē vītae. 6. Statuendum[2] vōbīs ante noctem est. 7. Licet mihi ex urbe ēgredī. 8. Nōs oportuit[3] hōc facere. 9. Trāditum est Scīpiōnem doctum fuisse. 10. Eādem nocte accidit ut esset lūna plēna. 11. Obsistitur illīs. 12. Cuī[4] parcī potuit? 13. Persuādētur cōnsulī.

[1] Compare **415.** 3 and 4.

[2] *The duty of deciding is to you* = *you must decide.* Compare **425.** 7.

[3] *It behooved us to do* = *we ought to have done.*

[4] See **343.**

[Observe that the following sentences are modelled closely on the foregoing, and on the illustrative examples. Cast each one into the Latin form before thinking of the Latin words; thus the fifth sentence will be changed to *It disgusts me of the folly*, etc.]

II. 1. It becomes us all to live well. 2. The battle will be fought bravely. 3. It followed that[1] the enemy were defeated. 4.[2] He was ashamed of his cowardice. 5. I am disgusted with the folly of the men. 6. What must we do? 7. What ought we to have done?[3] 8.[4] May I take the book? 9. It was reported to Cæsar that the enemy were approaching. 10. It resulted[5] from these circumstances[6] that[1] all were silent. 11. The winds are opposed with difficulty. 12. Can the soldier be spared? 13. Are not the laws of the republic obeyed?

**420.** VOCABULARY.

**decet,** 2, **decuit,** impers., *it is seemly, becoming, fitting.*

**ē-gredior,** 3, **-gressus [gradior],** *go out, go forth, march out.* Cf. **exeō.**

**fortiter,** adv. **[fortis],** *bravely, courageously.*

**licet,** 2, **-uit,** or **-itum est,** impers., *it is permitted, it is lawful, (one) may.*

**miseret,** 2, **-itum est,** impers. **[miser],** *it makes miserable, it excites pity, (one) pities.*

**ob-sistō,** 3, **-stitī, -stitum,** *oppose, withstand, resist,* w. dat.

**oportet,** 2, **-uit,** impers., *it is necessary, it behooves, (one) must* or *ought.*

**parcō,** 3, **peperci,** or **parsī,** ——, *spare,* w. dat.

**piget,** 2, **-uit,** or **-itum est,** impers., *it disgusts, (one) is disgusted.*

**pudet,** 2, **-uit,** or **-itum est,** impers., *it shames, (one) is ashamed.*

**pūgnō,** 1 **[pūgna],** *fight.*

**stultitia, -ae,** F. **[stultus,** *foolish***],** *folly.* (**345.** 11.)

**taedet,** 2, **-uit,** or **taesum est,** impers., *it disgusts, wearies, (one) is disgusted.*

**vix,** adv., *hardly, with difficulty.*

---

[1] A *result* clause, **ut,** etc.

[2] Compare **415.** 3.

[3] Compare I. 8.

[4] Compare **415.** 7.

[5] **Fiēbat.**

[6] **Rēs.**

## 2.

421. FOR TRANSLATION.*

### THE DEATH OF THE PET SPARROW.

Lugete, o Veneres Cupidinesque,
Et quantumst[1] hominum[2] venustiorum.
Passer mortuus est meae puellae,
Passer, deliciae meae puellae,
Quem plus illa oculis[3] suis amabat:
Nam mellitus erat suamque[4] norat[5]
Ipsa[6] tam bene quam puella matrem
Nec sese a gremio illius[7] movebat,
Sed circumsiliens modo huc modo illuc
Ad solam dominam usque pipiabat.
Qui[8] nunc it per iter tenebricosum
Illuc unde negant redire quemquam.[9]
At vobis male sit,[10] malae tenebrae
Orci, quae omnia bella[11] devoratis:
Tam bellum mihi[12] passerem abstulistis.
O factum male![13] io miselle passer!
Tua nunc opera[14] meae puellae[15]
Flendo turgiduli rubent[16] ocelli.—*Catullus.*

---

[1] For **quantum est.** Translate, *all ye lovely ones, whoever ye are.* What is it literally?

[2] Depends on **quantum.** See **340.**

[3] Ablative after the comparative **plūs.** See **212.**

[4] Supply **dominam.**

[5] For **nōverat,** but with the meaning of the imperfect.

[6] With **puella.**

[7] That is, **puellae.**

[8] Refers to **passer.**

[9] Subject acc. of **redīre.** See **401** and **279.** 6.

[10] *Ill betide you!*

[11] From **bellus.**

[12] Translate *my.*

[13] **Factum male,** *woful deed.* What is it literally?

[14] *On your account.*

[15] Genitive after **ocellī.**

[16] **Turgidulī rubent,** *are all swollen and red.*

# CHAPTER LXVI. 1.

## PERIPHRASTIC CONJUGATIONS.

### Future Active Participle. — Gerundive.

[*Review the participles of the regular and irregular verbs.*]

**422.** The future active participle with the verb **sum** forms the First, or Active Periphrastic Conjugation: **amātūrus sum, eram**, etc., *I am, was*, etc., *about to (going to, intending to) love.*

**423.** The gerundive with the verb **sum** forms the Second, or Passive Periphrastic Conjugation: **amandus sum, eram**, etc., *I am, was*, etc., *to be loved; I deserve, ought*, etc., *to be loved.*

**424.** PARADIGMS.

| | ACTIVE. | PASSIVE. |
|---|---|---|
| | Indicative. | |
| Pres. | **amātūrus sum** | **amandus sum** |
| Imper. | **amātūrus eram** | **amandus eram** |
| Fut. | **amātūrus erō** | **amandus erō** |
| Perf. | **amātūrus fuī** | **amandus fuī** |
| Plup. | **amātūrus fueram** | **amandus fueram** |
| F.P. | **amātūrus fuerō** | **amandus fuerō** |
| | etc. | etc. |

**425.** *Examine the following:* —

1. **Nōn dubitō quīn monitūrus sit**, *I do not doubt that he will advise.*
2. **Nōn dubitō quīn futūrum sit ut id fīat**, *I do not doubt that (it will happen that it be done) it will be done.*
3. **Sciēbam quid āctūrus essēs**, *I knew what you were going to do.*
4. **Pontem faciendum cūrat**, *he (takes care a bridge to be built) has a bridge built.*
5. **Dēlenda est Carthāgō**, *Carthage must be destroyed.*
6. **Caesarī omnia erant agenda**, *everything had to be done by Cæsar.*
7. **Mihi scrībendum est**, *(the duty of writing is to me) I must write.*

8. **Omnibus moriendum est,** (*the necessity of dying is to all*) *all must die.*

9. **Vōbīs jūdiciō ūtendum est,** (*the duty of using judgment is to you*) *you ought to use judgment.*

(1) The first three examples show how a future tense may be supplied for the subjunctive mood.

(2) Observe in the fourth example the use of the gerundive agreeing with a noun which is the object of **cūrō**, the whole expression denoting *to have a thing done.*

(3) The last five examples show some uses of the passive periphrastic conjugation. Notice that the idea of *necessity,* or *duty,* is prominent in these forms.

(4) In 8 and 9 **moriendum est** and **ūtendum est** are used impersonally, that is, without any personal subject, the gerundive being in the nominative singular neuter. This impersonal use belongs to verbs which do not take the accusative case. **Jūdiciō** is in the ablative after **ūtor**. See **304**.

(5) In the last four examples, **Caesarī, mihi, omnibus,** and **vōbīs,** denote in each case the person *to whom* there is a duty or necessity of doing something. This dative is most conveniently rendered with *by,* and is called the **Dative of Agent.**

**426.** Rule of Syntax. — **The dative is used with the gerundive to denote the person by whom the act must be done.**[1]

## 2.

**427.** EXERCISES.

I. 1. Quis dubitat quīn futūrī sītis doctī? 2. Quis dubitat quīn lūdōs vīsūrī sīmus? 3. Nōn erat dubium quīn lūdōs vīsūrus esset. 4. Nōlī dubitāre quīn crās ventūrus sim. 5. Cōgnōvī quid āctūrus sit. 6. Audiam quid āctūrus sīs. 7. Cōgnōveram quid āctūrī essent. 8. Dux castra mōtūrus est. 9. Scrībenda est mihi epistula. 10. Scrībenda erat

[1] How is the agent with a verb in the passive otherwise and commonly expressed?

tibi epistula. 11. Oppidum mīlitibus oppūgnandum erit. 12. Hīc liber mihi legendus est.

II. 1. There is no doubt that you are going to be a hero. 2. I doubt not that you will see the games. 3. Do not doubt[1] that he will be present. 4. Do you know what he is going to do? 5.[2] We ought to cultivate virtue. 6.[2] I must give the signal. 7.[2] We ought to read the poets. 8. The commander must be obeyed.[3] 9. The boy is not to be believed. 10. The town had to be fortified.

### 3.

428. EXERCISES.

I. 1. Quaesīvit ex ōrāculō Croesus utrum ipse superātūrus esset. 2. Nōn erat dubium quīn Faliscī sēsē Rōmānīs dēditūrī essent. 3. Nisi vīnum dēfēcisset, plūra et graviōra dictūrī fuimus. 4. Māgnam in spem veniēbat fore[4] ut pertināciā dēsisteret hostis. 5. Cum Scīpiō, graviter vulnerātus, in hostium manūs jamjam ventūrus esset, fīlius eum perīculō līberāvit. 6. Hōc cēnseō et Carthāginem esse dēlendam. 7. Aemilius līberōs Graecīs litterīs ērudiendōs[5] cūrāverat. 8. Caesarī dandum erat tubā sīgnum. 9. Mihi ūtendum est jūdiciō meō.[6] 10. Ita nōbīs vīvendum est, ut ad mortem parātī sīmus.

II. 1. I will ask of the general whether he is going to advance. 2. Who doubts that the Romans will surrender themselves to the Faliscans? 3.[7] If words had not failed, I was going to write a longer letter. 4. I think the enemy will be defeated. 5. When Cæsar was on the point of

[1] **Nōlī dubitāre.** How else may this be expressed?

[2] Express in two ways — by using **oportet**, and then by the gerundive.

[3] Lit. *it must be obeyed to the commander.* Cf. **415.** 6.

[4] **Fore** = **futūrum esse,** *to be about to be,* may be omitted in translation.

[5] Compare **425.** 4, and (2).

[6] See **425.** 9.

[7] Compare I. 3.

starting[1] for Rome, he received a letter from Pompey. 6. My opinion is[2] that the town ought to be besieged. 7. These things must not be despised by[3] us. 8. A wise man will have his boys trained[4] in Latin literature.[5] 9. The citizens[6] must obey the laws. 10. The soldiers must use their own judgment.

**429.** VOCABULARY.

**Aemilius, -ī,** M., *Æmilius,* a Roman consul.

**cēnseō,** 2, **-uī, -um,** *estimate; think, deem, be of opinion.*

**Croesus, -ī,** M., *Crœsus,* king of Lydia.

**dē-dō,** 3, **-didī, -ditum,** (*put away from one's self*) *surrender, deliver up.*

**dē-ficiō,** 3, **-fēcī, -fectum** [**faciō**], (*make away from*) *revolt; fail, be wanting.*

**dē-sistō,** 3, **-stitī, -stitum,** (*stand off* or *apart*) *leave off, cease, desist.*

**doctus, -a, -um,** adj. [P. of **doceō**], *learned.*

**gravis, -e,** adj., *heavy, serious.*

**graviter,** adv., *heavily, seriously.*

**ita,** adv., *thus, so.*

**jamjam,** adv., *already;* **jamjam ventūrus,** *on the point of coming.*

**jūdicium, -ī,** N. [**jūdicō**], *judgment, opinion.*

**op-pūgnō,** 1 [**ob**], *attack, assault, besiege.*

**ōrāculum, -ī,** N. [**ōrō**], *oracle.*

**parātus, -a, -um,** adj. [P. of **parō**], *ready, prepared.*

**pertinācia, -ae,** F. [**pertināx,** *persistent*], *perseverance, obstinacy.* (**345**. 11.)

**signum, -ī,** N., *mark, sign, signal.*

**ūtor,** 3, **ūsus,** *use, employ,* w. abl.

**utrum,** adv., *whether.* Cf. **num, 382.**

**jūdicō, cēnseō, existimō, arbitror, putō,** and **opīnor,** all mean *think;* but the first four imply more deliberation and reflection; primarily *think* as a judge, a magistrate, an appraiser, an arbiter; hence, in general, of official, authoritative opinion. **Putō** and **opīnor** imply rather private, personal judgment or opinion.

---

[1] *On the point of starting = already about to start.*

[2] *This I think.* Cf. I. 6.

[3] See **425**. (5).

[4] Cf. I. 7, and **425**. (2).

[5] Compare **232**. I. 4.

[6] **Ā cīvibus,** to distinguish the agent from the indirect object.

# CHAPTER LXVII.

## GERUND. — GERUNDIVE. — SUPINE.

**430.** Learn the gerunds and supines of the regular and irregular verbs.

### Gerund.

**431.** *Examine the following:* —

G. **Caesar loquendī fīnem facit,** *Cæsar makes an end of speaking.*

**Cupidus est tē audiendī,** *he is desirous of hearing you.*

D. **Aqua ūtilis est bibendō,** *water is useful for drinking.*

Ac. **Inter pūgnandum trīgintā nāvēs captae sunt,** *during the fight (amid the fighting) thirty ships were taken.*

Ab. **Mēns discendō alitur,** *the mind is strengthened by learning.*

1. The above examples illustrate the use of the gerund in its several cases. It will be seen that the gerund is used like the English verbal noun in *ing.* The nominative is supplied in Latin by the infinitive; *e.g.,* **vidēre est crēdere,** *seeing is believing.*

### Gerund and Gerundive.

**432.** *Examine the following:* —

| | | | |
|---|---|---|---|
| G. | **Cōnsilia** | **urbem dēlendī,**<br>**urbis dēlendae,** | *plans for (of) destroying the city.* |
| D. | **Operam dat** | **agrōs colendō** (rare)<br>**agrīs colendīs,** | *he devotes himself to tilling the fields.* |
| Ac. | **Vēnērunt ad** | **pācem petendum** (rare)<br>**pācem petendam,** | *they came to sue for peace.* |
| Ab. | **Occupātus sum in** | **litterās scrībendō** (rare)<br>**litterīs scrībendīs,** | *I was engaged in writing letters.* |

1. What is to be particularly studied in the above examples is the difference between the gerund and the gerundive construction, as shown within the braces. Observe (1) that *the* **gerund** *is put in the required case, and has its object in the accusative;* (2) that *the* **noun** *is put in the required case, and the gerundive agrees with it.*

2. Except in the genitive, where the two constructions are about equally common, the gerundive construction is almost always preferred.

3. Notice that the accusative of the gerund or gerundive with **ad** denotes a purpose. This construction is much used. In what other ways may a purpose be expressed?

## Supine.

**433.** *Examine the following:—*

1. **Lēgātī Rōmam veniunt pācem petītum,** *ambassadors come to Rome to sue for peace.*
2. **Id perfacile est factū,** *that is very easy to do,* or *to be done.*

Observe in the first example that the supine **petītum** has the same meaning as **ut petant, quī petant,** or **ad petendam**; that is, it expresses purpose. This use is common after verbs of motion.

**434.** Rule of Syntax.—**The supine in *um* is used after verbs of motion to express purpose.**

In the second example the supine in **ū** answers the question *in what respect?* **Perfacile factū,** *easy in respect to the doing.* This use is common after adjectives.

The supine in **ū** is really an *ablative of specification.* See **260.**

**435.** EXERCISES.

I. 1. Multī convēnēre studiō[1] videndae novae urbis. 2. Ars puerōs ēducandī difficilis est. 3. Ea[2] aquae causā[3] hauriendae dēscenderat. 4. Brūtus ad explōrandum cum equitibus antecēssit. 5. Mīlitēs ad domum custōdiendam ā rēge missī sunt. 6. Nēminī dubium est quīn Fabius rem Rōmānam cunctandō restituerit. 7. Is opportūnus vīsus est locus commūniendō praesidiō. 8. Omnis spēs ēvādendī adempta est. 9. Lēgātōs ad Caesarem mittunt auxilium rogātum. 10. Quod optimum est factū, faciam.

---

[1] *With the desire;* abl. of cause.

[2] *She.* See **270.** 2.

[3] The ablative **causā,** *for the sake of,* follows its genitive.

II. 1. You will have time to lead (of leading) out the army from that place. 2. He undertook the war for the sake[1] of destroying the republic. 3. Bodies are nourished by eating and drinking. 4. While drinking[2] we conversed about many things. 5. Many leaders had assembled to see[3] Scipio. 6. Night put[4] an end to the fighting. 7. This seems (to be) a suitable place for building a house. 8. The enemy had entertained[5] the hope of getting possession of the camp.[6] 9. A multitude of men came together to witness[3] the games. 10. It is difficult to say what he will do.[7]

**436.** VOCABULARY.

**ad-imō, 3, -ēmī, -ēmptum** [**emō**], *take away, remove.*

**alō, 3, -uī, -tum,** *nourish, strengthen, support.*

**ante-cēdō, 3, -cēssī, -cēssum,** *go before.*

**auxilium, -ī,** N. [**augeō**], *help, aid, support;* pl. *auxiliaries.*

**col-loquor, 3, -locūtus** [**com**], *speak together, converse.*

**com-mūniō, 4,** (*fortify strongly*) *secure, intrench.*

**con-veniō, 4, -vēnī, -ventum** [**com**], *come together, assemble.*

**cunctor, 1,** *linger, hesitate.*

**edō, edere** or **ēsse, ēdī, ēsum** or **ēssum,** *eat.*

**ex-plōrō, 1,** *search out, examine, explore; reconnoitre.*

**Fabius, -ī,** M., *Fabius,* a Roman general.

**hauriō, 4, hausī, haustum,** *draw (water), drain, drink up.*

**opportūnus, -a, -um,** adj., *fit, convenient, suitable; opportune.*

**re-stituō, 3, -uī, -ūtum** [**statuō**], (*replace*) *give back, return, restore.*

**sus-cipiō, 3, -cēpī, -ceptum** [**sub, capiō**], *undertake.*

[1] **Causā.** See p. 209, note 3.

[2] **Inter bibendum.**

[3] Express in three ways.

[4] *Put an end to = make an end of.*

[5] *Entertain the hope = come into the hope.*

[6] What case with **potior**?

[7] Why must the subjunctive be used? What tense of the subjunctive to express future time? What form expresses the immediate future?

# READING LESSONS.

## LETTERS: Cicero to his Wife Terentia.

**437.** B.C. 49.

Sī valēs, bene est, valeō.[1] Dā operam[2] ut convalēscās. Quod opus[3] erit, ut[4] rēs tempusque postulat, prōvideās[5] atque administrēs; et ad mē dē omnibus rēbus quam[6] saepissimē litterās mittās. Valē.

**438.** B.C. 49.

S. V. B. E. E.[7] V. Valētūdinem tuam velim[8] cūrēs[9] dīligentissimē.[10] Nam mihi et[11] scrīptum et nūntiātum est tē[12] in febrim subitō incidisse. Quod[13] celeriter mē fēcistī dē Caesaris litterīs certiōrem,[14] fēcistī mihi grātum. Item posthāc, sī quid[15] opus erit,[16] sī quid acciderit novī,[17] faciēs[18] ut sciam. Cūrā ut valeās. Valē.

---

1 The Romans often began their letters with these five words, or rather with the abbreviations S. V. B. E. V.

2 *Give labor = try.*

3 An indeclinable noun, *need;* **opus est,** *is necessary.*

4 What indicates that **ut** does not mean *in order that?*

5 The hortatory subjunctive. See **390**.

6 **Quam** strengthens the superlative; **quam saepissimē,** *as often as possible.*

7 For **ego.**

8 *I could wish;* **volō,** *I wish.*

9 Equivalent to **ut cūrēs.**

10 Notice the emphatic position of the adverb, after the verb.

11 **Et . . . et,** *both . . . and.*

12 Subj. of **incidisse.** See **401.**

13 *In that.*

14 **Fēcistī . . . certiōrem,** *made more certain = informed.*

15 *Anything;* **quid** is regularly used instead of **aliquid** after **sī, nisi, nē,** and **num.**

16 See note 3, above.

17 *Of new;* partitive genitive.

18 A future equivalent to the imperative. **Faciēs ut sciam,** *inform me.* What is it literally?

**439.** B.C. 46.

Sī valēs, bene est.[1] Cōnstituerāmus, ut[2] ad tē anteā scrīpseram, obviam Cicerōnem[3] Caesarī mittere; sed mūtāvimus cōnsilium, quia dē illīus[4] adventū nihil audiēbāmus. Dē cēterīs rēbus, etsi nihil erat novī,[5] tamen quid velīmus[6] et quid hōc tempore putēmus[6] opus[7] esse ex Siccā[8] poteris cōgnōscere. Tulliam adhūc mēcum teneō. Valētūdinem tuam cūrā[9] dīligenter. Valē.

**440.** B.C. 46.

[10]S. V. B. E. V. Nōs neque dē Caesaris adventū neque dē lītterīs quās Philotīmus habēre dīcitur, quidquam[11] adhūc certī[12] habēmus. Sī quid erit certī, faciam tē statim certiōrem.[13] Valētūdinem tuam fac[14] ut cūrēs. Valē.

---

1 Compare this form of beginning a letter with those of the two preceding.

2 Compare the use of **ut** in **437**, line 2.

3 That is, his son Cicero.

4 That is, Cæsar's.

5 Genitive neuter of **novus** depending on **nihil**. Compare the same word in **438**, and the note.

6 Translate the words **quid velīmus**, etc., just as they stand.

7 Compare **opus erit** in **437** and **438**, and the note.

8 A friend of Cicero.

9 Compare with this the beginning and the ending of **438**.

10 Observe how nearly this letter can be translated in the order of the Latin words.

11 *Anything at all.* To express *anything at all*, after a negative word, as here after **neque**, the Romans used **quidquam**, not **aliquid**. See **279**. 6.

12 Genitive neuter of **certus**, depending on **quidquam**. Compare **novī** in **438** after **quid**, and in **439** after **nihil**.

13 Compare **fēcistī certiōrem** in **438**, and the note.

14 See p. 150, note. **Fac ut cūrēs**, *be sure to take care.* What is the literal meaning? Compare with this the endings of the two preceding letters.

## FABLES.

**441.** DĒ VITIĪS HOMINUM.

Jūppiter nōbīs[1] duās pērās imposuit: alteram,[2] quae nostrīs vitiīs replēta est, post tergum nōbīs dedit; alteram[2] autem, quā[3] aliōrum vitia continentur, ante pectus nostrum[4] suspendit. Quārē nōn vidēmus quae[5] ipsī peccāmus; sī autem aliī peccant, statim eōs vituperāmus.

**442.** MULIER ET GALLĪNA.

Mulier quaedam habēbat gallīnam, quae eī[6] cotīdiē ōvum pariēbat aureum. Hinc suspicārī coepit illam[7] aurī massam intus cēlāre, et gallīnam occīdit. Sed nihil in eā repperit, nisi quod[8] in aliīs gallīnīs reperīrī solet.[9] Itaque dum mājōribus dīvitiīs inhiat,[10] etiam minōrēs[11] perdidit.

**443.** VULPĒS ET ŪVA.

Vulpēs ūvam in vīte cōnspicāta[12] ad illam subsiliit omnium vīrium suārum contentiōne,[13] sī eam forte attingere posset.

---

1 With **imposuit**; *has placed on us.*

2 **Alter . . . alter,** *the one . . . the other.*

3 **Quā = in quā pērā.**

4 Compare **ante pectus nostrum** with **post tergum nōbīs.**

5 *What we sin = what sins we commit.* On **ipsī,** see **270.** 4.

6 *For her.*

7 **Illam = illam gallīnam,** subject of **cēlāre.**

8 **Nisi quod = praeter id quod.**

9 *Is wont = is usually.*

10 *Gapes for = is greedy for.* Notice here a peculiarity of the Latin: the present is used after **dum,** though the perfect **perdidit** follows. The English idiom requires us to translate such a present by the imperfect, *was greedy for.*

11 Supply the Latin noun in the proper form.

12 Perfect participle of **cōnspicor,** agreeing with **vulpēs.** Translate by the present participle.

13 *With the exertion.*

Tandem dēfatīgāta inānī labōre discēdēns, "At nunc etiam," inquit, "acerbae[1] sunt, nec eās[1] in viā repertās[2] tollerem."[3]

**444.** RŪSTICUS ET CANIS FIDĒLIS.

Rūsticus in agrōs exiit ad opus suum. Fīliolum, quī in cūnīs jacēbat, relīquit canī[4] fidēlī atque validō custōdiendum.[5] Adrēpsit anguis immānis, quī puerulum exstinctūrus erat. Sed custōs fidēlis corripit eum dentibus acūtīs, et, dum eum necāre studet,[6] cūnās simul ēvertit super exstinctam anguem. Paulō post ex arvō rediit agricola; cum cūnās ēversās cruentumque canis rīctum vidēret,[7] īrā accenditur.[8] Temerē igitur custōdem fīliolī interfēcit ligōne, quem manibus tenēbat. Sed ubi cūnās restituit,[9] super anguem occīsum repperit puerum vīvum et incolumem. Paenitentia facinoris[10] sēra[11] fuit.

**445.** PUER MENDĀX.

Puer in prātō ovēs pāscēbat,[12] atque per jocum clāmitābat, ut sibi auxilium ferrētur, quasi lupus gregem esset adortus. Agricolae undique succurrēbant, neque[13] lupum inveniēbant. Ita ter quaterque sē ēlūsōs ā puerō vīdērunt. Deinde[14] cum ipse[15] lupus aggrederētur, et puer rē vērā[16] implōrāret au-

1 The plural, as if **ūvae** had been used.

2 **Eās repertās,** *them found* = *if I had found them.*

3 *Would I pick them up.*

4 The so called dative of the agent with **custōdiendum.** Translate, *left for his . . . dog to guard.*

5 Literally, *to be guarded.*

6 See p. 213, note 10.

7 For the subjunctive, see **373.**

8 Present for perfect, called *historical present.*

9 Translate as if it were **restituerat**; after **ubi, ut,** and **postquam,** meaning *when,* the perfect indicative is commonly used, but it is best rendered by the pluperfect.

10 Translate, *for the deed.*

11 *Too late.*

12 The imperfect, denoting customary action; render, *used to tend.*

13 *But . . . not.*

14 See p. 106, note 1.

15 *Really.* See **270. 6.**

16 **Rē vērā,** *in earnest.*

xilium, nēmō gregī subvēnit,[1] et ovēs lupī praeda[2] sunt factae. Mendācī hominī[3] nōn crēdimus, etiam cum vēra dīcit.

**446.** SENEX ET MORS.

Senex quīdam līgna in silvā cecīderat,[4] et, fasce in umerōs sublātō,[5] domum redīre coepit. Cum fatīgātus esset[6] et onere et itinere, dēposuit līgna, et, senectūtis[7] et inopiae[7] miseriās sēcum reputāns, clārā vōce invocāvit mortem, ut sē omnibus malīs[8] līberāret. Mox adest[9] mors et interrogat quid vellet. Tum senex perterritus: "Prō! hunc līgnōrum fascem, quaesō, umerīs[10] meīs impōnās."[11]

**447.** VULPĒS ET LEŌ.

Vulpēs nunquam leōnem vīderat. Cum huīc forte occurrisset, ita exterrita est, ut paene morerētur[12] formīdine.[13] Eundem cōnspicāta est iterum. Tum extimuit illa quidem, sed nēquāquam ut anteā. Cum tertiō[14] leōnī obviam facta esset, adeō nōn perterrita fuit,[15] ut audēret[12] accēdere propius et colloquī cum eō.

---

[1] Cf. **succurrō.** See **343.** How does the meaning *help* come from the primitive meaning?

[2] Predicate nominative.

[3] Why dative? See **343.**

[4] From **caedō,** not **cadō.**

[5] From **tollō,** not **sufferō.**

[6] For the subjunctive, see **373.**

[7] Notice the order: the genitives coming first are made emphatic.

[8] Abl. of separation. See **130.**

[9] See p. 214, note 8.

[10] **Umerīs . . . impōnās,** cf. **nōbīs . . . imposuit** in **441.**

[11] **Quaesō impōnās** = **quaesō ut impōnās.**

[12] Is this clause a *purpose* or *result* clause? See illustrative examples, **352** and **368.**

Are the clauses beginning with **cum** *temporal* or *causal?* Read again the illustrative examples, **372** and **374.**

[13] *Of fright.*

[14] *The third time.*

[15] *To such a degree was not frightened* = *was so far from being frightened.*

## CÆSAR'S TWO INVASIONS OF BRITAIN.

**448.** [In the latter part of the summer of B.C. 55, Cæsar brought his ships together into the country of the Morini, who occupied the seacoast from the modern Boulogne northward, and set sail for Britain.]

Caesar ipse cum omnibus cōpiīs in Morinōs proficiscitur, quod[1] inde erat brevissimus in Britanniam trājectus. Hūc nāvēs[2] undique ex fīnitimīs regiōnibus et quam[3] superiōre aestāte[4] effēcerat clāssem jubet convenīre.

Nactus[5] idōneam ad nāvigandum tempestātem, tertiā ferē[6] vigiliā solvit, equitēsque in ūlteriōrem portum prōgredī et nāvēs cōnscendere et sē sequī jūssit. Ipse hōrā[7] circiter diēī quartā cum prīmīs nāvibus Britanniam attigit, atque ibi in omnibus collibus expositās hostium cōpiās armātās cōnspexit. Hunc[8] ad ēgrediendum nēquāquam idōneum locum arbitrātus, dum reliquae nāvēs eō convenīrent, ad hōram nōnam in ancorīs[9] exspectāvit. Tum ventum et aestum ūnō tempore nactus secundum,[10] datō sīgnō et sublātīs ancorīs, circiter

---

1 *Because.*

2 Subject acc., together with **clāssem,** of **convenīre.**

3 Goes with **clāssem.** Translate aloud the whole sentence, first following strictly the order of the Latin words, and rendering **quam,** *what.* Probably the meaning will then be clear, and your translation can be recast into good English.

This method of discovering the meaning of a Latin sentence, as distinguished from that of trying to determine first the subject and predicate, and then the modifiers of each, will often be found very helpful.

4 Ablative of time when. See **136.**

5 From **nanciscor.** Cf. **nanctī,** p. 220, line 1.

6 See p. 154, note 1. In translating to **jūssit,** observe the suggestion in note 3.

7 Translate as if the order were **circiter quartā hōrā diēī,** but observe that **circiter** is here an adverb, and **hōrā** has the construction of **aestāte,** line 4, and **vigiliā,** line 6.

8 Goes with **locum.**

9 **In ancorīs,** *at anchor.*

10 Goes with **ventum** and **aestum.**

mīlia passuum septem ab eō locō prōgressus, apertō āc plānō lītore[1] nāvēs cōnstituit. At barbarī, cōnsiliō Rōmānōrum cōgnitō, nostrōs nāvibus ēgredī[2] prohibēbant.

[It seemed for a time as if Cæsar would not be able to effect a landing at all. The Britons, *barbari*, as Cæsar calls them, some standing on the edge of the shore, or advancing into the water, others driving in their horses with their two-wheeled chariots a little way, to get nearer to the ships, fought the Romans manfully. But they had to deal with an enemy as brave and determined as themselves, and the Romans were fighting under the eye of Cæsar. At last one daring soldier showed them how to conquer.]

Is[3] quī decimae legiōnis aquilam ferēbat contestātus deōs ut ea rēs[4] legiōnī fēlīciter ēvenīret, "Dēsilīte," inquit,[5] "mīlitēs, nisi vultis aquilam hostibus prōdere: ego certē meum[6] reī pūblicae atque imperātōrī officium praestiterō." Hōc cum[7] vōce māgnā dīxisset, sē ex nāvī prōjēcit atque in hostēs aquilam ferre coepit. Tum nostrī, cohortātī[8] inter sē, ūniversī ex nāvī dēsiluērunt.[9] Pūgnātum est ab utrīsque[10] ācriter. Nostrī tamen in hostēs impetum fēcērunt atque eōs in fugam dedērunt.

[As a result of this fight, and of some subsequent defeats, the Britons submitted to Cæsar, who soon after returned to Gaul.

---

1 We should expect **in lītore.**

2 *From disembarking.* Cf. **prōgressus, ēgrediendum, prōgredī,** above. It is by vigilant observation in reading, and comparison of different forms from the same root, rather than from incessant resort to vocabularies and dictionaries, that the task of getting a working knowledge of Latin words is to be accomplished. "Recollect that brains and common sense, not thumbs, should get most exercise."

3 Subject of **inquit.** Observe the suggestion of p. 216, note 3.

4 Do not translate *thing.*

5 Always placed after one or more of the words quoted.

6 **Meum . . . officium,** *my to the public and to the general duty.* Mark the order, and see how it gives emphasis to **meum.**

7 *When,* not *with.* See **373.**

8 **Cohortātī inter sē,** *encouraging each other.*

9 Cf. **dēsilīte,** above.

10 From **uterque.**

The following summer, B.C. 54, Cæsar prepared for a second invasion of Britain. With about 20,000 foot-soldiers and 2,000 horsemen, he set sail from Portus Itius, which is probably the modern Wissant, and landed in the neighborhood of Deal. There are many reasons for supposing that these were the places of the embarkation and landing of the preceding year.]

Caesar ad portum Itium, quō ex portū commodissimum[1] in Britanniam trājectum esse cōgnōverat, circiter[2] mīlium passuum trīgintā ā continentī, cum legiōnibus pervēnit. Ibi cōgnōscit sexāgintā nāvēs,[3] quae in Meldīs factae erant, tempestāte rējectās[4] cursum tenēre nōn potuisse atque eōdem unde erant profectae revertisse; reliquās parātās ad nāvigandum atque omnibus rēbus īnstrūctās invēnit. Eōdem equitātus tōtīus[5] Galliae convēnit numerō[6] mīlium quattuor, prīncipēsque ex omnibus cīvitātibus; ex quibus perpaucōs, quōrum in sē[7] fidem perspexerat,[8] relinquere in Galliā, reliquōs obsidum locō[9] sēcum dūcere dēcrēverat;[10] quod, cum ipse abesset, mōtum Galliae verēbātur.

Itaque diēs circiter vīgintī quīnque in eō locō commorātus, quod cōrus ventus nāvigātiōnem impediēbat, quī māgnam partem omnis temporis in hīs locīs flāre cōnsuēvit,[11] tandem idōneam nactus tempestātem[12] mīlitēs equitēsque cōnscendere[13] in nāvēs jubet.

---

1 **Commodissimum . . . trājectum.** Compare the order in line 2, p. 216, and 7, p. 217. In trying this first sentence, change mentally the order **quō ex** to **ex quō**; then observe the suggestion of note 3, p. 216.

2 Cf. **circiter mīlia passuum,** p. 216, line 13.

3 Subject acc. of **potuisse** and **revertisse.** Try this sentence by the method already recommended.

4 From **rēiciō.**

5 For irregularity of declension, see **200.**

6 *In number* = *to the number.* **260.**

7 **In sē,** *towards himself.*

8 Cf. **cōnspexit,** p. 216, line 9.

9 **Obsidum locō,** *in the place of hostages* = *as hostages.*

10 From **dēcernō.**

11 From **cōnsuēscō.**

12 **Idōneam nactus tempestātem.** Cf. p. 216, line 5.

13 **Cōnscendere in nāvēs.** Cf. **nāvēs cōnscendere,** p. 216, l. 7.

Labiēnō[1] in continente cum tribus legiōnibus et equitum mīlibus duōbus relīctō, ut portūs tuērētur et rem frūmentāriam prōvidēret, quaeque[2] in Galliā gererentur cōgnōsceret, cōnsiliumque prō[3] tempore et prō rē caperet, ipse cum quīnque legiōnibus[4] et parī numerō equitum quem[5] in continentī relinquēbat sōlis occāsū nāvēs[6] solvit; et lēnī Āfricō prōvectus, ortā lūce[7] sub sinistrā[8] Britanniam relīctam cōnspexit.

Accēssum[9] est ad Britanniam omnibus nāvibus merīdiānō ferē[10] tempore, neque in eō locō hostis est vīsus; sed, ut posteā Caesar ex captīvīs cōgnōvit, cum[11] māgnae manūs eō convēnissent, multitūdine nāvium perterritae, ā lītore discēsserant āc sē in superiōra loca abdiderant.[12]

Caesar, expositō exercitū et locō castrīs idōneō captō, ubi ex captīvīs cōgnōvit quō in locō[13] hostium cōpiae cōnsēdissent,[14] dē[15] tertiā vigiliā ad hostēs contendit. Noctū prōgressus mīlia passuum circiter duodecim hostium cōpiās cōnspicātus[16] est. Illī equitātū atque essedīs ad flūmen prōgressī ex locō superiōre nostrōs prohibēre et proelium committere coepērunt. Repulsī ab equitātū sē[17] in silvās

---

[1] **Labiēnō . . . relīctō.** See **412.**

[2] **Quaeque** = **et quae.** The **quo** connects **prōvidēret** and **cōgnōsceret:** *and might find out what was going on in Gaul.*

[3] **Prō tempore et prō rē,** *as the time and circumstances required.*

[4] **Quīnque legiōnibus.** See top of page 218.

[5] **Parī . . . quem,** *with a number equal (to that) which.*

[6] **Nāvēs solvit:** cf. p. 216, line 6.

[7] **Ortā lūce,** *light having arisen = at daybreak;* **ortā,** from **orior.**

[8] Supply **manū;** *under the left hand = on the left.*

[9] **Accēssum est ad,** *it was come to = they reached.* See **415** (2).

[10] See p. 154, note 1.

[11] Concessive. See **375.**

[12] From **abdō.**

[13] **Quō in locō,** *in what place.* Compare for order **quō ex portū,** p. 218, line 1.

[14] From **cōnsīdō.**

[15] *During.* Cf. p. 216, lines 5 and 6.

[16] Compare for meaning **cōnspexit,** line 7.

[17] **Sē abdidērunt:** cf. line 13.

abdidērunt, locum nanctī[1] ēgregiē et nātūrā et opere mūnītum. Ipsī ex silvīs rārī[2] prōpūgnābant nostrōsque intrā mūnītiōnēs ingredī[3] prohibēbant. At mīlitēs legiōnis septimae testūdine factā et aggere ad mūnītiōnēs adjectō,[4] locum cēpērunt eōsque ex silvīs expulērunt, paucīs vulneribus acceptīs. Sed eōs fugientēs longius[5] Caesar prōsequī vetuit, et[6] quod locī nātūram īgnōrābat, et quod māgnā parte diēī cōnsūmptā mūnītiōnī castrōrum tempus relinquī volēbat.

Postrīdiē ējus diēī māne tripartītō mīlitēs equitēsque in expedītiōnem mīsit, ut eōs quī fūgerant[7] persequerentur.

[While Cæsar was in pursuit of the enemy, messengers came to tell him that a violent wind had dashed his ships upon the shore and broken up many of them, so that he was obliged to return. Ten days were spent in hauling the ships up on land and strongly intrenching them; then, leaving men to guard and repair them, he resumed his advance.

Cæsar crossed the Thames where the river was fordable, at what point is uncertain, meeting all the time with a determined resistance from the Britons, but at last forcing them to submission. The brave Cassivellaunus, chief of the Britons, did his best to defend his country, and showed himself a worthy antagonist even of Cæsar; nor would he yield to the Roman till his principal dependents had dispersed with their troops and deserted him. The autumnal equinox was now at hand, and Cæsar thought it unsafe to remain longer in Britain.]

Obsidibus acceptīs exercitum redūcit ad mare, nāvēs[8] invenit refectās. Hīs dēductīs, quod et captīvōrum māgnum numerum habēbat, et nōnnūllae tempestāte dēperierant[9] nāvēs, duōbus commeātibus exercitum reportāre īnstituit, āc,

---

[1] Cf. p. 216, line 5, and note.

[2] *Here and there.*

[3] **Ingredī prohibēbant**: cf. **ēgredī prohibēbant**, p. 217, line 3, and note.

[4] From **adiciō.**

[5] *Too far.*

[6] *Both.*

[7] Distinguish between **fugiō** and **fugō.**

[8] We should expect **nāvēsque.**

[9] From **dēpereō.**

summā tranquillitāte cōnsecūtā, secundā initā[1] cum solvisset[2] vigiliā, prīmā lūce terram attigit omnēsque incolumēs nāvēs perdūxit.

---

## THE CUSTOMS AND HABITS OF THE BRITONS.

**449.** Britanniae pars interior ab iīs incolitur, quōs nātōs[3] in īnsulā ipsā memoriā prōditum[4] dīcunt; maritima pars ab iīs quī praedae āc bellī īnferendī[5] causā[6] ex Belgīs trānsierant. Hominum est īnfīnīta multitūdō crēberrimaque aedificia, ferē Gallicīs cōnsimilia; pecorum māgnus numerus. Ūtuntur aut aere,[7] aut nummō aereō, aut taleīs ferreīs ad certum pondus exāminātīs prō nummō. Nāscitur ibi plumbum album in mediterrāneīs regiōnibus, in maritimīs ferrum, sed ējus exigua est cōpia. Māteria cūjusque generis ut in Galliā est praeter fāgum atque abietem. Leporem et gallīnam et ānserem gustāre fās[8] nōn putant; haec tamen alunt animī voluptātisque causā.[9]

Ex hīs omnibus longē sunt hūmānissimī quī[10] Cantium incolunt, quae regiō est maritima omnis, neque multum ā Gallicā differunt cōnsuētūdine. Interiōrēs plērīque[11] frūmenta nōn serunt, sed lacte et carne[12] vīvunt, pellibusque sunt

---

1 From **ineō**; with **vigiliā**.

2 Cf. p. 216, line 6, and p. 219, line 6.

3 **Quōs nātōs,** *whom (to have been) born in the island itself, by memory (to have been) handed down, they say.* That is, *who, they say, according to tradition* (**memoriā prōditum**), *were born in the island itself.*

4 Supply **esse,** as also with **nātōs.**

5 How otherwise might this be?

6 **Praedae . . . causā.** See p. 209, note 1.

7 From **aes.**

8 Supply **esse.**

9 *For the sake of their mind and pleasure = for pastime.* Cf. for the order **praedae . . . causā,** note 6.

10 Understand **iī,** *those,* as the antecedent of **quī.** See p. 130, note 3.

11 **Interiōrēs plērīque,** *the people of the interior for the most part.*

12 From **carō.**

vestītī. Omnēs vērō sē Britannī vitrō īnficiunt, quod caeruleum efficit colōrem, atque hōc[1] horridiōrēs sunt in pūgnā adspectū;[2] capillōque[3] sunt prōmissō atque omnī parte[4] corporis rāsā praeter caput et labrum superius.

[1] *On this account.*

[2] *In appearance.* See **260**.

[3] **Capillō . . . prōmissō**: descriptive ablative (**341**). *They are with long hair = they let their hair grow long.*

[4] **Parte . . . rāsā**: another descriptive ablative. *They are with every part of the body shaven = they shave the whole body.* **Rāsā**, from **rādō.**

# VOCABULARIES.

# LATIN-ENGLISH VOCABULARY.

---

In this vocabulary words inclosed in brackets are, in most cases, those which are given in Latin lexicons and special vocabularies as the primitives of those against which they are set. But, except in compounds, it would be more correct to regard the bracketed words as *connected with the others in formation from a common root or stem*. It is on this ground that such instances will be found as *metus* referred to *metuō*, and *metuō* to *metus*. Neither is, strictly speaking, derived from the other, but both are formed from the stem *metu*.

Words printed in *Gothic Italic* type are at once derivatives and definitions. Many other more or less remotely derived words, not definitions, are added in SMALL CAPITALS.

It will be seen that comparisons of words in reference to meaning are much more frequent than is usual in special vocabularies. This has been done from the conviction that the pupil should make such comparisons frequently from the outset.

---



**ā** or **ab,** prep. w. abl., *away from, by.*

**ab-dō,** 3, -didī, -ditum, *remove, conceal.* Cf. cēlō.

**ab-dūcō,** 3, -dūxī, -ductum, *lead away, take off.*

**ab-eō,** -īre, -iī, -itum, *go from, go off, go away.* (327.)

**ab-iciō,** 3, -jēcī, -jectum [jaciō], *throw off, throw down.*

**abies,** -etis, F., *fir-tree.* (11. 4.)

**ab-sum,** -esse, āfuī, *be away, **absent**, distant;* with **ā** or **ab** and abl.

**āc,** conj., see atque.

**ac-cēdō,** 3, -cēssī, -cēssum [ad], *go* or *come near, approach.* ACCEDE. Cf. appropīnquō.

**ac-cendō,** 3, -dī, -cēnsum [ad, and supposed candō], *kindle, inflame.*

**accidō,** 3, -cidī, —— [ad, cadō], *fall upon, fall out, happen.* ACCIDENT. Cf. incidō and ēveniō.

**accipiō,** 3, -cēpī, -ceptum [ad, capiō], (*take to*), *receive, **accept**; suffer.*

**accūsō,** 1 [ad, causa], ***accuse.***

**ācer,** ācris, ācre, adj., *sharp, keen; active.* (150.) ACRID. Cf. acūtus.

**acerbus,** -a, -um, adj. [ācer], *bitter, sour, harsh.*

**aciēs,** -ēī, F. [ācer], *edge; order of battle.*

**ācriter,** adv. [ācer], *sharply, eagerly.*

**acūtus,** -a, -um, adj. [acuō, *sharpen*], *sharp.* Cf. ācer.

**ad,** prep. w. acc., *to, towards, near.*

**ad-eō,** adv., *to this, thus far; so, so very.*

**ad-eō,** -īre, -iī, -itum, *go to, approach, visit.* (327.)

**ad-ferō,** adferre, attulī, allātum (adl), *bear to, bring.* (321.)

**ad-hūc,** adv., *hitherto, up to this time.*

**ad-flō,** 1, *blow upon.*

**ad-iciō,** 3, -jēcī, -jectum [jaciō], (*throw to* or *against*), *add, join to.*

**ad-imō,** 3, -ēmī, -ēmptum [emō], (*take to one's self from another*), *take away, remove.*

**ad-ipiscor,** 3, adeptus [apiscor], *get, obtain.* Cf. potior.

**ad-jungō,** 3, -jūnxī, -jūnctum, *add, join.* ADJUNCT.

**ad-juvō,** 1, -jūvī, -jūtum, *aid, help.*

**ad-ministrō,** 1, *manage, do, perform,* ***administer.***

**ad-mīror,** 1, *wonder at,* ***admire.***

**ad-modum,** adv., *very.*

**ad-moveō,** 2, -mōvī, -mōtum (*move up* or *towards*), *apply, employ.*

**ad-orior,** 4, -ortus (*rise up against*), *attack.* Cf. aggredior.

**ad-rēpō,** 3, -rēpsī, -rēptum, *creep towards, steal slowly up.*

**ad-spiciō (asp),** 3, -spexī, -spectum [ad, speciō], *look at; look.*

**adspectus,** -ūs, M. [adspiciō], *sight, appearance,* ***aspect.***

**ad-sum,** -esse, -fuī (affuī), *be present, stand by, side with,* w. dat.

**adulēscēns,** -entis, M. and F. [adolēscō, *grow*], *youth, young person.* ADOLESCENCE. Cf. juvenis.

**ad-veniō,** 4, -vēnī, -ventum, *come to, arrive.* Cf. perveniō.

**adventus,** -ūs, M. [adveniō], *approach, arrival.* ADVENT.

**ad-versus,** prep. w. acc., *against, towards.*

**ad-versus,** -a, -um, adj. [P. of advertō], *opposite, opposed,* ***adverse;*** rēs adversae, ***adversity.***

**aedificium,** -ī, N. [aedificō], *building.* EDIFICE.

**aedificō,** 1 [aedis, faciō], *build.*

**aedis** (ēs), -is, F., *building, temple;* plur., *house.*

**aeger,** aegra, aegrum, adj., *sick, weak, feeble.*

**Aemilius,** -ī, M., ***Æmilius,*** *a Roman consul.* (79.)

**aequālis,** -e, adj. [aequus], ***equal;*** noun, *equal in age, companion.*

**aequus,** -a, -um, adj., *level,* ***equal;*** *calm.*

**āēr,** āeris, M., ***air.***

**aereus,** -a, -um [aes], *of copper, of bronze.*

**aes,** aeris, N., *copper, bronze; money.*

**aestās,** -ātis, F., *summer.*

**aestus,** -ūs, M., *tide.*

**aetās,** -ātis, F., ***age,*** *time of life.* (105.)

**af-flīgō,** 3, -xī, -ctum [ad], *cast down, prostrate, ruin.*

**Āfrica,** -ae, F., ***Africa.***

**Āfricānus,** -ī, M. [Āfrica], ***Africanus,*** *surname of Scipio.*

**Āfricus,** -ī, M., *south-west (wind).*

**ager,** agrī, M., *field, territory.* Cf. campus.

**agger,** -eris, M. [ad, gerō], (*what is carried to,* i.e.) *materials for a mound; mound, rampart.*

**aggredior,** 3, -gressus [ad, gradior], *go to; attack.* AGGRESSIVE. Cf. adorior.

**agitō,** 1 [frequentative of agō], *shake, disturb, vex, chase.* AGITATE.

**āgnōscō,** 3, -nōvī, -nitum [ad, (g)nōscō, *know*], *recognize.* Cf. cōgnōscō.

**agō,** 3, ēgī, āctum, *drive, lead;* ***act,*** *do.*

**agricola,** -ae, M. [ager, colō], *farmer.*

**agrī cultūra,** -ae, F. [ager, colō], ***agriculture.*** Cf. agricola.

**āla,** -ae, F., *wing.*

**albus,** -a, -um, adj., *white.* Cf. candidus.

**Alexander,** -drī, M., ***Alexander,*** *king of Macedon.*

**aliēnus,** -a, -um, adj. [alius], *belonging to another; another's.* ALIEN.

**alimentum,** -ī, N. [alō], *nourishment, food, provisions.*

**aliquandō,** adv. [alius], *at some time, ever; formerly, once.* Cf. ōlim.

**aliquis,** -qua, -quid (-quod), indef. pron., *some one, some.* (279.)

**alius,** -a, -ud, adj., *another, other;* alius . . . alius, *one . . . another.* (201.)

**al-loquor** [adl], 3, -locūtus [ad], *speak to, address.*

**alō,** 3, -uī, -itum and -tum, *nourish, support, strengthen; keep.*

**Alpēs,** -ium, F., *the Alps.*

**alter,** -era, -erum, adj., *the other (of two);* alter . . . alter, *the one . . . the other;* as num. adj., *second.* (200.)

**altus,** -a, -um, adj., *high, deep.*

**ambō,** -ae, -ō, num. adj., *both.*

**ambulō,** 1, *walk, take a walk.*

**America,** -ae, F., *America.*

**amīcitia,** -ae, F. [amīcus], *friendship.*

**amīcus,** -a, -um, adj. [amō], *friendly;* noun, *friend.*

**ā-mittō,** 3, -mīsī, -missum, *send away, let go, lose.* Cf. perdō.

**amnis,** -is, M., *river.* (172.)

**amō,** 1, *love, like, be fond of.* (319.)

**amplus,** -a, -um, adj., *large, splendid, renowned.* AMPLE.

**an,** conj., *or,* used in the second member of a double question.

**ancilla,** -ae, F., *maid-servant.*

**ancora,** -ae, F., *anchor.*

**Ancus,** -ī, *Ancus, fourth king of Rome.*

**Androclus,** -ī, M., *Androclus.*

**anguis,** -is, M., *snake, serpent.* (154.)

**angustiae,** -ārum, F. [angustus, *narrow*], *narrow pass.* Cf. Eng. "narrows."

**animal,** -ālis, N. [anima, *breath*], *living being, animal.* (149.)

**animus,** -ī, M., *mind, soul, spirit.* (273.)

**annus,** -ī, M., *year.* ANNUAL.

**ānser,** -eris, M., *goose.*

**ante,** prep. w. acc., *before.*

**anteā,** adv. [ante], *before.*

**ante-cēdō,** 3, -cessī, -cessum, *go before.* Cf. anteeō.

**ante-eō,** -īre, -iī, ——, *go before, surpass.* Cf. antecēdō.

**antīquus,** -a, -um, adj. [ante], *old, ancient.* ANTIQUITY. Cf. vetus.

**ānulus,** -ī, M., *ring, finger-ring.*

**aper,** aprī, M., *wild boar.*

**aperiō,** 4, -uī, -tum, *open.*

**apertus,** -a, -um, adj. [P. of aperiō], *uncovered, open.*

**ap-pellō,** 1 [ad], *address, call, name.* APPEAL.

**ap-petō,** 3, -īvī, or -iī, -ītum [ad], *seek after, strive for.*

**ap-propinquō,** 1 [ad], *come near, approach.* Cf. accēdō.

**aptō,** 1, *fit, apply, adjust.* ADAPT.

**apud,** prep. w. acc., *with, by, near, among.*

**Āpūlia,** -ae, F., *Apulia, a division of Italy.*

**aqua,** -ae, F., *water.* AQUATIC.

**aquila,** -ae, F., *eagle.*

**āra,** -ae, F., *altar.*

**arātrum,** -ī, N. [arō], *plough.*

**arbitror,** 1, *think, suppose, believe.* (429.)

**arbor,** -oris, F., *tree.*

**arceō,** 2, -uī, -tum, *keep off.*

**arcus,** -ūs, M., *bow.* ARC.

**Ariovistus,** -ī, M., *Ariovistus, king of a German tribe.*

**arma,** -ōrum, N. [armō], *arms, weapons, tools.*

**armō,** 1 [arma], *arm, equip.*

**arō,** 1, *plough.*

**Arpīnum,** -ī, N., ***Arpinum,*** *a town in Italy.*
**ars,** artis, F., ***art.***
**arvum,** -ī, N. [arō], *ploughed land, field.*
**arx,** arcis, F., *citadel.* (163.)
**Ascalaphus,** -ī, M., ***Ascalaphus.***
**Asia,** -ae, F., ***Asia.***
**asper,** -era, -erum, adj., *rough, harsh, severe.* ASPERITY.
**asȳlum,** -ī, N., *place of refuge,* ***asylum.***
**at,** conj., *but.* (393.)
**āter,** -tra, -trum, adj., *black, sable.*
**Athēnae,** -ārum, F., *Athens.*
**Athēniēnsis,** -e, adj., [Athēnae], *of Athens,* ***Athenian.***
**at-que** (before vowels and consonants, **āc** before consonants only) [ad, *in addition*], *and also, and especially, and.* Cf. et and -que.
**atrōx,** -ōcis, adj. [āter], *savage, fierce, harsh, cruel.* ATROCIOUS.
**Atticus,** -ī, M., ***Atticus,*** *a friend of Cicero.*
**attingō,** 3, -tigī, -tactum [ad, tangō], *touch, approach, arrive at, reach.*
**auctor,** -ōris, M. [augeō. *increase*], *maker,* ***author.***
**auctōritās,** -ātis, F. [auctor], *counsel, advice,* ***authority.***
**audācter,** adv. [audāx], *boldly.*
**audāx,** -ācis, adj. [audeō], *daring, bold.* (164). AUDACIOUS.
**audeō,** 2, ausus [audāx], *dare, be bold.* (p. 177, note 2.)
**audiō,** 4, *hear, listen.* (223.) AUDIENCE.
**au-ferō,** auferre, abstulī, ablātum [ab(s)], *bear off, carry away.* (321.) ABLATIVE.
**augeō,** 2, auxī, auctum, *increase, enlarge.*
**aureus,** -a, -um, adj. [aurum], *of gold, golden.*
**auris,** -is, F., *ear.*
**aurum,** -ī, N., *gold.*
**aut,** conj., *or;* **aut . . . aut,** *either . . . or.* Cf. vel.
**autem,** conj. (never the first word), *but, however, moreover.* (393.)
**autumnus,** -ī, M., ***autumn.***
**auxilium,** -ī, N. [augeō], *help, aid, support;* plur., ***auxiliaries.***
**avārus,** -a, -um, adj., *greedy, rapacious.* AVARICIOUS.
**ā-vertō,** 3, -tī, -sum, *turn away from,* ***avert.***
**avis,** -is, F., *bird.* (154.)
**avunculus,** -ī, M. [diminutive of avus], (maternal) ***uncle.***
**avus,** -ī, M., *grandfather.*

**barbarus,** -a, -um, adj., *foreign,* ***barbarous, barbarian.***
**beātus,** -a, -um, adj. [beō, *bless*], *blessed, happy.* BEATITUDE.
**Belgae,** -ārum, M., *the Belgae, a Gallic tribe.*
**bellō,** 1 [bellum], *war, carry on war.* Cf. bellum gerō.
**bellum,** -ī, N. [bellō], *war.*
**bellus,** -a, -um, adj., *pretty, charming, lovely.*
**bene,** adv. [bonus], *well.*
**beneficium,** -ī N. [bene, faciō], ***benefit,*** *favor.*
**benignē,** adv. [benīgnus], *kindly.*
**benīgnus,** -a, -um, adj. [bene, genus], (*of good birth*), *kind, good.* BENIGNANT.
**bēstia,** -ae, F., ***beast.***
**bibō,** 3, bibī, pōtum, *drink.* IMBIBE.
**bonum,** -ī, N. [bonus], *good thing, blessing;* plur., *goods, possessions.*

**bonus**, -a, -um, adj., comp. melior, superl. optimus; *good.* (208.)

**bōs**, bovis, M. and F., *ox, cow.* (262.)

**Bostonia**, -ae, F., *Boston.*

**bracchium**, -ī, N., *arm.*

**brevis**, -e, adj., *short, brief.*

**Britannī**, -ōrum, M., *the Britons.*

**Britannia**, -ae, F., *Britain.*

**Brūtus**, -ī, M., *Brutus, a Roman surname.*

**C.**, *abbreviation for Gājus.*

**cachinnō**, 1, *laugh aloud.* Cf. rīdeō.

**cadō**, 3, cecidī, cāsum, *fall.*

**caecus**, -a, -um, adj., *blind.*

**caedō**, 3, cecīdī, caesum, *cut, cut to pieces; kill.*

**caelum**, -ī, N., *sky, heaven.*

**caeruleus**, -a, -um, adj. [for caeluleus, from caelum], *dark-blue.*

**Caesar**, (J.), -aris, M., *Julius Caesar, a famous Roman.*

**Cāius**, -ī, M. See Gājus.

**calathus**, -ī, M., *basket.*

**calcar**, -āris, N. [calx, *heel*], *spur.* (149.)

**callēns**, -entis, adj. [P. of calleō, *be hard*], *hard, tough.*

**calliditās**, -ātis, F. [callidus, *cunning*], *shrewdness, cunning.*

**calor**, -ōris, M. [caleō, *be warm*], *heat, warmth.* CALORIC.

**Campānia**, -ae, F., *Campania, a division of Italy.*

**campus**, -ī, M., *field.* CAMP. Cf. ager.

**candidus**, -a, -um, adj. [candeō, *shine*], *bright, fair, white.* CANDID. Cf. albus.

**canis**, -is, M. and F., *dog.* (153.) CANINE.

**Cannae**, -ārum, F., *Cannae, a village in Apulia.*

**Cannēnsis**, -e, adj. [Cannae], *of Cannae.*

**Cantium**, -ī, N., *Kent (in Britain).*

**cantō**, 1 [canō], *sing.* CHANT.

**cantus**, -ūs, M. [canō], *singing, song.* (278.) CHANT.

**capillus**, -ī, M., *hair (of the head).* CAPILLARY.

**capiō**, 3, cēpī, captum, *take, seize* (235); cōnsilium capiō, *adopt a plan.* CAPTURE.

**captīvus**, -ī, M. [capiō], *captive, prisoner.*

**caput**, -itis, N., *head.* (105.) CAPITAL.

**Carbō**, -ōnis, M., *Carbo, a Roman.*

**carcer**, -eris, M., *prison.* INCARCERATE.

**careō**, 2, -uī, -itum, *be without, want.*

**carmen**, -inis, N., *song, poem.* (278.)

**carō**, carnis, F., *flesh.*

**carpō**, 3, -sī, -tum, *pluck.*

**carrus**, -ī, M., *wagon, cart.* CAR.

**Carthāginiēnsis**, -e, adj. [Carthāgō], *of Carthage, Carthaginian.*

**Carthāgō**, -inis. F., *Carthage, a town in Africa.*

**Carthāgō Nova**, *a town in Spain.*

**cārus**, -a, -um, adj., *dear, precious.*

**castra**, -ōrum, N., *camp.*

**cāsus**, -ūs, M. [cadō], *a falling; mischance, misfortune, chance.*

**catellus**, -ī, M. [diminutive of catulus], *little dog, puppy.*

**Catilīna**, -ae, M., *Catiline, a famous Roman conspirator.*

**Catō**, -ōnis, M., *Cato, a celebrated Roman censor.*

**cauda**, -ae, F., *tail.*

**causa**, -ae, F., *cause, reason;* **causā** (after a genitive), *for the sake.*

**caveō**, 2, cāvī, cautum, *beware, guard against.*

**cēdō**, 3, cēssī, cēssum, *go, depart, withdraw; grant.*

**celer**, -eris, -ere, adj., *swift.* (179.) CELERITY.

**celeriter**, adv. [celer], *swiftly.*

**cēlō**, 1, *conceal.* Cf. abdō.

**cēnseo**, 2, -uī, -um, *reckon; think, deem, be of opinion.* CENSURE. (429.)

**centum**, num. adj., indecl., *hundred.* CENT.

**Cerēs**, -eris, F., *Ceres, goddess of agriculture.* CEREAL.

**certē**, adv. [certus], *certainly, surely, of course.*

**certō**, 1, *contend, strive, vie with.*

**certus**, -a, -um, adj., *fixed, determined, certain, sure;* certiorem faciō, *make (one) more certain, inform.*

[**cēterus**], -a, -um, adj. (usually in plur.), *the other, the rest.*

**cibus**, -ī, M., *food.* Cf. pābulum.

**Cicerō**, -ōnis, M., *Cicero, a famous Roman orator.*

**Cimbrī**, -ōrum, M., *the Cimbri, a German tribe.*

**cingō**, 3, cinxī, cinctum, *bind, encircle, surround.*

**circiter**, adv. [circus, *circle*], *round about; about.*

**circum-dūcō**, 3, -dūxī, -ductum, *lead around.*

**circum-siliō**, 4, -iī, —— [saliō], *jump* or *hop around.*

**circum-veniō**, 4, -vēnī, -ventum, *surround; circumvent.*

**cīvis**, -is, M. and F., *citizen.* CIVIC.

**cīvitās**, -ātis, F. [cīvis], (*body of citizens*), *state; citizenship.* CITY.

**clādēs**, -is, F., *destruction, defeat, disaster.*

**clāmitō**, 1 [frequentative of clāmō], *cry out, call out.* Cf. exclāmō.

**clāmor**, -ōris, M. [clāmō], *shout, cry.* CLAMOR.

**clārus**, -a, -um, adj., *clear, renowned, famous; loud.*

**clāssis**, -is, F., *class of citizens; fleet.*

**cliēns**, -entis, M., *client.* (163.)

**coepī**, coepisse (defective verb, tenses from pres. stem wanting), *began.*

**coerceō**, 2, -uī, -itum [co(m), arceō, *inclose*], *confine, check, restrain.*

**cōgnōscō**, 3, -nōvī, -nitum [com, (g)nōscō], *learn, recognize, know.* Cf. āgnōscō.

**cōgō**, 3, -ēgī, -āctum [com, agō], *drive together, compel.*

**co-hortor**, 1 [co(m), intensive], *exhort, urge, encourage.*

**Collātīnus**, -ī, M., *Collatinus, surname of Lucius Tarquinius.*

**collēga** (conl), -ae, M. [legō], (*one who is chosen with another*), *colleague.*

**colligō** (conl), 3, -lēgī, -lectum [com, legō], *collect.*

**collis**, -is, M., *hill.* Cf. mōns.

**colloquium**, -ī, N. [colloquor], *conversation, colloquy.*

**col-loquor**, 3, -locūtus [com], *speak together, converse.*

**colō**, 3, coluī, cultum, *cultivate, till.* Cf. incola, agricola.

**colōnia**, -ae, F. [colōnus, *husbandman*, colō], *colony.*

**color**, -ōris, M., *color.*

**columba**, -ae, F., *dove.*

**com** (col, con, cor, co), primitive form of **cum**, a prefix denoting completeness or union; sometimes intensive.

**comes**, -itis, M. and F. [comitor (com, eō)], *comrade, companion.*

**comitor,** 1 [comes], *accompany, attend.*

**commeātus,** -ūs, M. [commeō, *go to and fro*], *passage, trip, expedition.*

**com-mittō,** 3, -mīsī, -missum, (*join together*), ***commit;*** proelium committere, *join battle, engage, begin fighting.*

**com-modus,** -a, -um, adj. (*that has proper measure*), *convenient, suitable.*

**com-moror,** 1, *stay, linger, delay, remain.*

**com-moveō,** 2, -mōvī, -mōtum, (*put in violent motion*), *shake, disturb, agitate.* COMMOTION.

**com-mūniō,** 4, (*fortify strongly*), *secure, intrench.*

**com-periō,** 4, -perī, -pertum, *ascertain, learn, find out.*

**com-pleō,** 2, -plēvī, -plētum, *fill out, fill up.* Cf. impleō.

**com-primō,** 3, -pressī, -pressum [premō], ***press*** *together; check,* ***suppress.***

**con-cutiō,** 3, -cussī, -cussum [com, quatiō], *shake violently.*

**cōn-ferō,** cōnferre, contulī, collātum (conl), [com], *bring together, collect;* sē cōnferre, *betake one's self.* CONFER.

**cōn-ficiō,** 3, -fēcī, -fectum [com, faciō], *make, accomplish, carry out.*

**con-fiteor,** 2, -fessus [com, fateor], ***confess.***

**cōn-flīgō,** 3, -xī, -ctum [com], *contend, fight.* CONFLICT.

**con-iciō,** 3, -jēcī, -jectum [com, jaciō], (*throw together*), *throw, hurl.*

**con-junx,** -jugis, M. and F. [com, jungō, *join*], *spouse, wife; husband.*

**cōnor,** 1, *attempt, try.*

**cōn-scendō,** 3, -dī, -scēnsum, [com, scandō, *climb*], ***ascend,*** *embark; go on board.*

**cōn-sequor,** 3, -cūtus [com], *follow close upon; follow.*

**cōn-sidō,** 3, -sēdī, -sēssum [com], (*sit together*), *encamp.*

**cōnsilium,** -ī, N. [cōnsulō, cōnsul], *advice,* ***counsel,*** *prudence; plan, design.*

**cōn-similis,** -e, adj., *very* ***similar,*** *quite like.*

**cōn-spiciō,** 3, -spexī, -spectum [com, speciō, *look*], *look at attentively; observe, see, behold.*

**cōn-spicor,** 1, [cōnspiciō], *see at a glance, descry, catch sight of.*

**cōnstāns,** -antis, adj., [P. of cōnstō], *firm, steady.*

**cōn-stat,** 1, -stitit, impers., *it is evident, clear.*

**cōn-stituō,** 3, -uī, -ūtum [com, statuō], (*place* or *put together*), *station, place; determine.*

**cōn-suēscō,** 3, -suēvī, -suētum [com], *become accustomed;* in perf., *be accustomed.*

**cōnsuētūdō,** -inis, F. [cōnsuētus], *habit,* ***custom.***

**cōnsul,** -ulis, M. [cōnsulō, *consult*], ***consul.*** (134.)

**cōnsulāris,** -e, adj. [cōnsul], *pertaining to a consul,* ***consular;*** noun, *ex-consul.*

**cōnsulātus,** -ūs, M. [cōnsul], *office of consul,* ***consulship.***

**cōn-sūmō,** 3, -sūmpsī, -sūmptum [com], *take up completely,* ***consume.***

**con-temnō,** 3, -psī, -ptum [com], *despise.* CONTEMN.

**contemplor,** 1, *look at, observe.* CONTEMPLATE.

**con-tendō**, 3, -dī, -tum [com], (*draw tight*), *exert one's self, strive; hasten*. CONTEND.

**contentiō**, -ōnis, F. [contendō], *struggle, exertion, effort*; ***contention***.

**contentus**, -a, -um, adj. [P. of contineō], ***contented***; w. abl.

**con-testor**, 1 [com, testis, *witness*], *call to witness, invoke*.

**con-tinēns**, -entis, F. [P. of contineō, sc. terra], ***continent***.

**con-tineō**, 2, -uī, -tentum [com, teneō], *hold together, hold*, ***contain***.

**contrā**, prep. w. acc., *against*.

**con-valēscō**, 3, -valuī ——, [com, valeō], *get well, grow strong*. CONVALESCENT. Cf. valeō.

**con-veniō**, 4, -vēnī, -ventum [com], *come together, assemble*.

**con-vertō**, 3, -tī, -sum [com], *turn around, turn, change*. CONVERT.

**cōpia**, -ae, F. [com, ops], *abundance, wealth*; plur., *troops, forces*.

**cor**, cordis, N., *heart*.

**cōram**, prep. w. abl., *in presence of*.

**Corinthus**, -ī, F., ***Corinth***. (11,4.)

**Coriolānus**, -ī, M., ***Coriolanus***, *surname of C. Marcius, a Roman consul*.

**Cornēlia**, -ae, F. ***Cornelia***, *mother of the Gracchi*.

**Cornēlius**, -ī, M., ***Cornelius***, *a Roman family name*.

**cornū**, -ūs, N., *horn*.

**corpus**, -oris, N., *body*. (140.) CORPSE.

**corrigō**, 3, -rēxī, -rēctum [com, regō], *make straight, reform*, ***correct***.

**corripiō**, 3, -uī, -reptum [com, rapiō], *seize, take hold of*.

**cor-rumpō**, 3, -rūpī, -ruptum, [com], *break in pieces, destroy*; ***corrupt***, *bribe*.

**cortex**, -icis, M. and F., *bark, shell, rind*.

**cōrus**, -ī, M., *north-west* (*wind*).

**cotīdiē**, adv. [quot, diēs], *daily*.

**crās**, adv., *to-morrow*.

**Crassus**, -ī, M., ***Crassus***, *a rich Roman, contemporary of Cæsar*.

**creātor**, -ōris, M. [creō], ***creator***.

**crēber**, -bra, -brum, adj., *frequent, numerous*.

**crēdō**, 3, -didī, -ditum, *trust, believe*; w. dat. CREDIT.

**creō**, 1, *make*, ***create***; *choose, elect*.

**Croesus**, -ī, M., ***Croesus***, *king of Lydia*.

**crūdēlis**, -e, adj., ***cruel***, *hard-hearted*.

**crūdēliter**, adv. [crūdēlis], ***cruelly***.

**cruentus**, -a, -um, adj. [cruor], *stained with blood, bloody*.

**cruor**, -ōris, M., *blood, gore*. Cf. sanguis.

**crūs**, crūris, N., *leg*.

**culpa**, -ae, F. [culpō], *blame, fault*. CULPABLE. Cf. vitium.

**culpō**, 1 [culpa], *blame, find fault with*.

**culter**, -trī, M., *knife*. COULTER.

**cum**, conj., *when; since, as; though, although*.

**cum**, prep. w. abl., *with*.

**Cumae**, -ārum, F., ***Cumae***, *a town in Campania*.

**cūnae**, -ārum, F., *cradle*.

**cunctātiō**, -ōnis, F. [cunctor], *delaying, delay*.

**cunctor**, 1, *linger, hesitate*.

**cupiditās**, -ātis, F. [cupidus, cupiō], *desire, eagerness*. CUPIDITY.

**Cupīdō**, -inis, M. [cupidus], ***Cupid***, *god of love*.

**cupiō**, 3, -īvī, or -iī, -ītum, *desire, be eager for*. Cf. dēsīderō.

**cūr**, adv. [quā, rē], *why, wherefore.*
**cūra**, -ae, F. [cūrō], *care, anxiety.*
**cūrō**, 1 [cūra], *care for, take care.*
**currō**, 3, cucurrī, cursum, *run.*
**currus**, -ūs, M. [currō], *chariot, car.*
**cursus**, -ūs, M. [currō], *a running, course.*
**curvus**, -a, -um, adj., *curved, bent; bending.*
**custōdiō**, 4 [custōs], *guard, protect, defend.*
**custōs**, -ōdis, M. and F. [custōdiō], *guardian, keeper.* CUSTODIAN.
**cymba**, -ae, F. *boat.* Cf. nāvicula.
**Cȳrus**, -ī, M., *Cyrus, king of Persia.*

**Daedalus**, -ī, M., *Daedalus, builder of the Labyrinth.*
**damnō**, 1, *condemn.*
**Dārēus**, -ī, M., *Darius, king of Persia.*
**Dātis**, -is, M., *Datis, a Persian general.*
**dē**, prep. w. abl., *from, about, concerning, of;* (of time), *in, during, about.*
**dea**, -ae, F., *goddess.* (p. 8, note 1).
**dēbeō**, 2, -uī, -itum, *owe, ought.* DEBIT, DEBT.
**decem**, num. adj., indecl., *ten.*
**December**, -bris, M. [decem], *December.* Often as adj.
**decem-plex**, -icis, adj. [plicō], *tenfold.*
**dē-cernō**, 3, -crēvī, -crētum (*separate from*), *decide, determine; decree.*
**dē-cerpō**, 3, -sī, -tum [carpō], *pluck off.*
**decet**, 2, decuit, impers., *it is becoming, fitting, proper.*
**decimus**, -a, -um, num. adj. [decem], *tenth.*
**dē-dō**, 3, -didī, -ditum (*put from one's self*), *surrender, deliver up.*
**dē-dūcō**, 3, -dūxī, -ductum, *lead away, draw down, launch.* DEDUCT.
**dē-fatīgō**, 1, *tire out, exhaust.*
**dē-fendō**, 3, -dī, -fēnsum [dēfēnsor], (*strike off from*), *defend, protect.*
**dēfēnsor**, -ōris, M. [dēfendō], *defender, protector.*
**dē-ferō**, -ferre, -tulī, -lātum (*bring from*), *deliver; report.*
**dē-fessus**, -a, -um, adj., *tired out, weary.*
**dē-ficiō**, 3, -fēcī, -fectum [faciō], (*make away from*), *revolt; fail, be wanting.*
**dē-formis**, -e, adj. [forma], *misshapen, ugly; base, disgraceful.*
**de-inde**, adv. (*from thence*), *then, afterwards.*
**dēlectō**, 1, *delight.*
**dēlēctus**, -ūs, M. [dēligō], *selection; levy.*
**dēleō**, 2, -ēvī, -ētum, *destroy.* DELETE.
**dēliciae**, -ārum, F., *delight, darling.*
**dē-migrō**, 1, *migrate from; emigrate, remove.*
**Dēmosthenēs**, -is, M., *Demosthenes, a famous Athenian orator.*
**dēnique**, adv., *finally, at last.*
**dēns**, dentis, M., *tooth.* DENTIST.
**dē-pereō**, 4, -iī, ——, *go to ruin, perish, be lost.*
**dē-pōnō**, 3, -posuī, -positum, *put down, put by, lay down.* DEPONENT.
**dē-scendō**, 3, -dī, -scēnsum [scandō, *climb*], *come down, descend.*
**dē-serō**, 3, -uī, -tum, *desert, abandon.*
**dēsīderō**, 1, *desire, long for, miss* (319). Cf. optō and cupiō.

**dē-siliō**, 4, -siluī [saliō, *leap*], *leap down*. Cf. subsiliō and trānsiliō.

**dē-sistō**, 3, -stitī, -stitum [*stand off* or *apart*], *leave off, cease; desist*.

**dē-spērō**, 1 [spēs], *be hopeless, despair*.

**dē-sum**, -esse, -fuī, ——, *be wanting, lack*; w. dat. Cf. dēficiō.

**dē-trahō**, 3, -traxī, -tractum, *draw off, take away*.

**deus**, -ī, M., *god*. (262.)

**dēvorō**, 1, *swallow up, devour*.

**Diāna**, -ae, F., *Diana, goddess of the chase*.

**dīcō**, 3, dīxī, dictum, *say, tell*.

**dictātor**, -ōris, M. [dictō, dīcō], *chief magistrate, dictator*.

**dictātūra**, -ae, F. [dictātor], *office of dictator, dictatorship*.

**dictitō** [frequentative of dīcō], *keep saying*.

**diēs**, -ēī, M. and F., *day*. (253.)

**dif-ferō**, differre, distulī, dīlātum [dis], *scatter, separate, put off; differ*. (321.)

**difficilis**, -e, adj. [dis, facilis, *far from easy*], *hard, difficult*. (207.)

**digitus**, -ī, M., *finger*. DIGIT.

**dignitās**, -atis, F. [dīgnus], *worth, dignity; office*.

**dīgnus**, -a, -um, adj., *worthy*.

**dīligēns**, -entis, adj. [P. of dīligō], *diligent, careful*.

**dīligenter**, adv. [dīligēns], *diligently*.

**dīligentia**, -ae, F. [dīligēns], *diligence, carefulness*.

**dī-ligō**, 3, -lēxī, -lēctum [legō], *esteem, love*. (319.)

**dīmicō**, 1, *fight, contend*. Cf. pūgnō.

**dī-midius**, -a, -um, adj. [medius], *half*.

**dī-mittō**, 3, -mīsī, -missum, *send away, let go*.

**dī-moveō**, 2, -mōvī, -mōtum (*move asunder*), *separate, drive away*.

**dī-ruō**, 3, dīruī, dīrutum, *tear asunder, destroy*. Cf. rescindō.

**dis, dī** (a prefix denoting separation), *asunder, apart, in different directions*. Cf. differō, discēdō, dissimilis, dīmittō, dīruō.

**Dīs**, Dītis, M., *Dis, another name of Pluto*.

**dis-cēdō**, 3, -cēssī, -cēssum, *depart, withdraw, go off*.

**discipulus**, -ī, M. [discō], *learner, scholar, pupil*. DISCIPLE.

**discō**, 3, didicī, ——, *learn*.

**dis-similis**, -e, adj., (*far from like*), *unlike, dissimilar*.

**diū**, adv., *for a long time, long*.

**dīves**, -itis, adj. (comp. dītior, superl. dīvitissimus), *rich*. (167. 3.)

**dīvitiae**, -ārum, F. [dīves], *riches, wealth*.

**dō**, dare, dedī, dătum, *give*.

**doceō**, 2, -uī, -tum, *teach, show*.

**doctus**, -a, -um, adj. [P. of doceō], *learned*. DOCTOR.

**dolor**, -ōris, M., *pain, grief*. DOLOROUS.

**dolus**, -ī, M., *trick, deceit*.

**domicilium**, -ī, N. [domus], *home, abode*.

**domina**, -ae, F. [dominus], *mistress*.

**dominor**, 1 [dominus], *be a lord and master, rule*. DOMINEER.

**dominus**, -ī, M. [domina], *lord, master*.

**domus**, -ūs, F., *house, home*; domī, *at home*. (262, 336.)

**dōnō**, 1 [dōnum], *give, present*. DONATE.

**dōnum**, -ī, N. [dō], *gift, present*.

**dormiō**, 4, *sleep*. DORMITORY.
**Drūsus**, -ī, M., *Drusus, a Roman*.
**dubitō**, 1 [dubius], *hesitate, doubt*. INDUBITABLE.
**dubium**, -ī, N. [dubius], *doubt*.
**dubius**, -a, -um, adj. [duo], *doubtful*. DUBIOUS.
**ducentī**, -ae, -a, num. adj. [duo, centum], *two hundred*.
**dūcō**, 3, -dūxī, -ductum [dux], *lead*.
**Duīlius** (C.), -ī, M., *Caius Duilius, a Roman general*.
**dulcis**, -e, adj., *sweet, pleasant*. DULCET. Cf. suāvis.
**dum**, adv., *while, as long as; until*.
**duo**, duae, duo, num. adj., *two*. (311. 4.)
**duo-decim**, num. adj., indecl. [decem], *twelve*.
**duo-dē-trīgintā**, num. adj., indecl., *twenty-eight*.
**dūrus**, -a, -um, adj., *hard*. ENDURE. Cf. difficilis.
**dux**, ducis, M. and F. [dūcō], *leader, general*. DUKE. Cf. imperātor.

**ecce**, interj., *lo! see! see there!*
**ē-dīcō**, 3, -dīxī, -dictum, *speak out, declare, proclaim*. EDICT.
**edō**, edere *or* ēsse, ēdī, ēsum *or* ēssum, *eat*.
**ēducō**, 1, *bring up, train, educate*.
**ē-dūcō**, 3, -dūxī, -ductum, *lead out, bring away*.
**ef-ferō**, efferre, extulī, ēlātum [ex], *bear out, bring forth*. (321.) ELATE.
**efficiō**, 3, -fēcī, -fectum [ex, faciō], *bring to pass, effect, complete; make, construct*.
**egēns**, -entis, adj. [P. of egeō], *in want, needy, destitute*.
**ego**, pers. pron., *I*. (264.)
**ē-gredior**, 3, ēgressus [gradior, step], *go out, go forth; disembark, land*. Cf. exeō.
**ēgregiē**, adv. [ēgregius], *remarkably, excellently*.
**ē-gregius**, -a, -um, adj. [grex], *remarkable, excellent*. EGREGIOUS.
**ēlegāns**, -antis, adj., *choice, elegant*.
**elephantus**, -ī, M., *elephant*.
**ē-lūdō**, 3, -sī, -sum, *deceive, mock; elude*.
**ē-mergō**, 3, -sī, -sum, *arise, come forth; emerge*.
**emō**, 3, ēmī, ēmptum, *buy, purchase*.
**enim**, conj. (never the first word), *for*. Cf. nam.
**Ennius**, -ī, M., *Ennius, father of Roman poetry*.
**ē-nūntiō**, 1, *say out, divulge, declare, report*. ENUNCIATE.
**ē**, see ex.
**eō**, adv. [is], *to that place, thither, there*.
**eō**, īre, iī, itum, *go*. (327.)
**eōdem**, adv. [īdem], *to the same place*.
**Ēpīrus**, -ī, F., *Epirus, a division of Greece*.
**epistula**, -ae, F., *letter, epistle*.
**eques**, -itis, M. [equus], *horseman, knight*.
**equester**, -tris, -tre, adj., [eques], (*pertaining to a horseman*), *equestrian*.
**equitātus**, -ūs, M. [equitō, eques], (*body of equites*), *cavalry*.
**equitō**, 1 [eques], (*be a horseman*), *ride*.
**equus**, -ī, M., *horse*.
**ergō**, adv., *therefore, accordingly*. Cf. igitur and itaque.
**ē-ripiō**, 3, -uī, -reptum [rapiō], *snatch out, seize and bear off*.
**errō**, 1, *wander; err, mistake*.

**ē-rudiō**, 4, [rudis, *rough*], *train, teach, instruct.*

**essedum**, -ī, N., *two-wheeled war-chariot.*

**et**, conj., *and;* et . . . et, *both . . . and.* Cf. atque, āc, and -que.

**etiam**, adv. and conj. [et, jam, *and now*], *also, even.*

**et-si**, conj., *though, although.*

**Eurōpa**, -ae, F., ***Europe.***

**ē-vādō**, 3, -vāsī, -vāsum, *go forth, escape.* EVADE.

**ē-veniō**, 4, -vēnī, -ventum, *come forth, turn out, happen.* EVENT. Cf. accidō and incidō.

**ē-vertō**, 3, -tī, -sum, *overturn, overthrow, destroy.*

**ē-volō**, 1, *fly away.*

**ex** or **ē**, prep. w. abl., *out of, from.*

**exāminō**, 1 [exāmen, *test*], *weigh out, weigh.*

**excelsus**, -a, -um, adj. [P. of excellō], *elevated, lofty, high.*

**ex-cipiō**, 3, -cēpī, -ceptum [capiō], *take out,* ***except;*** *receive, welcome.*

**ex-clāmō**, 1, *cry out,* ***exclaim.*** Cf. clāmitō.

**ex-cūsō**, 1 [causa], ***excuse.***

**ex-cutiō**, 3, -cussī, -cussum [quatiō], *shake out, strike off, drive away, cast out.*

**ex-eō**, -īre, -iī, -itum, *go out, come out.* EXIT. Cf. ēgredior.

**ex-erceō**, 2 [arceō], *keep busy, employ; train.* EXERCISE.

**exercitus**, -ūs, M. [exerceō], (*the thing trained*), *army.*

**exiguus**, -a, -um, adj., *scanty, small, slight.*

**expedītiō**, -ōnis, F. [expediō], *excursion,* ***expedition.***

**ex-pellō**, 3, -pulī, -pulsum, *drive out* or *away,* ***expel.***

**ex-perior**, 4, -pertus, *make trial of, test.* EXPERT.

**ex-plicō**, 1, -āvī, -ātum, and -uī, -itum, *unfold, explain.*

**explōrātor**, -ōris, M. [explōrō], *a searcher out,* ***explorer;*** *spy, scout.*

**ex-plōrō**, 1, *search out, examine,* ***explore;*** *reconnoitre.*

**ex-pōnō**, 3, -posuī, -positum, *put* or *set out,* ***expose;*** *draw up, marshal.*

**ex-pūgnō**, 1, *take by storm, assault.* Cf. oppūgnō.

**ex-sistō**, 3, -stitī, -stitum (*stand forth*), ***exist,*** *appear.*

**ex-spectō**, 1, *await, wait for,* ***expect.***

**ex-spīrō**, 1, *breath out, breath one's last,* ***expire.***

**ex-stinguō**, 3, -nxī, -nctum (*quench completely*), ***extinguish;*** *kill, destroy.*

**ex-terreō**, 2, -uī, -itum, *frighten, affright.*

**ex-timēscō**, 3, -timuī,—— [timeō], *fear greatly.*

**extrā**, prep. w. acc., *without, outside of.* Cf. intrā.

**ex-turbō**, 1, *thrust out, drive away.*

**faber**, -brī, M., *worker, carpenter.* FABRIC.

**Fabius**, -ī, M., ***Fabius,*** *a famous Roman general.*

**Fabricius**, -ī, M., ***Fabricius,*** *a famous Roman general.*

**fābula**, -ae, F. [for, *speak*], *story, tale,* ***fable.***

**facilis**, -e, adj. [faciō], (*that can be done*), *easy to do, easy.* FACILITY.

**facinus**, -oris, N. [faciō], (*the thing done*), *deed; crime.* Cf. scelus.

**faciō**, 3, fēcī, factum, *do, make.*

**fāgus**, -ī, F., *beech-tree.* (11. 4.)

**Faliscī**, -ōrum, M., the ***Faliscans***, *a people of Etruria.*

**falsō**, adv. [falsus], ***falsely.***

**falsus**, -a, -um, adj. [fallō, *deceive*], *deceptive*, ***false.***

**fāma**, -ae, F. [for, *speak*], *rumor;* ***fame***, *renown.*

**famēs**, -is, F., *hunger*, ***famine.***

**fās**, N., indecl. [for, *speak*], *divine law;* often translated as adj., *right, lawful.*

**fascis**, -is, M., *bundle.*

**fatīgō**, 1, *tire out, weary.* FATIGUE.

**fātum**, -ī, N. [for, *speak*], (*that which is spoken*), ***fate***, *destiny.*

**faveō**, 2, fāvī, fautum, *be favorable to*, ***favor***, *befriend;* w. dat.

**febris**, -is, F. [ferveō, *be hot*), ***fever.***

**Februārius**, -ī, M., ***February.*** Often as adj.

**fēlīciter**, adv. [fēlīx], *luckily, fortunately.*

**fēlīx**, -īcis, adj., *lucky, fortunate.*

**fera**, -ae, F. [ferus], *wild animal, wild beast.*

**ferē**, adv., *nearly, for the most part, almost, about.* Cf. paene.

**ferō**, ferre, tulī, lātum, *bear, bring;* ferunt, *they say.* (321.) Cf. portō and vehō.

**ferōx**, -ōcis, adj. [ferus], *fierce, impetuous.*

**ferreus**, -a, -um, adj. [ferrum], *of iron, iron.*

**ferrum**, -ī, N., *iron.*

**ferus**, -a, -um, adj., *wild, savage, cruel.*

**fidēlis**, -e, adj. [fidēs], *trusty, faithful.* Cf. fīdus.

**fidēliter**, adv. [fidēlis], *faithfully.*

**fidēs**, -eī, F. [fīdō, *trust*], *trust, faith.*

**fīdus**, -a, -um, adj. [fīdō, *trust*], *trusty, faithful.*

**fīlia**, -ae, F., *daughter.* (p. 8, note 1). Cf. nāta.

**fīliolus**, -ī, M. [diminutive of fīlius], *little son.*

**fīlius**, -ī, M., *son.* (79.) FILIAL.

**fīniō**, 4 [fīnis], *end*, ***finish.*** FINITE.

**fīnis**, -is, M., *end, boundary.*

**fīnitimus**, -a, -um, adj. [fīnis], *bordering on, neighboring.*

**fīō**, fierī, factus (supplies pass. to faciō), *be made, become.* (327.)

**firmō**, 1 [firmus], *make strong.*

**firmus**, -a, -um, adj. [firmō], *steadfast, strong.* FIRM.

**flagrō**, 1, *burn.*

**flectō**, 3, -xī, -xum, *bend, turn.*

**fleō**, 2, flēvī, flētum, *weep, cry.*

**flō**, 1, *blow.*

**flōs**, flōris, M., *flower.* FLORAL.

**flūmen**, -inis, N. [fluō], (*that which flows*), *river, stream.* (172.)

**fluō**, 3, flūxī, flūxum, *flow.*

**fluvius**, -ī, M. [fluō], (*the flowing thing*), *river, stream.* (172.)

**folium**, -ī, N., *leaf.* FOLIAGE.

**fōns**, fontis, M., *spring*, ***fount***, *fountain.*

**fore**, for **futurum esse.**

**formīdō**, -inis, F., *fear, terror.*

**forte**, adv. [fors, *chance*], *perchance, perhaps, possibly.*

**fortis**, -e, adj., *strong, brave, courageous.*

**fortiter**, adv. [fortis], *bravely, courageously.*

**fortitūdō**, -inis, F. [fortis], *strength, bravery, endurance*, ***fortitude.***

**fortūna**, -ae, F. [fors, *chance*], ***fortune.***

**forum**, -ī, N., *market-place;* ***forum.***

**frangō**, 3, frēgī, fractum, *dash in pieces, break.* FRACTION.

**frāter**, -tris, M., *brother.* FRATERNAL.

**frētus**, -a, -um, adj., *relying on, trusting to;* w. abl.

**frīgidus**, -a, -um, adj. [frīgeō, *freeze*], *cold, frigid.*

**frondōsus**, -a, -um, adj. [frōns], *covered with leaves, leafy.*

**frōns**, frondis, F., *leaf, foliage; garland of leaves.*

**frōns**, -tis, F., *brow, forehead.* FRONT.

**frūctus**, -ūs, M. [fruor], *fruit.* Cf. frūmentum.

**frūmentārius**, -a, -um, adj. [frūmentum], *pertaining to grain;* rēs frūmentāria, *grain-supply.*

**frūmentum**, -ī, N. [fruor], *corn, grain.* Cf. frūctus.

**fruor**, 3, frūctus, *enjoy;* w. abl. (304.)

**frūstrā**, adv., *in vain.*

(**frūx**), frūgis, F. (oftener plur.; gen. frūgum), [fruor], *fruit of the earth, fruits.* Cf. frūctus.

**fuga**, -ae, F. [fugiō, *flee*], *flight.*

**fugiō**, 3, fūgī, —— [fugō, fuga], *run away.* FUGITIVE.

**fugō**, 1 [fugiō, fuga], *put to flight, chase, drive.*

**fungor**, 3, fūnctus, *perform, discharge;* w. abl. (304.) FUNCTION.

**Gājus**, gen. Gāī (also written Cāius), M., *Caius, a Roman first name.*

**Galba**, -ae, M., ***Galba.***

**Gallia**, -ae, F., ***Gaul.***

**Gallicus**, -a, -um, adj. [Gallus], *belonging to the Gauls,* ***Gallic.***

**gallīna**, -ae, F. [gallus, *cock*], *hen.*

**Gallus**, -ī, M., *a* ***Gaul.***

**gaudeō**, 2, gāvīsus [gaudium], *be glad, rejoice.* (p. 177, note 2.)

**gaudium**, -ī, N. [gaudeō], *joy, delight.*

**gener**, -erī, M., *son-in-law.*

**gēns**, gentis, F., *clan, family.* GENTEEL.

**genū**, -ūs, N., *knee.* (245.)

**genus**, -eris, N., *birth, race; kind, nature.* GENDER.

**Germānus**, -a, -um, adj., ***German;*** noun, a ***German.***

**gerō**, 3, gessī, gestum, *bear, carry; wage, manage, do.*

**gladiātor**, -ōris, M. [gladius], (*swordsman*), ***gladiator.***

**gladius**, -ī, M., *sword.*

**glōria**, -ae, F., ***glory,*** *fame, renown.*

**gracilis**, -e, adj., *slender.* (207.)

**gradus**, -ūs, M., *step.* (245.) GRADE.

**Graecē**, adv. [Graecus], *in* ***Greek.***

**Graecia**, -ae, F., ***Greece.***

**Graecus**, -a, -um, adj., ***Grecian, Greek;*** noun, a ***Greek.***

**grāmen**, -inis, N., *grass.*

**grānum**, -ī, N., ***grain,*** *seed.*

**grātulor**, 1 [grātus], ***congratulate;*** w. dat.

**grātus**, -a, -um, adj., *acceptable, pleasing.* GRATEFUL.

**gravis**, -e, adj., *heavy, serious.* GRAVE.

**graviter**, adv. [gravis], *heavily, seriously.*

**gremium**, -ī, N., *lap, bosom.*

**grex**, gregis, M., *flock, herd.*

**gustō**, 1, *taste, eat.*

**habeō**, 2, *have, hold.*

**habitō**, 1 [frequentative of habeō], ***inhabit;*** *dwell, live.* (194.)

**Hannibal**, -alis, M., ***Hannibal,*** *a famous Carthaginian general.*

**Hasdrubal**, -alis, M., ***Hasdrubal,*** *a Carthaginian general, brother of Hannibal.*

**hasta**, -ae, F., *spear.*

**hauriō**, 4, hausī, haustum, *draw* (*water*), *drain.* EXHAUST.

**Hector**, -oris, M., ***Hector****, chief of the Trojan warriors.*

**Henna**, -ae, F., ***Henna****, a city of Sicily.*

**herī**, adv., *yesterday.*

**hic**, haec, hōc, dem. pron., *this, this of mine;* abl., hōc, *on this account;* as pers. pron., *he, she, it.* (275.)

**hiems**(hiemps), hiemis, F., *winter; storm.*

**hinc**, adv. [hīc], *from this place, hence.*

**Hispānia**, -ae, F., ***Spain.***

**Hispānus**, -ī, M., *a* ***Spaniard.***

**historia**, -ae, F., ***history.***

**hodiē**, adv. [hōc, diē], *to-day.*

**Homērus**, -ī, M., ***Homer****, the earliest and greatest Greek poet.*

**homo**, -inis, M. and F. (*human being*), *man.* (138.)

**honestās**, -ātis, F. [honestus], *honor, integrity,* ***honesty.***

**honōrificē**, adv., *honorably.*

**honor**, -ōris, M., ***honor.***

**honōrō**, 1 [honor], ***honor****, respect.*

**hōra**, -ae, F., ***hour.***

**Horātius**, -ī, M., ***Horatius, Horace.***

**horridus**, -a, -um, adj. [horreō, *shudder at*], *frightful, rough, wild.* HORRID.

**hortor**, 1, *urge,* ***exhort****, encourage.*

**hortus**, -ī, M., *garden.*

**hospes**, -itis, M. and F., ***host****, guest, guest-friend.* HOSPITAL.

**hostis**, -is, M. and F., *enemy.* (149, 172.) HOSTILE.

**hūc**, adv. [for old form hōc], *to this place, hither.*

**hūmānus**, -a, -um, adj. [homo], ***human****; cultivated, refined.*

**humilis**, -e, adj. [humus, *ground*], (*pertaining to* humus), *low, lowly,* ***humble****, poor.* (207.)

**ibi**, adv. [is], *in that place, there.*

**Īcarus**, -ī, ***Icarus****, son of Dædalus.*

**īdem**, eadem, idem, determ. pron. [is], *same.* (270.)

**idōneus**, -a, -um, adj., *fit, suitable, proper.*

**Īdūs**, -uum, F. plur., *the* ***Ides*** (*of the month*). The thirteenth, except in March, May, July, and October; in those months the fifteenth. (244. 1.)

**igitur**, conj. (seldom the first word), *therefore, then.* Cf. ergō and itaque.

**īgnāvia**, -ae, F. [īgnāvus], *laziness, idleness, cowardice.*

**īgnāvus**, -a, -um, adj. [in, *not*, gnāvus, *busy*], *lazy, idle, cowardly.*

**ignis**, -is, M., *fire.* (149.)

**ignōrō**, 1 [īgnārus, *ignorant*], *not know, be ignorant of.*

**ille**, -a, -ud, demon. pron., *that* (*yonder*); as pers. pron., *he, she, it.* (275.)

**illūc**, adv. [ille], *to that place, thither, there.*

**imāgō**, -inis, F., ***image****, likeness, picture.*

**imitor**, 1, ***imitate.***

**immānis**, -e, adj., *huge, immense, monstrous.* Cf. māgnus.

**impediō**, 4 [in, pēs], (*entangle the feet*), ***impede****, hinder, prevent.*

**im-pellō**, 3, -pulī, -pulsum [in], *urge on,* ***impel****, prompt.*

**imperātor**, -ōris, M. [imperō], *commander, general.* EMPEROR.

**imperium**, -ī, N. [imperō], *command, authority, power.* EMPIRE.

**imperō,** 1 [imperium], *order, command;* w. dat.

**impetrō,** 1, *accomplish; gain, procure, obtain.* Cf. adipiscor.

**impetus,** -ūs, M. [impetō, *rush upon*], *attack, onset.* IMPETUOUS.

**im-pleō,** 2, -ēvī, -ētum [in], *fill up, fill full, fill.* Cf. compleō.

**im-plōrō,** 1 [in], *cry out to, beseech, **implore**.*

**im-pōnō,** 3, -posuī, -positum [in], *put* or *place upon.*

**improbus,** -a, -um, adj. [in, *not,* probus, *good*], *bad, wicked.* Cf. malus.

**im-prō-vīsō,** adv. [videō], *unexpectedly.*

**im-pudēns,** -entis, adj. [in], *shameless, **impudent**.*

**in,** prep. w. acc. *into, to, against, for;* w. abl., ***in**, on.*

**in,** prefix, in composition with nouns, adjectives, and participles, often having negative sense. Cf. Eng. **un-**, **in-**, *not.*

**inānis,** -e, adj., *empty, useless.*

**in-cautus,** -a, -um, adj., ***incautious**, heedless.*

**in-certus,** -a, -um, adj., ***uncertain**.*

**in-cidō,** 3, -cidī, -cāsum [cadō], *fall into; happen, befall.* Cf. accidō and ēveniō.

**in-cipiō,** 3, -cēpī, -ceptum [capiō], (*take in hand*), *begin.* Cf. ordior.

**in-cōgnitus,** -a, -um, adj., *unknown.*

**incola,** -ae, M. and F. [incolō], *inhabitant.*

**in-colō,** 3, -uī, —— [incola], *dwell in, inhabit, live, dwell.* Cf. habitō and vīvō.

**incolumis,** -e, adj., *unharmed, safe.*

**inde,** adv. [is], *thence.*

**indicium,** -ī, N., *discovery, disclosure.*

**in-eō,** -īre, -iī, -itum, *go in, enter; begin.* (327.)

**inferī,** -ōrum, M. (īnferus, *below*], *inhabitants of the lower world, the dead.* INFERNAL.

**in-ferō,** īnferre, intulī, illātum (inl) (*bear in* or *against*), *cause;* bellum īnferre, *make war upon;* w. dat. (321.)

**infestus,** -a, -um, adj., *hostile, troublesome, dangerous.* INFEST.

**in-ficiō,** 3, -fēcī, -fectum [faciō], *stain, color.*

**in-fīnitus,** -a, -um, adj. [fīnis], *boundless, unlimited, **infinite**, vast.*

**in-flectō,** 3, -xī, -xum, *bend; change, alter.* INFLECT.

**in-gredior,** 3, -gressus [gradior, *step*], *enter.*

**in-hiō,** 1, *gape at, long for.*

**in-imīcus,** -a, -um, adj. [amīcus], *unfriendly, hostile;* noun, ***enemy**.* (172.) INIMICAL.

**initium,** -ī, N. [ineō], *beginning.* INITIAL.

**injūria,** -ae, F. [in, jūs], ***injustice**, injury, wrong.*

**injūstē,** adv. [injūstus], ***unjustly**.*

**inopia,** -ae, F. [inops, *without resources*], *want, poverty.*

**inquam,** defective verb, *say;* inquit (placed after one or more quoted words), *said he.*

**īn-stituō,** 3, -uī, -ūtum [statuō, *place*], *fix, determine, undertake.* INSTITUTE.

**īnstrūctus,** -a, -um [P. of īnstruō], *furnished, equipped.*

**īn-struō,** 3, -strūxī, -strūctum [struō, *build*], *build up, **instruct**, teach.*

**īnsula,** -ae, F., *island.* PENINSULA.

**īn-sum,** -esse, -fuī, ——, *be in, among;* w. dat. and *in* w. abl.

**intel-legō,** 3, -lēxī, -lēctum [inter], *see into; understand.* INTELLECT.
**inter,** prep. w. acc., *between, among, amid.*
**inter-eō,** -īre, -iī, -itum, *perish.*
**inter-dum,** adv., *sometimes.*
**inter-ficiō,** 3, -fēcī, -fectum [faciō], *kill, put to death.* Cf. necō and occīdō.
**interior,** -us, adj. [no positive], *inner, **interior.***
**inter-pellō,** 1, *interrupt; entreat, importune.*
**inter-rogō,** 1, *ask, inquire, question.* (382.) INTERROGATION.
**inter-sum,** -esse, -fuī, ——, *be present at* or *among;* w. dat. Cf. adsum.
**intrā,** prep. w. acc., *within.* Cf. extrā.
**in-tueor,** 2, *look towards, at,* or *upon.* INTUITION.
**intus,** adv. [in], *within, inside.*
**in-veniō,** 4, -vēnī, -ventum, *come upon, find, meet with, discover.* INVENT. Cf. reperiō.
**in-vicem,** adv., *by turns, in turn, alternately.*
**in-victus,** -a, -um, adj., *unconquerable, invincible.*
**invītō,** 1, ***invite.***
**invītus,** -a, -um, adj., *unwilling, reluctant.*
**in-vocō,** 1, *call upon, **invoke.***
**iō,** interj., *ah! oh!*
**ipse,** -a, -um, intens. pron., *self, very.* (270.)
**īra,** -ae, F., *anger, wrath; **ire.***
**ir-rīdeō,** 2, -rīsī, -rīsum [in], *laugh at, **ridicule**; jest, mock.*
**is,** ea, id, determ. pron., *that;* as pers. pron., *he, she, it.* (270.)
**iste,** -a, -ud, demon. pron., *that* (*of yours*). (275.)
**ita,** adv., *so, thus.* Cf. sīc.
**Ītalia,** -ae, F., ***Italy.***
**Italus,** -a, -um, adj., ***Italian.***
**ita-que,** conj., *and so, therefore.* Cf. ergō and igitur.
**item,** adv. [ita], *likewise, also.* ITEM.
**iter,** itineris, N. [eō], *way, road, march.* (262.) ITINERANT.
**iterum,** adv., *a second time, again.* ITERATION.
**Ithaca,** -ae, F., ***Ithaca,** an island in the Ionian Sea.*
**Itius,** M., ***Itius,** a port in Gaul.*

**jaceō,** 2, -uī, —— [jaciō], (*be thrown*), *lie.*
**jaciō,** 3, jēcī, jactum [jaceō], *throw, cast, hurl, fling.*
**jam,** adv., *already, now, at last.* Cf. nunc.
**jamjam,** adv., *already;* jamjam ventūrus, *on the point of coming.*
**jānua,** -ae, F. [Jānus], *door.* Cf. porta.
**Jānus,** -ī, M. [jānua], ***Janus,** the two-faced god.*
**jējūnium,** -ī, N. [jējūnus], *fast, hunger.*
**jējūnus,** -a, -um [jejūnium], *fasting, hungry, without food.*
**jocus,** -ī, M. (plur. jocī and joca), ***joke,** jest;* per jocum, *in jest, for a joke.*
**Jōhanniculus,** -ī, M., *little **John, Johnny,** Jack.*
**jubeō,** 2, jūssī, jūssum, *bid, order, command.* Cf. imperō.
**jūcundus,** -a, -um, adj., *pleasant, agreeable.*
**jūdex,** -icis, M. [jūdicō], ***judge.*** (105.)
**jūdicium,** -ī, N. [jūdicō], ***judgment,** opinion.*

**jūdicō**, 1 [jūdex], *judge*. (429.)
**Jūlius**, -ī, M., *Julius, a Roman family name.*
**Jūppiter**, Jovis, M., *Jupiter, the supreme deity of the Romans.* (262.)
**jūrō**, 1 [jūs], *swear, take an oath.*
**jūs**, jūris, N., *right, justice.* (140.) Cf. fās.
**jūssus**, -ūs, M. [jubeō], *command, order.*
**jūstē**, adv. [jūstus], *rightly, justly.*
**juvenis**, -is, M. and F., *youth, young person.* Cf. adulēscēns.
**juventūs**, -ūtis, F. [juvenis], *the season of youth, youth.*

**Labiēnus**, -ī, M., *Labienus, a lieutenant of Cæsar's.*
**labor**, M., -ōris, *labor.*
**labōrō**, 1 [labor], *work, toil.*
**labrum**, -ī, N., *lip.*
**lac**, lactis, N., *milk.* LACTEAL.
**Lacedaemoniī**, -ōrum, M., the *Lacedaemonians.*
**lacrima**, -ae, F., *tear.* LACRYMOSE.
**lacus**, -ūs, M., *lake, pond.*
**Laevīnus**, -ī, M., *Laevinus, a Roman consul.*
**lapis**, -idis, M., *stone.* LAPIDARY.
**Latīnē**, adv. [Latīnus], *in Latin.*
**Latīnus**, -a, -um, adj. [Latium], *Latin*; noun, *a Latin.*
**lātrō**, 1, *bark, bark at.*
**latrō**, -ōnis, M., *robber.*
**lātus**, -a, -um, adj., *broad, wide.* LATITUDE.
**latus**, -eris, N., *side.* LATERAL.
**laudō**, 1 [laus], *praise, laud.*
**laus**, laudis, F. [laudō], *praise, glory, fame.*
**lēgātus**, -ī, M. [lēgō, *depute*], *ambassador, lieutenant.* LEGATE.
**legiō**, -ōnis, F. [legō], (*a gathering*), *legion.*
**legō**, 3, lēgī, lēctum, *gather; select; read.*
**lēnis**, -e, adj., *soft, smooth, gentle.*
**leō**, -ōnis, M., *lion.* (134.)
**lepus**, -oris, M., *hare.*
**levis**, -e, adj. [levō], *light.* (150.)
**levō**, 1 [levis], *lift up, raise, lighten.*
**lēx**, lēgis, F., *law.* LEGAL.
**libenter**, adv. [libet, *it pleases*], *willingly, gladly*; libenter videō, *I am glad to see.*
**liber**, -brī, M., *book.*
**līber**, -era, -erum, adj., *free.* LIBERAL.
**Līber**, -erī, M., *Bacchus, god of wine.*
**līberē**, adv. [līber], *freely, fearlessly.*
**līberī**, -ōrum, M. [līber], *children.* (60.)
**līberō**, 1 [līber], *set free, free, liberate*; w. abl.
**lībertās**, -ātis, F. [līber], *freedom, liberty.*
**licet**, 2, licuit *or* licitum est, impers., *it is permitted, (one) may.*
**ligneus**, -a, -um, adj. [lignum], *of wood, wooden.*
**lignum**, -ī, N., *wood*; plur., *sticks of wood.*
**ligō**, -ōnis, M., *mattock, hoe.*
**līlium**, -ī, N., *lily.*
**lingua**, -ae, F., *tongue, language.*
**littera**, -ae, F., *letter* (*of the alphabet*); plur., *letter, epistle; literature.*
**lītus**, -oris, N., *shore, beach, bank.*
**locus**, -ī, M. (plur., locī and loca), *place, position, spot.* LOCAL.
**longē**, adv. [longus], *far off; widely, greatly, much, by much.*
**longus**, -a, -um, adj., *long.* LONGITUDE.
**loquor**, 3, locūtus, *speak, talk.*

**lūctus**, -ūs, M. [lūgeō], *mourning, lamentation.*
**lūcus**, -ī, M. [lūceō, *shine*], (*open place in a wood*), *wood, grove.*
**lūdō**, 3, lūsī, lūsum [lūdus], *play.* InterLUDE.
**lūdus**, -ī, M. [lūdō], *game, play.*
**lūgeō**, 2, lūxī, ——, *mourn, lament.*
**lūmen**, -inis, N. [lūceō, lūx], *light.* LUMINOUS.
**lūna**, -ae, F. [lūceō, lūx], *moon.* LUNA.
**lupus**, -ī, M., *wolf.*
**luscinia**, -ae, F., *nightingale.*
**lūx**, lūcis, F. [lūceō, *shine*], *light, daylight.*

**M.**, abbreviation of *Marcus, a Roman first name.*
**macte**, adj. [voc. of mactus], *be honored, be blessed; hail! well done!*
**maculō**, 1, *stain.*
**magis**, adv. [măg(nus)], *more.*
**magister**, -trī, M. [măg(nus)], *master, teacher.* Cf. praeceptor.
**magistrātus**, -ūs, M. [magister], (*the office of a* magister), ***magistracy, magistrate.***
**māgnificus**, -a, -um, adj. [māgnus, faciō], *splendid, **magnificent.***
**māgnitūdō**, -inis, F. [māgnus], *greatness, size, **magnitude.***
**māgnus**, -a, -um, adj. (comp. mājor, superl. māximus), *great, large.*
**mājor**, -us, comp. of māgnus. MAJOR.
**male**, adv. [malus], *badly, ill.* (219.)
**mālō**, mālle, māluī, —— [magis, volō], *be more willing, prefer, would rather.* (316.)
**malum**, -ī, N., *bad thing, evil.*
**mālum**, -ī, N., *apple.*
**malus**, -a, -um, adj. (comp. pējor, sup. pessimus), *bad, evil; baleful.* (208.) Cf. improbus.
**māne**, adv., *in the morning.*
**maneō**, 2, mānsī, mānsum, *stay, remain, await.*
**mānēs**, -ium, M., *departed spirits, souls.*
**Manlius**, -ī, M., ***Manlius**, a Roman.*
**manus**, -ūs, F., *hand; force, band.* (244, 1.) MANUAL.
**Mārcellus**, -ī, M., ***Marcellus**, a Roman general.*
**mare**, -is, N., *sea.* (149.) MARINE.
**maritimus**, -a, -um, adj. [mare], *belonging to the sea, bordering on the sea, **maritime.***
**Marius** (C.), -ī, M., *Gājus **Marius**, a famous Roman general.*
**Mārtius**, -ī, M. [Mārs], ***March.*** Often as adj.
**massa**, -ae, F., ***mass.***
**māter**, -tris, F., *mother.* MATERNAL.
**māteria**, -ae, F. [māter], (*mother-stuff*), ***materials**, timber.*
**mātrōna**, -ae, F. [māter], ***matron**, wife, lady.*
**mātūrō**, 1 [mātūrus, *ripe*], *hasten.*
**māximē**, adv. [māximus], *most, especially, greatly.* (219.)
**māximus**, -a, -um, superl. of māgnus. (208.)
**medicus**, -ī, M. [medeor, *cure*], *physician.* MEDICINE.
**mediterrāneus**, -a, -um, adj. [medius, terra], *midland, inland.* MEDITERRANEAN.
**medius**, -a, -um, adj., *middle;* often to be translated *midst.*
**Meldī**, -ōrum, M., *the **Meldi**, a people of Gaul.*
**melior**, -us, comp. of bonus. (208.)

**mellītus**, -a, -um, adj. [mel, *honey*], *honey-sweet, darling.*

**memor**, -oris, adj., *mindful.* (150.) MEMORABLE.

**memoria**, -ae, F. [memor], ***memory.***

**mendācium**, -ī, N. [mendāx], *lying, falsehood.*

**mendāx**, -ācis, adj., [mentior], *lying, deceitful.*

**mēns**, mentis, F., *mind, purpose.* (273.) MENTAL.

**mēnsa**, -ae, F., *table.*

**mēnsis**, -is, M., *month.*

**mentior**, 4 [mendāx], *lie, deceive.*

**Mercurius**, -ī, M., ***Mercury***, *messenger of the gods.* (79.)

**mereō**, **mereor**, 2, *be worthy of, deserve,* ***merit.***

**merīdiānus**, -a, -um, adj. [merīdiēs], *of* or *belonging to midday, noon;* ***meridian.***

**Metellus**, -ī, M., ***Metellus***, *a Roman general.*

**metuō**, 3, -uī, -ūtum [metus], *fear.* Cf. timeō.

**metus**, -ūs, M. [metuō], *fear, dread.* Cf. timor.

**meus**, -a, -um, poss. pron. (voc. sing. mas. mī), *my, mine.*

**migrō**, 1, ***migrate.***

**mīles**, -itis, M., *soldier.* (105.) MILITARY.

**mīlle**, num. adj., indecl. in sing.; in plur. mīlia, -ium, *thousand.* (311, 6.)

**Miltiadēs**, -is, M., ***Miltiades***, *a Greek general.*

**Minerva**, -ae, F., ***Minerva***, *goddess of wisdom.*

**minimē**, adv. [minimus], *least; no, by no means, far from it.*

**minister**, -tri, M. [minus], (*an inferior*), *servant.* (66.) MINISTER. Cf. magister.

**minor**, 1 [minae, *threats*], *threaten.*

**minor**, -us, comp. of parvus.

**minus**, adv. [minor], *less.*

**mīrābilis**, -e, adj. [mīror, *wonder at*], *to be wondered at; wonderful, extraordinary.*

**misellus**, -a, -um, adj. [diminutive of miser], *poor little.*

**miser**, -era, -erum, adj., *wretched, unhappy,* ***miserable.***

**miseret**, 2, -itum est, impers. [miser], *it makes miserable, it excites pity,* (*one*) *pities;* nōs miseret, *we pity.* (415.)

**miseria**, -ae, F. [miser], *wretchedness,* ***misery.***

**Mithridatēs**, -is, M., ***Mithridates***, *king of Pontus.*

**mittō**, 3, mīsī, missum, *send.* MISSION.

**modestia**, -ae, F. [modestus], ***modesty.***

**modius**, -ī, M. [modus], *measure; peck.*

**modo**, adv. [modus], *only;* modo . . . modo, *now . . . now.*

**molestus**, -a, -um, adj. [mōlēs, *pile*], *troublesome.* MOLEST.

**molliō**, 4 [mollis], *soften.* MOLLIFY.

**moneō**, 2, -uī, -itum, *remind, advise, warn.* MONITOR.

**mōns**, montis, M., ***mountain***, *hill.* Cf. collis.

**mōnstrō**, 1 [moneō], *show, point out.* DEMONSTRATE.

**monumentum**, -ī, N. [moneō], (*that which reminds*), *memorial,* ***monument.***

**mora**, -ae, F., *delay.*

**Morinī**, -ōrum, M., *the* ***Morini***, *a people of Gaul.*

**morior**, 3, mortuus [mors], (fut. part. moritūrus), *die.*

**mōrōsus**, -a, -um, adj. [mōs], *fretful, cross; morose.*
**mortālis**, -e, adj. [mors], (*liable to death*), *mortal.*
**mortuus**, -a, -um, adj. [P. of morior], *dead.*
**mors**, mortis, F. [morior], *death.*
**mōs**, mōris, M., *manner, habit, custom.* (140.) MORAL.
**mōtus**, -ūs, M. [moveō], *motion, movement; tumult, disturbance.*
**moveō**, 2, mōvī, mōtum, *move.*
**mox**, adv., *soon, presently.*
**mulier**, -eris, F., *woman.*
**multitūdō**, -inis, F. [multus], *multitude.*
**multum**, adv. [multus], *much.*
**multus**, -a, -um, adj., comp. plūs, superl. plūrimus, *much, many.*
**mundus**, -ī, M., *world, universe.* Cf. orbis terrārum.
**mūniō**, 4 [moenia, *fortifications*], *fortify, defend.*
**mūnitiō**, -ōnis, F. [mūniō], *fortification.* MUNITION.
**mūrus**, -ī, M., *wall.*
**mūtō**, 1, *change, alter.* MUTATION.

**nam**, conj., *for.* Cf. enim.
**nanciscor**, 3, nanctus *and* nactus, *get, obtain; find, meet with.*
**nārrō**, 1, *tell, relate, report, narrate.*
**nāscor**, 3, nātus, *be born; be found.*
**Nāsica**, -ae, M., *Nasica, surname of one of the Scipios.*
**nāta**, -ae, F. [P. of nāscor], *daughter.* Cf. fīlia.
**nātūra**, -ae, F. [nāscor], *nature.*
**nauta**, -ae, M. [for nāvita; nāvis], *sailor.*
**nāvicula**, -ae, F. [diminutive of nāvis], *little vessel, boat.* Cf. cymba.
**nāvigātiō**, -ōnis, F. [nāvigō], *a sailing; navigation.*
**nāvigō**, 1 [nāvis, agō], *sail, set sail.*
**nāvis**, -is, F., *ship.* (154.) NAVAL.
**nē**, conj., *that not, lest;* w. hortatory subjunctive, *not.*
**ne**, interrog. adv., enclitic. (p. 10, N. 2.) Cf. nōnne and num.
**necessārius**, -a, -um, adj. [necesse], *necessary.*
**necessitās**, -ātis, F. [necesse], *necessity, constraint.*
**necō**, 1, *kill, slay.* Cf. interficiō and occīdō.
**nectō**, 3, nexuī and nexī, nexum, *bind, weave.*
**negō**, 1 [nē, āiō, *say*], *say not, deny; refuse.*
**nēmō**, -inis, M. and F. [nē, homo], *no one.* For gen. and abl. use nūllīus, nūllō.
**Neptūnus**, -ī, M., *Neptune, god of the sea.*
**nē-quāquam**, adv., *by no means, not at all.*
**ne-que** *or* **nec**, *and not;* neque ... neque, *neither ... nor.*
**ne-sciō**, 4, *know not, be ignorant of.*
**neuter**, -tra, -trum, adj., *neither* (*of two*). (200.) NEUTRAL.
**niger**, -gra, -grum, adj., *black.* Cf. āter.
**nihil**, N., indecl., *nothing.*
**nimium**, adv., *too, too much.*
**ni-si**, conj., *if not, unless, except.*
**nix**, nivis, F., *snow.* (167, 2.)
**nōbilis**, -e, adj. [nōscō], *well-known, famous; noble.*
**noceō**, 2, -uī, -itum, *do harm to, hurt, injure;* w. dat. NOXIOUS. Cf. obsum.
**noctū**, adv. [nox], *by night, in the night.*

**nōlō**, nōlle, nōluī, ——, [nē, volō], *be unwilling, will not, not wish.* (316.)

**nōmen**, -inis, N. [nōscō], (*that by which a thing is known*), *name.* NOMINAL.

**nōminō**, 1 [nōmen], *name, call.*

**nōn**, adv. [nē, ūnum], *not.*

**nōn-ne**, interrog. adv., expecting an affirmative answer, *not?* Cf. -ne and num.

**nōn-nūllus**, -a, -um, adj. (*not none*), *some.*

**nōnus**, -a, -um, num. adj. [novem], *ninth.*

**noster**, -tra, -trum, poss. pron., *our, ours.* Nostrī, *our men.*

**nōtus**, -a, -um, adj. [P. of nōscō], *known.*

**novus**, -a, -um, adj., *new.* NOVELTY.

**nox**, noctis, F., *night.* (167. 2.) NOCTURNAL.

**nūbēs**, -is, F., *cloud.* (149.)

**nūllus**, -a, -um, adj. [nē, ūllus], *not any, no, none.* (200.) NULLITY.

**num**, interrog. adv., expecting a negative answer, *whether.* Cf. nōnne and -ne.

**Numa**, -ae, M., *Numa* (*Pompilius*), *second king of Rome.*

**numerus**, -ī, M., *number.*

**nummus**, -ī, M., *piece of money, coin.*

**nunc**, adv., *now.* Cf. jam.

**nunquam**, adv. [nē, unquam], *never.*

**nūntiō**, 1 [nūntius], *announce, report.*

**nūntius**, -ī, M. [nūntiō], *bearer of news, messenger.*

**nusquam**, adv. [nē, usquam], *nowhere.*

**nūtriō**, 4, *feed, nourish, support.* Cf. alō.

**ō**, interj., *O, Oh!*

**ob-eō**, -īre, -iī, -itum, *go to, reach, meet.*

**ob-ligō**, 1 [ligō, *bind*], *bind, oblige, put under obligation.*

**oblīvīscor**, 4, oblītus, *forget.*

**ob-ruō**, 3, -uī, -utum, *overwhelm, cover, bury.*

**obses**, -sidis, M. and F. [ob, sedeō], (*one who sits or remains as a pledge*), *hostage.*

**ob-sideō**, 2, -sēdī, -sēssum [sedeō], (*sit against*), *blockade, besiege.* Cf. oppūgnō.

**ob-sisto**, 3, -stitī, -stitum, *oppose, withstand, obstruct;* w. dat.

**ob-sum**, -esse, -fuī, ——, *be against, opposed to; injure;* w. dat. Cf. noceō.

**ob-temperō**, 1, *comply with, yield to;* w. dat.

**ob-viam**, adv., *in the way, towards;* with verb of motion, *meet;* w. dat.

**occāsus**, -ūs, M. [occidō], (*a sinking*), *setting.*

**occidō**, 3, -cidī, -cāsum [ob, cadō], *fall down, fall.*

**occīdō**, 3, -cīdī, -cīsum [ob, caedō, *cut*], *cut down, kill.* Cf. necō and interficiō.

**occupō**, 1 [ob, capiō], *take possession of, seize; occupy.* Cf. potior.

**oc-currō**, 3, -currī, -cursum [ob], *run to meet; meet, fall in with.* OCCUR.

**ōceanus**, -ī, M., *ocean.*

**ocellus**, -ī, M. [diminutive of oculus], *little eye.*

**octāvus**, -a, -um, num. adj. [octō], *eighth.*

**octō**, num. adj., indecl., *eight.*

**oculus**, -ī, M., *eye*. OCULAR.

**of-ferō**, offere, obtulī, oblātum [ob], (*bring before*), *present*, ***offer***. (321.)

**officium**, -ī, N. [opus, faciō], *service, duty*, ***office***.

**ōlim**, adv. [olle, old form of ille], (*at that time*); *formerly, once; at some time or other; hereafter*. Cf. aliquandō and quondam.

**omnis**, -e, adj., *whole, all, every*. Cf. tōtus.

**onus**, -eris, N., *load, burden*. ONEROUS.

**opera**, -ae, F. [opus], *labor, care, attention*; operam dare, *try*; operā, *on account of*. OPERATE.

**oportet**, 2, -uit, impers. [opus], *it is necessary, it behooves*; (*one*) *must* or *ought*.

**oppidānus**, -a, -um, adj. [oppidum], *of a town*; noun, *townsman*.

**oppidum**, -ī, N., *town*.

**op-pleō**, 2, -ēvī, -ētum [ob], *fill up; cover*.

**opportūnus**, -a, -um, adj., *fit, convenient, suitable*; ***opportune***.

**op-pūgnō**, 1 [ob], *attack, assault, besiege*. Cf. expūgnō and obsideō.

**[ops]**, opis, F., *aid, assistance*; plur., *power, strength, resources*.

**optimē**, adv. [optimus], *most excellently, best*. (219.)

**optō**, 1, *wish, desire, long for*. Cf. cupiō and dēsīderō.

**opus**, -eris, N., *work, labor* (140); as indecl. noun, *need, necessity*; opus est, *it is necessary*.

**ōrāculum**, -ī, N. [ōrō], ***oracle***.

**ōrātiō**, -ōnis, F. [ōrō], *prayer, plea; speech*, ***oration***.

**ōrātor**, -ōris, M. [ōrō], ***orator***, *ambassador*.

**orbis**, -is, M., *circle*, ***orb***; orbis terrārum, *earth, world*. Cf. mundus.

**orbus**, -a, -um, adj., *bereaved, childless*.

**Orcus**, -ī, M., ***Orcus***, *the lower world*; also *Pluto, the god of the lower world*.

**ordior**, 4, orsus, *begin, undertake*. Cf. incipiō.

**ōrdō**, -inis, M., *row, rank*; ***order***, *arrangement*.

**oriēns**, -entis, M. [P. of orior], *rising; east*.

**orior**, 4, ortus (pres. ind. of conj. 3, orĕris, orĭtur; imp. subj. orīrer or orĭrer. P. oritūrus), *rise, appear; begin*.

**ōrnāmentum**, -ī, N. [ōrnō], (*that which adorns*), ***ornament***, *jewel*.

**ōrnō**, 1, *adorn*, ***ornament***.

**ōrō**, 1 [ōs], *pray, beg*. Cf. petō and rogō.

**ōs**, ōris, N., *mouth, face*. ORAL.

**os-tendō**, 3, -dī, -ēnsum [ob(s)], (*stretch out before*), *show, display*.

**ōstium**, -ī, N. [ōs], *entrance, door*.

**ovis**, -is, F., *sheep*.

**ōvum**, -ī, N., *egg*. OVAL.

**pābulum**, -ī, N. [pāscō], *food, fodder*. Cf. cibus.

**paene**, adv., *nearly, almost*. Cf. ferē.

**paenitentia**, -ae, F. [paeniteō], *repentance*, ***penitence***. PENITENTIARY.

**palūs**, -ūdis, F., *swamp, marsh*.

**pār**, paris, adj., *equal*.

**parātus**, -a, -um, adj. [P. of parō], *ready*, ***prepared***.

**parcō**, 3, peperci (parsī), ——, spare; w. dat.

**parēns**, -entis, M. and F., ***parent***. (167. 1.)

**pāreō**, 2, -uī, ——, (*come forth, appear*), *be obedient to, obey;* w. dat.
**pariō**, 3, peperī, paritum *and* partum, *bring forth, lay.*
**pariter**, adv. [pār], *equally.*
**parō**, 1, *make ready, prepare, get.*
**pars**, partis, F., *part, piece, portion, share.*
**partior**, 4 [pars], *divide; part, share.*
**Parus**, -ī, F., *Paros, an island in the Ægean Sea.* (11. 4.)
**parvus**, -a, -um, adj. (comp. minor, superl. minimus), *small, little.*
**pāscō**, 3, pāvī, pāstum, *feed, tend; pasture.*
**passer**, -eris, M., *sparrow.*
**passus**, -ūs, M. [pateō], (*a stretching out of the feet in walking*), *step, pace.*
**pāstor**, -ōris, M. [pāscō], *feeder, keeper; shepherd.* (134.) PASTOR.
**pateō**, 2, -uī, ——, *lie open, be open.* P. patēns, *open.*
**pater**, -tris, M., *father.* (134.) PATERNAL.
**patienter**, adv. [patiēns], *patiently, with patience.*
**patior**, 3, passus, *bear, suffer, endure.* PASSION.
**patria**, -ae, F. [patrius, pater; sc. terra], *fatherland, native land, country.* EXPATRIATE.
**paucus**, -a, -um, adj. (generally plur.), *few, little.* PAUCITY.
**paulō**, adv. [paulus], *by a little, little.*
**paulus**, -a, -um, adj., *little.*
**Paullus**, -ī, M., *surname of Æmilius.*
**pauper**, -eris, adj., *poor.* (167. 3.)
**pāx**, pācis, F. (no gen. plur.), *peace.* PACIFY.
**peccātum**, -ī, N. [peccō], *mistake, fault, sin.*
**peccō**, 1, *make a mistake, commit a fault, sin.*
**pectus**, -oris, N., *breast.*
**pecus**, -oris, N., *cattle, herd.*
**pedes**, -itis, M. [pēs], *foot-soldier.*
**pējor**, -us, comp. of malus. (208.)
**pellis**, -is, F., *skin, hide.* PELT.
**pēnsum**, -ī, N. [P. of pendō], (*what is weighed out,* e.g. *wool, as a task for spinning*), *task; lesson, exercise.*
**per**, prep. w. acc., *through, by, by means of, on account of.*
**pēra**, -ae, F., *bag, wallet.*
**per-agrō**, 1 [ager], *wander through, pass over, traverse.*
**per-dō**, 3, -didī, -ditum, *destroy; lose.* Cf. amittō.
**per-dūcō**, 3, -dūxī, -ductum, *lead* or *bring through.*
**per-eō**, -īre, -iī, ——, *perish, be ruined.* (327.)
**per-fodiō**, 3, -fōdī, -fossum, *dig through, pierce, stab.*
**per-fringō**, 3, -frēgī, -fractum, [frangō], *break through, break.*
**per-fugiō**, 3, -fūgī, ——, *flee* (*for refuge*).
**pergō**, 3, perrēxī, perrēctum [per, regō], *go on, continue.*
**perīculum**, -ī, N. [perior, *try*], *trial, attempt; risk, danger, peril.*
**perītus**, -a, -um, adj. [P. of perior, *try*], (*having tried*), *skilful.*
**per-mittō**, 3, -mīsī, -missum, *allow, grant, suffer, permit.* Cf. sinō.
**per-paucus**, -a, -um, adj. (generally plur.), *very few.*
**Persae**, -ārum, M., *the Persians.*
**per-sequor**, 3, -cūtus, *follow persistently, follow up.*
**per-spiciō**, 3, -spexī, -spectum, [speciō], *see through, see into; perceive, observe.* PERSPECTIVE.

**per-stō,** 1, -stitī, -stātum, *stand fast, persevere, persist.*

**per-terreō,** 2, -uī, -itum, *thoroughly frighten.*

**pertinācia,** -ae, F. [pertinā x], *perseverance; obstinacy.* PERTINACITY.

**per-veniō,** 4, -vēnī, -ventum (*come through to the end*), *arrive.* Cf. adveniō.

**pēs,** pedis, M., *foot.* (105.) PEDAL.

**petō,** 3, -īvī *or* -iī, -ītum, *seek, demand, beg.* PETITION. Cf. ōrō and rogō.

**Philotimus,** -ī, M., *Philotimus.*

**piger,** -gra, -grum, adj., *slow, lazy, indolent.*

**piget,** 2, -uit *or* -itum est, impersonal, *it disgusts,* (*one*) *is disgusted.*

**pigritia,** -ae, F. [piger], *laziness, sloth, indolence.*

**pīlum,** -ī, N., *javelin.*

**pīpiō,** 1, *chirp.*

**placeō,** 2, -uī, -itum [placidus], *please;* w. dat.

**placidē,** adv. [placidus], *softly, gently, quietly.* PLACIDLY.

**placidus,** -a, -um, adj. [placeō], *gentle, quiet, calm.* PLACID.

**plānitiēs,** -ēī, F. [plānus, *even, level*], (*a flatness*), *level ground, plain.*

**plānus,** -a, -um, adj. [plānitiēs], *even, flat, level, plain.*

**Plataeēnsēs,** -ium, M., *the Plataeans, inhabitants of Platæa.*

**plēbs,** plēbis, F., *the common people, multitude.* PLEBEIAN.

**plēnus,** -a, -um, adj. [pleō, *fill*], *full.*

**plērusque,** -aque, -umque, adj. (generally plur.), *very many, most, the greater part.*

**plumbum,** -ī, N., *lead;* plumbum album, *tin.*

**plūs,** plūris, adj., comp. of multus. (208.)

**Plūtō,** -ōnis, *Pluto,* M., *god of the lower world.*

**pōculum,** -ī, N., *cup, bowl.*

**poēma,** -atis, N., *poem.*

**poena,** -ae, F. [pūniō], *quit-money, fine, punishment.* PENAL.

**Poenī,** -ōrum, M., *the Carthaginians.*

**Poeniceus,** -a, -um, adj. [Poenī], *Carthaginian.* See Pūnicus.

**poēta,** -ae, M., *poet.*

**polliceor,** 2, *promise.* Cf. prōmittō.

**Polyphēmus,** -ī, M., *Polyphemus, a Cyclops.*

**Pompējus,** -ēī, M., *Pompey, a famous Roman general.*

**pōmum,** -ī, N., *fruit.*

**pondus,** -eris, N. [pendō, *weigh*], *weight.*

**pōnō,** 3, posuī, positum, *put, place, set.* POSITION.

**pōns,** -ntis, M., *bridge.*

**Popēdius,** -ī, M., *Popedius, a Latin.*

**populus,** -ī, M., *people.*

**Porcius,** -ī, M., *a Roman family name.*

**Porsena,** -ae, M., *Porsena, an Etruscan king.*

**porta,** -ae, F., *gate, door.* PORTAL. Cf. jānua.

**portō,** 1, *carry, bring.* Cf. ferō and vehō.

**porticus,** -ūs, F. [porta], *portico.*

**portus,** -ūs, M., *harbor, port.*

**possum,** posse, potuī, —— [potis, *able,* sum], *be able, can.* (292.)

**post,** prep. w. acc., *after, behind;* as adv., for posteā, *afterwards, after.*

**post-eā,** adv., *afterwards.*

**posterus**, -a, -um, adj. [post] (comp. posterior, superl. postrēmus *or* postumus), *following*, *next*.

**post-hāc**, adv., *after this time*, *hereafter*, *henceforth*.

**postrīdiē**, adv. [posterō diē], *on the day after*, *the following day*.

**postulō**, 1, *ask*, *demand*. Cf. quaerō and rogō.

**potēns**, -entis, adj., [P. of possum], *able*, *powerful*; ***potent***.

**potior**, 4 [potis, *able*], *become master of*, *get*, *get possession of*; w. gen. or abl. Cf. adipiscor.

**praebeō**, 2 [prae, habeō], *hold forth*, *offer*, *furnish*.

**praeceps**, -ipitis, adj. [prae, caput], *head-foremost*, *headlong*; *rash*, ***precipitate***.

**praeceptor**, -ōris, M. [praeceptum], *teacher*, ***preceptor***. Cf. magister.

**praeceptum**, -ī, N. [praeceptor], *maxim*, ***precept***.

**praeda**, -ae, F., *booty*, *spoil*, ***prey***. PREDATORY.

**praedicō**, 1 [prae, dicō, -āre, *make known*], *proclaim*, *boast*.

**prae-eō**, -īre, -iī, -itum, *go before*; *be at the head*. (327. 2.)

**praemium**, -ī, N., *reward*, *prize*. PREMIUM.

**praesidium**, -ī, N. [prae, sedeō, *sit before*], *defence*, *help*; *troops*, *garrison*.

**praestāns**, -antis, adj. [P. of praestō], *pre-eminent*, *distinguished*.

**prae-stō**, 1, -stitī, -stitum (stātum), *stand before*; *surpass*; *fulfil*, *discharge*, *perform*.

**prae-sum**, -esse, -fuī, ——, *be before*, *at the head of*, *command*; w. dat.

**praeter**, prep. w. acc., *beyond*, *besides*, *except*.

**praeter-eō**, -īre, -iī, -itum, *go by*, *pass by*, *omit*. (327. 2.) PRETERITE.

**praetōrius**, -a, -um, adj. [praetor], (*pertaining to a prætor*), ***prætorian***; noun, *ex-prætor*.

**prātum**, -ī, N., *meadow*.

**premō**, 3, pressī, pressum, ***press***; with **ōre**, *bite*, *eat*.

[**prex**], precis, F. (used mostly in plur.), *prayer*, *entreaty*.

**prīmus**, -a, -um, adj. [superl. with comp. prior, no pos.], *first*, *foremost*. PRIME.

**prīnceps**, -ipis, adj. [prīmus, capiō], (*taking the first place*), *first*, *chief*; noun, *chief*, *leader*. (105.) PRINCE.

**prius-quam**, conj., *before that*, *before*.

**prīvō**, 1, ***deprive***; w. abl.

**prō**, interj., *O!*

**prō**, prep. w. abl., *before*, *in behalf of*, *for*; *considering*.

**prō-cēdō**, 3, -cēssī, -cēssum, *go forward*, *advance*, ***proceed***. Cf. prōgredior.

**procul**, adv., *far*, *far from*.

**prō-dō**, 3, -didī, -ditum, *give forth*; *hand down*; *give up*, *betray*.

**prō-dūcō**, 3, -dūxī, -ductum, *lead forth*.

**proelium**, -ī, N., *battle*, *combat*. Cf. pūgna.

**proficīscor**, 3, -fectus, *set out*, *march*, *go*. Cf. exeō and ēgredior.

**pro-fiteor**, 2, -fessus [fateor], *acknowledge*, *confess*, *declare*. PROFESS.

**prō-flīgō**, 1, *overthrow*, *destroy*, *ruin*. PROFLIGATE.

**profundus**, -a, -um, adj., *deep*, ***profound***.

**prō-gredior**, 3, -gressus [gradior,

*step*], *go forward, advance.* PROGRESS. Cf. prōcēdō.

**pro-hibeō,** 2 [habeō], (*hold in front of*), *hold back, check, hinder, prevent, prohibit.*

**prō-iciō,** 3, -iēcī, -iectum [iaciō], *throw forward, cast away, cast.* PROJECT.

**prō-mittō,** 3, -mīsī, -missum [*let* or *send forth*], *promise; let grow.* Cf. polliceor.

**prope,** prep. w. acc., and adv. (comp. propius, superl. proximē), *near, near to; nearly, almost.*

**prō-pōnō,** 3, -posuī, -positum, *put before, set forth; make known, declare.* PROPOSE.

**prōpositum,** -ī, N. [prōpōnō], *purpose, design, resolution.* PROPOSITION.

**proprius,** -a, -um, adj., (*one's*) *own.* PROPER.

**prō-pūgnō,** 1 (*fight in front*), *rush out to battle, make sorties.*

**prō-sequor,** 3, -cūtus, *follow, pursue.* PROSECUTE.

**Prōserpina,** -ae, F., *Proserpina, daughter of Ceres.*

**prō-sternō,** 3, -strāvī, -strātum, *overthrow, destroy; prostrate.*

**prō-sum,** prōdesse, prōfuī, ——, *be useful to, benefit;* w. dat. (293.)

**prō-vehō,** 3, -vexī, -vectum, *carry forward, convey;* in pass., *ride, sail.*

**prō-videō,** 2, -vīdī, -vīsum, (*see forward*), *provide.*

**prōvincia,** -ae, F., *province.*

**proximus,** -a, -um (superl. with comp. propior, no pos.), *nearest, next.* PROXIMITY.

**prūdēns,** -entis, adj. [for prōvidēns], *wise, sagacious, knowing, prudent.* (164.)

**prūdenter,** adv. [prūdēns], *wisely, prudently.*

**prūdentia,** -ae, F. [prūdēns], *foresight, sagacity, wisdom, prudence.*

**pūblicus,** -a, -um, adj. [populus], (*pertaining to the people*), *public.*

**Pūblius,** -ī, M., *Publius, a Roman first name.*

**pudet,** 2, puduit *or* puditum est, impers., *it shames,* (*one*) *is ashamed.*

**puella,** -ae, F. [diminutive of puer], *girl, maiden.*

**puellāris,** -e, adj. [puella], *girlish.*

**puer,** -erī, M., *boy, child.* PUERILE.

**puerulus,** -ī, M. [diminutive of puer], *little boy.*

**pūgna,** -ae, F. [pūgnō], *battle, contest.* PUGNACIOUS. Cf. proelium.

**pūgnō,** 1 [pūgna], *fight.* Cf. dīmicō.

**pulcher,** -chra, -chrum, adj., *beautiful, fair, comely.*

**pulchritūdō,** -inis, F. [pulcher], *beauty.*

**pulvis,** -eris, M., *dust.* PULVERIZE.

**Pūnicus,** -a, -um, adj. [Poenī], *Carthaginian, Punic;* mālum Pūnicum, *pomegranate.* See Poeniceus.

**pūniō,** 4 [poena], *punish.*

**putō,** 1, *think, believe, reckon.* (429.)

**Pyrēnaeus,** -a, -um, adj., *Pyrenaean, Pyrenees.*

**Pyrrhus,** -ī, M., *Pyrrhus, king of Epirus.*

**quadrāgintā,** num. adj., indecl. [quattuor], *forty.*

**quadringentī,** -ae, -a, num. adj. [quattuor, centum], *four hundred.*

**quaerō,** 3, quaesīvī or -iī, quaesītum, *seek, ask, inquire.* (382.)

**quaesō,** 3, -īvī, *or* -iī, —— [old form of quaerō], *beg, pray.*

**quam,** adv.; interrog., *how, how much?* rel., *as much, as, than;* quam saepissimē, *as often as possible.*

**quantus,** -a, -um, adj. [quam], *how great, how much; as great as, as much as.*

**quā-rē,** adv. (*on account of which thing*), *wherefore.*

**quartus,** -a, -um, num. adj. [quattuor], *fourth.* QUART.

**qua-si,** adv., *as if.*

**quater,** num. adv. [quattuor], *four times.*

**quattuor,** num. adj., indecl., *four.*

**quattuor-decim,** num. adj. [decem], *fourteen.*

**-que,** conj. enclitic, *and.* Cf. et, atque, and ac.

**quercus,** -ūs, F., *oak.* (11. 4.)

**quī,** quae, quod, rel. and adj. pron., *who, which, what, that.* (279.)

**quia,** conj., *because.* Cf. quod.

**quīdam,** quaedam, quid(quod)-dam, indef. pron., *certain, a certain one, a.* (279. 4.)

**quidem,** adv. (never the first word), *indeed, certainly, in truth;* nē . . . quidem, *not even.*

**quīn,** conj. [quī, nē], *but that, that.*

**quīngentī,** -ae, -a, num. adj., indecl. [quīnque, centum], *five hundred.*

**quīnquāgintā,** num. adj., indecl. [quīnque], *fifty.*

**quīnque,** num. adj., indecl., *five.*

**quīntus,** -a, -um, num. adj. [quīnque], *fifth.*

**quīntus decimus,** num. adj., *fifteenth.*

**quis,** quae, quid, interrog. pron., *who? which? what?* (279.)

**quisquam,** quidquam (no fem. or plur.), indef. pron., *any, any one (at all).* (279. 4.)

**quisque,** quaeque, quid(quod)que, indef. pron., *each one, each, every.* (279. 4.)

**quō,** adv., *where, whither.*

**quod,** conj., *because.* Cf. quia.

**quondam,** adv., *once, formerly.* Cf. aliquandō and ōlim.

**quoniam,** adv. [cum (quom), jam], *since, because.* Cf. cum.

**quoque,** adv. (following the emphatic word), *also, too.*

**quot,** interrog. and rel. adj., indecl., *how many; as many as.*

**radius,** -ī, M., *beam, ray.*

**rādō,** 3, rāsī, rāsum, *shave.* RAZOR.

**rāna,** -ae, F., *frog.*

**rapāx,** -ācis, adj. [rapiō], *snatching, greedy, ravenous.* RAPACIOUS.

**rapiō,** 3, -uī, -tum [rapāx], *seize, snatch, drag away.* RAPTURE.

**rārus,** -a, -um, adj., *far apart, dispersed, single.* RARE.

**ratiō,** -ōnis, F., *plan, method; reason.*

**re-cipiō,** 3, -cēpī, -ceptum [capiō], *take back, get again, receive.* Sē recipere, *withdraw, retreat.*

**recitō,** 1, *read aloud, recite.*

**re-creō,** 1 [creō, *make*], *refresh, recreate.*

**rēctē,** adv. [rēctus], *rightly.*

**red-eō,** -īre, -iī, -itum [re(d)], *go back, return.* (327. 2.)

**reditus,** -ūs, M. [redeō], *return.*

**re-dūcō,** 3, -dūxī, -ductum, *lead back, bring back.* REDUCE.

**re-ferō,** -ferre, rettulī, -lātum, *carry back, bring back.* (321.) REFER. Cf. reportō.

**re-ficiō,** 3, -fēcī, -fectum [faciō], *make again; repair, restore, rebuild.*

**rēgīna,** -ae, F. [regō], (*the ruling one*), *queen.*

**regiō,** -ōnis, F., *region.*

**rēgnō,** 1 [rēgnum, rēx], *be king, rule, reign.*

**rēgnum,** -ī, N. [rēx], *kingdom.*

**regō,** 3, rēxī, rēctum [rēx], *rule.*

**Rēgulus,** -ī, M., ***Regulus,*** *a Roman consul.*

**re-iciō,** 3, -jēcī, -jectum [jaciō], *throw back, drive back.* REJECT.

**re-linquō,** 3, -līquī, -lictum [reliquus], *leave behind, leave.* RELINQUISH.

**reliquus,** -a, -um, adj. [relinquō], *remaining, the rest.*

**re-mittō,** 3, -mīsī, -missum, *send back.* REMIT.

**rēmus,** -ī, M., *oar.*

**Remus,** -ī, M., ***Remus,*** *twin brother of Romulus.*

**re-pellō,** 3, reppulī, repulsum, *drive back, **repel, repulse.***

**re-periō,** 4, repperī, repertum [pariō, *procure*], *find, discover, ascertain.* Cf. inveniō.

**re-petō,** 3, -petīvī *or* -iī, -petītum, *seek again, demand back;* rēs repetō, *demand restitution.*

**re-pleō,** 2, -ēvī, -ētum, (*fill again*), *fill up, fill.* REPLETE.

**re-portō,** 1, *bring back, carry back.* Cf. referō.

**re-prehendō,** 3, -dī, -hēnsum, *hold back, restrain, reprove.* REPREHENSIVE.

**re-putō,** 1, (*count over*), *reckon; think over.*

**rēs,** reī, F., *thing, event, circumstance, affair* (254); rēs pūblica, ***republic,*** *state, commonwealth.*

**re-scindō,** 3, -scidī, -scissum, *tear away, break down.* RESCIND.

**re-spondeō,** 3, -dī, -spōnsum, (*promise in return*), *answer, reply, **respond.***

**re-stituō,** 3, -uī, -ūtum [statuō], *replace; give back, return, restore.* RESTITUTION.

**re-stō,** 1, restitī, ——, *stop behind, stand still, remain.*

**re-tineō,** 2, -tinuī, -tentum [teneō], *hold back, restrain, **retain.***

**re-vertor,** 3, -tī, -sum (deponent in pres. imp. and fut.), *turn back, return.* REVERT.

**re-vocō,** 1, *call back, recall.*

**rēx,** rēgis, M. [regō], (*ruler*), *king.* (105.)

**Rhēa Silvia,** -ae, F., ***Rhea Silvia,*** *mother of Romulus and Remus.*

**Rhēnus,** -ī, M., *the **Rhine.***

**Rhodus,** -ī, F., ***Rhodes,*** *an island in the Ægean Sea.*

**rictus,** -ūs, M. [ringor, *open the mouth*], *jaws wide open; jaws.*

**rīdeō,** 2, rīsī, rīsum, *laugh.* Cf. cachinnō. DERIDE.

**rīsus,** -ūs, M. [rīdeō], *laughter.*

**rīvus,** -ī, M., *brook, stream.* RIVAL.

**rōbur,** -oris, N., *strength.*

**rogō,** 1, *ask, question.* Cf. interrogō. (382.)

**Rōma,** -ae, F., ***Rome.***

**Rōmānus,** -a, -um, adj. [Rōma], ***Roman;*** noun, *a Roman.*

**Rōmulus,** -ī, M., ***Romulus,*** *first king of Rome.*

**rosa,** -ae, F., ***rose.***

**rōstrum,** -ī, N. [rōdō, *gnaw*], *beak of a vessel.* ROSTRUM.

**rubeō,** 2 [ruber], *be red.*

**ruber,** -bra, -brum, adj. [rubeō], *red.* RUBY.

**ruina,** -ae, F. [ruō, *fall*], (*a falling down*), *downfall, disaster, **ruin.***

**rūpēs,** -is, F. [ru(m)pō, *break*], (*the broken thing*) *cliff, rock.*

**rūrsus,** adv. [re-vorsus, revertō], (*turned back*), *back, again.*

**rūs,** rūris, N., *the country.*

**rūsticus**, -ī, m. [rūs], *countryman, peasant.* Rustic.

**sacer**, -cra, -crum, adj., ***sacred.***

**saepe**, adv., *often, frequently.*

**sagitta**, -ae, f., *arrow.*

**Saguntum**, -ī, n., ***Saguntum,*** *a town in Spain.*

**Sallustius**, -ī, m., ***Sallust,*** *a Roman historian.*

**salūs**, -ūtis, f., ***safety,*** *welfare.* Salutary.

**Samnīs**, -ītis, m., *a* ***Samnite.***

**sanguis**, -inis, m., *blood.* Sanguinary. Cf. cruor.

**sapiēns**, -entis, adj. [sapiō, *be wise*], *wise, sensible.*

**sapienter**, adv. [sapiēns], *wisely.*

**satis**, adv., *enough.* Satisfy.

**Sāturnus**, -ī, m., ***Saturn,*** *god of agriculture.*

**saxum**, -ī, n., *rock.*

**schola**, -ae, f., ***school.***

**sciō**, 4, scīvī, scītum, *know, know how.* Science.

**Scīpiō**, -ōnis, m., ***Scipio,*** *a famous Roman general.*

**scrība**, -ae, m. [scrībō], (*one who writes*), *clerk.* Scribe.

**scrībō**, 3, scrīpsī, scrīptum [scrība], *write.* Scribble.

**scrīptor**, -ōris, m. [scrībō], *writer, author.*

**scrīptum**, -ī, n. [scrībō], *writing, written work.* Script.

**scūtum**, -ī, n., *shield.*

**sē-cēdō**, 3, -cēssī, -cēssum, *go apart, withdraw, retire;* ***secede.***

**secundus**, -a, -um, adj. [sequor], *following, next;* ***second;*** *favorable.*

**sed**, conj., *but.* (393.)

**sedeō**, 2, sēdī, sēssum, *sit.* Session.

**sēdēs**, -is, f. [sedeō], *seat, abode.*

**semper**, adv., *always, ever.*

**sempiternus**, -a, -um, adj. [semper], *everlasting.*

**senātor**, -ōris, m. [senex], ***senator.***

**senātus**, -ūs, m. [senex], *council of elders,* ***senate.***

**senectūs**, -ūtis, f. [senex], *old age.*

**senex**, senis, adj., *old;* noun, *old man.* (262.) Senile.

**senior**, -ōris, adj. [comp. of senex], *elder, old person.*

**sēnsus**, -ūs, m. [sentiō], *feeling,* ***sense,*** *perception.*

**sententia**, -ae, f. [sentiō], *opinion, purpose.* Sentence.

**sentiō**, 4, sēnsī, sēnsum [sēnsus], *feel, know (by the senses), see, perceive.*

**septem**, num. adj., indecl., *seven.*

**September**, -bris, m. [septem], ***September.*** Often as adj.

**septem-decim**, num. adj. [decem], *seventeen.*

**septiēs**, num. adv. [septem], *seven times.*

**septimus**, -a, -um, num. adj. [septem], *seventh.*

**sequor**, 3, secūtus, *follow.* Sequence.

**serō**, 3, sēvī, satum, *sow, plant.*

**serta**, -ōrum, n. [serō, *plait*], *garlands, wreaths of flowers.*

**sērus**, -a, -um, adj., *late.*

**serviō**, 4. [servus], *be a slave to,* ***serve;*** w. dat.

**servitūs**, -ūtis, f. [servus], *slavery,* ***servitude.***

**servō**, 1, *save, keep;* ***preserve.***

**servus**, -ī, m. [serviō], *slave,* ***servant.*** (66.)

**sexāgintā**, num. adj., indecl. [sex], *sixty.*

**sextus**, -a, -um, num. adj. [sex], *sixth.*

**sī,** conj., *if, whether.*

**sic,** adv., *so, thus, in this manner.* Cf. ita.

**Sicca,** -ae, M., *Sicca, a friend of Cicero.*

**Sicilia,** -ae, F., *Sicily.*

**sīdus,** -eris, N., *star, constellation.* SIDEREAL. (301.)

**sīgnum,** -ī, N, *mark, sign, signal.*

**silva,** -ae, F., *wood, forest.* SILVAN.

**similis,** -e, adj. [simul], *like, resembling, similar.*

**simplex,** -icis, adj., *simple, plain, artless.*

**simul,** adv. [similis], *at the same time.*

**sin,** conj. [sī-nē], *but if, however, if.*

**sine,** prep. w. abl., *without.*

**singulī,** -ae, -a, num. adj., *separate, single, one by one.* (311. 8.)

**sinister,** -tra, -trum, adj., *left (hand).* SINISTER.

**sinō,** 3, sīvī, situm, *allow, permit.* Cf. permittō.

**sinus,** -ūs, M., *bosom, lap, folds of a garment.*

**sitis,** -is, F. (acc. -im, abl. -ī), *thirst.*

**socer,** -erī, M., *father-in-law.*

**socius,** -ī, M., *ally, companion.* ASSOCIATE.

**Sōcratēs,** -is, M., *Socrates, a famous Greek philosopher.*

**sōl,** sōlis, M., *sun* (no gen. plur.). SOLAR.

**soleō,** 2, solitus, *be accustomed, wont.* (p. 177, note 2.)

**Solōn,** -ōnis, M., *Solon, the great lawgiver of Athens.*

**sōlus,** -a, -um, adj., *alone, single; sole.* (200.)

**solvō,** 3, solvī, solūtum, *loose, loosen; break; weigh anchor, set sail.* SOLVE.

**somnus,** -ī, M., *sleep.*

**soror,** -ōris, F., *sister.*

**sors,** -tis, F., *lot, condition.* SORT.

**sortior,** 4 [sors], *draw lots, obtain by lot.*

**spargō,** 3, -sī, -sum, *strew, scatter.* SPARSE.

**Spartacus,** -ī, M., *Spartacus, a gladiator.*

**spatium,** -ī, N., *room, space; period.*

**spectō,** 1 [speciō, *look*], *look at, behold, witness.* SPECTACLE.

**speculor,** 1, *spy out, watch.*

**specus,** -ūs, M., *cave, den.*

**spērō,** 1 [spēs], *hope, hope for.*

**spēs,** speī, F. [spērō], *hope, expectation.*

**spoliō,** 1, *rob, plunder, spoil, despoil.*

**statim,** adv. [stō], *(standing there), on the spot, immediately, at once.*

**statua,** -ae, F. [statuō], *(the thing set up), statue.*

**statuō,** 3, -uī, -ūtum, *put, place; determine, think, believe.*

**stella,** -ae, F., *star.* (301.) STELLAR.

**stō,** 1, stetī, statum, *stand.*

**strāgēs,** -is, F., *slaughter, carnage.*

**stringō,** 3, -nxī, strictum *(draw tight), graze; draw, unsheath.*

**studeō,** 2, -uī, —— [studium], *be eager, strive earnestly for; study;* w. dat.

**studium,** -ī, N. [studeō], *zeal, eagerness; study.*

**stultitia,** -ae, F. [stultus], *folly.*

**stultus,** -a, -um, adj., *foolish, silly.*

**suāvis,** -e, adj., *sweet, delightful.* Cf. dulcis. SUAVITY.

**suāviter,** adv. [suāvis], *sweetly, delightfully.*

**sub-dūcō,** 3, -dūxī, -ductum, *draw from under, draw up.*

**subeō,** -īre, -iī, -itum, *go under* or *up to, enter; undergo.* (327.)

**subitō**, adv. [subeō], *suddenly, unexpectedly.*

**sub-moveō**, 2, -mōvī, -mōtum (*move from beneath*), *remove, drive away.*

**subsidium**, -ī, N. [subsideō], *aid, support, relief, assistance.*

**sub-siliō**, 4, -uī, —— [saliō, *leap*], *jump up.* Cf. dēsiliō and trānsiliō.

**sub-veniō**, 4, -vēnī, -ventum (*come to one's relief*), *help, aid, assist.* Cf. succurrō.

**suc-currō**, 3, -currī, -cursum [sub], (*run up to*), *help, aid,* ***succor.***

**suf-ferō**, sufferre, sustulī, sublātum [sub], *bear up under, undergo.* SUFFER.

**suī**, reflex. pron., *of himself* (*herself, itself, themselves*). (264.)

**Sūlla**, -ae, M., ***Sulla,*** *a famous Roman general and statesman.*

**sum**, esse, fuī, ——, *be, exist.*

**summus**, -a, -um, adj., superl. of superus, *highest.*

**sūmō**, 3, sūmpsī, sūmptum, *take, take up;* ***assume.***

**super**, prep. w. acc. and abl., *over, above, on top of.*

**superbē**, adv. [superbus], *proudly, haughtily.*

**superbus**, -a, -um, adj. [super], *proud.* SUPERB.

**superior**, -us, adj., comp. of superus, *higher,* ***superior.***

**superō**, 1 [super], *pass over; surpass, overcome; conquer.*

**super-sum**, -esse, -fuī, ——, *remain over; survive, exist.*

**suprēmus**, -a, -um, adj., sup. of superus, *highest; last.*

**suscipiō**, 3, -cēpī, -ceptum [sub, capiō], *undertake.*

**sus-pendō**, 3 -dī, -pēnsum [sub], *hang up,* ***suspend.***

**suspicor**, 1 [suspiciō, *look askance at*], *mistrust, suspect.*

**sustineō**, 2, -tinuī, -tentum [sub, teneō], *hold up, bear, endure;* ***sustain.***

**suus**, -a, -um, poss. pron. [suī], *his, hers, her, its, theirs, their* (*own*).

**taceō**, 2, tacuī, tacitum, *be silent, be silent about.* TACIT.

**taedet**, 2, taeduit, taesum est, impers., *it disgusts, wearies;* (*one*) *is disgusted, wearied.*

**tālea**, -ae, F., *thin bar.*

**tam**, adv., *so;* tam . . . quam, *as . . . as.* Cf. ita and sīc.

**tamen**, adv., *yet, but, nevertheless.*

**tandem**, adv. [tam], (*just so far*), *at length, finally.*

**tangō**, 3, tetigī, tactum, *touch.*

**tantō**, adv. [tantus], *by so much, so much the* (with comparatives).

**tantum**, adv. [tantus], *only.*

**tantus**, -a, -um, adj., *so great.*

**Tarentīnus**, -a, -um, adj., *of Tarentum,* ***Tarentine.***

**Tarquinius**, -ī, M., ***Tarquin the Proud,*** *seventh king of Rome.*

**tectum**, -ī, N. [tegō, *cover*], *covering, shelter, roof.*

**tēlum**, -ī, N., *weapon.*

**temerārius**, -a, -um [temerē], *rash, inconsiderate.*

**temerē**, adv., *rashly, inconsiderately.*

**temeritās**, -ātis, F. [temerē], *chance; rashness,* ***temerity.***

**tempestās**, -ātis, F. [tempus], (*state* or *condition of time*), *weather; stormy weather, storm,* ***tempest.***

**templum**, -ī, N., ***temple.***

**tempus**, -oris, N., *time.* TEMPORAL.

**tenebrae**, -ārum, F., *darkness, shades.*

**tenebricōsus**, -a, -um, adj. [tenebrae], (*full of darkness*), *dark, gloomy*.

**teneō**, 2, -uī, tentum, *hold, keep, have;* memoriā tenēre, *remember*.

**tener**, -era, -erum, adj., *soft, delicate, **tender***.

**tenuis**, -e, adj., *thin, light*.

**ter**, num. adv. [trēs], *thrice, three times*.

**Terentius**, -ī, M., *a Roman family name*.

**tergum**, -ī, N., *back*.

**terra**, -ae, F., *earth, land*. TERRACE.

**terreō**, 2 [terror], *frighten, alarm, **terrify***.

**terror**, -ōris [terreō], ***terror**, alarm*.

**tertiō**, adv. [tertius], *the third time*.

**tertius**, -a, -um, num. adj. [trēs], *third*.

**tertius decimus**, num. adj., *thirteenth*.

**testimōnium**, -ī, N. [testor, *bear witness*], *witness, evidence, **testimony***.

**testūdō**, -inis, F. [testa, *shell*], *tortoise; shed* or *covering to protect besiegers*.

**Teutonēs**, -um, M., *the **Teutons**, a German tribe*.

**Thalēs**, -is, M., ***Thales**, a Greek philosopher*.

**Themistoclēs**, -is, M., ***Themistocles**, a famous Athenian*.

**Tīcīnus**, -ī, M., *the **Ticinus**, a river of Italy*.

**tigris**, -is, *or* -idis, ***tiger***.

**timeō**, 2, -uī, —— [timor], *fear, be afraid of*.

**Tīmoleōn**, -ontis, M., ***Timoleon**, a Corinthian general*.

**timor**, -ōris, M. [timeō], *fear, dread, alarm*. TIMOROUS.

**tolerō**, 1, *bear, endure*. TOLERATE.

**tollō**, 3, sustulī, sublātum, *lift, raise, pick up; weigh (anchor)*.

**tot**, adj., indecl., *so many*. Cf. quot.

**tōtus**, -a, -um, adj., *whole, all, entire*. (200.) TOTAL.

**tractō**, 1 [trahō], *handle, manage, **treat***.

**trā-dō**, 3, -didī, -ditum [trāns], *give over, deliver; relate, recount*. TRADITION.

**trahō**, 3, traxī, -ctum, *draw, drag; derive*.

**trā-iciō**, 3, -jēcī, -jectum [trāns, jaciō], *throw across; pass over, cross*.

**trājectus**, -ūs, M. [trāiciō], *a crossing over, passage*.

**tranquillitās**, -ātis, F. [tranquillus], *calmness, **tranquillity**; a calm*.

**trāns**, prep. w. acc., *across, beyond, over*.

**trān-scendō**, 3, -dī, -scēnsum [scandō, *climb*], *step* or *pass over; cross*. TRANSCEND.

**trāns-eō**, -īre, -iī, -itum, *go over, cross*. (372.)

**trāns-fīgō**, 3, -fīxī, -fīxum, *pierce through, pierce, stab; **transfix***.

**trān-siliō**, 4, -iī, *and* -uī, —— [saliō, *leap*], *leap over* or *across*. Cf. dēsiliō and subsiliō.

**trecentī**, -ae, -a, num. adj. [trēs, centum], *three hundred*.

**tredecim**, num. adj., indecl. [trēs, decem], *thirteen*.

**trēs**, tria, num. adj., *three*. (311. 4.)

**tribūnus**, -ī, M. [tribus, *tribe*], ***tribune***.

**trīgintā**, num. adj., indecl. [trēs], *thirty*.

**tripartītō**, adv. [trēs, partior], *in three divisions*.

**trīstis**, -e, adj., *sad, gloomy.*
**triumphus**, -ī, *triumph.*
**tū**, pers. pron., *thou.* (264.)
**tuba**, -ae, F., *trumpet.*
**tueor**, 2, tuitus, *and* tūtus, *look at; watch, defend, guard.* Cf. dēfendō.
**Tullia**, -ae, F., *Tullia, Cicero's daughter.*
**tum**, adv., *at that time, then.*
**tunc**, adv. [tum], *at that time, then.*
**turgidulus**, -a, -um, adj., *swollen.* TURGID.
**turpis**, -e, adj., *ugly, foul; base, disgraceful, shameful.*
**turpiter**, adv. [turpis], *foully, basely, shamefully.*
**turpitūdō**, -inis, F. [turpis], *ugliness, baseness.*
**turris**, -is, F., *tower.* (149.)
**tūtus**, -a, -um, adj. [P. of tueor], *safe.*
**tuus**, -a, -um, poss. pron., *thy, thine; your, yours* (of only one).
**tyrannus**, -ī, M., *tyrant.*

**ubi**, adv., *where, when.*
**ūllus**, -a, -um, adj. [for ūnulus, diminutive of ūnus], *any, any one.* (200.)
**ūlterior**, -us, adj., comp. (no positive), *further.*
**ūltimus**, -a, -um, adj. (superl. of ūlterior), *furthest, last.* ULTIMATE.
**umerus**, -ī, M., *shoulder.*
**unde**, adv., *whence.*
**undi-que**, adv., *from all parts, on all sides, everywhere.*
**ūni-versus**, -a, -um, adj., (*turned into one*), *all together.*
**unquam**, adv., *at any time, ever.*
**ūnus**, -a, -um, num. adj., *one; alone.* (200).
**urbs**, -is, F., *city.* (163.) SUBURBS.
**urgeō**, 2, ursī, ——, *press, drive, impel, urge.*
**usque**, adv., *all the time, continually.*
**ut** *or* **utī**, adv. and conj., *how, as; that, in order that, so that.*
**uter**, -tra, -trum, interrog. pron., *which of two.* (200.)
**uterque**, utraque, utrumque, indef. pron., *each of two, both.* (200.)
**ūtilis**, -e, adj. [ūtor], *useful, advantageous.*
**uti-nam**, adv., *would that, O that, I wish that.*
**ūtor**, 3, ūsus, *use, employ;* w. abl.
**utrum**, adv., *whether;* used chiefly in double questions.
**ūva**, -ae, F., *grape, bunch of grapes.*
**uxor**, -ōris, F., *wife.* Cf. conjunx.

**vagor**, 1, *go to and fro, wander.* VAGRANT.
**valeō**, 2, -uī, -itum, *be strong* or *well;* valē, *farewell, good by.* Cf. convalēscō.
**valētūdō**, -inis, F. [valeō], *state of health, health.*
**validus**, -a, -um, adj. [valeō], *strong, stout, sturdy.* VALID.
**vallis** (or vallēs), -is, F., *valley, vale.*
**varius**, -a, -um, adj., *different, changeable, various.*
**Varrō**, -ōnis, M., *Varro, a Roman consul.*
**vastō**, 1 [vastus, *waste, desolate*], *lay waste, ravage.*
**vehō**, 3, vexī, vectum, *carry, draw, convey;* pass., *ride, sail.*
**vēlōx**, -ōcis, adj., *swift, fleet, quick.* (179.) VELOCITY.
**vēnātor**, -ōris, M. [vēnor, *hunt*], *hunter.*

**venēnum**, -ī, N., *poison.* VENOM.
**venia**, -ae, F., *indulgence, mercy, kindness.* VENIAL.
**veniō**, 4, vēnī, ventum, *come.*
**ventus**, -ī, M., *wind.*
**Venus**, -eris, F., ***Venus**, goddess of love.*
**Venusia**, -ae, F., ***Venusia**, a town in Apulia.*
**venustus**, -a, -um, adj. [Venus], *lovely, charming.*
**vēr**, vēris, N., *spring.* VERNAL.
**verbum**, -ī, N., *word.* VERB.
**vereor**, 2, *reverence, respect, fear.*
**vērō**, adv. and conj. [vērus], *in truth, in fact, but in fact.*
**vērum**, -ī, N. [vērus], *the truth.*
**vērus**, -a, -um, adj., *true, real.*
**vester**, -tra, -trum, poss. pron., *your, yours* (of more than one).
**veterrimus**, -a, -um, adj., superl. of vetus.
**vestiō**, 4 [vestis, *garment*], *clothe.*
**vetō**, 1, -uī, -itum, *forbid, prevent.* VETO.
**vetus**, -eris, adj., *old.* (144, 208.) VETERAN. Cf. antīquus.
**vetustior**, -us, adj., comp. of vetus.
**via**, -ae, F., *way, road, street.*
**vīcīnus**, -a, -um, adj. [vīcus], *near, neighboring.* VICINITY.
**victor**, -ōris, M. [vi(n)cō], *conqueror, **victor**.*
**victōria**, -ae, F. [victor], ***victory**.*
**vīcus**, -ī, M., ***village**.*
**videō**, 2, vīdī, vīsum, *see, perceive;* pass., *be seen, seem.* VISION.
**vigil**, adj. [vigeō, *be lively*], *watchful.* (151. 4.) VIGILANT.
**vigilia**, -ae, F. [vigilō, vigil], *a watching, watch,* i.e., *the fourth part of the night.*
**vigilō**, 1 [vigil], *watch.*
**vīgintī**, num. adj., indecl., *twenty.*
**vinciō**, 4, vinxī, vinctum, *bind.*
**vincō**, 3, vīcī, victum, *conquer, defeat.* (186.)
**vindicō**, 1, *claim; avenge, punish.* VINDICATE.
**vīnum**, -ī, N., ***wine**.*
**viola**, -ae, F., ***violet**.*
**vir**, virī, M., *man, hero.* (138, 262.)
**virgō**, -inis, F., *maiden, **virgin**.*
**virtūs**, -ūtis, F. [vir], (*manliness*), *courage, bravery; **virtue**.*
**vīs**, vīs, F. (gen. and dat., rare), *strength, power.* (262.)
**vīta**, -ae [vīvō], *life.* VITAL.
**vītis**, -is, F. [vieō, *twist together*], *vine.*
**vitium**, -ī, N. [vītis], (*a moral twist*), *fault, blemish, **vice**.* Cf. culpa.
**vītō**, 1, *avoid, shun.*
**vitrum**, -ī, N., *woad, a dye.*
**vituperō**, 1, *blame, censure.* VITUPERATION. Cf. culpō.
**vīvō**, 3, vīxī, vīctum [vīvus], *live.* (194.)
**vīvus**, -a, -um, adj. [vīvō], *alive, living.*
**vix**, adv., *hardly, with difficulty.*
**volō**, velle, voluī, ——, *wish, be willing, desire, intend.* (316.)
**voluptās**, -ātis, F., *pleasure, enjoyment.*
**vōx**, vōcis, F. [vocō, *call*], ***voice**.*
**vulnerō**, 1 [vulnus], *wound, hurt, injure.* VULNERABLE.
**vulnus**, -eris, N. [vulnerō], *wound.*
**vulpēs**, -is, F., *fox.*
**vultus**, -ūs, M., *countenance, looks, features.*

**Zama**, -ae, F., ***Zama**, a town in Africa.*

# ENGLISH-LATIN VOCABULARY.



**a,** *commonly not translated;* quīdam, quaedam, quoddam (279. 5).
**able (be),** possum (292).
**about,** dē, *w. abl.*
**absent (be),** absum (297).
**accept,** accipiō, 3.
**accompany,** comitor, 1.
**accord (own),** ipse, -a, -um (270. 6).
**accuse,** accūsō, 1.
**across,** trāns, *w. acc.*
**act,** agō, 3.
**admire,** admīror, 1.
**admonish,** moneō, 2 (112).
**adorn,** ōrnō, 1.
**advance,** prōcēdō, 3; prōgredior, 3.
**advice,** cōnsilium, -ī, N.
**advise,** moneō, 2 (112).
**afar,** longē.
**affair,** rēs, reī, F. (254.)
**afraid (be),** metuō, 3; timeō, 2.
**Africa,** Āfrica, -ae, F.
**after,** post, *w. acc.;* cum, *w. subj.;* postquam, *w. ind.*
**afterwards,** posteā, deinde.
**again,** iterum, rūrsus.
**against,** adversus, contrā, in, *w. acc.*
**age (old),** senectūs, -ūtis, F.
**agriculture,** agrī cultūra, -ae, F.
**aid,** auxilium, -ī, N.
**air,** āēr, āeris, M.
**Alexander,** Alexander, -drī, M.
**alive,** vīvus, -a, -um.
**all,** omnis, -e; tōtus, -a, -um (200)
**Alps,** Alpēs, -ium, F.
**alone,** sōlus, -a, -um (200).
**aloud (read),** recitō, 1.
**altar,** āra, -ae, F.
**always,** semper.
**ambassador,** lēgātus, -ī, M.; ōrātor, -ōris, M.
**among,** in, *w. abl.;* inter, *w. acc.*
**ancient,** antīquus, -a, -um; vetus, -eris (141).
**and,** et; atque, *or* āc; -que.
**Androclus,** Androclus, -ī, M.
**anger,** īra, -ae, F.
**angrily,** cum īrā (144).
**animal,** animal, -ālis, N. (149).
**another,** alius, -a, -ud (201); *one . . . another,* alius . . . alius.
**another's,** aliēnus, -a, -um.
**answer,** respondeō, 2, *w. dat.*
**any,** ūllus, -a, -um (200); aliquis, -qua, -quid, *or* -quod (279); quis (p. 211, note 15); quisquam, ——, quidquam (279. 6).
**approach,** appropinquō, 1, *w. dat., and* ad, *w. acc.*
**arm,** *n.,* bracchium, -ī, N.
**arm,** *v.,* armō, 1.
**arms,** arma, -ōrum, N.
**army,** exercitus, -ūs, M., *the general word; on the march,* āgmen, -inis, N.; *in order of battle,* aciēs, -ēī, F.
**Arpinum,** Arpīnum, -ī, N.
**arrangement,** ōrdō, -inis, M.

**arrival,** adventus, -ūs, M.
**arrow,** sagitta, -ae, F.
**art,** ars, artis, F.
**as,** ut; *as . . . as*, tam . . . quam; *same . . . as*, īdem . . . quī; (= *since*), cum, *w. subj.*; (= *when*) cum.
**Asia,** Asia, -ae, F.
**ashamed (be),** pudet, 2 (415).
**ask of,** quaerō, 3.
**assemble,** conveniō, 4.
**at,** in, *w. acc. or abl.*; ad, *w. acc.*; apud, *w. acc.*; *in combination w. verbs* (*wonder at, etc.*), *see the verbs*; *w. names of towns, locative case* (334).
**Athenian,** Athēniēnsis, -e.
**Athens,** Athēnae, -ārum, F.
**attentively,** dīligenter.
**author,** auctor, -ōris, M.
**away (go),** abeō (327); discēdō, 3.
**away from,** ā *or* ab, *w. abl.*; ē *or* ex, *w. abl.*

**back (bring or carry),** referō (321); reportō, 1.
**bad,** malus, -a, -um; improbus, -a, -um.
**basely,** turpiter.
**battle,** pūgna, -ae, F.; proelium, -ī, N.
**be,** sum (73).
**bear,** ferō (321); vehō, 3; tolerō, 1; **(off),** auferō.
**beast,** bēstia, -ae, F.
**beautiful,** pulcher, -chra, -chrum.
**beauty,** pulchritūdō, -inis, F.
**because,** quod; quia.
**become,** fīō (327); **it becomes,** decet, 2 (415).
**beg,** petō, 3; ōrō, 1.
**begin,** incipiō, 3; ordior, 4.
**believe,** crēdō, 3; *w. dat.*
**benefit,** *n.*, beneficium, -ī, N.
**benefit,** *v.*, prōsum (293), *w. dat.*
**besiege,** obsideō, 2; oppūgnō, 1.
**best,** optimus, -a, -um.
**better,** melior, -us, *compar. of* bonus (208).
**between,** inter, *w. acc.*
**big,** māgnus, -a, -um.
**bind,** vinciō, 4.
**bird,** avis, -is, F. (154).
**black,** niger, -gra, -grum; āter, ātra, ātrum.
**blame,** vituperō, 1; culpō, 1.
**blind,** caecus, -a, -um.
**blood,** sanguis, -inis, M.; cruor, -ōris, M.
**boar,** aper, aprī, M.
**boat,** nāvicula, -ae, F.; cymba, -ae, F.
**body,** corpus, -oris, N.
**bold,** audāx, -ācis.
**boldly,** audācter.
**book,** liber, -brī, M.
**booty,** praeda, -ae, F.
**born (be),** nāscor, 3.
**Boston,** Bostonia, -ae, F.
**both** (*each of two*), uterque, utraque, utrumque (200); *both . . . and*, et . . . et.
**boy,** puer, -erī, M.
**bow,** arcus, -ūs, M. (247).
**brave,** fortis, -e.
**bravely,** fortiter.
**bravery,** fortitūdō, -inis, F.
**break,** frangō, 3; **(through)** perfringō, 3.
**breeze,** ventus, -ī, M.; aura, -ae, F.
**bribe,** corrumpō, 3.
**bridge,** pōns, pontis, M.
**bring,** portō, 1; ferō (321); **(up),** ēducō, 1.
**Britain,** Britannia, -ae, F.
**broad,** lātus, -a, -um.
**brook,** rīvus, -ī, M.

**brother,** frāter, -tris, M.
**Brutus,** Brūtus, -ī, M.
**build,** aedificō, 1.
**burden,** onus, -eris, N.
**but,** at; autem; sed (393); **(that),** quīn.
**buy,** emō, 3.
**by,** ā, ab, *w. abl.*; *(denoting means or instrument)*, *w. abl. alone.*

**Cæsar,** Caesar, -aris, M.
**call,** nōminō, 1; appellō, 1; vocō, 1.
**calm,** aequus, -a, -um.
**camp,** castra, -ōrum, N.
**Campania,** Campānia, -ae, F.
**can,** possum (292).
**care,** cūra, -ae, F.
**carefully,** dīligenter; cum cūrā (144).
**carry,** portō, 1; ferō (321); **(back),** referō; *carry on war,* bellum gerere.
**cart,** carrus, -ī, M.
**Carthage,** Carthāgō, -inis, F.
**Cato,** Catō, -ōnis, M.
**certain (a),** quīdam, quaedam, quid(quod)dam (279. 4); *sure,* certus, -a, -um.
**chance,** fors, -tis, F.; cāsus, -ūs, M.
**change,** mūtō, 1.
**cherish,** colō, 3.
**chief,** prīnceps, -cipis, M.
**children,** puerī, -ōrum, M.; līberī, -ōrum, M. (60).
**Cicero,** Cicerō, -ōnis, M.
**Cimbri,** Cimbrī, -ōrum, M.
**circumstance,** rēs, reī, F.
**citadel,** arx, arcis, F.
**citizen,** cīvis, -is, M. *and* F.
**city,** urbs, -is, F.
**clerk,** scrība, -ae, M.
**cliff,** rūpēs, -is, F.
**clothe,** vestiō, 4.
**cold,** *adj.*, frīgidus, -a, -um.
**cold,** *n.*, frīgus, -oris, N.
**Collatinus,** Collatīnus, -ī, M.
**come,** veniō, 4; **(down),** dēscendō, 3; **(out),** ēgredior, 3; **(together),** conveniō, 4; **(off),** abeō (327).
**coming,** *n.*, adventus, -ūs, M.
**command,** imperō, 1, *w. dat*; iubeō, 2, *w. acc.*; praesum, *w. dat.*
**commander,** imperātor, -ōris, M.; dux, ducis, M.
**commonwealth,** rēs pūblica, reī pūblicae, F.
**comrade,** comes, -itis, M. *and* F.
**companion,** comes, -itis, M. *and* F.
**compel,** cōgō, 3.
**condemn,** damnō, 1.
**conquer,** superō, 1; vincō, 3 (186).
**consul,** cōnsul, -is, M.
**consulship,** cōnsulātus, -ūs, M.
**contemplate,** contemplor, 1.
**contented,** contentus, -a, -um, *w. abl.*
**converse,** colloquor, 3.
**Corinth,** Corinthus, -ī, F.
**Cornelia,** Cornēlia, -ae, F.
**correct,** corrigō, 3.
**counsel,** cōnsilium, -ī, N.
**country** *(fatherland)*, patria, -ae, F.; *(not city)*, rūs, rūris, N.
**courage,** virtūs, -ūtis, F.
**covered with leaves,** frondōsus, -a, -um.
**cowardice,** īgnāvia, -ae, F.
**cowardly,** īgnāvus, -a, -um.
**create,** creō, 1.
**creator,** creātor, -ōris, M.
**cross,** *tr.*, trānscendō, 3; *tr.* and *intr.*, trānseō (327).
**cruelly,** crūdēliter.
**cultivate,** colō, 3.
**Cumae,** Cūmae, -ārum, F.
**cunning,** *n.*, calliditās, -ātis, F.

**cup,** pōculum, -ī, N.
**Cyrus,** Cȳrus, -ī, M.

**Dædalus,** Daedalus, -ī, M.
**daily,** cotīdiē.
**danger,** perīculum, -ī, N.
**daughter,** fīlia, -ae, F.
**day,** diēs, -ēī, M. *and* F. (254).
**daybreak (at),** prīmā lūce.
**dear,** cārus, -a, -um.
**death,** mors, -tis, F.
**deep,** altus, -a, -um; profundus, -a, -um.
**defeat,** *n.*, clādēs, -is, F.
**defeat,** *v.*, vincō, 3; superō, 1 (186).
**defend,** dēfendō, 3.
**defender,** dēfēnsor, -ōris, M.
**delay,** mora, -ae, F.
**delight,** dēlectō, 1.
**deliver,** dēferō (321).
**demand restitution,** rēs repetō, 3.
**Demosthenes,** Dēmosthenēs, -is.
**depart,** discēdō, 3; exeō (327).
**deprive,** prīvō, 1; *w. abl.*
**descend,** dēscendō, 3.
**desert,** dēserō, 3.
**deserve,** mereō, mereor, 2.
**design,** cōnsilium, -ī, N.
**desire,** volō (316); dēsīderō, 1 (319); cupiō, 3.
**despair,** dēspērō, 1.
**despise,** contemnō, 3.
**destroy,** dēleō, 2.
**difficult,** difficilis, -e.
**difficulty (with),** vix.
**diligently,** dīligenter.
**discharge,** fungor, 3, *w. abl.*
**disclose,** ēnūntiō, 1.
**disgraceful,** turpis, -e.
**disgusted (be),** piget, 2 (416).
**divide,** dīvidō, 3; (*share*), partior, 4.
**do,** faciō, 3; agō, 3.
**dog,** canis, -is, M. *and* F.
**doubt,** *n.*, dubium, -ī, N.
**doubt,** *v.*, dubitō, 1.
**doubtful,** dubius, -a, -um.
**dove,** columba, -ae, F.
**down (tear),** rescindō, 3; **(come)** dēscendō, 3.
**draw,** trahō, 3; **(up),** subdūcō, 3.
**drink,** bibō, 3.
**drive,** agō, 3; **(off),** submoveō, 2.
**duty,** officium, -ī, N.
**dwell,** habitō, 1; vīvō, 3 (194).

**each (one),** quisque quaeque, quid(quod)que (279. 4); **(of two),** uterque utraque, utrumque (200).
**eagle,** aquila, -ae, F.
**earth,** terra, -ae, F.
**easily,** facile.
**easy,** facilis, -e.
**eat,** edō, 3.
**egg,** ōvum, -ī, N.
**eight,** octō.
**eighth,** octāvus, -a, -um.
**either . . . or,** aut . . . aut.
**elegant,** ēlegāns, -antis.
**elephant,** elephantus, -ī, M.
**else,** alius, -a, -ud (201).
**embark,** cōnscendō, 3.
**employ,** admoveō, 2; ūtor, 3, *w. abl.*
**encircle,** cingō, 3.
**end,** *n.*, fīnis, -is, M.
**end,** *v.*, fīniō, 4.
**endure,** patior, 3; ferō (321), tolerō, 1.
**endurance,** fortitūdō, -inis, F.
**enemy,** hostis, -is, M. *and* F.; inimīcus, -ī, M. (172).
**enjoy,** fruor, 3, *w. abl.*
**Ennius,** Ennius, -ī, M.

**enough,** satis.
**enter,** ingredior, 3; ineō (327).
**entertain the hope,** veniō in spem.
**entreaty,** precēs, -um, F.
**Epirus,** Ēpīrus, -ī, F.
**equally,** pariter.
**equanimity,** aequus animus, M.
**Europe,** Eurōpa, -ae, F.
**even,** etiam; ipse (270. 6).
**evident (it is),** cōnstat, 1.
**excellently,** optimē.
**explain,** explicō, 1.
**expulsion,** *P. of* expellō.
**eye,** oculus, -ī, M.

**Fabricius,** Fabricius, -ī, M.
**fact,** rēs, reī, F.
**fail,** dēficiō, 3; dēsum (297).
**fair,** pulcher, -chra, -chrum.
**faithful,** fīdus, -a, -um; fidēlis, -e.
**faithfully,** fidēliter.
**Faliscans,** Faliscī, -ōrum, M.
**famous,** clārus, -a, -um.
**far and wide,** longē lātēque.
**farmer,** agricola, -ae, M.
**father,** pater, -tris, M.
**father-in-law,** socer, -erī, M.
**fault,** vitium, -ī, N.; culpa, -ae, F.; *find fault with,* vituperō, 1; culpō, 1.
**favor,** faveō, 2, *w. dat.*
**fear,** *n.*, metus, -ūs, M.
**fear,** *v.*, timeō, 2; metuō, 3.
**few,** paucī, -ae, -a.
**fidelity,** fidēs, -eī, F.
**field,** ager, agrī, M.
**fierce,** atrōx, -ōcis.
**fiftieth,** quīnquāgēsimus, -a, -um.
**fifty,** quīnquāgintā.
**fight,** pūgnō, 1; dīmicō, 1.
**fill,** impleō, 2, -ēvī, -ētum; compleō, 2.
**finally,** dēnique.
**find,** reperiō, 4; inveniō, 4.
**finger,** digitus, -ī, M.
**finish,** fīniō, 4; cōnficiō, 3.
**fire,** īgnis, -is, M.
**first,** prīmus, -a, -um.
**fit,** aptō, 1.
**five,** quīnque.
**five hundred,** quīngentī, -ae, -a.
**flee,** fugiō, 3.
**fleet,** clāssis, -is, F.
**flight,** fuga, -ae, F.
**flock,** grex, gregis, F.
**flow,** fluō, 3.
**flower,** flōs, flōris, M.
**fodder,** pābulum, -ī, N.
**follow,** sequor, 3.
**folly,** stultitia, -ae, F.
**food,** cibus, -ī, M.
**foot,** pēs, pedis, M.
**foot-soldier,** pedes, -itis, M.
**for,** *conj.*, nam; enim (*not the first word*).
**for,** *sign of dative; prep.*, dē, prō, *w. abl.; of time, space, purpose,* in, *w. acc.*
**forces,** cōpiae, -ārum, F.
**forget,** oblīviscor, 3.
**forgetful,** oblītus, -a, -um.
**former (the),** ille (275. 6).
**forth (go),** exeō (327); ēgredior, 3.
**fortify,** mūniō, 4.
**fortune,** fortūna, -ae, F.
**forty,** quadrāgintā.
**forum,** forum, -ī, N.
**forward (go),** prōcēdō, 3; prōgredior, 3.
**foully,** turpiter.
**fourteen,** quattuordecim.
**fourth,** quartus, -a, -um.
**free,** līber, -era, -erum.
**free from,** līberō, 1; *w. abl.*
**friend,** amīcus, -ī, M.
**frighten,** terreō, 2.

**frog,** rāna, -ae, F.
**from,** dē, *w. abl.*; *away from*, ā *or* ab, *w. abl.* *out of*, ē *or* ex, *w. abl.* **(afar),** longē.
**fruit,** frūctus, -ūs, M.
**full,** plēnus, -a, -um
**furnish,** praebeō, 2.

**Galba,** Galba, -ae, M.
**game,** lūdus, -ī, M.
**garden,** hortus, -ī.
**Gaul,** Gallia, -ae, F.
**Gauls,** Gallī, -ōrum, M.
**general,** dux, ducis, M. *and* F.; imperātor, -ōris, M.
**Germans,** Germānī, -ōrum, M.
**get,** adipiscor, 3; **(possession),** potior, 4, *w. abl.*; **(by lot),** sortior, 4.
**gift,** dōnum, -ī, N.
**girl,** puella, -ae, F.
**give,** dō, 1.
**glory,** glōria, -ae, F.
**go,** eō (327) **(forth** *or* **out),** exeō; **(off** *or* **away)** abeō; discēdō, 3; **down)** dēscendō, 3.
**God,** Deus, -ī, M. (262).
**goddess,** dea, -ae, F.
**gold,** aurum, -ī, N.
**golden,** aureus, -a, -um.
**good,** bonus, -a, -um (208).
**good thing,** bonum, -ī, N.
**grain,** frūmentum, -ī, N.
**great,** māgnus, -a, -um.
**greatly,** māximē.
**Greece,** Graecia, -ae, F.
**Greek,** Graecus, -a, -um.
**guard,** *n.*, custōs, -ōdis, M. *and* F.
**guard,** *v.*, custōdiō, 4.

**hand,** manus, -ūs, F.
**handsome,** pulcher, -chra, -chrum.
**Hannibal,** Hannibal, -alis, M.
**happy,** beātus, -a, -um; fēlīx, -īcis.
**hard,** dūrus, -a, -um; *(difficult)*, difficilis, -e.
**hasten,** contendō, 3.
**haughtily** superbē.
**have,** habeō, 2.
**he,** is, hīc (270); ille (275).
**head,** caput, -itis, N.; *be at the head of*, praesum (297).
**headlong,** praeceps, -cipitis.
**hear,** audiō (223)
**heart,** cor cordis, N.
**heat,** calor, -ōris, M.
**heaven,** caelum, -ī, N.
**heavy,** gravis, -e.
**Hector,** Hector -oris, M.
**hero,** vir, virī, M. (262).
**hesitate,** dubitō, 1; cunctor, 1.
**high,** altus, -a, -um.
**hill,** collis, -is, M.
**himself,** *see* self.
**his,** ējus (270); illīus (275); **(own),** suus, -a, -um.
**history,** historia, -ae, F.
**hold,** habeō, 2 teneō, 2.
**home,** domicilium, -ī, N.; domus, -ūs, F. (262).
**Homer,** Homērus, -ī, M.
**honor,** *n.*, honestās, -ātis, F.
**honor,** *v.*, honōrō, 1.
**hope,** spēs, -eī, F.
**Horatius,** Horātius, -ī, M.
**horn,** cornū, -ūs, N.
**horse,** equus, -ī, M.
**horseback (ride),** in equō vehī; equitō, 1.
**horseman, horse-soldier,** eques, -itis, M.
**hour,** hōra, -ae, F.
**house,** domus, -ūs, F. (262).
**how,** quam **(many),** quot.
**huge,** māgnus, -a, -um; immānis, -e; ingēns, -entis.

**human,** hūmānus, -a, -um.
**hundred,** centum.
**hunger,** famēs, -is, F.
**hunter,** vēnātōr, -ōris, M.
**hurl,** coniciō, 3.
**hurtful (be),** noceō, 2, *w. dat.*
**hustle,** exturbō, 1.

**I,** ego (264).
**Icarus,** Īcarus, -ī, M.
**if,** sī; *if not,* nisi.
**ignorant (be),** nesciō, 4; īgnōrō.
**illustrious,** clārus, -a, -um.
**imitate,** imitor, 1.
**immediately,** statim.
**in,** in, *w. abl.*
**increase,** augeō, 2.
**inhabitant,** incola, -ae, M. *and* F.
**inhabit,** habitō, 1; incolō, 3.
**injure,** noceō, 2, *w. dat.*
**instruct,** ērudiō, 4; doceō, 2.
**intend,** in animō est; *w. dat.*
**into,** in, *w. acc.*
**invite,** invītō, 1.
**iron (of),** ferreus, -a, -um.
**island,** īnsula, -ae, F.
**it,** is, ea, id (270).
**Italian,** Italus, -ī, M.
**Italy,** Ītalia, -ae, F.
**itself,** *see* self.

**Janus,** Jānus, -ī, M.
**javelin,** pīlum, -ī, N.
**jewel,** ōrnāmentum, -ī, N.
**joy,** gaudium, -ī, N.
**judge,** jūdex, -icis, M. (105).
**judgment,** jūdicium, -ī, N.
**Julius,** Jūlius, -ī, M.
**Jupiter,** Jūppiter, Jovis, M. (262).
**justly,** jūstē.

**keen,** ācer, ācris, ācre.
**keep off,** arceō, 2.
**kill,** necō, 1; interficiō, 3; occīdō, 3.
**kind,** benīgnus, -a, -um.
**king,** rēx, rēgis, M.
**kingdom,** rēgnum, -ī, N.; imperium, -ī, N.
**knife,** culter, -trī, M.
**know, know how,** sciō, 4.
**known,** nōtus, -a, -um.

**labor,** labor, -ōris, M.
**lack,** dēsum (297)
**Lævinus,** Laevīnus, -ī, M.
**lake,** lacus, -ūs, M. (247).
**land,** ager, agrī, M.; terra, -ae, F.
**language,** lingua, -ae, F.
**large,** māgnus, -a, -um.
**last,** suprēmus, -a, -um.
**Latin,** Latīnus, -a, -um.
**latter (the),** hīc, haec, hōc (275. 5).
**laugh,** rīdeō, 2; **(at),** irrīdeō, 2; **(aloud),** cachinnō, 1.
**law,** lēx, lēgis, F.
**lazy,** piger, -gra, -grum.
**lead,** dūcō, 3; **(out),** ēdūcō, 3.
**leader,** dux, ducis, M. and F.
**leaf,** folium, -ī, N.
**leap over,** trānsiliō, 4.
**learn,** discō, 3.
**leg,** crūs, crūris, N.
**legion,** legiō, -ōnis, F.
**lesson,** pēnsum, -ī, N.
**let,** *sign of subj. or imperative.*
**letter,** epistula, -ae, F.; litterae, -ārum, F.
**levy,** dēlēctus, -ūs, M.
**life,** vīta, -ae, F.
**light,** *adj.,* levis, -e (150).
**light,** *n.,* lūx, lūcis, F.; lūmen, -inis, N.
**like,** amō, 1.
**likeness,** imāgō, -inis, F.
**line of battle,** aciēs, -ēī, F.

**lion,** leō, -ōnis, M. (134).
**listen,** audiō, 4 (223).
**literature,** lītterae, -ārum, F.
**little,** parvus, -a, -um.
**live,** vīvō, 3 habitō, 1 (194).
**long,** longus, -a, -um; *a long time,* diū.
**longer (no),** jam, *w. neg.*
**look at,** spectō, 1.
**lose,** āmittō, 3; perdō, 3.
**lot (obtain by),** sortior, 4.
**loud (laugh out),** cachinnō, 1.
**love,** amō, 1 (319).
**low,** humilis, -e.
**lucky,** fēlīx, -īcis.

**maiden,** puella, -ae, F.
**make,** faciō, 3; **(trial of),** experior, 4.
**man,** vir, virī, M. (262); homo, -inis, M. (138).
**Manlius,** Manlius, -ī, M.
**manner,** mōs, mōris, M.
**many,** multī, -ae, -a.
**Marcellus,** Mārcellus, -ī, M.
**marshal,** īnstruō, 3.
**master,** dominus, -ī, M.; magister, -trī, M.
**may,** licet; *w. dat.*
**means** (*by means of*), *use abl.*
**meet,** obeō (327); *go to meet,* obviam eō, *w. dat.*
**memory,** memoria, -ae, F.
**messenger,** nūntius, -ī, M.
**migrate,** migrō, 1.
**mind,** animus, -ī, M.; mēns, mentis, F. (273)
**mindful,** memor, -oris (150).
**mine,** meus, -a, -um (266).
**Minerva,** Minerva, -ae, F.
**miserable,** miser, -era, -erum.
**miss,** dēsīderō, 1.
**Mithridates,** Mithridātēs, -is, M.
**modesty,** modestia, -ae, F.
**month,** mēnsis, -is, M.
**monument,** monumentum, -ī, N.
**moon,** lūna, -ae, F.
**more,** plūs (208), magis.
**most,** plūrimus, -a, -um (208).
**mother,** māter, -tris, F.
**mountain,** mōns, montis, M.
**move,** moveō, 2.
**much,** multus, -a, -um (208).
**multitude,** multitūdo, -inis, F.
**must,** oportet, 2; *gerundive.*
**my,** meus, -a, -um (266).

**name,** nōmen, -inis, N.
**nation,** gēns, gentis, F.
**native land,** patria, -ae, F.
**near,** prope, *w. acc.*
**neighboring,** fīnitimus, -a, -um.
**Neptune,** Neptūnus, -ī, M.
**never,** nunquam.
**new** novus, -a, -um.
**night,** nox, noctis, F.
**nightingale,** luscinia, -ae, F.
**ninety,** nōnāgintā.
**ninth,** nōnus, -a, -um.
**no,** nūllus, -a, -um (200).
**nobody, no one,** nēmō, -inis, M. *and* F. (286); *that no one* (*neg. purpose*), nē quis.
**no longer,** jam, *w. neg.*
**not,** nōn.
**nothing,** nihil, *indecl.*
**nourish,** alō, 3; nūtriō, 4.
**now,** nunc; jam.
**Numa,** Numa, -ae, M.
**number,** numerus, -ī, M.
**nurture,** nūtriō, 4.

**oak,** quercus, -ūs, F.
**obey,** pāreō, 2, *w. dat.*
**obtain,** adipiscor, 3; potior, 4, *w. abl.*; **(by lot),** sortior, 4.
**ocean,** ōceanus, -ī, M.

**of**, *sign of genitive;* dē, *w. abl.;* (*out of*), ē *or* ex, *w. abl.*
**offer**, prōpōnō, 3; offerō (321); praebeō, 2.
**often**, saepe.
**old**, antīquus, -a, -um; vetus, -eris (141); (**man**), senex, -is (262); (**age**), senectūs, -ūtis, F.
**on**, in, *w. abl.*; (*of time*), *abl.*
**one**, ūnus, -a, -um (200); *one . . . another*, alius . . . alius; *the one . . . the other*, alter . . . alter.
**open**, *adj.*, patēns, -entis.
**open**, *v.*, aperiō, 4.
**opinion**, jūdicium, -ī, N.
**oppose**, obsistō, 3; *w. dat.*
**orator**, ōrātōr, -ōris, M.
**order**, *v.*, imperō, 1, *w. dat.*; jubeō, 2, *w. acc.*
**order** (*in order to*), ut, *w. subj.*
**other**, alius, -a, -ud (201); *some . . . others*, aliī . . . aliī; (*of two*), alter, -era, -erum.
**ought**, dēbeō, 2; oportet, 2; *gerundive.*
**our**, noster, -tra, -trum.
**ourselves**, *see* self.
**out**, *in combination w. verbs, see the verbs.*
**out of**, ē *or* ex, *w. abl.*
**over**, *in combination w. verbs, see the verbs.*
**overcome**, vincō, 3; superō, 1 (186).
**owe**, dēbeō, 2.
**own**, proprius, -a, -um; (**his, her, their**), suus, -a, -um; (**my**), meus, -a, -um; (**our**), noster, -tra, -trum; (**your**), vester, -tra, -trum; (**thy**), tuus, -a, -um.

**pain**, dolor, -ōris, M.
**parent**, parēns, -entis, M. *and* F.
**part**, pars, partis, F.
**pass** (**narrow**), angustiae, -ārum, F.
**pass by**, praetereō (327).
**patience** (**with**), patienter. *See also* 144.
**patiently**, patienter.
**peace**, pāx, pācis, F.
**people**, populus, -ī, M.; (**common**), plēbs, -is, F.
**peril**, perīculum, -ī, N.
**perish**, pereō (327).
**Persians**, Persae, -ārum, M.
**physician**, medicus, -ī, M.
**place**, *n.*, locus, -ī, M., *in plur* M. *and* N.
**place** *v.*, pōnō, 3.
**plain**, plānitiēs, -ēī, F.
**plan**, cōnsilium, -ī, N.
**pleasant**, grātus, -a, -um.
**pleasing**, grātus, -a, -um.
**pleasure**, voluptās, -ātis, F.; (**with**), libenter.
**pledge**, fidēs, -eī, F.
**plough**, *n.*, arātrum, -ī, N.
**plough**, *v.*, arō, 1.
**poem**, poēma, -atis, N.
**poet**, poēta, -ae, M.
**point** (**be on the**), *see* 422.
**Polyphemus**, Polyphēmus, -ī, M.
**Pompey**, Pompējus, Pompēī, M.
**poor**, miser, -era, -erum; pauper, -eris (167. 3).
**possess**, habeō, 2; potior, 4, *w. abl*
**possession** (*get possession of*) potior, 4, *w. abl.*; adipiscor, 3
**postpone**, differō (321).
**power**, imperium, -ī, N.
**praise**, *n.*, laus, laudis, F.
**praise**, *v.*, laudō, 1.
**precept**, praeceptum, -ī, N.
**prefer**, mālō (316).
**present** (**be**), adsum, *w. dat.*
**pretty**, pulcher, -chra, -chrum.
**prevent**, prohibeō, 2.

**prisoner,** captīvus, -ī, M.; captīva, -ae, F.
**proceed,** prōcēdō, 3.
**proclamation (make),** ēdīcō, 3.
**promise,** polliceor, 2; prōmittō, 3.
**property,** bona, -ōrum, N.
**proud,** superbus, -a, -um.
**province,** prōvincia, -ae, F.
**prow,** rōstrum, -ī, N.
**prudence,** prūdentia, -ae, F.
**punish,** pūniō, 4.
**punishment,** poena, -ae, F.
**pupil,** discipulus, -ī, M.
**purpose** (*for the purpose of*), ut or quī, *w. subj.*; ad, *w. gerund or gerundive*; *supine.*
**put (to flight),** fugō, 1; **(off),** differō (321); **(by),** dēpōnō, 3; **(an end to),** fīniō, 4.
**Pyrrhus,** Pyrrhus, -ī, M.

**queen,** rēgīna, -ae, F.
**quickly,** celeriter.

**raise,** tollō, 3; levō, 1.
**rather (wish),** mālō (316).
**read,** legō, 3; **(aloud),** recitō, 1.
**receive,** recipiō, 3; accipiō, 3; excipiō, 3.
**recite,** recitō, 1.
**recognize,** āgnōscō, 3.
**red,** ruber, -bra, -brum.
**refresh,** recreō, 1.
**Regulus,** Rēgulus, -ī, M.
**reign,** rēgnō, 1.
**relate,** trādō, 3; nārrō, 1.
**relieve,** līberō, 1; *w. abl.*
**remain,** maneō, 2.
**remember,** memoriā teneō.
**remove** (= *emigrate*), dēmigrō, 1.
**Remus,** Remus, -ī, M.
**render aid,** auxilium ferō.
**renown,** fāma, -ae, F.
**renowned,** amplus, -a, -um; clārus, -a, -um.
**report,** nūntiō, 1.
**republic,** rēs pūblica, reī pūblicae, F.
**respect,** vereor, 2.
**respects (in all),** omnibus rēbus.
**rest (the),** cēterī, -ae, -a.
**restitution (demand),** rēs repetō, 3.
**restrain,** coerceō, 2.
**results (it),** fit (327).
**retain,** retineō, 2.
**retreat,** sē recipiō, 3.
**return,** redeō, (327).
**reward,** praemium, -ī, N.
**Rhine,** Rhēnus, -ī, M.
**Rhone,** Rhodanus, -ī, M.
**rich,** dīves, -itis (167. 3).
**ride,** *pass. of* vehō, 3; equitō, 1.
**rightly,** rēctē.
**rise,** orior, 4.
**river,** amnis, -is, M.; flūvius, -ī, M.; flūmen, -inis, N. (172).
**road,** via, -ae, F.
**rob,** spoliō, 1; prīvō, 1; *w. abl.*
**robber,** latrō, -ōnis, M.
**Roman,** Rōmānus, -a, -um.
**Rome,** Rōma, -ae, F.
**Romulus,** Rōmulus, -ī, M.
**rose,** rosa, -ae, F.
**rough,** asper, -era, -erum.
**ruddy,** ruber, -bra, -brum.
**rule,** regō, 3 (180); rēgnō, 1.

**sad,** trīstis, -e.
**safe,** tūtus, -a, -um.
**sagacious,** prūdēns, -entis.
**sail,** *pass. of* vehō, 3; nāvigō, 1.
**sailor,** nauta, -ae, M.
**sake** (*for the sake*), causā, *w. gen.*
**Sallust,** Sallustius, -ī, M.
**same,** īdem, eadem, idem (270).
**Samnite,** Samnīs, -ītis.

**Saturn,** Sāturnus, -ī, M.
**save,** servō, 1.
**say,** dīcō, 3; (*keep saying*), dictitō, 1.
**scare,** terreō, 2.
**school,** schola, -ae, F.
**Scipio,** Scīpiō, -ōnis, M.
**sea,** mare, -is, N.
**see,** videō, 2; (**through**), perspiciō, 3.
**second,** secundus, -a, -um.
**seek,** petō, 3; quaerō, 3.
**seem,** videor, 2.
**seize,** rapiō, 3.
**self,** ipse, -a, -um (270); suī (264).
**send,** mittō, 3; (**back**) remittō, 3.
**senate,** senātus, -ūs, M.
**September,** September, -bris, M.
**servant,** minister, -trī, M.; servus, -ī, M. (66).
**set out,** proficīscor, 3.
**seven,** septem.
**seventh,** septimus, -a, -um.
**share,** partior, 4.
**sharply,** ācriter.
**she,** ea, ējus, F.
**sheep,** ovis, -is, F.
**shepherd,** pāstor, -ōris, M.
**shield,** scūtum, -ī, N.
**ship,** nāvis, -is, F. (154).
**shore,** lītus, -oris, N.
**short,** brevis, -e.
**shout,** clāmor, -ōris, M.
**Sicily,** Sicilia, -ae, F.
**sick,** aeger, -gra, -grum.
**side,** latus, -eris, N.
**signal,** sīgnum, -ī, N.
**silent (be),** taceō, 2.
**since,** cum, *w. subj.*
**sing,** canō, 3; cantō, 1.
**sister,** soror, -ōris, F.
**sit,** sedeō, 2.
**sixth,** sextus, -a, -um.
**skillful,** perītus, -a, -um.
**slave,** servus, -ī, M. (66).
**slavery,** servitūs, -ūtis, F.
**slay,** necō, 1; interficiō, 3; occīdō, 3.
**sleep,** *n.*, somnus, -ī, M.
**sleep,** *v.*, dormiō, 4.
**small,** parvus, -a, -um.
**smith,** faber, -brī, M.
**Socrates,** Sōcratēs, -is, M.
**soldier,** mīles, -itis, M.
**Solon,** Solōn, -ōnis, M.
**some one,** aliquis, -qua, (quid) -quod (279. 2); quīdam, quaedam, quod(quid)dam (279. 5); *some . . . others,* aliī . . . aliī; (*of two parties*), alterī . . . alterī; *often not expressed.*
**something,** aliquid.
**son,** fīlius, -ī, M.
**song,** cantus, -ūs, M.; carmen, -inis, N. (278).
**son-in-law,** gener, -erī, M.
**soon,** mox.
**soothe,** molliō, 4.
**source,** fōns, fontis, M.
**Spain,** Hispānia, -ae, F.
**spare,** parcō, 3; *w. dat.*
**speak,** loquor, 3; dīcō, 3; *speak to,* alloquor, 3.
**spear,** hasta, -ae, F.
**spiritedly,** ācriter.
**spring,** fōns, fontis, M.
**spy,** explōrātor, -ōris, M.
**stab,** trānsfīgō, 3.
**stain,** maculō, 1.
**star,** stella, -ae, F. (301).
**start** (= *set out*), proficīscor, 3.
**state,** cīvitās, -ātis, F.
**statue,** statua, -ae, F.
**step,** gradus, -ūs, M. (245).
**story,** fābula, -ae, F.
**street,** via, -ae, F.
**strong,** validus, -a, -um; fortis, -e.
**study,** *n.*, studium, -ī, N.

**study,** *v.*, studeō, 2, *w. dat.*
**sturdy,** validus, -a, -um.
**successfully,** optimē; fēlīciter.
**suddenly,** imprōvīsō.
**suffer,** patior, 3; tolerō, 1; sufferō (321).
**suitable,** opportūnus, -a, -um.
**summer,** aestās, -ātis, F.
**summon,** invītō, 1.
**sun,** sōl, sōlis, M.
**surpass,** superō, 1; vincō, 3 (186).
**surrender,** dēdō, 3.
**surround,** cingō, 3; circumveniō, 4.
**survive,** supersum (297).
**swear,** jūrō, 1.
**sweet,** dulcis, -e; suāvis, -e.
**swift,** vēlōx, -ōcis; celer, -eris, -ere (179).
**sword,** gladius, -ī, M.

**table,** mēnsa, -ae, F.
**tail,** cauda, -ae, F.
**take,** capiō, 3; sūmō, 3; *take a walk,* ambulō, 1.
**tall,** altus, -a, -um.
**Tarentine,** Tarentīnus, -ī, M.
**Tarquin,** Tarquinius, -ī, M.
**task,** pēnsum, -ī, N.
**teach,** doceō, 2.
**teacher,** magister, -trī, M.; praeceptor, -ōris, M.
**tear down,** rescindō, 3.
**tedious,** longus, -a, -um.
**tell,** nārrō, 1; dīcō, 3.
**temple,** templum, -ī, N.
**tender,** tener, -era, -erum.
**tenth,** decimus, -a, -um.
**terrify,** terreō, 2.
**terror,** terror, -ōris, M.
**than,** quam; *abl.* (212).
**that,** *conj.* (*in purpose or result clauses*), ut; (*after verbs of fearing*), nē; (**not**), nē; (*after expressions of doubt*), quīn; *after verbs of saying and the like, not translated.*
**that,** *pron.* (*determ.*), is, ea, id (270); (*demon.*), ille, -a, -ud (275); iste, -a, -ud (275); (*rel.*), quī, quae, quod (279).
**their,** *gen. plur. of* is; (**own**), suus, -a, -um.
**themselves,** *see* self.
**then,** tum; deinde.
**there,** ibi; *as an expletive, not translated.*
**thing,** rēs, -eī, F.
**think,** arbitror, 1; putō, 1 (429).
**thirst,** sitis, -is, F. (*acc.* -im, *abl.* -ī).
**thirty,** trīgintā.
**this,** (*determ.*), is, ea, id (270); (*demon.*), hīc, haec, hōc (275).
**thou,** tū.
**though,** cum, *w. subj.*
**thousand,** mīlle (311. 6).
**three,** trēs, tria (311. 4).
**three hundred,** trecentī, -ae, -a.
**thrust forth,** exturbō, 1.
**through,** per, *w. acc.*
**throw,** jaciō, 3; coniciō, 3.
**time,** tempus, -oris, N.
**tired,** dēfessus, -a, -um.
**to,** *sign of dative;* ad, in, *w. acc.;* (*expressing purpose*), ut, *w. subj.;* ad, *w. gerund or gerundive; supine.*
**to-day,** hodiē.
**together with,** cum, *w. abl.*
**toil,** labōrō, 1.
**to-morrow,** crās.
**too,** quoque; (**much**), nimium.
**touch,** tangō, 3.
**towards,** ad, in, *w. acc.*
**tower,** turris, -is, F. (149).

**town,** oppidum, -ī, N.
**townsman,** oppidānus, -ī, M.
**train,** exerceō, 2.
**tree,** arbor, -oris, F.
**trial (make),** experior, 4.
**true,** vērus, -a, -um.
**trumpet,** tuba, -ae, F.
**truth,** vērum, -ī, N.
**try,** experior, 4; cōnor, 1.
**turn,** convertō, 3; **(from),** āvertō, 3; **(out),** ēveniō, 4.
**twenty,** vīgintī.
**two,** duo, -ae, -o (311. 4); **(which of),** uter, -tra, -trum; **(each of),** uterque, utraque, utrumque.
**tyrant,** tyrannus, -ī, M.

**uncertain,** incertus, -a, -um.
**undertake,** suscipiō, 3; cōnor, 1.
**unwilling (be),** nōlō (316).
**up,** *in combination w. verbs, see the verbs.*
**upon,** in, *w. acc. or abl.*
**use,** ūtor, 3; *w. abl.*
**useful,** ūtilis, -e.

**vain (in),** frūstrā.
**valley,** vallis (*or* vallēs), -is, F.
**valor,** virtūs, -ūtis, F.
**very,** *superl. degree;* admodum.
**victorious,** vīctor, -ōris, M.
**victory,** vīctōria, -ae, F.
**virtue,** virtūs, -ūtis, F.
**voice,** vōx, vōcis, F.

**wage (war),** gerō, 3.
**wagon,** carrus, -ī, M.
**walk** (= *take a walk*), ambulō, 1.
**wall,** mūrus, -ī, M.
**wander,** vagor, 1.
**want** (= *wish*), volō (316); dēsīderō, 1.
**want** (= *lack*), careō, 2.
**war,** bellum, -ī, N.
**warn,** moneō, 2.
**watch,** vigilō, 1.
**watchful,** vigil, -is (151. 4).
**water,** aqua, -ae, F.
**way,** via, -ae, F.; (= *respect*), rēs, reī, F.
**weapon,** tēlum, -ī, N.
**weary,** dēfessus, -a, -um.
**weep,** fleō, 2.
**welcome,** excipiō, 3.
**well,** bene.
**well (be),** valeō, 2.
**what,** *interrog.*, quis, quae, quid (quod) (279); (= *that which*), id quod.
**when,** cum.
**whether,** num; utrum.
**which,** quī, quae, quod (279); (*of two*), uter, utra, utrum (200).
**while,** dum.
**white,** albus, -a, -um; candidus, -a, -um.
**who,** *rel.*, quī, quae; *interrog.*, quis, quae (279).
**whole,** tōtus, -a, -um (200).
**why,** cūr.
**wide,** lātus, -a, -um.
**wife,** uxor, -ōris, F.
**wild,** ferus, -a, -um.
**wild beast,** fera, -ae, F.
**wind,** ventus, -ī, M.
**wine,** vīnum, -ī, N.
**wing,** āla, -ae, F.
**winter,** hiems, -is, F.
**wise,** sapiēns, -entis.
**wisely,** sapienter.
**wish,** volō (316).
**with,** cum, *w. abl.; sometimes abl. alone.*
**without,** sine, *w. abl.*
**witness,** spectō, 1.
**wonder,** mīror, 1; **(at),** admīror, 1.

**wooden,** līgneus, -a, -um.
**woods,** silva, -ae, F.
**word,** verbum, -ī, N.
**work,** *n.*, labor, -ōris, M.; opus, -eris, N.
**work,** *v.*, labōrō, 1.
**world,** mundus, -ī, M.
**worthy,** dīgnus, -a, -um.
**would rather,** mālō (316).
**would that,** utinam.
**wound,** *n.*, vulnus, -eris, N.
**wound,** *v.*, vulnerō, 1.
**wretched,** miser, -era, -erum.
**write,** scrībō, 3.
**writing,** scrīptum, -ī, N.
**wrong,** injūria, -ae, F.

**year,** annus, -ī, M.
**yesterday,** herī.
**yonder (that),** ille, -a, -ud (275. 3).
**you,** *sing.* tū, *plur.* vōs.
**young man,** adulēscēns, -entis, M.; juvenis, -is, M.
**your,** *sing.* tuus, -a, -um; *plur.* vester, -tra, -trum.

**Zama,** Zama, -ae, F.
**zeal,** studium, -ī, N.

# GLOSSARIUM GRAMMATICUM.



**ablative,** ablātīvus, -ī, M.; (*of instrument*) īnstrūmentī; (*of agent*) agentis; (*of manner*) modī; (*of specification*) respectūs; (*of separation*) sēparātiōnis; (*of description*) quālitātis.
**absolute,** absolūtus, -a, -um.
**accent,** accentus, -ūs, M.
**accusative,** accūsātīvus, -ī, M.
**active,** āctīvus, -a, -um.
**adjective,** adjectīvum, -ī, N.
**adverb,** adverbium, -ī, N.
**agent,** agēns, -entis, M.
**agree,** congruō, 3; *w. abl.;* concordō, 1.
**agreement,** concordātiō, -ōnis, F.
**alphabet,** alphabētum, -ī, N.
**answer,** *n.*, respōnsum, -ī, N.
**answer,** *v.*, respondeō, 2.
**antecedent,** antecēdēns, -entis, N.
**apposition,** appositiō, -ōnis, F.; (**be in**) appōnō, 3.

**cardinal,** cardinālis, -e.
**case,** cāsus, -ūs, M.
**clause,** clausula, -ae, F.
**common** *or* **appellative,** appellātīvus, -a, -um.
**comparative,** comparātīvus, -a, -um.
**comparison,** comparātiō, -ōnis, F.
**compound,** compositus, -a, -um.
**concessive,** concēssīvus, -a, -um.
**condition,** hypothesis, -is, F.; conditiō, -ōnis, F.
**conditional,** hypotheticus, -a, -um; conditiōnālis, -e.
**conjugation,** conjugātiō, -ōnis, F.
**conjunction,** conjunctiō, -ōnis, F.
**consonant,** līttera cōnsonāns, -antis, *or* cōnsonāns, -antis, F.
**construction,** cōnstrūctiō, -ōnis, F.
**conversation,** colloquium, -ī, N.
**correct,** *adj.*, rēctus, -a, -um.
**correct,** *v.*, corrigō, 3; ēmendō, 1.
**correctly,** rēctē.

**dative,** datīvus, -ī, M.
**declension,** dēclīnātiō, -ōnis, F.
**decline,** dēclīnō, 1.
**declinable,** dēclīnābilis, -e.
**defective,** dēfectīvus, -a, -um.
**degree,** gradus, -ūs, M.
**demonstrative,** dēmōnstrātīvus, -a, -um.
**deponent,** dēpōnēns, -entis.
**derive,** trahō, 3.
**description (abl. of),** quālitās, -ātis, F.
**determinative,** dēfīnītus, -a, -um.
**difference,** discrīmen, -inis, N.
**diminutive,** dēminutīvum, -ī, N.
**diphthong,** diphthongus, -ī, M.
**direct,** dīrēctus, -a, -um; rēctus, -a, -um.
**discourse,** ōrātiō, -ōnis, F.
**discuss,** tractō, 1.
**dissyllable,** dissyllabus, -ī, M.
**distributive,** distribūtīvus, -a, -um.

**end,** *v.*, dēsinō, 3.
**English,** Anglicus, -a, -um.
**English (in),** Anglicē.
**etymology,** etymologia, -ae, F.
**example,** exemplum, -ī, N.; **(for)** ut; exemplī causā.
**exception,** exceptiō, -ōnis, F.

**feminine,** fēminīnus, -a, -um.
**finite,** fīnītus, -a, -um.
**formation,** formātiō, -ōnis, F.
**future,** futūrum, -ī, N.
**future perfect,** futūrum exāctum.

**gender,** genus, -eris, N.
**genitive,** genetīvus, -ī, M.
**gerund,** gerundium, -ī, N.
**gerundive,** gerundīvum, -ī, N.
**govern,** regō; *pass. of* jungō *or* conjungō, *foll. by* cum *w. abl.*
**grammar,** grammatica, -ae, F.

**imperative,** modus imperātīvus *or* imperātīvus, -ī, M.
**imperfect,** imperfectum, -ī, N.
**impersonal,** impersōnālis, -e.
**increase,** crēscō, 3.
**indicative,** modus indicātīvus, -ī, M., *or* indicātīvus, -ī, M.
**indeclinable,** indēclīnābilis, -e.
**indirect,** indīrēctus, -a, -um; oblīquus, -a, -um.
**infinitive,** modus īnfīnītīvus *or* īnfīnītīvus, -ī, M.
**instrument,** īnstrūmentum, -ī, N.
**interjection,** interjectiō, -ōnis, F.
**interrogative,** interrogātīvus, -a, -um.
**intransitive,** intrānsitīvus, -a, -um.
**irregular,** irrēgulāris, -e; anōmalus, -a, -um.

**Latin,** Latīnus, -a, -um.
**Latin (in),** Latīnē.
**lesson,** pēnsum, -ī, N.
**letter,** littera, -ae, F.
**limit,** *v.*, limitō, 1.
**liquid,** liquidus, -a, -um.
**locative,** locātīvus, -ī, M.
**long,** longus, -a, -um; prōductus, -a, -um.

**manner,** modus, -ī, M.
**masculine,** masculīnus, -a, -um.
**mean,** sīgnificō, 1.
**meaning,** sīgnificātiō, -ōnis, F.
**mistake,** *n.*, error, -ōris, M.
**mistake,** *v.*, errō, 1.
**monosyllable,** monosyllabum, -ī, N.
**mood,** modus, -ī, M.
**mute,** mūtus, -a, -um.

**negative,** negātīvus, -a, -um.
**neuter,** neuter, -tra, -trum.
**nominative,** nōminātīvus, -ī, M.
**noun,** nōmen, -inis, N.; substantīvum, -ī, N.
**numeral,** numerālis, -e.

**object,** objectum, -ī, N.
**ordinal,** ordinālis, -e.

**paradigm,** paradigma, -atis, N.
**participle,** participium, -ī, N.
**particle,** particula, -ae, F.
**partitive,** partītīvus, -a, um.
**passive,** passīvus, -a, -um.
**perfect,** perfectum, -ī, N.
**person,** persōna, -ae, F.
**personal,** persōnālis, -e.
**phrase,** phrasis, -is, F.
**pluperfect,** plūsquamperfectum, -ī, N.

**plural**, plūrālis, -e.
**positive**, positīvus, -a, -um.
**preposition**, praepositiō, -ōnis, F.
**present**, praesēns, -entis, N.
**principal**, prīncipālis, -e.
**pronoun**, prōnōmen, -inis, N.
**proper**, proprius, -a, -um.

**quantity**, quantitās, -ātis, F.
**question**, interrogātiō, -ōnis, F.

**reflexive**, reciprocus, -a, -um; reflexīvus, -a, -um.
**regular**, rēgulāris, -e.
**relative**, relātīvus, -a, -um.
**remember**, memoriā teneō.
**review**, recōgnōscō, 3; **(lesson)** pēnsum recōgnōscendum.
**root**, rādīx, -īcis, F.
**rule**, rēgula, -ae, F.

**school**, schola, -ae, F.
**sentence**, sententia, -ae, F.
**separation**, sēparātiōnis.
**sequence**, cōnsecutiō, -ōnis, F.
**short**, brevis, -e; correptus, -a, -um.
**sibilant**, sībilus, -a, -um.
**singular**, singulāris, -e.
**sound**, sonus, -ī, M.
**specification**, respectus, -ūs, M.
**speech (part of)**, ōrātiō.
**stem**, basis, -is, F.
**study**, *n.*, studium, -ī, N.
**study**, *v.*, studeō, 2.
**subject**, subjectum, -ī, N.
**subjunctive**, modus subjunctīvus, -ī, M., *or* subjunctīvus, -ī, M.
**substantive**, substantīvum, -ī, N.
**substantively**, substantīvē.
**superlative**, superlātīvus, -a, -um.
**supine**, supīnum, -ī, N.
**syllable**, syllaba, -ae, F.
**syntax**, syntaxis, -is, F.

**teacher**, praeceptor, -ōris, M.; magister, -trī, M.; magistra, -ae, F.
**tense**, tempus, -oris, N.
**termination**, terminātiō, -ōnis, F.
**transitive**, trānsitīvus, -a, -um.
**treat (= discuss)**, tractō, 1.

**verb**, verbum, -ī, N.
**vocabulary**, vōcābulārium, -ī, N.
**vocative**, vōcātīvus, -ī, M.
**voice**, vōx, vōcis, F.; genus, -eris, N.
**vowel**, littera vōcālis, -is, F., *or* vōcālis, -is, F.

**wish**, optātiō, -ōnis, F.
**word**, verbum, -ī, N.; vōcābulum, -ī, N.; vōx, vōcis, F.

**yes**, certē, certissimē; vērō; ita est, ista sunt; *verb of question repeated.*

Presswork by Ginn & Co., Boston.

Printed in Great Britain
by Amazon

72559771R00167